CHICANA/O REMIX

# CHICANA/O REMIX

Art and Errata since the Sixties

KAREN MARY DAVALOS

▐▌ NEW YORK UNIVERSITY PRESS  New York

NEW YORK UNIVERSITY PRESS
New York
www.nyupress.org

Book designed and typeset by Charles B. Hames

Library of Congress Cataloging-in-Publication Data
Names: Davalos, Karen Mary, 1964– author.
Title: Chicana/o remix : art and errata since the sixties / Karen Mary Davalos.
Description: New York : New York University Press, 2017. |
Includes bibliographical references and index.
Identifiers: LCCN 2016052434 | ISBN 9781479877966 (cl : alk. paper) |
ISBN 9781479821129 (pb : alk. paper)
Subjects: LCSH: Hispanic American art—20th century. |
Hispanic American art—21st century. | Art—Historiography.
Classification: LCC N6538.H58 D38 2017 | DDC 704.03/68—dc23
LC record available at https://lccn.loc.gov/2016052434

Manufactured in the United States of America

10 9 8 7 6 5 4 3 2 1

Also available as an ebook

# CONTENTS

# LIST OF ILLUSTRATIONS

*C hicana/o Remix: Art and Errata since the Sixties* emerged from my considerable immersion in Chicana/o art. Starting in 2007 at the invitation of Chon A. Noriega, and following an established methodology in Chicana/o and feminist studies to reconstitute subjugated knowledge, I conducted seventeen life history interviews for the CSRC Oral Histories Series, a major project of the Chicano Studies Research Center (CSRC) at the University of California, Los Angeles (UCLA), with funding from the Getty Foundation and other sources. Oral history has emerged as the central method for investigating fifty years of Chicana/o art.[1] I gathered over 130 hours of an archive previously undocumented: it includes the life stories of Judith Baca, Charles "Chaz" Bojórquez, David Botello, Barbara Carrasco, Leonard Castellanos, Yreina D. Cervántez, Roberto "Tito" Delgado, Richard Duardo, Margaret Garcia, Juan "Johnny" Gonzalez, Judithe Hernández, Leo Limón, Alma López, Gilbert "Magu" Sánchez Luján, Monica Palacios, John Valadez, and Linda Vallejo.[2] In addition to the extensive oral history interviews with artists, I worked with them for dozens of additional hours correcting transcripts in an effort to publish the archive and get their story as accurate as possible. The life history interviews, which average ten hours per artist, left me with a strong impression that my view of Chicana/o art was likely incorrect, and from these sonic archival documents I began to envision the unmapped territory and new cartography that could accommodate the latest information.

Not only did I participate in the excavation, creation, and preservation of the archive, I assisted in its interpretation. The book draws on ten years of coparticipatory research, a method central to Chicana/o art history since its inception, although it has never been described as such because its leading scholars, such as Shifra M. Goldman and Tomás Ybarra-Frausto, were less invested in a distinction between researcher and informant. Refuting the myth of the detached social analyst, the term *coparticipatory research* captures the extensive involvement of the researcher and the collaborative relationship between the researcher and people whose lives, experiences, and activities are central to the topic of study.[3] Goldman, Ybarra-Frausto, Amalia Mesa-Bains, Terezita Romo, and Holly Barnet-Sánchez, the paramount shapers of the field and authors of foundational scholarship in Chicana/o art history, consistently worked in curation, criticism, advocacy, and archival documentation.

Building the archive was a central project of Goldman, who invited Ybarra-Frausto to join her in the production of *Arte Chicano: A Comprehensive Annotated Bibliography of Chicano Art* (1985).[4] The materials they amassed for the reference book served and informed their own intellectual work and that of others; later, public institutions acquired their private archives, allowing public access to their collections, which they had independently built over several decades.[5] Mesa-Bains works as art historian, artist, and curator. With a MacArthur Fellowship in 1992, she also served as a cultural ambassador and helped introduce numerous Chicana/o artists to curators, collectors, philanthropic foundations for the arts, and critics. Romo has also held multiple roles in the arts: curator, critic, developer of the archive, and advocate. In 1972 she was among the student leaders who founded La Raza Bookstore, which later expanded into La Raza Galería Posada, a project of the Royal Chicano Air Force of Sacramento.[6] Barnet-Sánchez was present at the formation of *Chicano Art: Resistance and Affirmation, 1965–1985*, the major traveling exhibition and catalog that continues to serve as a reference. Goldman and her colleagues developed a coparticipatory methodology for investigating Chicana/o art that relied on immersion into the process and practice.

Following this coparticipatory approach, I undertook a research method that involved me in various roles and created a dense and broad understanding of Chicana/o art in Los Angeles. I volunteered as curator and advocate and I worked as part of a research team at UCLA that supported multiple exhibitions of Chicana/o art. However, my major use of coparticipatory research started in 2003, when I began attending weekly opening and closing receptions for art exhibitions; visiting with artists and sharing transportation, food, and leisure time with them; and attending public forums on Chicana/o art. I also gathered hundreds of ephemeral items and purchased rare and precious catalogs from exhibitions produced by arts organizations.

In addition to regular attendance at art exhibitions, I explored fifty years of Chicana/o art exhibitions through archival materials.[7] Mary Salinas Durón and Armando Durón, noted collectors and arts advocates, graciously allowed me to study their private collection of ephemera, which they have been gathering since 1977. Using their collection of over twelve linear feet of postcards, flyers, and broadsides gathered in massive three-ring binders, I was able to survey approximately 1,950 exhibitions in Los Angeles that included Chicana/o artists. Simultaneously, the UCLA Chicano Studies Research Center provided me with a database it was creating for the exhibition *Mapping Another L.A.: The Chicano Art Movement* (2011), and by combining these materials I generated a comprehensive list of over 2,300 exhibitions of Chicana/o art in the Los Angeles area since 1945. For this project I focused on Los Angeles–area exhibitions produced since 1963, recording over two thousand visual art exhibitions of Chicana/o artists.[8] Using this substantial record of expressive visual practice, I examine the errata exhibition, one of many patterns within the Chicana/o arts critical discourse (see chapter 2).

The coparticipatory methodology also took me to curation. During the research phase, I curated three exhibitions and wrote gallery or catalog essays for four local venues: Tropico de Nopal Gallery Art-Space, Avenue 50 Studio, Fremont Gallery, and the nationally recognized Self Help Graphics & Art. For these projects, I spoke at length with artists Linda Arreola, Margaret Garcia, CiCi Segura Gonzalez, Poli Marichal, Marianne Sadowski, and Linda Vallejo, as well as with artists, curators, and artistic directors Kathy Gallegos and Reyes Rodriguez. Curation brought me into a close circle of Chicana/o artists and advocates who were willing to provide me with insight and direction. It helped me consider the challenges of presence and the conditions under which Chicana/o art is made visible. It also made me more visible in the curatorial landscape of Los Angeles, and as a result of these projects I was invited to sit on panels as an expert on the local Chicana/o art scene, to recommend artists for exhibitions, and to identify scholars for catalog essays. Therefore, I was asked to describe and analyze the field as I was in the midst of investigating it, breaking the cardinal rules of Western social science research—its false separation between Self and Other and its mystified relationship between knowledge and power. Because coparticipatory research emerges from ethnic and feminist studies and from the social movements that gave rise to these interdisciplinary projects, it does not imagine a neutral research site or a detached observer. Indeed, it questions these assumptions as veils for social inequality, privilege, and knowledge production as an attempt to reproduce the status quo.

The life history interviews were vital in the development of *Mapping Another L.A.*, an exhibition at the UCLA Fowler Museum that traced the dynamic activities and relationships among nine arts institutions and collectives. Through my work on this exhibition I was immersed in part of the major Getty Foundation initiative Pacific Standard Time: Art in L.A. 1945–1980. For the Getty's considerable economic and art historical stimulus package, the UCLA Chicano Studies Research Center proposed the four-part exhibition *L.A. Xicano*, curated by Chon A. Noriega, Pilar Tompkins Rivas, and Terezita Romo. I was a research associate working with the team of scholars and artists, including Sandra de la Loza, who conducted research, wrote catalog essays, and provided consultation for *L.A. Xicano*.[9] This experience provided me with invaluable insights into the cultural politics of arts institutions in Los Angeles and the exhibitions I examine here. It also means that Noriega, Romo, de la Loza, and others are simultaneously colleagues, subjects and objects of analysis, and interlocutors. This aspect of the present project places it squarely in the scholarship of ethnic and feminist studies, which has moved past the myth of neutrality and the contributory model. *Chicana/o Remix* advocates for a critical engagement with one's subject without seeking a contributory narrative. The contributory model feeds the myth and ideology of assimilation by reassuring nativists, patriots, and citizens that *those* racial or ethnic groups are participating in and celebrating American society. Assimilationist ideology requires the absence of a critique of power. To avoid the contributory model, the book advances a decolonial method for Chicana/o art history.

# ACKNOWLEDGMENTS

I could not have ventured into an investigation of Chicana/o art without the support of artists Linda Arreola, Judith Baca, Charles "Chaz" Bojórquez, David Botello, Barbara Carrasco, Leonard Castellanos, Isabel M. Castro, Yreina D. Cervántez, Ernesto de la Loza, Sandra de la Loza, Roberto "Tito" Delgado, Richard Duardo (rest in peace), Kathy Gallegos, Margaret Garcia, CiCi Segura Gonzalez, José Luis "Joe" Gonzalez, Juan "Johnny" Gonzalez, Yolanda Gonzalez, Wayne Alaniz Healy, Judithe Hernández, Leo Limón, Gilbert "Magu" Sánchez Luján (rest in peace), Poli Marichal, Reyes Rodriguez, Marianne Sadowski, Peter Tovar, John Valadez, and Linda Vallejo. I could not have completed the project without the generous support of Eric C. Zinner, editor-in-chief of New York University Press. I also recognize the earlier support of the Chicano Studies Research Center, especially Rebecca Epstein, Rebecca Fraizer, Lizette Guerra, Connie Heskett, Marissa K. López, Chon A. Noriega, Yolanda Retter (forever smiling), Darling Sianez, Michael R. Stone, Cathy Sunshine, Christopher Anthony Velasco, and Jenny Walters.

As this book was produced during and through my teaching activities at Loyola Marymount University (LMU) and UCLA, I owe recognition to a cadre of students: Haydee Budrecki, Carlos Cardenas, Lauro Cons III, Adán Duarte, Jackeline Estrada, Lorena (Flores) Galaviz, Araceli Palafox, Frank J. Romo, and Nickolas Smith. Citlaly Orozco assisted with securing permissions, organizing the images, and drafting the captions. Khanh Nguyen, Lourdes Karina Olivares, and Lupe Zepeda were UCLA undergraduate students with amazing professional research skills. I benefited from the labor of Mirasol Riojas, a graduate student who compiled the database of the first four hundred exhibitions that informed the analysis in chapter 2.

I began thinking about this project in 2003 while a fellow at the UCLA Institute of American Cultures and the Chicano Studies Research Center. A sabbatical from LMU in 2010–11 allowed me to complete the bulk of research and the first drafts of the book. The University of Minnesota supported the book in its final stages of production and provided a subvention to reproduce color images.

Several colleagues inspired coherence from chaos. I acknowledge the insights of Armando Durón, who read the manuscript at each stage and provided me access to the Durón Family Collection. He was like a graduate research assistant when he took notes for me, and like a dissertation adviser when he read and commented on everything *twice*. I thank Harry Gamboa Jr. for long conversations about art and Los Angeles. I owe Tere Romo gratitude for consistently inspiring my analysis. I thank Arlene Dávila for reading and commenting on versions of the manuscript and for being present at every stage of the writing process, especially when it was difficult. Tomás Ybarra-Frausto and Shifra M. Goldman jointly and independently taught me to love the archive and to build it. Constance Cortez and the MALCS Writing Workshop participants, Marivel T. Danielson, Rosa Furumoto, Adriana P. Nieto, and Mariela Nuñez-Janes, provided extensive comments and suggestions on an earlier version of chapter 5. Bryan Jay Wolf inspired me to dive deeply into a single work of art. His brilliant book, *Vermeer and the Invention of Seeing*, gave me *susto* because he fearlessly discusses in the finest detail a work of art by Rembrandt (not Vermeer!).

Audiences of various conferences gave important feedback on specific chapters. I acknowledge the contributions of the third and fourth Biennial Latino Art Now! national conferences, 2010 and 2013, for helpful suggestions about artistic influence and remixing. The audience of the National Association for Chicana and Chicano Studies (NACCS) Chicana Caucus plenary in 2012 graciously listened to me singing sarcastically about misrepresentations of Chicana/o art.

Librarians, archivists, and technicians assisted me with the research. At LMU, Elaine Coates, Matt Frank, Sheilah Jones, Nick Mattos, Enrique Sandoval, and David Scozzaro provided technical support, and the

Department of Archives and Special Collections helped me track down obscure information about art exhibitions at LMU. Karen Rapp, former director, and Victor Parra of the Vincent Price Art Museum at East Los Angeles College gave me access to the museum's archives. Matthew Cook and Kristen LaBonte at the California State University Channel Islands Library and Simon Elliott of UCLA Library Special Collections provided important assistance. Sal Güereña, director of the California Ethnic and Multicultural Archives (CEMA) at the University of California, Santa Barbara, gave me access to preprocessed materials in the Shifra Goldman Papers. Sal had the insight in the 1980s to preserve the art history of Chicanas and Chicanos. Callie Bowdish, former computer resource specialist at CEMA, shared with me all the wonderful treasures Goldman had found.

Any wise Chicana will also acknowledge her family. I begin with my partner, David G. Stanton, who shaped the larger argument of the book and must be acknowledged for taxiing me to hundreds of art exhibitions. Our daughter, M. Olivia, brought to my attention the way Graciela Iturbide smuggled Chicana/o art into the Getty Center. Our son, Glennon, taught me to appreciate the relationship that children of collectors have with the art in their homes. His critical mind motivates me to work harder. My brother and sisters and cousins are a constant source of support—and they never tire of cheering for me even as I make a fool of myself at family gatherings. My brother-in-law, David Gaylord, proofed the manuscript. My parents read multiple drafts of the manuscript, and my mother, Mary Catherine Davalos, functioned as my copy editor, providing publication facts, confirming citations, and verifying consistency in the book. She nearly memorized two chapters. When she needed a second pair of eyes—she did this work in her seventies—my father joined the team. I am grateful for Ruben M. Davalos and his temperament. He taught me to maintain my cool when the work was stalled. When they came to town to help me, my aunt Angelina Souza provided them with a room. You see, for Chicana academics, a book is a family affair.

# INTRODUCTION

Reframing Chicana/o Art

A certain anxiety accompanies archeological excavation. Besides fearing accidental destruction in the process of discovery, archeologists also worry about the effect of time. Scholars of history and cultural anthropology become similarly anxious when attempting to recover previously lost stories and documents that face a scarcity of opportunities to "speak." As I researched Chicana/o art since the 1960s, looking for materials that would corroborate the individual memories that I had recorded, I was less concerned about an artist's inability to recall the past than the fate of the stuff that the artists kept in their basements, garages, and studios. Were moisture, insects, and chemicals destroying precious documents beyond recognition? What if someone decided to trash them before I was granted access? How much more digging would alleviate the fear that I had missed a crucial story?

These anxieties are multiplied when one is working in a field that has been invisible. Compared to other areas of Chicana/o cultural production, the critical examination of the visual arts is largely underdeveloped.[1] Awareness of this invisibility produces a "burden of representation," as Kobena Mercer has observed about black visual arts. He reflects on the burden of getting the entire story told at the first chance because a partial account will not satisfy the urgency of the political moment, an urgency triggered by the cavernous gap in the record. In the end, Mercer urges us to decline this responsibility even though he recognizes that the burden of representation is a product of the "structures of racism" that have "historically marginalized [our] access to the means of cultural production."[2]

While I agree with Mercer that the regulation of visibility is a form of institutionalized racism within the public space of museums and galleries and within art history, I am not willing to dismiss the burden of representation.[3] If I were to put aside the encumbrance, I would feel as if I were no longer accountable to the histories and structures of racism and other concurrent forms of oppression, sexism and homophobia among them. Contesting hegemony is an ongoing struggle, and the context is too politically charged for me to feel that my choices are merely academic, made in the name of good organization and coherence. If this book appears "particularly anxious" about the recovery of Chicana/o art history, it is because I am keenly aware that the "primary work of cultural excavation" that literary scholar Silvio Torres-Saillant describes is still under way, and that it is an enormous task.[4] The pressure to "get it right" is intense because I imagine the potential of equity within the arts.[5]

I am convinced that Chicana/o art is a distinct category because of its structural location—how it has been, and continues to be, positioned in terms of social contexts and political and economic power. I also recognize that identity-based art is so vilified that it gets dismissed even before it is understood. Thus *Chicana/o Remix* engages with art critics and art historians who argue that the category of Chicana/o art should be retired because it is no longer relevant in the so-called postidentity moment.[6] I join a range of scholars, including Jennifer A. González, Miwon Kwon, Kate Mondloch, and Amelia Jones, who observe that visual arts discourse is still haunted by essentialist models.[7] The dispute turns on acceptance of a binary that separates art that is "ethnic" from art that is "universal," or art that is "political" from art that is "global." While González and Jones appear more comfortable with the idea that artists participated at one point in "these narrow categorical frameworks," I am not yet convinced that the majority of Chicana/o artists promoted or practiced "narrow" identities or produced work that activated this binary.[8] In addition to challenging mainstream art criticism for its limitations, this book proposes a new and better method of theorizing the artistic production of people of Mexican descent.[9] In my refusal to disregard Chicana/o art because it appears troublesome or unfashionable, I address the politics of visibility, allowing me to develop a method that does not appropriate or reify.

The debate among Chicana/o art historians over identity versus postidentity art is, ironically, linked to the ubiquitous dualist taxonomy within Chicana/o art discourse. This discursive coherence is most clearly articulated in earlier writings by Shifra M. Goldman and Tomás Ybarra-Frausto and later by Terezita Romo, Amalia Mesa-Bains, Victor Zamudio-Taylor, and George Vargas, all of whom characterized Chicana/o art in binary terms, dividing it into two periods and styles.[10] The first period, 1968 to 1975, is "marked by a totally noncommercial, community-oriented character in the attitudes and expectations of the individuals and groups" who produced the work and in "the purposes they served."[11] Work of this period is often described as political art, agitprop, or people's art, evoking Maoist principles. The second period, from 1975 to the mid-1980s, is not as neatly specified, but it is generally considered less politically charged and more commercial, arising from individual rather than collective concerns.[12] In the late 1990s Ybarra-Frausto introduced a third phase, one dominated by the millennial generation of artists, but it simply continues and reconfirms the waning of political themes and the transcendent importance of the individual that apparently characterized the second period.[13] This polarized classificatory scheme gave rise to what has been perceived as a public debate between Shifra M. Goldman and artists Malaquias Montoya and Lezlie Salkowitz-Montoya. Although they appeared to value different aesthetic practices, the Montoyas and Goldman called for a politics of accountability as an aspect of historical and aesthetic recognition, or the more current term, *visibility*. They called on artists to engage in the struggle against multiple forms of oppression, although the Montoyas emphasized capitalism.[14] For them, artists are agents of social change. As Romo notes in one of her reformulations of the dualist methodology, the Montoyas advanced "agency (action)" as the defining aspect of Chicana/o art, rather than "artwork (object) and intent (message)," which had been the focus of previous scholarship.[15]

I do not take issue with the claim that Chicana/o art challenges the notion that art is autonomous—that its meaning is internal, referring only to the work itself ("art for art's sake," perhaps). But in this book I do intervene to argue against the dualist approach, which has generally ruled Chicana/o art history since the mid-1970s. I am especially interested in what is left out when one relies on a binary taxonomy of Chicana/o art and in how its dualistic terms of representation narrow the interpretation, reception, and documentation of Chicana/o art. Chon

A. Noriega offers a partial lesson about this bifurcating methodology in his observation of "touchstone Chicano art surveys since the 1980s." He states that "curatorial binaries" have supported a narrow interpretation of Chicana/o art that contrasts "cultural politics versus art market" orientations and "conceptual versus realist" styles.[16] I extend Noriega's observation and expose not only the cultural politics of institutional and exhibition settings but also the ways the methodology of Chicana/o art history has consistently turned to a binary to characterize Chicana/o art and artists in the following ways: political versus commercial art, folk versus fine art, parochial versus cosmopolitan art or global aesthetics, representational versus conceptual art, older or *veterano* artists versus younger ones, women versus men, feminist versus Chicano art (in this case, the authentic category is structured as patriarchal), historical documents versus aesthetic objects, untrained versus formally trained artists, ethnic-identified versus postethnic artists, and Chicana/o versus Mexican artists. The polarities are coupled so that the existence of one requires the existence of the other. Often, however, that other is assumed or imagined: the opposing category is rarely present within an exhibition or scholarly work.[17] The most troubling aspect of the binary is its ability to excuse serious research.

My burden of representation is to repair the "entrenched, polarizing accounts" and explain how Chicana/o art "might bridge or even exceed these categories."[18] Thus my goal in *Chicana/o Remix* is to challenge the art historian, curator, or critic who has classified Chicana/o art as parochial, separatist, political, "too ethnic," or not ethnic enough. In presenting this new scholarship, I hope to broaden the ways Chicana/o visual art is interpreted and theorized and to expand the arenas in which critical debate takes place. Read comparatively with the existing scholarship, this book offers a revision of accepted Mexican, Latin American, and American art histories, one built on a broader, more representative base that does not conform to normative phantoms. I do so by documenting the multifaceted, intertwined, and generative visual culture of Chicana/o art in Los Angeles since 1963.

Los Angeles serves as an ideal case study for investigating Chicana/o art and its terms of visibility for several reasons. The metropolitan area may not be unique in the quality and quantity of its Chicana/o visual arts, but it is exemplary in the resources and collective energy that can be harnessed for its documentation. Los Angeles is home to three major centers of Chicana/o art production and criticism—Self Help Graphics & Art, Social and Public Art Resource Center (SPARC), and Plaza de la Raza—that originated during the Chicano movement and continue a sustained and expansive engagement with the visual arts. Los Angeles is also one of only a few urban centers with a rich material archive. The region allows for extensive archival investigation of its own history, thanks to the private collection of postcards and other exhibition ephemera gathered and preserved by Mary Salinas Durón and Armando Durón, the archival materials, art, and life history interviews of artists at the UCLA Chicano Studies Research Center, and the California Ethnic and Multicultural Archives (CEMA) at the University of California, Santa Barbara, which houses the institutional materials of multiple arts organizations located in Los Angeles and the private files of Shifra M. Goldman.[19]

Los Angeles has been home to some of the most important exhibitions of Chicana/o art, and these have given rise to extensive archival documentation and popular criticism. The foundational show *Chicano Art: Resistance and Affirmation, 1965–1985* emerged in 1990 from faculty and students at UCLA. The metropolitan area is home to internationally recognized Chicana/o artists, including Carlos Almaraz, Judith Baca, Chaz Bojórquez, Barbara Carrasco, Yreina D. Cervántez, Harry Gamboa Jr., Gronk, Gilbert "Magu" Sánchez Luján, John Valadez, and Patssi Valdez. Their work is exhibited, collected, documented, and archived, although not at the level of other midcareer American artists.

The most recent phenomenon that makes Los Angeles important is the unprecedented season in which six exhibitions of Chicana/o art were produced by mainstream institutions with support from the Getty Foundation's Pacific Standard Time (PST) initiative.[20] Starting in 2002, the Getty provided over $11 million to support research, exhibitions, programs, and publications on the LA postwar art scene. This initiative launched an unparalleled six-month collaboration with over sixty institutions that presented the art of Los Angeles in a series of public programs and exhibitions that began in the fall of 2011. Six of the exhibitions focused on Chicana/o art. *Asco: Elite of the Obscure* was curated by Rita Gonzalez and C. Ondine Chavoya and was presented by the Los Angeles County Museum of Art (LACMA) with the Williams College Museum of Art. *MEX/LA: Mexican Modernism(s) in Los Angeles 1930–1985* was curated by Rubén Ortiz-Torres (with Jesse Lerner) at the Museum of Latin American Art in Long Beach. The umbrella project *L.A. Xicano*, organized by the Chicano Studies Research Center, presented four exhibitions: *Art along the Hyphen: The Mexican-American Generation* (lead curator, Terezita Romo) at the Autry National Center; *Mural Remix: Sandra de la Loza*, an installation conceived and designed by the artist at LACMA; and, at UCLA's Fowler Museum, *Mapping Another L.A.: The Chicano Art Movement* and *Icons of the Invisible: Oscar Castillo*. PST represented a milestone in the United States, not just Los Angeles.[21] The exhibition of Chicana/o art in Los Angeles has often involved joint efforts between community-based or artist collectives, college- and university-based programs, and mainstream institutions. For instance, the 1975 coproduced group show *Chicanismo en el Arte* debuted at East Los Angeles College and LACMA and involved a large cohort of Chicana/o artists and arts advocates. The quality and quantity of exhibitions that are generated by collaborations or debates between Chicana/o arts cultural centers and mainstream institutions are probably unique to Los Angeles, and create an extensive discursive and institutional archive.

*Chicana/o Remix* also elucidates the analysis of Chicana/o, Latina/o, and Latin American art beyond Los Angeles. Forms of and approaches to art are not unique to Chicana/o Los Angeles but are also found among Nuyorican artists in New York City, Mexican artists in Chicago, and Tejana/o artists in San Antonio. The troubled relations between Los Angeles mainstream art museums and community-based arts organizations— the debates, the tensions, and the uneven collaborations—apply to other sites of Latina/o cultural production. Most important, although the critical frames for visibility emerge from Los Angeles–based exhibition and curatorial practices, the amalgamated theoretical discourse can apply across a range of Chicana/o art cultural production. Los Angeles does not hold a monopoly on the use of exhibition and curation as a site of art criticism or as a methodology for canon critique. In this way, the book contributes to an understanding of Chicana/o and Latina/o art that is based on a broader national and international perspective.

## The Wisdom of *Action Portraits*

I begin my project with an analysis of Sandra de la Loza's *Action Portraits* (2011). This groundbreaking work, which de la Loza created in collaboration with Joseph Santarromana, visually expresses the methodology and framework for my engagement with Chicana/o art. Simply put, de la Loza brings to the foreground of art discourse previously ignored or undocumented styles of Chicana/o murals painted in the 1970s. In her "double role as artist and curator," she functions as a "performative archivist" who instructs us to return to the archive with eyes wide open.[22] A component of the exhibition *Mural Remix: Sandra de la Loza* at the Los Angeles County Museum of Art (LACMA) in 2011, *Action Portraits* covered an entire wall of the Samuel H. Kress Foundation Gallery on the second floor of LACMA's Ahmanson Building. In the three-channel video installation, six contemporary East Los Angeles muralists—identified as Fabian Debora, Roberto Del Hoyo, Raul Gonzalez, Liliflor, Sonji, and Timoi—are shown larger than life, painting their nude bodies with kaleidoscopic designs. Each muralist works methodically and somewhat theatrically, moving a large paintbrush over torso, arms, hands, neck, and face. As the brush moves, multichromatic patterns appear on the skin. De la Loza created these designs from samples drawn from color slides in the Nancy Tovar Murals of East Los Angeles Slide Collection.[23] The motifs that make up the designs—natural landscapes, supergraphics, organic shapes, elements of nature, text, and symbols of life force, as well as spirals, concentric circles, and geometric and psychedelic patterns—are from the backgrounds of extant and destroyed murals, painted in the 1970s, that "animated and activated" the walls of an important Chicana/o neighborhood.[24]

To create *Action Portraits*, de la Loza filmed the six muralists dipping their brushes into a bucket positioned off-screen and coating their bodies with green paint. De la Loza and Santarromana then digitally inserted the designs into the painted areas.[25] The portraits of the sitters vary in duration, and in the three-panel display the portraits appear on the wall in a random loop sequence, occupying one or two of the three "canvases" at a time. The result is a seemingly infinite number of combinations, which thwart expectation and compel the viewer to watch actively. Unlike conventional portrait subjects, the muralists participate in their self-making. They determine how, at what speed, and where to apply the brush and move it across their bodies. Once completely covered, they stare directly at the camera, which captures their figures from waist to face. Raul Gonzalez starts his first stroke below his navel, at the body's center of gravity, pulls the brush vertically to his neck, and then rapidly makes two horizontal swipes across his face (fig. 1.1). He pauses before the next stroke, gazing into the camera as if to acknowledge his aware-

1.1 Sandra de la Loza, in collaboration with Joseph Santarromana, *Action Portraits* (still from digital video), 2011. Image courtesy of the artist.

1.2 Sandra de la Loza, in collaboration with Joseph Santarromana, *Action Portraits* (still from digital video), 2011. Image courtesy of the artist.

ness of the viewer's inspection. The "paint" on his face recalls Holly-wood's depictions of Indian warriors and shamans, and in that moment he looks ready for battle or ritual. Fabian Debora also conveys his recognition of public scrutiny. After he completes his portrait, Debora holds the paintbrush like a weapon of defiance, firmly gripping the handle and staging the brush below his waist (fig. 1.2).[26]

*Action Portraits* points to the invisibility of psychedelia, supergraphics, organic shapes, text, and nature motifs in art historical accounts of Chicana/o murals—an absence that was produced by scholars' overemphasis on political realism as the only significant aesthetic produced during the Chicano movement. Similarly, by directing us to the multiplicity of these motifs, de la Loza undercuts the anticipated and conventional art discourse. By manipulating and reframing the very objects—East Los Angeles murals—that have become canonized as Chicana/o art, or that have been dismissed as cliché in some circles, *Action Portraits* invites a re-thinking of Chicana/o art history and the historical, social, and aesthetic frameworks that make Chicana/o cultural production visible. We come to recognize, as de la Loza did in her study of the Tovar Collection, that Chicana/o artists of the 1970s applied a range of styles, techniques, and designs to their East LA murals.

Following de la Loza's methodology, I look closely at Chicana/o art since the 1960s to identify and theorize the ignored, forgotten, or un-documented aspects of cultural production. *Chicana/o Remix* documents and analyzes works, artists, experiences, and practices that have been overlooked due to prevailing theoretical conventions and disciplinary boundaries. I put these conventions aside to investigate anew artistic production, interpretation, curatorial practice, and collecting in multiple arenas. This research presents a panorama of Chicana/o art between 1963 and 2013 that includes exhibitions, institutions, private collections, and artists' aesthetic experiences, as well as curatorial discourse and art criticism. I demonstrate how each of these functions as an important site of knowledge and cultural production.

Because this is the first book to look at Chicana/o art from the 1960s through the first decade or more of the twenty-first century, and because it accounts for processes and practices across the so-called political and commercial phases of Chicana/o art, I am able to interrogate assumptions about Chicana/o art during and after the Chicano movement. For example, what is accomplished when a contemporary Chicana artist confronts the expectations about her identity? In *Action Portraits*, the arbitrary combination of portraits within the triptych calls attention to the multiple and complex subject positions—societal placements determined by prevailing discourses of race, gender, and so on—of what we recognize as "community" and "self" as well as "art" and "artist." In this work de la Loza breaks out from the singular index.[27] As brown skin, tattoos, and faces are covered, personal identity is obscured and collective subjectivity is amplified as the "portrait" is completed.[28] As multichromatic images cover brown flesh, the viewer is forced to focus on the mural motifs, and the muralists' bodies become the canvas that holds the image. The muralists participate in the obfuscation of their self-portraits. For instance, the female muralists appear with their breasts already painted, an act that disguises sex and gender and denies sexualized viewing (see fig. 1.1). By withholding racialized and gendered readings of the muralists' bodies, de la Loza increases the resonance of a communal location and place.[29]

The tension between public and private representation and performance of the self is built into the work through the placement of the camera and the framing of the muralists' bodies. The spectator observes several muralists, for example, painstakingly painting each finger, making sure that no flesh is exposed. Once the portraits are complete, however, the muralists' hands fall outside the video frame. The covering of the body—the action—is meant for the viewer, but the entire figure is not intended for the viewer's gaze. The work tacitly forbids the appropriation of the artist and the community. De la Loza reinforces the act of withholding by omitting the muralists' voices from the video. The viewer cannot hear the cheerful conversation Timoi is having with someone off-screen. Her lips shape words, her face opens into a smile, and her eyes respond to conversation, but the viewer hears nothing. De la Loza recognizes that public and private visibility are connected without collapsing the distance between them. Portraiture yes, but self-representation is not offered for wholesale consumption. The work makes the viewer aware that "the visual field cannot provide full knowledge of a person," as Amelia Jones observes about Rachel Garfield's video installation *So You Think You Can Tell* (2000).[30] When the muralists in *Action Portraits* gaze at the camera or hold the brush as a weapon, they tacitly acknowledge the forces that have shaped their self-making, recalling Bryan Jay Wolf's observation that "art comes into being *not* by naming its sources, the forces which make it possible, but by effacing, erasing them." It is the art historian's task, recommends Wolf, "to understand the anxieties, tensions, contradictions, overdeterminations, and resolutions (both personal and social)" that an artwork does not display.[31]

In *Action Portraits* de la Loza insists that the muralists' bodies—and the public memories of East Los Angeles—are not meant for appropriation. A relevant art history must insist on the visibility of Chicana/o artists and their work, but not as exotic, foreign, primitive, or other. Previous efforts to analyze Chicana/o art have resulted in the untenable charges that Chicana/o art is "too ethnic," "too female," or "not Chicano enough," proclamations that do little to illuminate the aesthetic process, its social conditions, or the work itself. In this way, *Action Portraits* pushes us to a theoretical framework that acknowledges Chicana/o art as a historically contingent and spatially informed process of self-making, even as it extends beyond the process. *Action Portraits* additionally signals that Chicana/o art has emerged from an epistemology that is grounded in spatial, embodied, affective, and relational meaning. The muralists perform the activity of self-making with great intensity and concentration. They place the brush deliberately, their hands seeking the sensation their bodies know—a patch of flesh is showing on the underside of the arm, a spot on the forehead needs another coat of paint, or the brush moves systematically across the torso in a series of horizontal strokes as the mind's eye traces a grid. *Action Portraits* suggests that the artists' proprioception is not only physical, providing them with an awareness of their bodies in space and the relative location of each limb, but also societal: they are aware of a sense of place, whether within the city of Los Angeles, or the field of Chicana/o art, or American art history more generally. Their knowledge of place is indistinguishable from their knowledge of themselves. When this social proprioception includes attentiveness to power dynamics, it becomes what Chela Sandoval identifies as oppositional consciousness, a critical awareness and strategy for action that intertwines ways of thinking to respond to inequality and injustice.[32]

Sandra de la Loza's remix of the visual record tells us that what we thought we knew about Chicana/o art is likely insufficient, if not mistaken. The sampling, the kaleidoscope technique, and the remixing of background as foreground remind us that art histories are social constructions that can legitimate some works and some artists while rendering others invisible. Her engagement with the archive becomes a form of critical interrogation of the subjective quality of knowledge production and of the framing of Chicana/o art. *Action Portraits* skillfully rejects an essentialist reading of the very art form that has been employed to support the narrow interpretation or dismissal of Chicana/o art. By subverting the anticipated iconography, de la Loza refocuses our gaze without apology. Similarly, this book intervenes in standard discourses of American, Latin American, and Chicana/o art history by remixing the exhibition record as well as the critical weight of specific exhibitions. It also offers new information—for example, about artists' travel in Europe and Asia, the for-profit activities of arts organizations, the advocacy of private collectors—without dismissal or apology. *Chicana/o Remix*, too, functions as canon critique.

In the end, Sandra de la Loza's *Action Portraits* demonstrates that the visibility of Chicana/o art is tied to the historicization of the work. She holds scholars accountable to the historical context, but she does not pretend to have resolved the postmodern dilemma, which asks, "Whose history?" Nevertheless, the artist consistently directs the viewer to a counterhistory rather than the status quo. In her new approach to the art historical record, de la Loza does not dismiss the social and political mobilizations that activate Chicana/o communities, and she does not disregard the conditions that gave rise to mural production in Los Angeles. *Action Portraits* operates not in the space of shame, ambivalence, or apology, but as an ethical challenge intended to open the discourse and expand, not contract, how we consider Chicana/o art. If we make Chicana/o art visible, then it must be seen in terms that take account of the artist's proprioception (expanded to include their knowledge of themselves and their relative location within art history), the actual context and content of the work, and the hegemonic imperatives of coloniality, patriarchy, and racism that caused its invisibility. Sandra de la Loza may not have intended a reorientation of the field, but she offers a model for challenging the tools that have conventionally been used to animate the field.

### Introducing Anzaldúan Thought to Art History

Following Sandra de la Loza's visual charge, I aim to historicize Chicana/o art in Los Angeles in ways that push beyond the current limits of American and Chicana/o art histories. My project relies on Emma Pérez's notion of the "decolonial imaginary."[33] I begin by following tactics and spaces in which Chicana/o art is visible, analyzed, and theorized. I also consider topics that other critics describe as parochial or anachronistic in an effort to disqualify those charges that I interpret as a practice of invisibility. Decolonial theory posits that invisibility—in this case that of Chicana/o art within the fields of American and Latin American art, and even in some cases within the field of Chicana/o art—is rooted in the histories of colonialism, imperialism, material and political dispossession, and legal and discursive exclusion from citizenship. A decolonial framework recognizes that the "master's tools" have been inadequate to reveal, let alone dismantle, the hegemonic framework of art criticism.[34] The historical and contemporary racialization of Mexicans as criminals, perpetual foreigners, and immigrants who are straining the economy and cultural fabric of the nation; the militarization of the southern geopolitical border; the long-term detention of hundreds of thousands of migrants at deportation centers, away from public and legal scrutiny, in the name of national security; gendered violence against Mexican women and Chicanas in the health care system and institutions ostensibly designed to uphold democracy and liberty; the subtractive language model of K–12 public education, which leads to the loss of Spanish proficiency within five years of schooling; the segregation of the labor market and housing; the contemporary disavowal or commercial appropriation of identity and culture—all create the conditions that obscure or reject Chicana/o art. This obfuscation and rejection have served racial, material, gender, sexual, and other hierarchies and privileges in American society and scholarship.

I intentionally employ historical description and formal analysis in my exploration of largely uncharted territory because this interdisciplinary method supports a politics of visibility—that is, it attends to the political and cultural conditions under which Chicana/o art critics, historians, curators, teachers, and collectors engage the work. As Priscilla Wald reminds us, "History [needs] to be rewritten not only to register past injustices but also because history—the story of the past—justifies the institutions and structures of the present."[35] My goal is to question art history's structures, methods, and institutions. If I am successful, my narration will draw attention to the ways Chicana/o art is a decolonial practice. This book is itself a function of the decolonial imaginary and "a form of reparation."[36] At the heart of this project is the exposure of a myth: that artists and art exist outside history. Although I do not directly engage with this premise, this book works as a counternarrative to the dismissal of identity-based art.[37] For a broad range of scholars, curators, and critics, identity, as well as subjectivity and positionality, is "something we might be better off without."[38] This suggests that the universal legibility of cultural production occurs when artists rise above local meaning. I suggest instead that the power of Chicana/o art originates in its ability to access local meaning. Equally important is its ability to register with viewers who are outside the immediate context of Chicana/o experiences. I am fascinated by the ways Chicana/o art blends and exceeds the categories of local and global, regional and universal, or collective distinction and individuality.

A politics of visibility is intertwined with notions of accountability. This insistence on accountability is not a gatekeeping function or claim to authenticity, nor does it seek political isolation. It is simply an acknowledgment of the dynamics that made the body of work known as Chicana/o art invisible within American and Latin American art historiography. Visibility cannot be achieved without a recognition of the conversations under way within critical ethnic and feminist studies, and it cannot require the denial of the proper name of this art in any of its formations and negotiations, including Mexican American, Chicano, Xicana, Jotería, Indígena, Latinx, or Latin@. The current model of accommodation and assimilation—gaining access, seeking integration, achieving economic success—risks the further appropriation of Chicana/o art and, tragically, its further exclusion from its place within American and Latin American art historiography. My aim is to make the presence of Chicana/o art within mainstream or authorizing museums, collections, and criticism serve the collective project of emancipation, social justice, dignity, and empowerment. To do otherwise would only boost assimilationist rhetoric, the lifeblood of American cultural hegemony, and extend its articulation within art history. Chicana/o art cannot gain critical acceptance only to be used as reinforcement for negative stereotypes of Mexicans, a patriarchal or homophobic gaze, or racial and cultural hierarchies that dehumanize Chicanas/os and privilege whiteness. At the deepest level, then, *Chicana/o Remix* confronts the ideological and material dimensions of white racial primacy and its ability to inhabit and control knowledge production. This study is a reparative measure because it recognizes that our public institutions of art—

whether involved in education, art production, or art preservation—are unsustainable. The demography of the United States, as actor and collector Cheech Marin proudly points out, has shifted, and Chicanos and Chicanas are currently "the mainstream" simply by their numeric presence and transcultural influence.[39]

This book also considers *mestiza* consciousness, which Gloria Anzaldúa describes as taking shape at the moment when the terms *domestic* and *foreign*—or *self* and *other*—have "lost their semantic tidiness."[40] However, I do not assume that the terms were tidy during an earlier period and become less tidy in the twenty-first century. Although Anzaldúan scholarship has yet to take up permanent residency within art history, I aim to join these intellectual discourses.[41] While few art historians would support the statement that culture is bounded by race/ethnicity or gender, this dated notion consistently appears as an undercurrent in discussions about nonwhite artists who are conceived as completely separate or inherently distinct from a white population.[42] Specifically, art history lacks a theory of the borderlands—one that ventures beyond simplistic understandings of cultural assimilation or separatism—and this omission supports the current vilification of ethnic-identified artists and their work. By linking my work to Anzaldúan social analysis, I contribute to the practice of ending what Chela Sandoval has called "academic apartheid."[43] In this way, *Chicana/o Remix* aims to bridge disciplinary distinctions that privilege European and European American social critics over feminists of color in the United States.

As AnaLouise Keating demonstrates, Anzaldúan thought provides an analytic lens for comprehending local and global movement and dispersal across racialized, gendered, sexed, and material borders.[44] By considering the local and international movement of not only people but also ideas and cultural products across racialized and material borders, it also explores transhistorical subjectivities, such as Xican@ indigeneity and the desire of Xican@ people to claim a native presence in the nation, in the past, and in contemporary cultures.[45] In the Americas transnational flows take many forms, most of which are unacknowledged or denied by nationalistic rhetoric, which promotes a singular body politic. Many Chicana/o artists follow a different cultural logic: a willingness to extend temporally (transhistorically) and spatially (transnationally) across the Americas, and to do so in ways that exceed national identifiers that guide the current methods and boundaries of art history.

By tracing art exhibitions, arts organizations, artists' lives and work, and collections, *Chicana/o Remix* attempts a more capacious art history. As I grapple with the limits, errors, and omissions of a field of study, I extend the recuperative project that began in the 1960s to bring the voices of Chicana/o artists, curators, and advocates into view and to understand their agency as theory. I aim to reposition from the margins the art, the work, organizations, and practices of Chicana/o art. The book is expansive, with an investigative reach of five decades, even as its spatial location is precise. Although focused solely on the Los Angeles area, it delves deeply into each of its topics: presentations of art, the ways artists construct an infrastructure to present or sell their work, the paths of discovery as the artists formulate their aesthetic styles, and the ways collectors and mainstream arts institutions respond to the broad range of Chicana/o art.

## Organization of the Book

In this wide-ranging study, each chapter offers new material and ways of thinking about Chicana/o art and can stand on its own as a case study of Chicana/o art. Chapter 2 documents the appearance of a counter-discourse since 1975 to argue that Chicana/o art criticism is produced through the "errata exhibition," a term I have coined to describe a type of visual arts practice that challenges interpretations made by the so-called public museum and offers critical and visual engagement with mainstream art museums.[46] By staging errata exhibitions, Chicana/o arts organizations offer alternative knowledge production, art criticism, and history of Chicana/o art. Using an interdisciplinary method that combines formalism with sociohistorical analysis, the chapter describes the conceptual frame for visibility that I employ throughout the book.

Chapter 3 travels into uncharted territory regarding Chicana/o arts organizations. Following the methodology of Sandra de la Loza, I return to the archive and bring new or previously ignored information to the forefront. Focusing on the period 1969–78, the chapter illustrates how the earliest ventures operated with complex and nuanced views about commerce, politics, community, and the arts. This chapter documents how Goez Art Studios and Gallery and Mechicano Art Center moved between for-profit and nonprofit endeavors, linking commerce and art, engaging in cross-cultural collaboration, and advocating for social transformation and the potentiality of Chicana/o art and the communities from which it emerges.

Chapter 4 also takes the reader to unmapped territory by analyzing the international influences that inform the work of Chicana/o artists. Very little has been written about the impact of non-Chicana/o or non-Mexican aesthetics on the artwork produced by Chicanas/os. Researchers overlook how European art influences Chicana/o artists. For instance, during an oral history interview for the Smithsonian Institution, Jeffrey Rangel disregards Gilbert "Magu" Sánchez Luján's remark that he was stationed for three years in England. Magu states that he joined the Air Force specifically for the GI Bill and "to go overseas and see the world," but at this point Rangel changes the subject.[47] By taking up a topic that has been dismissed since the earliest formations of Chicana/o art history, I argue that any analysis of Chicana/o art must recognize the social proprioception of the artist. This attentiveness to self-in-relation produces a new language and framework for comprehending the realities of aesthetic influence while acknowledging the politics of visibility. Looking closely at specific works of art, I show that Chicana/o artists craft a visual language that is both local and global, even combining visual aesthetic practices across historical moments.

In chapter 5 I argue that Chicana/o art collectors in Los Angeles embody the public emplacement of Chicana/o art, offering a new map for understanding cultural production. Their collecting practices are living corrections to the art historical record housed inside local and national museums that claim to safeguard the aesthetic achievements of the region, nation, or world. It is within private collections that the archive of Chicana/o art is maintained, preserved, and protected. Collectors in Los Angeles have created informal and formal groups to share and celebrate their work, and in this way, I argue, Chicana/o art collectors function as "critical witnesses" to the national and international injustice of neglect and invisibility.[48]

Chapter 6 expands the methodology of Sandra de la Loza, presenting a remix of the Chicana/o art exhibitions produced in the first decade of the twenty-first century. *The Road to Aztlan: Art from a Mythic Homeland* (2001) and *Asco: Elite of the Obscure, A Retrospective, 1972–1987* (2011) are the main focus. This remix allows new narratives and visual aesthetics, and it brings forgotten histories into the foreground—specifically that of the early exhibition *4 Chicano Artists* (1970–71).

*Chicana/o Remix* concludes with an invitation to create, expand, and explore the archive of Chicana/o art. Unlike Chicana/o literary criticism, which can be distinguished by a variety of interpretative frameworks such as cultural nationalist, poststructuralist, Marxist, feminist, queer, and gothic, scholarly work on American and Chicana/o art has taken a much narrower approach. Therefore we have much work ahead of us. In raising this call, I recognize the difficulty of dismantling ideological and structural fortresses that have made it difficult to see Chicana/o art. I am inspired by the art itself, especially its arrival in unexpected places. Therefore, the bulk of the closing chapter is devoted to three delightful tales about Chicana/o art exhibitions and what they foretell for the future and the questions we are asking about art.

# ERRATA EXHIBITIONS

## The Sites of Chicana/o Art Discourse

Opening at the SPARC Gallery in March 1989, *Errata: Not Included* disputed the art historiography of *Hispanic Art in the United States: Thirty Contemporary Painters and Sculptors*, the intra-continental touring exhibition that had arrived at the Los Angeles County Museum of Art a month earlier.[1] With portable murals, mural sketches, and paintings of explicit and potent political commentary, *Errata: Not Included* insisted on the social function of art. Additionally, guest curator Maria Luisa de Herrera aimed a spotlight on the very art form—the mural—that had been ignored by *Hispanic Art* curators Jane Livingston and John Beardsley, who insisted on an exclusive emphasis on painting and sculpture that was colorful and fanciful and neo-expressionist or abstract.[2] De Herrera featured five prolific Los Angeles muralists—Judith Baca, David Botello, Wayne Alaniz Healy, Willie Herrón III, and George Yepes—in *Errata: Not Included*, documenting the importance of muralism as a national form of Chicana/o visual expression. The exhibition acknowledged the mural as the most widely recognized genre of Chicana/o art, one that has flourished since the late 1960s. *Errata: Not Included* challenged Livingston and Beardsley's curatorial silence about politics and art and claimed that the historic significance of the mural lay in its integration of politics and art. It clarified that one could not separate the "artistic" from the "sociological," as Livingston and Beardsley had proposed.[3]

One example from *Errata: Not Included* illustrates this position of integration. Willie Herrón III's portable mural *Sueños Hechos Realidad*

**2.1** Willie Herrón III, *Sueños Hechos Realidad*, 1972. Portable mural, acrylic on Masonite, 8 x 8 feet. Image courtesy of Social and Public Art Resource Center (SPARC). © 1972 Willie Herrón III.

(1972) is a surreal aesthetic achievement that metaphorically—and satirically, given the work's title, "Dreams Come True"—details the trauma and frustration within Chicana/o communities (fig. 2.1). A multiheaded figure fills the mural canvas, and one central *calavera* focuses its gaze directly at the viewer while the five other distorted faces are in profile at right and left. The chest cavity of the figure is exposed, and the red and blue veins pump precious blood. A flail swings from the figure's left hand, and another hand grips a grenade. It is unclear whether the hand is tossing it away or pulling it inside the exposed body, suggesting that

ERRATA EXHIBITIONS

strategies of resistance are both destructive and constructive. Herrón's portable mural visualizes the brutal attacks on Chicano dreams of belonging and safety as well as the creative arts as a tactic of resistance against injury, exploitation, and suppression.

## The Errata Exhibition: The Site of a New Art Criticism

*Errata: Not Included* is an ideal starting point for a remixing of Chicana/o art discourse. Following Sandra de la Loza, I bring to the foreground the exhibition activities at SPARC that are generally overlooked in order to rethink art criticism. SPARC's ongoing contribution to public art, notably the creation and preservation of mural monuments in Southern California, overshadows its significant exhibition record. Yet since its founding, the SPARC Gallery has evidenced a consistent oppositional consciousness and critical position that are intertwined with the regional arts and social scene.[4] While the exhibition space has launched the careers of dozens of LA Chicana/o and other nonwhite and women artists, the gallery was never intended as a springboard into market success. As SPARC's artistic director, Judith Baca, states, the organization's presentation venue was conceived as a means to promote "social change" and provide a "desperately needed alternative to the commercial-valued art world."[5] SPARC's executive director, Debra Padilla, observes that the gallery functions as a space of critical engagement in which to expand aesthetic discourse, inspire civic dialogue, and present visual art that is not dependent on nationalistic, patriarchal, or homophobic expectations.[6]

I coin the term *errata exhibition* to honor SPARC's role in shaping, fostering, and naming this critical genre. This mode of exhibition has come into sharp focus because of *Errata: Not Included*, although the strategy predates the 1989 show. The term *errata exhibition* distinguishes a type of visual arts presentation that aims to overturn the art criticism that accompanies mainstream exhibitions and calls into question the artificiality of cultural authority and discernment by intervening against and analyzing the claims made by other arts institutions.[7] It is a timely visual and public challenge to American art criticism, methods, and category formation, particularly the narrow constructions of "Chicana/o art" and "American art." For its producers, the errata exhibition provides what is immediately missing from the prevailing arts discourse. Although an errata exhibition participates in the larger site of contestation (the critical reviews, audience reception, and scholarly analysis of a show), the errata exhibition is centrally concerned with its interlocutor, the mainstream exhibition. I showcase the errata exhibition because its critical contribution has received relatively little acknowledgment and, thus, is ephemeral when compared to the reviews and analyses generated within the mainstream of American art history and criticism.[8] Thus, the bulk of my interdisciplinary analysis engages only selectively with the exhibitions that triggered the errata interventions that I discuss, focusing on their design or layout, the official press releases, the catalog essays and didactic labels, and the general hubbub about a show. As Sandra de la Loza demonstrates, remixing can recenter the discourse, and therefore my aim is to insert the errata exhibitions more permanently into the "book" of American art criticism. I deliberately shift the margin to the center, but I do not wish to imply that the errata are somehow uncomplicated and unmediated truths of art historical discourse. This emphasis is not ideological; it is a pragmatic desire to build the archive. The errata exhibitions and the overwhelming majority of Chicana/o art exhibitions in the Los Angeles metropolitan region that are produced by arts organizations with budgets under one million dollars rarely receive public reviews, media attention, or critical analysis. I begin my investigation of each errata exhibition by looking at the issues raised by the intervention, and I detour when formal analysis will help illuminate the critical discourse of the errata exhibition. My strategy allows me to document aspects of Chicana/o art production that are otherwise invisible.

I argue that given the relative absence of Chicana/o art within American art criticism and authorizing institutions, the errata exhibition has become a powerful form of intervention.[9] As a critical strategy, the errata exhibition announces problematic interpretations, or, more accurately, recognizes systematic flaws in the art historical method that do not allow for an accounting of its own coloniality. This coloniality is reflected in part in the dichotomous approach that considers art production as either high or low, fine or folk, modern or primitive, and postethnic or ethnic. As a public critique, the errata exhibition holds the potential to rectify myths of whiteness as well as untenable representations of Chicana/o art and culture, such as those that separate art and politics. In this way, the errata exhibition is a social space of opposition and activity that invites public discussion among multiple audiences. However, the errata exhibition also demonstrates that an oppositional consciousness is not isolationist. It clarifies how binary thinking misunderstands Chicana/o art practices.

Although the insights produced by the errata exhibition are related to earlier forms of institutional critique created by Fluxus artists in the 1960s and 1970s, as well as the challenges artists made to the white cube—the typical white-walled gallery—in the 1970s and 1980s, the errata exhibition is concerned most directly with the ideological apparatus of the museum and its creation of "visual regimes that support cultural, racial and class hierarchies."[10] In her review of "museumist art"—art that challenges traditional approaches to collecting and display—Lisa G. Corrin astutely observes that critique of the museum as an institution "often inadvertently reasserts the validity of the museum." The work of artists such as "Michael Asher, Louise Lawler, Judith Barry, Andrea Fraser, and Hans Haacke" has "increasingly become politically neutralized, now comfortably coexisting within the archetypal white cube it intended to critique." For Corrin, the co-optation of museumist art occurs because the artists "have had to avoid direct discussion of the relation of a commissioning museum to issues of race."[11] The errata exhibition works within the dissent tradition of American arts but with an attention to an aesthetic politics that emerges from the very topics usually disallowed in the museum, such as race, ethnicity, class, gender, sexuality, language, or white privilege. Furthermore, the errata exhibition does not attempt to "coexist comfortably" with the institutions and ideologies it interrogates but instead offers new terms, new sites, and new epistemologies of visibility.

The errata exhibition is a form of institutional critique that is similar to Fred Wilson's "critical, materialist investigation of museums."[12] It questions the racial logic that determines how museums preserve and display art and artifacts. Its purpose parallels that of James Luna's performances and multimedia works, which challenge the ongoing colonialist display of Native American art and culture, and Ken Gonzales-Day's Profiled series, a set of photographs that juxtapose sculptures from several encyclopedic museums to create a visual discourse on race, representation, and the role of Western collections in the formation of racial difference and racial hierarchies. The errata exhibition also resonates with Renée Green's multimedia interrogations of the residue of colonial contact and the codetermination of race and gender and with artists working independently of the authorizing institutions, such as the

Guerrilla Girls, who lampoon museum conventions that ignore gender, racial, and class privileges.

The errata exhibition has much in common with *Spray Paint LACMA* (1972), also referred to as *Project Pie in De/Face*, a well-known critique of LACMA. Performed and documented by Asco, the Los Angeles artist collective initially composed of Harry Gamboa Jr., Gronk, Willie Herrón III, and Patssi Valdez (with the frequent participation of Humberto Sandoval), *Spray Paint LACMA* contested notions of authority and authorship. Using spray paint, Gamboa, Gronk, and Herrón signed their names on one of LACMA's exterior walls and came back the next morning to photograph the event with Valdez. Both the act and the image dispute the meaning of the art object and the structures that determine valuation. Their protest was, as Chon A. Noriega notes, "in accordance with the terms of institutional critique being developed at the time." However, as Noriega elaborates, Asco's institutional critique was distinct from other local challenges to the museum, such as Edward Ruscha's *The Los Angeles County Museum on Fire* (1965–68), because Asco insisted on the annihilation of the racial and class conventions that underwrite the so-called universal aesthetic and produce the judgments that are a major aspect of curation. In both the act and the image, Asco exposed "the larger system of organized practices that produce racialized subjects" and thus "the underlying racial and class dynamics that exclude Chicano artists."[13] As collective critical discourse, errata exhibitions extend this form of dissent.

Chicana/o arts organizations in Los Angeles have staged critical conversations by producing over 2,200 exhibitions between 1963 and 2013. The overwhelming majority of these exhibitions were produced by Self Help Graphics & Art, SPARC, Plaza de la Raza, Goez Art Studios and Gallery (1969–81), and Mechicano Art Center (1969–78), and by several more institutions that opened near the end of the twentieth century: Palmetto Gallery (1988–94), organized by David Botello and Wayne Alaniz Healy; Galería Las Americas (1990–2001), operated by Linda Vallejo, and its predecessor, Galería Nueva (1989–91), which Vallejo co-owned with Ramses Noriega; Tropico de Nopal Gallery Art-Space (2000–present), founded by Reyes Rodriguez and Marialice Jacob; and Avenue 50 Studio (2001–present), founded by Kathy Gallegos.[14] Indeed, it can be argued that Chicana/o art exhibitions largely function as a counterbalance to the Eurocentric art establishment in their claims to space, belonging, history, and culture that are not permitted under the cultural hegemony of the United States.[15] However, these sites from which the subaltern speaks "might bridge or even exceed" American and European aesthetics, as artists have made use of the cultures in which they participate.[16] Nevertheless, the arts organizations were critical of the authority and exclusionary power that accumulate due to the codetermined privileges of American and European art and art criticism. This chapter focuses on six errata exhibitions and their ability to disrupt interpretations of art as well as spur a rethinking of Chicana/o visual arts practice and production.[17] I select these six because curatorial statements are available through documents or interviews, although my analysis does extend beyond the curators' goals when I offer formal analysis of the work on display. The interdisciplinary methods, and even my own detours, illustrate how a flexible methodology can document a rich field of Chicana/o art criticism that has heretofore been largely invisible. Indeed, my focus on the errata exhibition rather than the event that prompted it is a productive intervention against the undocumented nature of Chicana/o art. An emphasis on the errata exhibition, particularly the art, is an intervention that is prudent at this historical juncture.

I begin with the first errata exhibitions in Chicana/o Los Angeles, which appeared in 1975 and 1976. During the Chicano movement, Chicanas questioned claims of ethnic and stylistic coherence and inclusion, voicing feminist critique through visual art production. Under the title *Las Chicanas*, a group of these artists produced a set of errata exhibitions that challenged the patriarchal bias of Chicano art and untenable claims regarding comprehensiveness. At least three were produced on the Eastside, and another, *Las Chicanas: Las Venas de la Mujer*, was showcased at the Woman's Building in downtown Los Angeles. Taking advantage of its extensive archival record, I focus the analysis on *Las Chicanas: Las Venas de la Mujer*. It is an important starting point for this discussion because exhibitions in mainstream art museums in the early twenty-first century continue to overlook the complex, multimodal, and polyvocal aesthetic and critical discourse of the 1970s.

In the 1990s, Chicana feminists echoed in powerful ways the errata exhibitions of the 1970s by commenting on gender balance and stylistic omissions in the seminal exhibitions of the decade, particularly *Chicano Art: Resistance and Affirmation, 1965–1985*, known by its acronym, *CARA*. Chicana feminist artists not only introduced errata as a genre of exhibition, they also brought to public attention the critical lens of borderlands theory, which would guide and inform Chicana/o art exhibitions in Los Angeles for close to fifty years. *Image and Identity: Recent Chicana Art from "La Reina del Pueblo de Los Angeles de la Porciúncula"* (1990) was the first show to systematically register borderlands theory as a key feature of Chicana/o art criticism.

The chapter then turns to an investigation of two errata exhibitions that each contest interpretations of Chicana/o art that emerged from LACMA. *Other Footprints to Aztlan: Works from the Collection of Mary and Armando Durón* (2001), presented by SPARC, was the errata to the county art museum's *Road to Aztlan: Art from a Mythic Homeland* (2001). *Vaguely Chicana* (2008), a solo exhibition of Linda Arreola's work that was curated by Reyes Rodriguez at Tropico de Nopal Gallery Art-Space, was one of a series of corrigenda to *Phantom Sightings: Art after the Chicano Movement* (2008). Although this final section detours from the documentation of the errata exhibition, my methodology illuminates previously undocumented debates and describes the power of local arguments to shake up curatorial statements. By shifting away from the conventions of American art criticism and drawing on borderlands theory, my analysis reveals that Chicana/o art is complex, polyvocal, multireferential, and yet historically contingent.

## Challenging Sexism and Aesthetic Exclusion

*Chicanismo en el Arte* (1975) and *Chicanarte* (1975) were major art exhibitions that helped bring attention to the flourishing Chicana/o art movement in Los Angeles. Both shows were designed as "comprehensive cultural statement[s]," and to that end, each included over a hundred artists and was accompanied by a catalog.[18] Both received considerable local and national media coverage. Given the tenor of the times, it is significant that both debuted at public institutions. *Chicanismo en el Arte* opened at the Vincent Price Art Museum (formerly the Vincent Price Gallery) at East Los Angeles College (ELAC) in March before traveling west to LACMA.[19] *Chicanarte* opened at the Los Angeles Municipal Art Gallery at Barnsdall Park in September. Both included community collaboration, although Chicana/o artists, advocates, and university and college faculty predominantly organized *Chicanarte*.[20] The two exhibitions are frequently considered the events that launched California Chicana/o artists into the national spotlight.[21]

Although the exhibitions were described as "comprehensive," patriarchy undermined principles of equality, inclusion, belonging, and accountability, informing the decisions made for each exhibition. *Chicanismo* may have presented a balance of young men and women when it premiered at the Vincent Price Art Museum; this is difficult to determine, since an exhibition checklist could not be found. Nevertheless, when the show traveled to LACMA, *Chicanismo* was reduced from over two hundred to seventy works, and only four Chicanas—Irma Peña, Thelma H. Sanchez, Maricella Segura, and Patssi Valdez—were among the selected artists. *Chicanarte* featured seventeen female artists, including Yreina D. Cervántez, Gloriamalia Flores, Diane Gamboa, Yolanda M. López of San Diego, Rosalyn Mesquita, Olga Muñiz, Xochitl Nevel, and Josefina Quezada, but it made serious omissions. Judith Baca, Isabel M. Castro, Carmen Lomas Garza, Ester Hernandez, and Judithe Hernández had been producing public art, prints, and paintings since the early 1970s, but they were not included.

Responding to the absence of women artists in these two major shows, Chicana artists decided to present "women's perspectives" and created exhibitions at Plaza de la Raza in Lincoln Park and Mechicano Art Center in East Los Angeles.[22] The errata exhibition *Las Chicanas* debuted in spring 1975 at Plaza's Boathouse Gallery and featured Baca, Castro, Judithe Hernández, Muñiz, and Quezada, as well as Sylvia Moreno. It was reprised in June and, to make a more substantial corrective intervention, it showcased several additional artists: Victoria Del Castillo-Leon, Gloria Florez, filmmaker Sylvia Morales, Celia Tejada, and Patssi Valdez. According to Judithe Hernández, the artists conceptualized *Las Chicanas* with a structure parallel to that of *Los Four*, a traveling exhibition that debuted in 1973 and showcased four (or possibly more) Chicana/o artists. The artists and the works that were included in *Las Chicanas* changed from show to show, but using the consistent title fortified the identity of the loosely affiliated group for audiences.[23] The circulation and repetition of this errata exhibition suggest that Chicana artists achieved some recognition of their reassessment of gender imbalance and their effort to register "women's perspectives" in Chicana/o cultural production.

In addition to the *Las Chicanas* exhibitions in Mexican American neighborhoods, Chicana artists presented *Las Chicanas: Las Venas de la Mujer* (September 16–October 15, 1976) as an errata exhibition at the Woman's Building on North Spring Street near Chinatown. This setting allowed the artists to build critical dialogue across the city and to join with other women who were challenging patriarchy in the arts. It also articulated a then emergent theory of identity and community formation known as intersectionality, a notion that gender, race, class, and other social identities are mutually constitutive.

Using their experiences as sources of knowledge and critical insight, Chicana artists—and writers and activists—began in the 1970s to question the claims of cultural unity, solidarity, and coherence in the face of sexism and racism.[24] For instance, Baca had been collaborating with Christina Schlesinger, who "had come from Boston [to participate in] the Feminist Studio Workshop," which had been founded by artist Judy Chicago, graphic designer Sheila Levrant de Bretteville, and art historian Arlene Raven. Baca and Schlesinger met in 1973 when Schlesinger volunteered for one of Baca's mural teams. Schlesinger subsequently invited Baca to attend a slide-lecture presentation by Raven, and for Baca "it was one of those revelatory, amazing experiences. . . . [Raven] showed slide after slide after slide of women. . . . From Mary Cassatt to . . . Georgia O'Keeffe." This feminist sensibility was further supported by the consciousness-raising workshops Baca attended in Venice, California. Yet neither women's group included what Baca identified as *comadres*, working-class women of Mexican heritage who shared her interest in self-determination and image making. Like her contemporaries, Baca sought artist collectives that could nurture feminist sensibilities, but the Chicano art centers lacked space for her and her development of a feminist art practice.

*Las Chicanas: Las Venas de la Mujer* was a deliberate redress to the omission of Chicanas and Mexican women from Anglo feminist circles as well as the gender imbalance and patriarchy within Chicano artist groups. In *Las Chicanas: Las Venas de la Mujer*, Baca, Castro, Hernández, Muñiz, and Quezada underscored the errata of *Chicanismo* and *Chicanarte* by reinterpreting female icons and the roles to which Mexican American women are assigned (fig. 2.2). Through paintings, drawings, installations, performance, and aerosol and graffiti murals, the exhibition registered a Chicana feminist social criticism against the racial and gendered expectations found within the LA women's movement and the Chicano movement. For instance, the announcement for the exhibition, as Michelle Moravec observes, featured a photograph of the artists in *tableau vivant*, "costumed as various mythohistorical figures."

# Opening: Las Venas de la Mujer

September 16, 8:00 p.m.

Las Chicanas is a group of five women artists: Josephina Quesada, Judith Hernandez, Judy Baca, Olga Munez, and Isabel Castro. Las Chicanas have been showing throughout the community for a period of about a year. *Las Venas de la Mujer* will be a retrospective on what had made the Chicana today. The exhibition will be a multimedia two-dimensional (mural painting) as well as three-dimensional environments.

The metamorphosis of highlighting historical events will be the prevailing theme of the environmental exhibition *Las Venas de la Mujer*. Five Chicana artists will collectively depict the conception of the Chicana and trace her development through time and space to finally give birth to a unique contemporary existence. The execution of this environment will be translated simultaneously in two-dimensional (muralistic painting) which Chicanos have inherited from our Mexican ancestors, as well as three-dimensional traditional settings found in the homes of our culture. The exhibition will open September 16, 1976, which will mark the dual celebration of Mexico's Independence Day as well as the attemtp to explain the traditional, social, and political roles of the Chicana experience.

**2.2 Photograph from brochure for the exhibition** *Las Chicanas: Las Venas de la Mujer*, **1976.**

Judithe Hernández appears as La Llorona, the weeping mother who mourns the loss of her children, while Josefina Quezada appears as La Catrina, the satirized "fashionable lady" who reflected the "good" woman's complicity with corrupt politics. Olga Muñiz highlighted the indigenous roots of the mestiza, perhaps as Malintzin/Malinche, the native woman who served as Cortes' translator, gave birth to his child, and became the symbolic mother of all Mexicans. Judy Baca appears as Malintzin's modern incarnation of the Pachuca who flouted propriety and claimed her sexuality. Isabel Castro dressed as [one of the] "Adelitas," who fought to liberate Mexico.[25]

The photographic tableau initiated the alternative Chicana subjectivity proposed by each work in the exhibition. As Moravec suggests, the artists presented a historicized context for Chicana womanhood by embodying mythohistorical female figures who had been invisible or objectified. The staging of the women's bodies commented on and challenged patriarchy by replacing the male pantheon with a matrilineage. Furthermore, the artists' costumes, which could be removed and changed, implied the constructed nature of gender norms. The artists' bodies became sites of transformation and defiance as the artists dismantled the mythical histories of patriarchy.

More significant was the artists' use of styles and formats, such as installation and performance art, not typically associated with Chicana/o social realism. *Las Venas de la Mujer* was avant-garde in its incorporation of tableau and assemblage and its emphasis on the recontextualization of everyday objects as art. However, this Chicana avant-garde style recoupled politics and art and thereby diverted from the depolitical American avant-garde movement and its masculine gestures. Blurring the boundaries between life and art, Muñiz re-created the environment of a sweatshop; Castro designed an installation that criticized Chicano movement politics and culture using posters and newspapers—the very materials of *el movimiento*; and Quezada explored female invisibility through a minimalist vignette of a spider web and human silhouettes. Baca staged a performance with her interactive mixed-media piece *Las Tres Marias*, a triptych composed of three panels: one with a painting of a chola, one with a painting of a pachuca, and one, the central panel, with a mirror that reflected the viewer's image.

I detour here to introduce into the art historical record evidence of how these Chicana artists were experimenting with a range of visual forms as they engaged a feminist critique of Chicano cultural production, Anglo feminist practice, and arts organizations. Indeed, this documentation is vital to the expansion of Chicana/o art history. Studies conducted in the past several years have not rectified the errors or filled the gaps in the art historical record. Even the research completed for Pacific Standard Time: Art in L.A. 1945–1980—the Getty Foundation initiative that aimed to exhibit, document, and reinterpret Los Angeles art—fell short. For instance, the initiative did not overturn the assertion that Baca and Asco occupied contrasting creative spheres, with Baca identified as the standard bearer for Chicana/o social realism, and Asco as the pioneering force for the Chicana/o avant-garde.[26] Yet a closer examination of *Las Venas de la Mujer* reveals aesthetic innovations that animated the feminist message of the errata exhibition. I suggest that the experimental styles of the artists further complicate Chicana womanhood by presenting critiques that moved beyond gender balance. Similar to second-wave feminism among white women, Chicana feminism sought to reclaim and reinterpret images of women. *Las Venas de la Mujer* deliberately staged new visions of "Mexican and Chicana cultural icons," presenting avant-garde forms for such rearticulations.[27] While Chicana/o art history frequently portrays Asco as singular in its use of hybridity and as having "launch[ed] the Chicano avant-garde," *Las Venas de la Mujer* serves to expose and challenge such an observation by documenting the hybrid aesthetics within Chicana feminist practices of the 1970s.[28]

Close inspection of Hernández's installation, which could easily be mistaken for a traditional Mexican home altar, illustrates how the artist broke with cultural and aesthetic conventions. For Hernández, the three-level altar installation recognized women as "artistic curators of a family history."[29] She intermingled in an altar format Catholic religious figures, indigenous icons, and photographs of contemporary women and men, objects of urban vernacular, and her own art. As in the installation created by Muñiz, the boundaries of art and daily life were ambiguous in Hernández's work, not only calling into question the notion of the object and beauty but also replacing the cultural authority of the art world with the knowledge and judgment embodied in altars. According to Hernández, the installation was a "riff on my grandmother's altars" and on the artist's recent experimentation with the altar form. A previously constructed assemblage from 1973 appears on the top left platform. A wooden crate houses a miniature La Catrina, but this female figure, which was originally designed by José Guadalupe Posada, is homely. It is constructed of a whiskbroom; the short handle serves as the neck and the bristles form the body, which is dressed in a string of lace. This assemblage reinforces the "irony, humor, and darkness" found in Posada's work. Hernández states that the calavera represents the "integration of sociopolitical commentary of my generation with those of the past." It reinforces the spatial and temporal layering she was trying to achieve in the work, thereby tying together the conventional altar and the avant-garde installation.

Additionally, because the format of Hernández's installation does not emphasize the symmetry and balance that are frequently found among

**2.3** Isabel M. Castro, *Untitled* (detail), 1976. Mixed-media installation for the exhibition *Las Chicanas: Las Venas de la Mujer*, Woman's Building, Los Angeles, September 16–October 15, 1976. Image courtesy of the artist.

Mexican American *altares*, her neo-baroque design with its layering, exuberant abundance, and excessive detail restages the images of the divine and of contemporary Chicanas/os as an intertwined sacred community. The layering and spatial distribution of holy figures, family, and friends unite their sacred value and aesthetic message. The work's composition reflects a conceptual maneuver that touched on every aspect of the errata exhibition: to reimagine living Chicanas as divine, a strategy that Yolanda M. López would articulate with her Guadalupe series.[30] It is also a powerful conceptual gesture in its use of traditional media to offer radically new subjectivities and epistemologies, linking the work to that of Faith Ringgold and her quilts, Consuelo Jimenez Underwood and her textile installations, and Bently Spang and his Modern Warrior series of mixed-media portrayals of Native Americans.

Isabel M. Castro's untitled work is an excellent example of the Chicana feminist avant-garde, and it evidences the innovative and critical sensibilities of the exhibition. She created an installation, an art form that employs repurposed and found objects and is connected to readymades.[31] The text-image work legitimates Chicana resistance as part of a longer history of women's public activism, independence, and agency. Castro surrounded a raised platform and wall with tall fencing and barbed wire and placed a chair on the platform to represent the physical architecture of repression, such as the detention center and the interrogation seat (fig. 2.3). The wall is plastered with a collage of Chicano movement posters, flyers, and newspaper articles (most covering events in Nicaragua and El Salvador), and painted across the face of the collage in red lettering is a militant message in Spanish that proclaims "¡Ya Basta!" (Enough!). In this way, Castro raised her voice against the rhetorical form and content of Chicano politics and culture, which are represented by the posters announcing the Chicano Moratorium and other contemporary events. She felt that their aggressive and hostile tone undermined solidarity. In addition, the installation expresses women's resistance to the Chicano movement's suppression of women's leadership. Her text calls out to Chicanas as "las adelitas" and "hermanas," historicizing contemporary calls for sisterhood, a feminist mobilization strategy, and contextualizing a call for hemispheric solidarity across Latin America.

Baca's piece visually reformulated Chicana womanhood while participating in the performance art practice that was emerging at the Woman's Building. Baca's multipart work consisted of a spray-paint and graffiti mural created by cholas from Pacoima—the community of Baca's youth—along with a vanity table and the triptych *Las Tres Marias*. The mirrors of the vanity table and the triptych were strategically placed so that the audience could see Baca's ritual performance reflected in the triptych's central panel. Sitting behind the vanity table and in front of *Las Tres Marias*, Baca "turned [herself] into the 'chuca." As she recalls, "I . . . shaved my eyebrows and ratted my hair and did that whole thing." For the errata exhibition, the artist became the third Maria, the reflection in the mirror. Baca states that the performance was

about the roles of women. . . . In the vanity table mirror was this projection—a rear projection—of me going through the process of starting as Judy Baca and turning into the pachuca. I was looking at the facades [available to Chicanas], but I was doing it, you know, as I transformed myself. It was this incredible thing. . . . The face and the tight skirts and the Mary Janes—all of that was like a battle [suit]. [I was] putting on . . . the warrior garb.

For Baca, the public transformation was empowering because through her creation of a modern pachuca she embodied the qualities she identified with a pachuca: invincibility, bravery, and fearlessness. Therefore, unlike the heterosexual patriarchal placement of Chicanas as either virgins or whores, the performance dramatized how pachucas and their contemporary counterparts, cholas, transgress gender norms and construct empowered subjectivities.[32] In this staged ritual of self-becoming, Baca embodied the transformation from the subordinated Chicana into a strong figure "putting on . . . the warrior garb." Each of the side panels of the triptych featured a figure whose stance announced "Don't mess with me," even as the artist performed the slippery nature of self-fashioning. By watching the performance, the audience was implicated in the construction of the self.

While the critical force and relevance of Chicana feminist errata exhibitions of the 1970s shifted the discursive terrain, the exhibitions could not eliminate patriarchal bias within Chicana/o cultural production and American art. However, they did raise the level of debate and opened space for public criticism of masculinity and sexist assumptions and of narrow expectations about art produced by Chicanas. When in 1990 Chicana feminist criticism was again articulated as an errata exhibition, the exhibition was produced with greater support. A catalog was published, and the show generated media coverage, neither of which had occurred with the previous errata exhibitions. The 1990 exhibition, *Image and Identity: Recent Chicana Art from "La Reina del Pueblo de Los Angeles de la Porciúncula,"* was a response to several group shows. Each had been noted in its time as seminal and vanguard, and each eventually came to be treated as a sort of sacred cow. *Image and Identity*, curated by Sybil Venegas and presented at the Laband Art Gallery of Loyola Marymount University, repaired the gender imbalance of *Chicano Art: Resistance and Affirmation, 1965–1985* (1990), which had 43 women out of 185 artists; *Hispanic Art in the United States* (1987–89), which exhibited only 3 women out of 30 artists; the European exhibition *Le Démon des Anges* (1989), which had 4 women out of 16 artists; and *Aqui y Alla* (1990), a show at the Los Angeles Municipal Art Gallery that ran concurrently with *Image and Identity* and presented 4 women among 14 artists. It was this social convergence of masculine privilege, not the specific male-female ratio of each exhibition, that inspired the errata exhibition at Loyola Marymount University.

Venegas was determined to address the narrow presentation of Chicana/o art in these four influential exhibitions. *Image and Identity* filled the aesthetic gaps by presenting alternate works by five artists who were represented in the other exhibitions: Laura Aguilar, Barbara Carrasco, Diane Gamboa, Margaret Garcia, and Dolores Guerrero Cruz. These works documented the range of issues with which Chicana artists were engaged. Cherríe Moraga's observation about *CARA* captures the problems Venegas aimed to rectify:

> What was missing in [*CARA*] was the rage and revenge of women, the recognition that the violence of racism and misogyny has distorted our view of ourselves. What was missing was a portrait of sexuality for men and women independent of motherhood and machismo: images of the male body as violador *and* vulnerable, and of the female body as the site of woman-centered desire.[33]

Venegas extended the discourse around "resistance and affirmation" (the subtitle of CARA) by exploring negotiations of patriarchy, racism, and sexuality.

The work of Gamboa conveys the "rage and revenge of women," particularly in *Bloody Coffee* (1990), while Garcia's sublime portraits of women, such as *Portrait of Dolores Cruz, Artist* (1990) and *Portrait of Anita Holguin, Educator* (1990), visualize female grace, dignity, and women-centered communities without reference to patriarchy or motherhood. Garcia's titles deliberately announce the sitter's profession (artist, educator, actress), not her family identity as defined by a man (mother, wife). This absence of the male rule of law opens a space for women-centered desire. Aguilar's photography presents the possibility of lesbian desire as well as "the violence of racism and misogyny." Joining art and text within the image, Carrasco framed two works with words that conveyed her concerns about internalized gender and ethnic oppression. In her Serape Series, Guerrero Cruz resisted the depiction of human figures to portray a sense of place. Working within the art historical trajectory of landscape paintings or interior portraits, she visualized Chicanas' isolation in and departure from the domestic setting as well as our cultural memory. The "Mexican serapes draped over pieces of furniture" create "homeplace," the term bell hooks coined to register the site of comfort, security, and resistance against social violence.[34] Guerrero Cruz's colorful paintings are simultaneously documents of absence and presence, the very complexity that Moraga found missing in *CARA*.

The series that Carrasco produced for the errata exhibition requires further elaboration, as it addressed the internalized oppression within Mexican American communities and serves as rich evidence of the ways Chicana artists expanded the themes and styles that were registered in the four seminal exhibitions. Carrasco's *Milk the Pass* (1990) comments on skin color preferences in the United States and within Chicano communities, as well as on the artist's personal history (fig. 2.4). The surrealistic painting suggests a neatly assimilating Mexican American household through a strategically placed larger-than-life chili on top of a red and white checkered tablecloth. The table is the platform for the artist's central image, a white female figure who is gasping for breath as she struggles to free herself from a huge milk bottle. The milk bottle is uncannily alive and animated, and it seems to have swallowed the female figure, whose arms and body are trapped inside the vessel. The woman, entirely white and dripping with milk, has been submerged in the liquid, and the shallow space of the scene dramatizes the woman's struggle to break free of the milk bottle. The sunny yellow curtains that frame the composition belie the distress of the woman and suggest that the trauma originates in the home. Another Carrasco painting in the errata exhibition, *Names Do Hurt Me* (1990), also gestures toward the psychological violence that can occur in the home. In both works, the backdrop—whether curtains or wallpaper—is patterned with the silhouettes of cockroaches, suggesting the dirty secret of internalized racism and skin colorism within Mexican American households. Carrasco conveys the unfortunate reality for people of color in the United States, who are told explicitly and implicitly to pass for white—as if the denial of self will guarantee success and inclusion—but who learn that passing requires a total submersion that washes away all cultural identity, community affiliation, and historical memory. As *Milk the Pass* implies, some of this pressure comes from inside Chicana/o families. Carrasco's pain, however, also came from her ability to appear white in a group of non-Chicanos, who felt safe in publicly deriding and

2.4 Barbara Carrasco, *Milk the Pass*, 1990. Acrylic on canvas,
12 x 24 inches. Collection of Dr. Cheryl Mendoza. Image
courtesy of the artist. © 1990 Barbara Carrasco.

disparaging Mexican Americans when they thought none were present to hear their racist comments.[35]

Through the errata exhibition, Aguilar, Carrasco, Gamboa, Garcia, and Guerrero Cruz, expanded styles, themes, and approaches to Chicana/o aesthetics and politics. Together their work demonstrates how the errata exhibitions of Chicana feminists advance a critical commentary about Chicano cultural politics, such as patriarchal gender expectations, skin color privilege, and heteronormativity. Venegas intervened against Chicana/o art criticism using an expansive curatorial strategy that did not anticipate or limit the issues of importance to Chicana artists. Working from a feminist orientation that understands the complexities of multiple subject positions—including gender, race, ethnicity, skin color, language, class, and sexuality—and the codetermined processes of these subjectivities, Venegas describes the work as "primarily representational, often overtly political, yet at the same time intensely personal, revealing and honest."[36] Venegas presented no contradiction in joining the two sites of struggle: political and personal. This Chicana feminist paradigm of bridging seemingly disparate spaces, systems, and processes has become the most significant contribution to twentieth-century criticism, particularly in Chicana/o and American art history.[37]

## Other Footprints Making Roads to Aztlán

Although Chicana feminist thought had successfully transformed the field of ethnic studies by the mid-1980s and continued to have an impact on other disciplines in the 1990s, social identity theory with its expectation of complexity and multiplicity has yet to influence authorizing arts institutions and American art history. One example of an exhibition that slipped into essentialism even as it proposed a complex view of identity formation, community, and culture was *The Road to Aztlan: Art from a Mythic Homeland*, which debuted at LACMA in 2001. In response to this exhibition, SPARC produced *Other Footprints to Aztlan: Works from the Collection of Mary and Armando Durón* (2001), which outlined an alternative discourse about culture, memory, belonging, and community. *The Road to Aztlan* was an exploration of the "art derived from and created about the legendary area that encompasses the American Southwest and portions of Mexico"—namely, Aztlán. Curators Virginia M. Fields and Victor Zamudio-Taylor were interested in the geographic borderlands as a "unified cultural area," and they presented material evidence from the pre-Columbian era, the colonial period, and contemporary times to document two thousand years of coalescing cultural achievement and aesthetics.[38] It was a comprehensive exhibition because of its broad historical and geographic focus. I look at the exhibition design of *The Road to Aztlan* and the curators' critical assessment of Chicana/o art and Aztlán because they inspired the errata exhibition at SPARC.[39] My consideration of *Other Footprints* draws attention to the theoretical and conceptual argument of transnationalism, offering a complex and nuanced understanding about Chicana/o art and life. This errata exhibition underscores the multifaceted nature of the transnational phenomenon, specifically its contemporary and historical components, a central point made by the content of *The Road to Aztlan* but diminished by the curators' comments about Aztlán, Mesoamerican references, and Chicana/o artists.

On the topic of Aztlán as the site of cultural heritage, the Chicana/o writers and visual artists affiliated with *The Road to Aztlan* could claim significant theoretical ground. Foundational Chicana/o thought was acknowledged in several components of the exhibition: the catalog essays discussed the historical patterns of shared material culture across the region and across time periods; didactic labels described the region as unified; and the layout of the exhibition encouraged visitors to visualize cultural and aesthetic consistency. As visitors walked through the gallery, they moved from the past to the present, and this chronology implied a developmental model from ancient to contemporary times. The placement of contemporary art by Chicana/o and Mexican artists in the final gallery suggested that they had emerged from the earlier aesthetic forms on display. The importance of shared culture was reinforced at the opening ceremony: LACMA had invited a group of Los Angeles–based artists and spiritual leaders to perform a "Chicana-Indigenous" blessing; the term *Chicana-Indigenous* itself signaled a foundational aspect of Chicana/o thought: personhood is inclusive, transnational, rooted in the Americas, and also contingent on contemporary US culture. I was invited to present a lecture on Chicano art and the history of Chicano art exhibition. In the presentation, I observed that the exhibition design and the exhibition checklist were consistent with Chicano historiography and its transhistorical and transnational theory of belonging and space.

In general, the curators affirmed what Chicana/o artists, creative writers, philosophers, and historians had been claiming publicly since the late 1960s: Aztlán is their homeland, and its territory and history span both sides of the geopolitical border. More important for museum studies and art historical discourse, the exhibition reconsidered the conventional distinction between art and artifact, echoing Chicana/o criticism that had challenged this binary since the 1970s.[40] *The Road to Aztlan* enacted a Chicana/o orientation to space and belonging, and this positioning proved successful for LACMA, a museum in a municipality whose Latino population had reached 44 percent. The exhibition broke attendance records, attracting approximately 140,000 people.[41]

However, while *The Road to Aztlan* validated transnational and transhistorical influence and reconsidered the disciplinary divide over art and artifact, the curatorial commentary was unfortunately confined by art historical conventions that invested heavily in nationalist distinctions and cultural hierarchies. More serious is the fact that the curators did not account for the dynamic relationships between Mexican and Chicana/o cultures. Although the leaders of SPARC and Armando Durón, the curator, were not initially inspired to counter the claims of the exhibition, once they read the curators' introductory essay, they became convinced that *Other Footprints* was an imperative.

The introductory essay, written by Fields and Zamudio-Taylor, reaffirms national identifications without critically attending to the constructions and hierarchies of difference. The two curators unabashedly praise Mexican artists in the exhibition, arguing that

> Mexican and Chicano/a artists have viewed pre-Columbian art and culture differently. Mexican artists tend to be *more ironic* and less direct than their Chicano/a contemporaries in their engagement with these themes, establishing a *more complex* relationship to pre-Columbian canons. The Chicano/a engagement with the pre-Columbian past, by contrast, reflects a grassroots origin and is community-oriented. For Chicano/a artists, the concept of Aztlan has served as a means of asserting identity and claiming a history, whereas for Mexican artists, consideration of the pre-Columbian past has prompted a *more philosophical* investigation of the construction of identity over time and its deployment in national narratives.[42]

This one short passage undermines the rich content of the exhibition as well as the other, multifaceted catalog essays written by notable scholars in the fields of archeology, anthropology, art history, Chicana/o studies, and American history. Fields and Zamudio-Taylor unconsciously reproduced Aristotle's elevation of tragedy (and irony) over history for its so-called universal message and potential for forecasting the future through their unabashed praise for Mexican artists. The passage mishandles the tremendous philosophical intervention that is made when Chicana/o artists claim a pre-Columbian past against two nationalist agendas that fully erase the possibility of such a relationship across time and space.[43] By favoring Mexican over Chicana/o art, the curators could not account for the considerable feat of creating an oppositional consciousness and subjectivity without the benefit of a national or patriarchal narrative. They could not account for artistic expression that works against two nations, even as Chicana/o art borrows from both nations' visual and social histories.

Specifically, Fields and Zamudio-Taylor's comparative method could not account for the art included in the exhibition that was attributed to Chicanas/os. For instance, the minimalist work by David Avalos (*Hubcap Milagro #4*, 1986), the installation by Amalia Mesa-Bains (*Reflections on a Transparent Migration*, 2001), the text-image collage prints by Yreina D. Cervántez (*The Nepantla Triptych*, 1995), and the photographic triptych by James Luna (*Half Indian/Half Mexican*, 1991) express a postcolonial and postmodern approach to the past, belonging, and race representation. These works are allegorical, complex, and nuanced in their connections to Mexico and the United States; they could be described as philosophical and ironic. However, the passage paints Chicana/o artists as inadequate cultural producers (*los pochos*) within the Mexican aesthetic context. Moreover, this comparative methodology of more versus less validates an imaginary conceptual refinement of lowbrow representational art and political realism. In this passage, Fields and Zamudio-Taylor duplicated well-known preferences in American and Latin American art history that were otherwise rejected by the content of the exhibition.[44]

Another essay, this one authored individually by Zamudio-Taylor, suggests the origin of this critical preference for Mexican artists. It too became a point of contention for SPARC leadership and Durón. In this essay Zamudio-Taylor clarifies his critical commentary against the concept of a Chicana/o Aztlán. Aztlán, he writes, had "served a valuable and necessary function as a didactic vehicle that forged traditions and reinvented a mythic past. *Today*, however, such practices appear clichéd and restrictive." His dismissal further submerges Chicana/o aesthetics under Mexican ones. He notes that "from a post-Chicano/a perspective, themes and formal endeavors that address and refer to the pre-Columbian past" are not "obsolete," simply an anachronism. References to Aztlán were fine during the Chicano movement, but today they are old-fashioned and parochial. In effect, a Chicano perspective is an "essentializing discourse" and thus inappropriate.[45] References to Aztlán, a mythic past, or even contemporary indigenous culture are reframed as "restrictive," "cliché," and "obsolete," while Mexican artists' use of irony and satire in their references to a pre-Columbian past positions them as "postmodern." Similarly, those works or artists that function from a "post-Chicano" orientation "articulate contemporary and global concerns with a consciousness of modernism and postmodernism." Announcing that Mexican and post-Chicano artists are cosmopolitan, Zamudio-Taylor reproduces the inaccurate assumption that identification with something other than the so-called universal or global aesthetic disables critical distance and the ability to conceptualize one's experience.[46]

*Other Footprints to Aztlan* focused on this reductionist and disparaging view of Chicana/o art. Durón was particularly concerned with the assessments that Chicana/o art was "cliché" and "restrictive" in its references to what he sarcastically called "this boogeyman word—Aztlan."[47] On a broader discursive level, *Other Footprints* also functioned as the erratum to the collecting practices of the authorizing art museum. In the press release, SPARC announced the show as an errata exhibition by stating, "Chicano art, having no permanent public space in Los Angeles, has largely been left for private collectors to make decisions that would otherwise be made by museums, critics and scholars."[48] It is within private collections that Chicana/o art has been interpreted, preserved, and even exhibited. It is the private collections that enable the work of public curators who aim to develop inclusive art historical analyses. The full title of the errata exhibition, *Other Footprints to Aztlan: Works from the Collection of Mary and Armando Durón*, shamed the county museum because of its failure to function as an institution for the public good and in the public interest. It has not systematically collected Chicana/o art, but the Duróns and others have (see chapter 5).

In a more immediate way, the errata exhibition took critical aim at the LACMA exhibition by positing the concept of Aztlán as an expansive view of cultural memory, belonging, and influence. Durón selected works that are ironic or have other qualities that Fields and Zamudio-Taylor had attributed to Mexican art. In particular, he used the work of Gilbert "Magu" Sánchez Luján to counter Fields and Zamudio-Taylor's anachronistic understanding of Aztlán and to provide leverage for his alternative view. The capstone of *The Road to Aztlan* was Magu's *Trailing los Antepasados* (2000), a mixed-media installation. For *Other Footprints*, Durón selected a serigraph by Magu, *Returning to Aztlan* (1983), with the same theme. In both works, Magu depicts a cool Aztec lowrider traveling from central Mexico to Los Angeles. The roads in these two works suggest an open, continuously used route between an ancient and a contemporary site. While visitors to either exhibition could see that Magu was depicting a journey between the two sites, it was where they encountered the installation at LACMA—at the end of the exhibition—that troubled Durón. Its location seemed to express a singular direction of influence (fig. 2.5). Moreover, Magu's installation was isolated—it was the last work in the exhibition and it was placed near the exit—and this layout reinforced Zamudio-Taylor's interpretation of Chicano indigenous aesthetics as "restrictive" and "obsolete." The placement of the installation physically expressed Zamudio-Taylor's commentary about Aztlán: it was a cultural dead end.

On the other hand, Durón felt that both the installation and the print conveyed the transnational and multidimensional cultural contacts that characterize the US-Mexico borderlands. At the opening reception and in the small catalog for the show, Durón argued that "there is no *one* direction we are all headed toward; instead, we are seemingly headed in all directions at the same time."[49] Durón reinforced this understanding of culture and belonging through the exhibition design. Unlike the exhibition layout of *The Road to Aztlan*, the layout at SPARC was not chronological or developmental, eschewing a hierarchical relationship between past and present, or between Chicana/o and Mexican artists. Durón invited viewers to experience the art on a circular path, as if leading to *and* from Aztlán, and Magu's print was the starting and the ending point. In this way, *Other Footprints* articulated a complex subjectivity and hybridity and rejected a static and linear view of culture and identity. Indeed, it called for a sophisticated rereading of Aztlán as an aesthetic reference that critically, ironically, and philosophically questions the grounds of nationalism and geopolitical boundaries. The art proposed an agility not considered by Zamudio-Taylor.

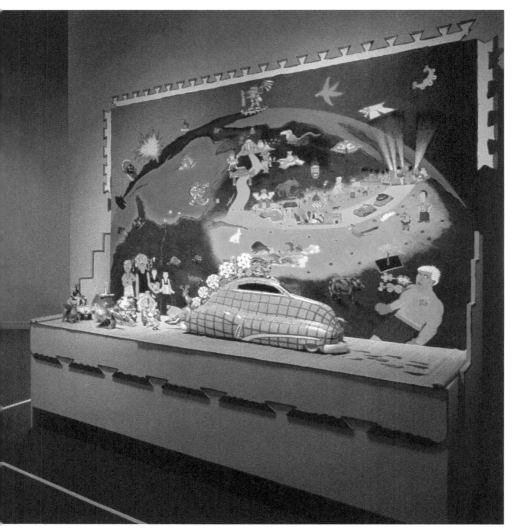

**2.5** Gilbert "Magu" Sánchez Luján, *Trailing los Antepasados*, 2000. Mixed-media installation for the exhibition *The Road to Aztlan*, Los Angeles County Museum of Art, May 13–August 26, 2001. Reproduced with permission from The Estate of Gilbert "Magu" Luján. Image © Museum Associates/LACMA.

The installation and the serigraph complicate notions of culture, belonging, and influence through a speculative or hypothetical view of the colonial past.[50] A fuller, formal analysis of the works illuminates this interpretation of Aztlán. For example, the installation includes a car sculpture that travels on a road made from reed. Behind this is a painting that depicts a band of traveling *locos* on the road from Mexico City to Los Angeles, a city of light, gloss, and high-rise pyramids. The composition of the painting echoes the sculptural elements of the car, and each is embellished in a style that blends the aesthetics of American hot-rods and lowriders. Using Zamudio-Taylor's interpretation, the direction of the vehicles and the architectural elements of the two cities suggest that Los Angeles is a derivative and anachronistic version of Mexico City. Durón, on the other hand, emphasized the transnational and dynamic references in the work in both the design of the exhibition and his curatorial comment. The collector was excited about the way both works suggest that Mexican artists who migrate north are influenced by Chicana/o aesthetics *before* they embark on their tour. Both cars have the classic lines and dropped chassis of a lowrider, a form of cultural expression that was perfected in the Chicano communities of the American Southwest, not in Mexico. Indeed, the sculpture is a customized, classic lowrider "Bomb," an American car produced from the 1930s through the 1950s that sported sideboards, fender skirts, and sun visor. Chicano car enthusiasts refer to it as the original lowrider style.

It is Magu's speculative visual narrative or hypothetical history to which I draw the reader's attention. The installation and the serigraph imply a rereading of the past and pre-Columbian references, a perspective Magu suggests in the spatial composition of the globe. In both works, Magu disrupts the conventions of Western cartography, flipping north and south and locating Mexico above the United States. The entire Southern Hemisphere is in the top register of each composition. He depicts an imaginary world in which the Spanish and US conquests did not produce an indigenous cultural genocide or Eurocentric cultural hegemony. From this hypothetical history, Indian revivalism becomes a postmodern aesthetic that traces the broad transnational and transhistorical network of influence among the contemporary inheritors of indigenous cultures. In Magu's imagination, the West did not establish global and spatial hierarchy, although a barbed wire fence does cut the landscape at a place recognized as the US-Mexico border. Yet Zamudio-Taylor could not account for this complex speculative narrative; for him, *Trailing los Antepasados* was passé because of its indigenous references.

By placing *Returning to Aztlan* in a position of prominence, Durón seemed to emphasize conjunctive existence across the Americas. Echoes of pre-Columbian material culture are not clichéd but transnational. The composition of both works underscores an open, fluid, holistic, and hybrid view of cultures. In *Trailing los Antepasados*, a figure wearing a war bonnet steps across a single strand of barbed wire that separates Mexico from the United States. Several more figures congregate at the border, hailing one another from either side of the barbed wire and their home, which sits at the border. In *Returning to Aztlan*, the eagle-clutching snake from the Aztec legend is flying toward the United States. The barbed wire fence is broken and pulled back at several points along the border, as if the crossing originated on both northern and southern sides. These figures are not retracing the path of the Mexica who traveled from their homeland; they are moving in all directions. In this way, the aesthetic hierarchy that privileged Mexican artists over Chicanas/os is undercut.

As its title suggests, the errata exhibition proposed that the route to Aztlán has never lost its significance. Foremost, the errata exhibition positioned Chicano-landia as a significant spatial homeland and site of place-based identity for contemporary Chicanas/os. SPARC's leadership and Durón would not accept LACMA's pronouncement that Aztlán was irrelevant in the contemporary moment. For Durón, however, the evidence was expressed not solely in art but also in popular culture, commerce, and literature. One display case contained novels and other books, flyers, business cards, and announcements from current businesses with "Aztlán" in their titles. On the entire back wall of the SPARC Gallery, Durón displayed a monumental photograph of an eighteen-wheel truck from the Aztlan Trucking School, its massive size symbolic of the contemporary importance of the homeland and notions of resistance. The curator's discussion of the photo revealed the connection between the concept of Aztlán and economic autonomy and self-determination: "The Aztlan Trucking School, located in South Central Los Angeles, was founded by George M. Ricchezze with three other partners around 1970 as a direct result of the Chicano Moratorium marches. Ricchezze, an Argentine Jew, proposed that people [receive training] in driving equipment."[51] In contrast to the art history of Zamudio-Taylor, which posited a relevant but nevertheless mythical and anachronistic Aztlán that is beyond the reach of contemporary inhabitants, *Other Footprints* illustrated, as Durón notes, the "millennial trail unbroken" and the multidirectional cultural journey.[52]

Apart from the work by Magu, Durón selected several works for the exhibition that possess the qualities Fields and Zamudio-Taylor identified as lacking in Chicana/o art. Three that are mentioned in the catalog essay by Durón—*Migra Mouse* (1994) by Lalo Alcaraz, *New World Order* (1994) by Chaz Bojórquez, and *Brown Power* (2000) by Monique Prieto— are ironic and complex and present a philosophical position about nation, belonging, and resistance. *Brown Power* is an abstract painting that signifies through color and composition the force exerted by people of color on American society. Organic but intimidating brown shapes dominate the flat composition and press toward a smaller, gray form whose color is symbolic of neutrality, age, formality, or power. The shapes seem animated by the space between them, which shifts the power dynamic toward the brown forms. The work foretells the demographic weight of Chicanas/os in the United States, the historical presence of indigenous people in the Americas, and the cross-race coalition that fights back against oppression.[53] Prieto's work also demonstrates that abstract art is another aesthetic path to Aztlán.

*Migra Mouse* draws on pop culture, duplicating the cartoon style of Alcaraz's syndicated comic strip *La Cucaracha*. Beneath an image of the famous mouse, the caption, "Disney Co. $upport$ Wilson," points to campaign contributions from "the happiest place on earth" to the campaign coffers of Pete Wilson, the former governor of California and the leading elected official advocating for Proposition 187, a 1994 ballot initiative that aimed to end social services to immigrants. Alcaraz uses irony and satire to warn Chicanas/os that they could be unknowingly supporting the anti-immigrant legislation. As Durón comments in the exhibition catalog, "Alcaraz wants Latinos to know that when they patronize Disney products, they are paying for their own oppression."[54]

Bojórquez's well-known serigraph *New World Order* turns Spanish colonists into vandals who destroy a pre-Columbian temple with their *placas*, thereby subverting the power dynamic between contemporary descendants of Europe and indigenous civilizations of the Americas. Similar to Magu's speculative visual narrative, the Bojórquez work depicts another world—both past and future—in which the colonial invasion did not lead to indigenous genocide but merely resulted in futile claims for space and cultural hegemony. The unwelcome invaders ironically use street calligraphy or graffiti, the very form of representation rejected by the nation-state, to visually present European power and assertions of belonging. Thus, Bojórquez subtly calls into question the ability of contemporary graffiti writers to claim space and authority beyond the surface of the wall on which their names appear.

Two other works in the errata exhibition are worth mentioning for their feminist interrogations of the construction of identity and cultural solidarity. Durón's selection of feminist art further underscores the narrow interpretation of Chicana/o art endorsed by Zamudio-Taylor since an anti-sexist orientation is conceptually linked to a complex, contemporary, expansive, nonparochial, or non-anachronistic understanding of community and belonging. *Unidos* (1993) by Victor Estrada and *Mnesic Myths* (1999) by Alma López take a critical position against any notion of Chicano unity that subverts women's experiences or desires, extending the theoretical implications and interpretive discourse of Chicana feminist errata exhibitions. Yet the two artists do not appear to forgo Chicana/o identity, as Zamudio-Taylor expects of a post-Chicano orientation. They raise a philosophical question about the cost of cultural solidarity: What is lost when the community's needs are put before those of Chicanas? Estrada's lithograph is filled with the kind of doodling that a 1970s-era high school student might have made on a Pee-Chee folder, complete with well-practiced designs for *placas* and scantily clad women. The ironic title, *Unidos*, suggests that the objectifying imagery of Chicana/o popular culture, in which women are simply objects of heterosexual male desire, does little to empower women and thereby undermines cultural solidarity.

Operating in the zone of feminist empowerment, López restages the patriarchal myth of Popocatepetl and Ixtaccihuatl with two Chicana lesbians who are dressed in the fashion of urban Chicana youth. In this reclaimed Mexican legend of forbidden love, the two women are literally surrounded by the icons of female power: the figure of Coatlicue is in the background, the reclining body lies on the Aztec stone monolith of Coyolxauhqui, and the flowery designs from Our Lady of Guadalupe's gown frame the composition. Each icon, particularly Coyolxauhqui, has been appropriated by Chicana feminists "as the symbol of identity reclamation," as art historian Judith Huacuja explains: "For feminists, [Coyolxauhqui] represents recovery of the physical and intellectual body, earlier mutilated by sexist attitudes against women's pleasure and power.

For Mexicanas and Chicanas, [Coyolxauhqui] embodies the Indigenous concept of spirituality dismembered by colonizing powers."[55] Homeland is not a place of containment, but one expanded to include Chicana lesbians and other women empowered as agents of their desire. These works break gender and sexual boundaries enforced by patriarchy, nationalism, heteronormativity, and coloniality.

## Errata to the Binary

Postethnic art exhibitions that questioned Chicana/o identification have been emerging in Los Angeles and elsewhere since the beginning of the millennium. In Southern California, *Leaving Aztlán: Redux* (2006) and *Xican@ Demiurge: An Immediate Survey* (2006) both attempted to visualize a postidentity aesthetic for art attributed to people of Mexican descent. In the case of *Phantom Sightings: Art after the Chicano Movement* (2008), the exhibition's title gave some critics and artists pause, particularly in light of the preceding shows in the region. The preposition *after* denotes temporality (subsequent to, following on, as a consequence of) and suggests a sequence, as does the prefix *post*. This temporal reading of *after* inspired the errata exhibition *Vaguely Chicana*.[56] An exhibition of paintings and mixed-media work by Linda Arreola at Tropico de Nopal Gallery Art-Space in Los Angeles, *Vaguely Chicana* directly confronted the idea that a critique of a cultural identity is necessarily a sign of moving away from cultural identification. Curator Reyes Rodriguez presented a series of works by Arreola that are abstract, geometric, conceptual, and largely devoid of the human figure, characteristics that denied the assumption that the term *Chicana art* (or *Chicano art*) obliged the artist to create works that incorporated the particular styles and images associated with Chicano movement cultural production.

Prudence is required in any comparison of *Vaguely Chicana* and *Phantom Sightings* because of their differences in scale, scope, and depth. *Phantom Sightings* was a comprehensive group exhibition curated by three people, Rita Gonzalez, Howard Fox, and Chon A. Noriega, and each from a different field and with differing backgrounds; *Vaguely Chicana* was a solo exhibition organized by one person. I do not suggest that they are similar representational forms. However, *Vaguely Chicana* is an erratum because it is an intentional dialogue with *Phantom Sightings*, and I argue that it exposes a critical remixing of the discourse. Working ethnographically, with undocumented sources—conversations in galleries, observations at public events, and nonverbal communication—I came to understand how Rodriguez and others positioned *Vaguely Chicana* as an errata exhibition. More importantly, a formal analysis of the art provides the framework for rethinking the category "Chicana/o art." Because *Vaguely Chicana* and *Phantom Sightings* were very different in many respects, I detour from my method of looking closely at the show to which the errata exhibition responded. I do not examine the art, exhibition design, or didactic labels of *Phantom Sightings*. When I turn to the catalog essays, my analysis is very focused, and it is for the purpose of tracking down which of the published statements may have inspired Rodriguez to produce the errata exhibition. What follows is an examination of the perceived orientation of *Phantom Sightings*; my analysis is only obliquely concerned with the curators' goals and directly concerned with the ways the curators reflect popular thought.[57]

Identifying the work of Asco as a starting point, *Phantom Sightings* intended to challenge conventional definitions of Chicana/o art and offer a strategy for interpreting "conceptual art and urbanism" produced by artists who came of age after the Chicano movement.[58] Curators Gonzalez, Fox, and Noriega stated that the temporal curatorial model of art produced *after something* allowed them "the freedom to follow an idea, rather than represent a constituency."[59] Admittedly working from "different generational [and disciplinary] perspectives," the curators agreed to focus on "the distinctive features of recent Chicano art: that which privileges conceptual over representative approaches, and articulates social absence rather than cultural essence."[60] In addition, the curators were acutely aware of the infrequent presentation of Chicana/o art, particularly its omission from major exhibitions that were focused on styles or aesthetic trends in American art. Their aim was "to explore the gray zone between . . . inclusion and exclusion."[61] The introductory essay is the only common ground, as the individually authored essays use different strategies and present different arguments. While the curators knew that their decision would "occasion considerable debate," they could not have anticipated how their strategy would cause confusion. Some people praised the show for its postethnic orientation, and others felt that the exhibition affirmed a specifically Chicana/o art. Shortly after the close of *Phantom Sightings*, Rodriguez admitted at a public forum that he was "still uneasy about the underlying message that was sent by some of the artists [who] didn't feel that the c-word [euphemism for *Chicano*] belonged in the show." He acknowledged that the curators had claimed otherwise, but he wondered aloud, "Is it post-Chicano or not?"[62] Throughout the exhibition's run, reported Rodriguez, several artists included in *Phantom Sightings* conveyed their desire to distance themselves from ethnic identifiers, effectively overpowering the curatorial claims that it was not a postethnic show. In several circles the question about identity or postidentity overpowered attention to the works themselves. Indeed, few people spoke to me about the art; nearly all discussions debated whether the exhibition endorsed postethnic or identity-based art. The binary ruled the local conversation.[63]

While Rodriguez's conversations with the artists may have been the original source for his question, the catalog essays restage important aspects of the undocumented but lively debates in Los Angeles and elsewhere about Chicana/o art. For this discussion, I focus on claims that informed Rodriguez's decision to produce *Vaguely Chicana*. For example, Noriega argues that conceptual art appeared *during* the movement (an argument I explore in chapter 4). He claims that "Chicano art" is "an unruly category" because it is more expansive than the adjective implies: "The artworks attributed to this category often do much more than illustrate an agenda of a social protest movement, define the boundaries of a community, or express an identity in search of recognition."[64] Demonstrating the ways Chicana/o artists of the earlier period expressed the types of complexities illustrated by *Phantom Sightings*, he closely examines the work of Yolanda M. López, Malaquias Montoya, Mel Casas, and César Martínez. He notes that local and global events influenced their work, and they engaged in "dialog with art history and artistic influences" and also made use of styles other than "didactic realism."[65] His essay reiterates the value of the category "Chicano art" even as he observes that the term produces invisibility ("phantoms") or misunderstanding within American and Chicano art history. His essay articulates not only a positive endorsement of Chicana/o identification but also a worry: Does the category produce its own disappearance?

Rita Gonzalez does not endorse a postethnic orientation in her essay, but she acknowledges artists who disassociate themselves from the cultural identifier. She does not provide clarity about which artists use the term *Chicana/o*, or any other identifier, to describe their work, but one of her statements performs the very binary that troubles Rodriguez. In stating the parameters of her work, Gonzalez notes that she "discusses artists in the exhibition who come after the Chicano movement and *either* have moved away from identifying themselves as Chicano/a artists *or* have attempted to complicate what that term means at this historical juncture."[66] This statement, like many I heard, cannot account for artists such as Linda Arreola who became active as artists after the movement, who identify as Chicana/o, *and* who complicate the identifier. More important for my purposes, Gonzalez fails to consider artists who came of age during the movement and to question whether they "move[d] toward" identification and complicated the term in the moment. Given her attention to feminist and queer theory as sources for social transformation, the reader can anticipate that Judy Baca, Judithe Hernández, and other artists who exhibited under the title Las Chicanas in order to "complicate what the term means" would not surprise Gonzalez. Yet the statement echoes what I learned from many museum visitors: a postethnic orientation depends upon critical distance from "Chicana/o" identification.

In the final essay, Howard Fox proposes that the "observer who believes in the concept of essential cultural, ethnic, or national identity"—an imaginary spectator who represents the dominant view within American art history—will be confused by *Phantom Sightings*.[67] Anticipating or even craving an authentic, bounded, or coherent object, exhibition, or community, such an observer, Fox reports, will not be satisfied by the show. Fox identifies several trends among the works and how each trend confounds notions of essentialism, pointing to intervention, appropriation, transformation, hybridity, and the use of trickery. The last approach is the most challenging for Fox's imaginary observer because "reality" is "outside of common knowledge." This phrase betrays Fox's comfort with normative thinking, as "reality" is perceived from the position of a normative imaginary spectator.[68] Ticket sales indicate that *Phantom Sightings* was overwhelmingly popular, so it is far from clear that the actual observers found the exhibition as unsatisfactory as Fox's hypothetical observer might have.[69]

The essays present a range of perspectives about art, with each curator expressing an aspect of the local, and perhaps national, debates about Chicana/o art. Although these differences are intriguing, it was this lack of curatorial coherence—a gray zone—that led to *Vaguely Chicana*. The work of Linda Arreola visually answered Rodriguez's question,

"Is it post-Chicano or not?" with a complexity that refused the binary. The errata exhibition not only intervened against the conventional view that Chicana/o art is unmediated, transparent, and coherent, but it also proposed an experience of identity that affirmed the complex processes of identity formation.[70] The works in *Vaguely Chicana* present the negotiations and maneuvers that are expressed in Chicana art and illustrate the intersection of Chicana subjectivity and spirituality.[71] It affirmed not only the generative quality of Chicana subjectivity but also the critical analysis of it, without calling for a move to forgo the identification. It expanded narrow subjectivities and brought fallacies of Chicana/o art historiography to public attention.[72]

The exhibition showcased a series of Arreola's mixed-media paintings on wood that offer a refreshing take on human experience, racial formation, belonging, and identity-based art. A Los Angeles–based artist with a background in sculpture and architecture, Arreola emphasized minimalist sculptural works constructed of wood and steel cable early in her career. She went on to explore painting, installation, and printmaking, studying the latter at Self Help Graphics & Art. Each of the paintings in *Vaguely Chicana* contains a grid, which is the foundation on which Arreola builds and layers her paintings. The grid expresses the three-dimensional quality of beauty, life, and humanity and suggests an interconnection between all things. As Arreola notes, "I believe there is a connection between the domestic and the sublime, the commonplace and the spiritual, and the material and the soul. This has been the nature of my work."[73] The artist finds pleasure in the structure of the grid, but the grid is neither dogmatic nor reductive. She conveys this through the careful placement of circles and other shapes, color, and stenciled numbers and letters. Circles that are quadrated by the intersecting lines of the grid are an important element of many of these works. Arreola applies different colors to define certain quadrants. Others are empty of color, revealing the wood support; often these quadrants have been pierced, leaving a single hole. The addition of color, shapes, and text disrupts the grid's rigid form. With each glance, the eye sees new patterns and new contingent but unexpected structures. At times the eye stops seeing patterns, and fluidity and movement fill the frame.

This blending of form and freedom is easily observed in *Almost* (2008), a mixed-media painting that uses the letters of the title in multiple arrangements across the foreground. Some letters cluster and others float independently, but the viewer seeks a pattern, searching for the six letters that form the word. The eye creates order from the chaos, symbolic of the art historical method that attempts to sort and categorize even before it has the capacity to bring works into focus or create meaning from what has been unknown. The word *ALMOST*, ten times larger than the other symbols, is emblazoned across the raw wood in the midsection. It too is not completely visible, as the letters *L* and *M* are nearly obscured by the clutter of circles, shaded quadrants, letters, and matching blue foreground and background. Meaning is always almost in view. This shadowed and fragmented visibility conveys Anzaldúan thought regarding Chicana/o subjectivity.

Catalog essayist Laura E. Pérez describes the series as experiments in repetition and serendipity.[74] These two conditions are not paradoxical within Chicana feminist thought; they describe a subjectivity that can be simultaneously mapped and unknown. As scholars have documented, the expressive culture of the borderlands indicates that hybridity and resilience, aesthetically identified as *rasquachismo*, are common strategies and epistemologies. Arreola's *Glyph #1* (2007) evokes this borderlands culture (fig. 2.6). She fills the picture space with a network of lines and quadrated circles on a yellow field. In the top two-thirds of the field, quadrants in each row are colored with red, black, or green, and white dots are precisely positioned in the space between each group of four circles. In the lower third, every circle has one black quadrant, creating a sense of darkness and accumulation. The entire network of lines, circles, and dots is framed in black, and five red circles anchor the composition at the bottom. None of the red circles are sectioned or punctured; this, combined with the intensity of their hue, suggests another structure, one not yet mapped. Here the work gestures to multiplicity through a series of overlapping contingent and independent positions within the network created by the grid. On a larger level, the work in *Vaguely Chicana* suggests a challenge to art historiography. What appears to be an obligatory element of the composition—the grid—is symbolic of the realist and political qualities attributed to *movimiento* art. It is also a response to the structures of inequality and power. In *Vaguely Chicana*, Chicana/o art is presented as ethically accountable to the forces that render some human lives less valuable than others. How the artist responds has changed, as indicated by Arreola's use of color and shape, but the immediacy of the response has not.

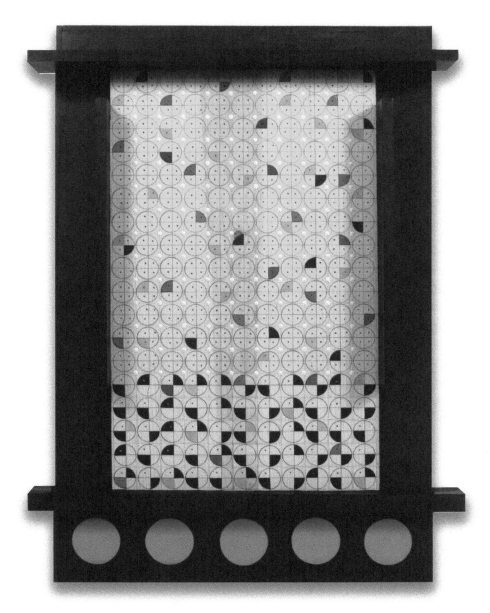

**2.6** Linda Arreola, *Glyph #1*, 2007. Mixed media, 24.5 x 17.5 inches. Image courtesy of the artist.

"Vaguely Chicana" is a phrase originally meant to insult, wound, or punish female artists who do not match a narrow definition of cultural membership, gender expectations, or aesthetic style. It would exclude their work from the canon of Chicano art. In this errata exhibition, the phrase is reclaimed for its ability to signal indeterminate, indefinite, and unfixed qualities. It also, however, signals the indefinite without rhetorically or visually calling for the rejection of a culturally specific and gendered identity; it does not apologize, sidestep, or deny historically contingent subjectivities or notions of womanhood. Arreola demonstrates how an artist can "complicate" the identification while identifying herself as Chicana.

Another work, a massive sculptural installation titled *The Wall*, furthers this Anzaldúan notion. Built by hand from wood blocks, the installation consists of two parts: a symmetrical step pyramid, cut along its vertical axis to expose its interior, and a second construction that frames the resulting facade and follows, yet distorts, the pyramid's outline (fig. 2.7). The doubled form represents the artist's socially constructed and historically rooted identity and signifies the rebuilding of cultural memory, identity, and self within a specific site, history, framework, and geographic place. The back of the piece projects several feet into the gallery, which references Mesoamerican temples through the stepped construction of the interior pyramid. The work is symbolic of Arreola's heritage: it is handmade and massive; it represents a symbol of Mexico, indigeneity, and Chicanismo. An intertextual reading is useful since the title, when considered alone, might suggest criticism of the perceived obligatory content of Chicana/o art. In the gallery the sculpture was delicately lit, as if it were an altar to Mesoamerican heritage, and the stepped incline implied cultural ascension. Arreola uses the idiom of the pyramid to participate in the cultural community of Chicanas/os even as the art exemplifies an expansion of that community. The "wall," therefore, can refer to hegemonic citations of Chicana/o art—the imposed structures—which relegate it to the margins, or the fortifying histories that provide a genealogy, strategies for upward mobility, and platforms for intervention.

Arreola creates new spaces of identity that track chaos, beauty, structure, and mystery. She simultaneously reaffirms the elemental aspects of life and contests the conventional views of what and who can be Chicana. This errata exhibition calls for a recognition of the heterogeneity of Chicana and Chicano experiences and recasts identity as playful

2.7 Linda Arreola, *The Wall*, 2008. Douglas fir, 81 x 138 x 56 inches. Installation view for the exhibition *Vaguely Chicana*, Tropico de Nopal Gallery Art-Space, Los Angeles, April 12–May 17, 2008. Photograph by Reyes Rodriguez. Image courtesy of the artist.

and mysterious while posing larger human questions of belonging and positionality. One is vaguely Chicana only if identity is singular, homogeneous, and essentialized. The Chicana feminist position articulated by this errata exhibition requires an understanding of race, gender, and culture as "historically codependent and mutually determinative."[75] Arreola suggests that some of our multiplicity, the complex and diverse subject positions of Chicanas, comes from experiences that are not yet mapped (such as the artists' tours of Europe and Asia explored in chapter 4) but that are encountered, real, and situated.

## Critical Significance: Borderlands Theory

Because Chicana/o art criticism has not kept up with Chicana/o art production, I have shifted the site of analysis to the exhibition of Chicana/o art in order to document and investigate the interpretive discourse about

Chicana/o art. Within a realm of abundant cultural production—more than 2,200 exhibitions were produced between 1963 and 2013—the errata exhibition has served as a critical discursive site that creates visibility and cultural authority. We come to recognize, as did Sandra de la Loza in her study of the Tovar Collection, that Chicana and Chicano artists draw on and create a range of styles, techniques, and approaches to art. Moreover, the errata exhibitions under review produced expansive interpretations and contextualizations of Chicana/o aesthetics, supporting in particular a decolonial imaginary for borderlands arts. While this framework has achieved recognition since the 1990s and drives much current Chicana/o scholarship, it is new within art criticism and especially within the authorizing spaces of public museums. For this reason, I look at errata exhibitions across several decades to illustrate the utility of the decolonial framework and its versatility across time. The borderlands lens is productive because it allows for an analysis of identity and identification that is broad rather than narrow. The errata exhibitions theorize a borderlands paradigm for Chicana/o art, emphasizing its fluid, hybrid, and historically contingent qualities. In this regard, Sandra de la Loza's art is again instructive. She reminds us that Eurocentric paradigms and Chicana/o art historiography crumble under the weight of the visual evidence and that the visual evidence challenges long-held assumptions, privileges, and power.

As each errata exhibition discussed herein makes clear, Chicana/o art is a site that criticizes American racism and sexism, Mexican nationalism, material inequality, and/or patriarchy, while nonetheless residing inside such strategies of power. The errata exhibitions constitute and are constitutive of the borderlands—places, ideas, and practices that contest and reverse operations of power and oppression. Errata exhibitions represent an art criticism that remains fluid and highly conscious of its relationship to its object of study. Eurocentric art criticism has had difficulty understanding art that resists and contests power while not completely shedding Western cultural hegemony. In addition, the methodologies of art history, particularly the reliance on geographic distinctions, artists' birthplace, and evolutionary models that privilege Europe, render Chicana/o art invisible, derivative, or inconsequential because it does not fit into the established order. As long as Eurocentric art criticism demands the dismissal of cultural, racial, or gender identity and politics, a practice that is part of the colonial project, reclaiming identity or adhering to a counterhegemonic politics is a decolonial act.

It is important to acknowledge that errata exhibitions focus on the representation of cultural, racial, and gender identities. Chicana/o art, particularly as expressed through errata exhibitions, does not follow unswervingly a single positionality. Multiplicity is a central aspect of the errata exhibition, and those documented here articulate a breadth of concerns that indicate a new criticality against narrow notions of identity, representation, and art classification and methods. *Errata: Not Included* and *Other Footprints* called for a historical methodology that recognizes hemispheric dynamics and tensions. *Vaguely Chicana* offered a new interpretation of authenticity and obligation, pointing to a negotiation of resistance against ongoing structures of racial and gender violence rather than foregrounding social realism and Mexican iconography. *Las Venas de la Mujer* announced with the photograph of artists-cum-archetypes that identities are social constructions, not unmediated or coherent roles. Race and identity are not the only, or even the primary, focus of errata exhibitions and the art that is shown; rather, it is the logic of racism and sexism that underlies the set of conditions that give rise to errata exhibitions. Erasure and dismissal are the contexts in which the artists work, and their work offers new ways of thinking about identity and representation. The errata exhibition dismantles monolithic categories, unequal processes, and the social hierarchies that contain the artists and the work, and it challenges the critics and commentators who presume that the artists speak for specific communities.

The Chicana feminist errata exhibitions discussed here evidence the fact that Chicana/o art is imprinted by both hegemonic and borderlands spaces. These intertwined locations give meaning to the works that were displayed, especially when the exhibition was collective and public. Chicana/o culture and identity was thus proposed, negotiated, and constructed by human agents operating within specific contexts not necessarily of their own making, to paraphrase Marx. In the mid-1970s, during the explosion of US Third World feminism and its influence across multiple disciplines, Chicana feminist errata exhibitions were among the first to theorize a codetermined intersection of race and gender, to challenge the image of the singular female and male, and to acknowledge racism within the women's movement and sexism within the Chicano movement. Illustrating intersectionality was not the curators' only objective in these errata exhibitions; they proposed and conceptualized identity in complex and multiple ways, suggesting that the subjective experience of gender and race "*always* depends fundamentally on relations to other social identities."[76] Chicanas always inhabit a racialized body, as Barbara Carrasco illustrates in *Milk the Pass* and as the artists of *Las Venas de la Mujer* captured through the incarnation of female archetypes that challenge the virgin/mother/whore imperative of coloniality, patriarchy, and racism. In some ways, the works in these errata exhibitions expanded the parameters of the social movement among Chicanas/os to the transnational stage, connecting women's labor in Latin America to Chicana labor in the United States, as in the installations by Josefina Quezada and Isabel M. Castro. Finally, the Chicana feminist errata exhibitions visualized interconnectedness in displays of art that evoke the sacred and the divine, such as Judithe Hernández's altar installation and Margaret Garcia's portraits, which were designed to inspire awe and admiration of the female sitters, who appear to coinhabit celestial and mundane worlds.

The errata exhibitions referenced the multiple and hybrid identities rooted in Chicana/o experiences. By advocating for an aesthetic of resistance and continuity, difference and solidarity, the errata exhibitions formulated an art criticism that embraced the "divisions, splits, ruptures, gaps, silences, wounds, and absences" of Anzaldúa's borderlands, of living in-between.[77] This specifically Chicana/o commentary challenged, and simultaneously was positioned within, American art historiography. This is precisely the space occupied by Asco, as Amelia Jones observes in her study of avant-garde aesthetics in the East Los Angeles milieu of poverty, miseducation, and police brutality (including the form of state-sponsored harm that disproportionately drafts men of color to the frontlines of battle).[78] The errata exhibitions' dismantling of art taxonomies in the moment that they were being used or renovated—an untying and crossing of disciplinary boundaries—was a major aesthetic advancement with simultaneous political and theoretical ramifications. The art criticism enacted through errata exhibitions was consistently responsive to strategies of containment, holding firm to a politics of accountability. Curators acknowledged the errata in locations that served Chicana/o constituents and residents, but they continued to query who belongs and who decides. The errata exhibitions testify to an expansive interpretation and representation of art, one with political utility.

More important for Chicana/o art criticism, when errata exhibitions wield expansive, multiple, and complex subjectivities or the "dismemberment, or fragmentation of the body," they prompt a "new introspection and renewed awareness." The polyvalent subject is not theorized for its pathology, thus precluding a diagnosis that understands fragmentation as cultural schizophrenia or failed assimilation.[79] The borderlands are conceptually a site and source of knowledge and struggle, but they are also a conduit of creativity and a place of negotiation. As Anzaldúa recognizes in her analysis of visual artists and creative writers, struggle is the source of *la facultad*, a knowledge that emerges from oppression and the sixth sense that the dispossessed develop to survive.[80] In this way, the notions of community and culture are not rejected, but are expanded, complicated, and reconfigured with an ability to recover repressed aesthetics and experiences. The borderlands are generative rather than obligatory, inclusionary rather than exclusionary, diverse rather than singular. By linking errata exhibitions from the 1970s to those of the twenty-first century, I demonstrate the longevity of borderlands theory.

In short, the errata exhibition is important because it intervenes against erasure, dismissal, inaccuracies, and confusion, making public discourse accountable to the history of exclusion and the context of inclusion and pointing to the structures of the art world as the source of exclusion. If public museums are sites that regulate raced and gendered artistic production (a point I make in *Exhibiting Mestizaje*), then the errata exhibition holds the public museum accountable, demanding that it offer equitable access and resources to all publics. The errata exhibition must be seen as a site of radical intervention.

# LOOKING AT THE ARCHIVE

## Mechicano Art Center and Goez Art Studios and Gallery

Leonard Castellanos, artist and a director of the Mechicano Art Center, received classical training in high school from David Ramirez, whom he credits with facilitating his acceptance at Chouinard Art Institute on full scholarship. Ramirez required his students to understand and execute the painting techniques of Renaissance artists, such as Michelangelo and Leonardo da Vinci; to read canonical works, such as *Principles of Art History* by Heinrich Wölfflin, for their theories of composition and color; and to approach figure drawing through the study of anatomy. Castellanos learned to understand the composition of all things through "the interior flow of the body" and "the gesture of the body."[1] Continuing his technical training at Chouinard, Castellanos studied with master printer and neo-Dadaist Connor Everts, abstract surrealist Emerson Woelffer, and Disney animator Donald Graham.[2]

Castellanos excelled in printmaking, but the various and diverse media of sculpture—metal, Plexiglas, wood, paint, Styrofoam, resin, glass—drew his attention while he was enrolled in the master of fine arts (MFA) program at California State University, Los Angeles, where again he was closely mentored by faculty, particularly printmaker Leonard Edmondson. Out of economic necessity, Castellanos leveraged his technical skills to start a business with Everts (by then his close friend), forming C&C Press Recovery Company. The venture gave him increasing skill with metal casting and experimentation in media, which he put to use in his MFA thesis project in 1968 on "modular spatial arrangement."[3] The culminating work consisted of "thirty to forty modular three-dimensional forms" whose "arrangement . . . was infinite." This conceptual and interactive sculpture featured eighteen-inch boxes, constructed of wood but painted, primed, and sealed to look like glass. The "fine finish"— Castellanos's words to describe the high polish of the sealant—places his style squarely within the aesthetics of West Coast minimalism, particularly the light and space movement. This work engaged the viewer and artist with its infinite combinations, as he notes: "You could, literally, randomly arrange [the work] and never do the same thing twice."[4]

Castellanos brought this wide-ranging understanding of techniques (such as classical drawing, printmaking, and photomontage) and styles (such as conceptual, minimalist, and abstract art), plus barrio and Mexican aesthetics, to his curatorial work for Mechicano. One of the organization's early group shows blended the personal experiences of Chicana/o artists with European aesthetics, evoking the ideological and epistemological process that Chicana feminist scholar Gloria Anzaldúa identifies as mestiza consciousness.[5] Running from May 28 through June 8, 1973, at the Junior Art Center in Barnsdall Park, the show contained thirty works from fifteen artist members of Mechicano. Castellanos selected pieces that conveyed the artists' range and their various approaches to art. For example, the art of Guillermo Martinez and Ray Atilano drew on the work of Mexican muralists and surrealists; Manuel Cruz's rough sculpture of General Douglas MacArthur with smeared red lipstick engaged Mexican folk art and political satire, expanding José Guadalupe Posada's social commentary to three-dimensional form; Oscar Castillo's photographs of a blond mannequin and a Rolls Royce grill suggested the critical documentary style of Walker Evans and Paul Strand as well as contemporaries Martha Rosler and Allan Sekula; and Carlos Almaraz's painting with its "brilliant pink, overlapping letters and trickles of color" was reminiscent of "bright, chalky pastel colors common to East LA buildings and graffiti-like forms common to East LA walls" and Jasper Johns.[6] While one reviewer found the affinity with Johns unsurprising, another was troubled by the use of styles that were supposedly outside Chicana/o experience, dismissing the fact that these artists had been trained in US institutions of higher learning or the notion that they could grapple with multiple influences and still identify as "Chicano."

With its wide range of styles and visions for creating art, this early exhibition could be read as an irregularity within Chicana/o art history.

Following Sandra de la Loza's cue, I propose instead a remixing of the archive that will amend our understanding of the art produced by the arts organizations that participated in the Chicano movement. This chapter investigates Mechicano from 1969 to 1978 and Goez Art Studios and Gallery during its years of collaborative creative activity, from 1969 to 1982, when it was on East First Street in East Los Angeles.[7] The two organizations developed simultaneously at the beginning of the Chicana/o art movement. As case studies of the 1960s and 1970s, Goez and Mechicano illustrate how arts organizations moved between for-profit and nonprofit endeavors, supported a wide range of styles, and animated new relationships between culture and politics. Following an analysis of the flourishing of cultural centers as well as the anchoring ideologies and practices that informed arts production, I turn to the formation and development of critical education and heritage tourism by Goez and Mechicano. In addition, the chapter documents collaborations the two arts organizations undertook with a broad range of constituents—a largely successful effort, although gender equity was not collectively pursued. I explore how Goez and Mechicano operated with complex and nuanced views about commerce, politics, culture, and the arts.[8] Artists in these institutions promoted a highly mobile and flexible view of economic and political empowerment—major tenets of the civil rights movements. Through their art, they worked toward an alternative view of society, one in which art and politics are overlapping. My examination of Mechicano and Goez reveals that both engaged in complex negotiations and orientations, forcing a rethinking of the dominant critical framework that contrasts civil rights initiatives with for-profit endeavors.

William Wilson's review of the Mechicano group show for the *Los Angeles Times* illustrates how critical discourse can constrain how Chicana/o art is perceived. It also reveals that "postidentity postures" were operating decades before the election of Barack Obama and that Chicana/o arts organizations emerged in a context that required tenacity to gain traction among artists, collaborators, and residents.[9] Wilson complained that the artists had nothing unique or new to add because they "fail[ed] to make any ethnic connection."[10] His statement betrays the narrow presumptions of art historians and critics who understood ethnicity and race as bounded and who promoted the assumption that only human figuration could project racial themes.[11] Wilson's comments about Almaraz's painting constitute a case in point. Wilson noted that its colors and text-like gestures echo the architecture and urban aesthetics of East Los Angeles, but the composition also reminded him of Jasper Johns's gestural abstraction. For Wilson, this bicultural sensibility was not only problematic but also a sign of the artist's invisibility or lack of distinction. Consciously or not, Wilson subscribed to Western notions of race and ethnicity as characterized by difference, essence, or biology, and the critical energy of his review was not focused on the art. He concluded with the following observation: "In a curious way the evident inability of specialized groups to produce a specialized art is a monument to the homogenizing tendencies of American democracy."[12] Working within and wielding the rhetoric of racial containment, Wilson saw the artists on exhibition only as expressions of assimilation and American exceptionalism. This framework ignores how Chicana/o artists "moved adeptly through neoclassical approaches, Mexican social realism, neo-Dadaist principles, hard-edge abstraction and graffiti aesthetics" to practice a borderlands aesthetic.[13]

While absurd, Wilson's statement of American triumphalism—America as the great melting pot—advanced the view that because it is neither all-American nor sufficiently "specialized," Chicana/o art is illegible. The hybridity of the Mechicano artists disqualified their claims to rights and visibility within the art world.[14] Wilson's so-called *art* review should be recognized as a claim for whiteness and its guise of normative, yet unmarked, status and the concatenate privilege of naming others as inherently backward or different. It affirmed the autonomous authority to set the discursive limits of art history. Wilson employed notions of democracy to undermine the demands of the artists for self-determination, recognition, and the redistribution of public space. These were precisely the goals of Mechicano when it opened at its first location near La Cienega Boulevard, the center of the Los Angeles art scene, in 1969; when it made its home on Whittier Boulevard in East Los Angeles between 1971 and 1976; and later when it relocated to North Figueroa Street in Highland Park under the leadership of Joe D. Rodriguez before closing two years later.[15] Mechicano was also deeply invested in exploring an "aesthetic alternative" that was experimental rather than definitive.[16] Wilson could not comprehend how community formation and the construction of the self through cultural production are inextricably connected to politics. He could not account for the ways a historically marginalized identity could function within American aesthetic traditions even as it gave rise to alternative modes of expression.[17] Wilson's

LOOKING AT THE ARCHIVE

inability to see an expressly Chicana/o art was based on a myth of essentialism for nonwhite people and the art they create.

Mechicano and Goez advocated for cross-cultural collaboration and developed a politics of accountability that turned the sites of and activities for aesthetic presentation into spaces of social transformation. One of the ways the two organizations accomplished this was by linking art and commerce. Investigating this link is of particular importance since many Chicana/o art historians have viewed for-profit activity with skepticism if not outright contempt. This view develops directly from a periodization of Chicana/o cultural production that divides it into political art from the 1960s and 1970s and more recent commercial concerns. I aim to complicate the picture because for-profit activities, including graphic design and merchandising, were a vital part of the formation of Chicana/o cultural production at Goez and Mechicano, and the interweaving of art and commerce continues to be practiced by Chicana/o arts organizations in Los Angeles and elsewhere. Furthermore, the community orientation and attention to collective transformation rather than personal aspirations persisted long after 1975, which is generally considered the final year of political art. A significant historical legacy has been buried under the conventions of Chicana/o cultural politics, and this erasure has resulted in stale retellings and narrow understandings of Chicana/o visual cultural production.[18]

Admittedly, I have participated in this erasure. When I learned about Goez, I initially dismissed it from my investigation because it was a commercial enterprise, which in my mind disqualified it from the Chicana/o body politic. Other scholars reinforced this perspective when they relegated Goez to a few sentences in Chicana/o art history, briefly describing the arts institution as "commercial" or a "for-profit gallery."[19] This silence implies that the institution diverged from Chicana/o cultural politics and the discourse of self-determination. A similar bias applies to Mechicano. Although it is generally celebrated as the counterpoint to the profit-oriented Goez, Mechicano was largely a commercial venture during its first year, and this usually receives little attention. A closer look shows that Mechicano continued its collaborations with commercial institutions well after it relocated to Mexican American neighborhoods. Mechicano also expanded the conventional model for commercial art dealers by providing studio art classes at its locations in East Los Angeles and Highland Park, blurring the lines between a commercial establishment and a community organization. This exploration of Goez and Mechicano reveals that ideological complexities that are typically associated with activism and art after the Chicano movement were at play during the Chicano movement.

This chapter rejects and challenges several clichés about Chicana/o art in Los Angeles, and I expect that most of the misperceptions I expose can be discovered for similar organizations throughout the United States. The chapter disputes the conventional wisdom that Chicana/o arts organizations of the 1960s and 1970s stridently opposed for-profit endeavors, were separatist in practice and politics, and developed and supported an obligatory aesthetic style. The connection between art and economic empowerment is significant because in the case of Goez and Mechicano it was expressed through for-profit ventures that were not separate from cultural affirmation and aesthetic control. Self-representation— the authority to determine one's subjectivity and image—was informed by a critical consciousness that rejected the Eurocentric and American devaluation of Mexican and indigenous history and cultural heritage, and this critical consciousness in turn shaped the creation of murals, posters, tours of public art, festivals, and other claims to space. The results cannot be anticipated by current conventions in Chicana/o studies, American art history, or Latin American visual criticism, which typically render Chicana/o art as insufficient in its universal appeal, lacking in cosmopolitan influence, or simply out of fashion.

By blending critical education with heritage tourism, Goez and Mechicano used for-profit strategies to promote Chicana/o cultural production without acquiescing to forms that degraded it through the political economy of race and culture. The arts organizations avoided the co-opting or profiteering strategies of capitalism while simultaneously promoting the economic and cultural capital of artists. The artists of Goez and Mechicano strove to be accountable to their Chicana/o communities by attempting to empower them with economic development that would sustain culture even as it transformed it.

### Building a Space for Art and Politics: Context of Goez and Mechicano

Goez and Mechicano produced a range of programs and activities: mural creation, studio art classes, heritage tourism, graphic design, and plans to reconfigure public urban space. These diverse practices integrated a broad array of collaborators, audiences, and influences while supporting Chicana/o aesthetics. Established in 1969, Mechicano and Goez were the first venues to support Chicana/o artists in Los Angeles, but they did not form in a vacuum. In the 1970s Chicana/o Los Angeles witnessed the birth of dozens of cultural centers and artist groups. As foundational players in the Chicano movement, these organizations created a dynamic period of Chicana/o cultural production. Those currently documented include Nosotros (founded in 1969), Self Help Graphics & Art (SHG, working as early as 1970 and formally incorporated in 1973), Plaza de la Raza (incorporated in 1970), Centro Joaquin Murrieta de Aztlan (founded in 1970), Mexican American Center for the Creative Arts (founded in 1970), Asco (founded in 1971), United Chicano Artists (founded in 1972), Los Four (founded in 1973), Social and Public Art Resource Center (SPARC, operating as early as 1974 and officially incorporated in 1976), Los Dos Streetscapers (founded in 1975), Artists Union for Revolutionary Arts (founded in 1975 and known by the acronym AURA), Aldama House/Corazon Productions (founded in 1975), Centro de Arte Público (CAP, founded in 1976), and EastLos Gallery (founded in 1978). Collectively these fourteen arts organizations and artist collectives increased civic engagement and creative vitality within the city and surrounding region. While it is generally understood that three institutions, Plaza de la Raza, SPARC, and Self Help Graphics & Art, have sustained the legacy of the civil rights movement since the 1970s by consistently offering arts education, supporting art production, sponsoring exhibitions, and advocating for the arts and artists, it is important to recognize how the institutions that no longer exist also shaped critical consciousness about art, politics, representation, vernacular aesthetics, and urban space.[20]

The activities of several of these organizations were driven by the artists' debates about representation and appropriation. CAP, SPARC, SHG, and Centro Joaquin Murrieta, a nonprofit organization directed by Josefa Sanchez and Alfonso Baez in East Los Angeles, advocated for a relevant aesthetic style and practice and rejected the premise of the art market system. For example, to gain more autonomy over images and the process of mural production, Judy Baca and her cofounders Donna Deitch and Christina Schlesinger formally incorporated SPARC as a non-profit organization independent of the Citywide Mural Program, which was funded by the city of Los Angeles. Muralism is one of the most provocative challenges to the art market system because it systematically refuses participation in the commodification of art. Similarly, artists of Centro Joaquin Murrieta advocated for art that did not rely on financial transactions by producing "chalk-ins" in Belvedere Park.

While a critique of profiteering certainly was present among Chicana/o activists in Los Angeles, artists were also challenging the influence of public and private agencies that supported the arts. Similar to Goez, which distrusted municipal grants, CAP was a significant cultural experiment that tried to work outside the public funding circuit and its accompanying limits on representation.[21] CAP members understood firsthand the restrictive role that public funding played at various *centros*, including Mechicano and SHG. In founding CAP, artists championed the view that artistic production should not be compromised or appropriated. This vision of an art not dependent on bureaucracy was central to artist collectives across the globe during times of social dissent dating from the 1900s, but CAP managed to avoid the pitfalls and entanglements of "avant-gardist romanticism" by refusing the art markets and institutions they criticized.[22] Unlike other avant-garde artists in New York and Los Angeles, CAP and its contemporaries could not enjoy an idealistic relationship to or affiliation with corporate sponsors and authorizing arts institutions because generally the artists were underemployed and their work remained outside the fine arts market. Aesthetic and political independence translated into experimentation, and for CAP and Goez it took the form of a small business venture. In general, arts organizations advocated for cultural pride and self-determination for the Mexican-heritage community and the creation and exhibition of art while also promoting employment and financial stability for artists.

Despite their for-profit status, CAP and Goez supported intense artistic dialogues and debates that unfolded at sites like Aldama House, a commune in the Highland Park neighborhood of northeast Los Angeles. These colloquies drew artists such as Carlos Almaraz and activists such as Patricia Parra. The vigorous discussions, whether formally staged or spontaneously embraced, spanned art, politics, and the role of the artist. Some of the meetings were serendipitous gatherings of artists. Others were formal, as artists sought to explore a new visual language and develop networks. The statewide clearinghouse Concilio de Arte Popular was established as a result of these discussions. This creative energy and desire to work collectively helped support several arts organizations even when funding was scarce, allowing artists to share ideas and resources, comment on one another's work, and experience the somatic and transcendent qualities of art making.[23] The freewheeling discussions in the context of art making, which took place also at Mechicano, Goez, and SHG, served to further explore what it meant to be *un centro cultural*—a space that allowed for a firestorm of creative energy and supported the aesthetic processes of a broad range of artists.

While the atmosphere of Chicana/o arts organizations was dynamic, patriarchy was the authoritative code and women's roles were limited.[24] Some centers, nevertheless, included women from the beginning. At Goez, Esperanza Martinez and Josefina Quezada, both critically acclaimed, were among the artists who exhibited their work, and Alicia and Rebecca Gonzalez, sisters of the founding members, helped manage the gallery. At Mechicano, Mura Bright was an essential patron; other women exhibiting and contributing to Mechicano included Isabel M. Castro, Sonya Fe, Judithe Hernández, Lucila Villaseñor Grijalva, Susan Saenz, and Maria Elena Villaseñor.[25] In 1976 Fe was hired to run Mechicano's silk-screen workshop. At SHG, Linda Vallejo was hired to manage the Barrio Mobile Art Studio, which was launched in 1975. SPARC was particularly significant because women cofounded it. The creation of ideological and visual feminist space within arts organizations and artist collectives was a challenge for women as well as men, and SPARC was known for its ongoing feminist agency. The literary magazine *Chismearte*, housed at CAP and elsewhere, played an important role in valuing women artists and art historians. Two special issues about women supported Chicana feminist consciousness. The special issue titled "La Mujer," published in 1977, included two articles by Sybil Venegas, "The Artists and Their Work—The Role of the Chicana Artist" and "Conditions for Producing Chicana Art," which are considered the first to articulate Chicana art history.[26] The art of Barbara Carrasco was selected for the cover of the second special issue, and she used the space to visually express Chicanas' agency in transforming and empowering womanhood within Chicana/o communities.[27]

The output of artists and the concurrent demand for space required legal and social action to create facilities. A community campaign to save the boathouse in Lincoln Park in 1969 led to the formation of Plaza de la Raza and a campaign to design and build a larger cultural center. Plaza de la Raza was the only arts organization whose physical facility was built from the ground up. More frequently, as with Goez, Mechicano, CAP, and SPARC, artists formed the demolition and construction crews that renovated vacant buildings, transforming them into offices, studios, and galleries for exhibition. While land use and the reclamation of public space were vital to the Chicana/o art movement, a social sense of belonging was also generated through public and communal activities. The cofounder of

SHG, Sister Karen Boccalero, advanced printmaking rather than muralism, but it was her strategic vision that resulted in SHG's most influential arts program, which was centered around Día de los Muertos.[28] SHG's Day of the Dead activities became the organization's unique contribution to cultural life in Los Angeles, one that made a permanent change in the city's use of urban space, as witnessed by the celebrations for the dead that have occurred throughout the region since the mid-1980s. However, this most phantasmagorical of Chicana/o arts has not entered art history discourse, as it is interpreted as merely folkloric. Nevertheless, hosting citywide events was foundational to SHG's and Mechicano's success in generating a sense of belonging within Los Angeles.

Part of this elastic practice emerged from a desire to advocate for art as vital to daily experience, not just as a tool to communicate the goals of *el movimiento*. Several arts organizations envisioned artists in K–12 classrooms as pedagogues who would design and deliver content as well as instruct, in the community as inventors of the character and meaning of public space, and in the labor force as valued workers. Mechicano, Plaza de la Raza, Mexican American Center for the Creative Arts, Nosotros, and Centro Joaquin Murrieta provided multidisciplinary arts instruction, offering classes in visual arts, dance, music, theater, and creative writing. The curricula emphasized indigenous arts, Mexican aesthetics, and Chicana/o urban vernacular. United Chicano Artists aimed to place Chicana/o artists in the public school system, a strategy that SHG pursued through the Barrio Mobile Art Studio.[29] The cofounders of Centro Joaquin Murrieta conceived a plan for Chicano University, an autonomous institution that would employ local artists to design and teach bilingual and bicultural courses in the performing arts, fine arts, and communications (the plan never bore fruit).

The intensity of the moment, driven by political and social unrest, arts activism, and a groundswell of artistic talent, supported numerous organizations, which in turn reinforced experimentation. More common than a narrow set of expectations about Chicana/o aesthetics was a collective critical resistance to formalizing a specifically Chicana/o art. For instance, early in 1971 Goez hosted a Chicana/o art symposium at the gallery that was organized by Gilbert "Magu" Sánchez Luján. This event, along with a second symposium in April at the International Institute on Boyle Avenue that was also organized by Magu, gathered artists to discuss the boundaries of Chicana/o art. The intense discussion did not result in agreement.[30] I propose that the artists understood the "dilemma in forming an alternative, counterhegemonic movement" in the context of a national ideology that structurally and rhetorically overlooked its difference.[31] As Castellanos notes about Mechicano artists, the ideological shift produced during this period depended upon a belief "that art is a very fundamental part of your existence. That it has to be part of your environment."[32] Artists found agreement in an approach to art that recognized it as central to life and in experimentation that supported complexity and ambiguity.

Indeed, the cofounders of Goez responded to the unresolved debate by placing a sign, "Barrio Art," in the window to characterize the hybrid approach that was central to Goez's cultural production. The organization was housed in an old meatpacking warehouse that was remodeled by the cofounders and their family and friends. They designed horseshoe arches in the style of the Great Mosque of Córdoba in Andalucía, Spain, and used a large wooden "walk-in freezer" to stage the office as "the captain's quarters of a Spanish galleon."[33] A display of imported goods from Spain and furniture and wood carvings from Tijuana, Mexico, formulated a complex Chicana/o aesthetic. This combination of Spanish, Mexican, and US aesthetic references produced a flexible, transnational, and innovative decorative style. "Barrio Art" announced the location of this sensibility and greeted visitors to the inaugural exhibition in December 1971.[34] In short, Goez's cultural authority hinged on its spatial location within a materially and transnationally configured space. In what follows, I explore more deeply how Mechicano and Goez resisted narrowly defined arts practices and negotiated cosmopolitan sites and forms of cultural production.

## Creating Goez Art Studios and Gallery and Mechicano Art Center

From 1969 through the 1970s, Goez and Mechicano were central to the visual arts activity in East Los Angeles and throughout the city. Both organizations achieved tremendous success for arts institutions that had to create from scratch what it meant to serve Chicanas/os. The origin of each foretells how it was able to navigate social and cultural conditions that empowered Los Angeles elites and authorized dominant aesthetics.

Goez Art Studios and Gallery was a for-profit business cofounded in November 1969 by two brothers, José Luis and Juan "Johnny" Gonzalez, and David Botello.[35] The company title, Goez, comes from the first and last two letters of the brothers' family name, Gonzalez, and José Luis hoped it would intrigue Anglo Americans but not trigger a prejudiced reaction. Located in a warehouse that needed extensive work before the cofounders could open for business, Goez was a multipurpose company that simultaneously functioned as an art studio, gallery, dealership, clearinghouse for muralists, import business, fine arts restoration service, advertising agency, visual arts school, and cosponsor of citywide cultural festivals.[36] It began as an import business, selling Spanish and Mexican furniture, leatherwork, replicas, and tapestry on consignment, but the revenue was not sufficient to sustain the company. Within a year of operation, the cofounders reframed their original emphasis on merchandise and fine art sales to include heritage tourism, community beautification through public art, graphic design, and a school for the visual arts, which incorporated as a separate entity with Juan at the helm. From its location on East First Street, Goez advanced the key characteristics of centros culturales: critical education, errata exhibitions, and spatial and ideological claims to cultural primacy through murals, maps, and heritage tourism. Goez is a pioneer in Chicana/o art history because of its early promotion of public art as a component of heritage tourism, an economic model intended to benefit local economies by increasing state, county, and city revenues. Goez's focus on heritage tourism predates the urban policies that emerged in the late 1980s and 1990s to promote postmodern urban reform and development. It was also a distinct form of cultural tourism because it did not authenticate a romantic Mexican past, as does Olvera Street, a tourist attraction in central Los Angeles.[37] Goez's commercial venture, therefore, reinforced self-representation and affirmation, the central tenets of the Chicano movement.

Mechicano Art Center was the product of a collaboration between Victor Franco, a community organizer, and Mura Bright, a former set designer, illustrator, and decorator who had lived in Mexico for ten years.[38] Their first independent venture was Mechicano Gallery on Melrose Place near La Cienega Boulevard, which represented artists Ray Atilano, Ray Bojórquez, Leonard Castellanos, Xavier Lopez, Frank Martinez, Alex Rodriguez, and Benny Venegas. Franco and Bright produced an exhibition of Chicano art in September 1969, but after a successful inauguration, Mechicano Gallery could not maintain the rent and closed its doors in June 1970.[39] The relocation of Mechicano to East Los Angeles allowed Franco to pursue his original plan for a multimedia center that would produce theater, music, and visual and performing arts.[40] He selected an old laundromat on Whittier Boulevard because it could accommodate a gallery, studios, classrooms, and a space for musicians to gather. It was also near Doctors Hospital, a major supporter of the arts in East Los Angeles. With an "organizing nucleus" that included Atilano, Bojórquez, Bright, Martinez, Rodriguez, Venegas, singer-songwriter Willie G, and later Castellanos, Mechicano became a collective that organized exhibitions and provided members with studio space.[41]

Goez was a commercial gallery and Mechicano consistently collaborated with authorizing arts organizations, but both institutions were fundamental to the establishment of critical education for the Chicana/o community. Critical education provides constituents with the tools to challenge domination, particularly race, class, and gender oppression, through the collection of new information, the development of new interpretations, and the employment of new methods of engagement. Through their exhibitions in particular, Goez and Mechicano consistently introduced innovative and alternative commentary about racial and aesthetic hierarchies and about the ways aesthetic standards are embedded within the codes of racial and class domination.[42]

Mechicano's exhibitions were marked by its strategy of collaboration. It joined with other galleries, community institutions, colleges, universities, K–12 schools, public libraries, and even banks to produce exhibitions of Chicana/o art for a broad constituency and in a variety of sites.[43] The wide network made it possible for Mechicano to produce exhibitions throughout California, Washington, and Arizona. This enhanced the value of the works not only as objects but also as American art. Mechicano's network proved especially useful during periods in which it lacked a home but continued to produce exhibitions in college venues.[44]

Documentary photographs and reviews suggest that the exhibitions organized by Mechicano and Goez included a range of aesthetic styles. For instance, two major group shows of Mechicano artists at local universities featured abstract expressionism, portraiture, realism, and conceptual art. *Chicano Art: The Artists of the Mechicano Art Center of East Los Angeles* ran from November 29 through December 17, 1971, at the Vincent and Mary Price Gallery (now the Vincent Price Art Museum) at East Los Angeles College, and *Mechicano at USC* appeared in September 1973 at the University of Southern California's Fisher Gallery. Both received media coverage that commented on the stylistic variety of the works shown.[45] The exhibition at the Fisher Gallery included William Bejarano's "bright abstractions" and "works by Ernesto Palomino, Guillermo Martinez, and Antonio Victorin [which] range from psychedelic compulsion to social realism."[46] Exhibitions at Goez supported a wide range of aesthetic styles, techniques, and approaches. On display in Goez's inaugural exhibition in 1971 were "classical, contemporary, abstract and modern painting, nail relief, copper relief, wood relief, metal sculpturing, wood sculpture, marble sculpture, tapestry, sand paintings, and graphic arts."[47] A brochure produced in the mid-1970s contains photographs of the gallery that show the same range of works: classical portraits, abstract sculpture, a reproduction of the sixteenth-century Guadalupe portrait, and a large wood-relief image of an Aztec god. By the end of the decade Goez boasted of representing over three hundred artists whose works expressed a variety of styles and techniques.[48]

An important aesthetic direction at Mechicano was indicated by a photography exhibition in April 1971, which was possibly the first show at the East Los Angeles location. It came eight months after the national Chicano Moratorium on August 29, 1970, in which tens of thousands of Chicanas and Chicanos in Los Angeles protested the Vietnam War and the disproportionate number of Mexican Americans being drafted and dying on the battlefield. Mechicano produced a pictorial interrogation of the Los Angeles County Sheriff's Department, whose officers had been implicated in the violence that erupted at the protest and in the death of journalist Ruben Salazar as he covered the demonstration for television station KMEX. Originally published in *La Raza* magazine, the photographs of police brutality, bloodied protesters, and teargassed crowds, and the condemning image of a deputy shooting into the Silver Dollar café—where Salazar was killed—was a visual challenge to the official inquest, which had exonerated the deputy, and to the Sheriff's Department's code of impunity.

Cultural production at Mechicano also supported avant-garde sensibilities. Harry Gamboa Jr. photographed at least one performance in which Willie Herrón III painted an "untitled acrylic interior mural on plaster and plywood at Mechicano Art Center. This work was painted for temporary duration and was whitewashed within 30 days by its creator."[49] Similar to the critical commentary for which Gamboa, Herrón, and their Asco collaborators were known, Herrón's experimental performance suggests the simultaneous criticism of municipal censorship of Chicana/o public art and the self-imposed silencing within Chicana/o mural expression. Staged inside Mechicano, it indicates that the members, particularly the muralists, were aware of the internal forces that suppressed cultural production. At the same time, the temporary presence of Herrón's mural implies that muralists emphasized the process rather than the product, signaling how the creation of public art functions as a pedagogical strategy for mobilizing a community and transforming its social environment.[50] In fact, the murals on the exterior of Mechicano's Whittier Boulevard facility were ephemeral works, further supporting an interpretation of murals as social transformation rather than object. In 1972 Mechicano initiated a monumental public art project in the Ramona Gardens housing development under the direction of Armando Cabrera. The artists planned to create 105 murals, and by 1975 they had completed fifteen for the housing project.[51] One of the works was a massive surrealistic mural by Herrón that filled the interior walls of an administrative office.[52]

Community art classes were another aspect of critical education at Mechicano and Goez. From its inception, the classes at Mechicano favored normative visual arts curricula, but the instruction did not approach art from Western conventions. By 1972 Mechicano was offering classes in drawing, painting, and photography, and it also provided instruction in graphic art, silk-screen printing, and mural production. It also held informal jazz sessions twice a month.[53] Mechicano's silk-screen program, supported initially by a "self-help grant" from the Catholic Campaign for Human Development and then by a grant from the National Endowment for the Humanities, was conceptually part of the avant-garde trend against art for art's sake.[54] As Castellanos reports, the silk-screen program reinforced a critical orientation against the modernist image of the individual artistic genius. "The silk-screen poster operation is more than just a poster operation," explained Castellanos in a 1973 interview. "We want to share our talents and abilities" with the community. Castellanos stated that Mechicano was "willing to train children, people, organizations that want posters [for] free," and he added that the center would "lend them our facilities."[55] His cofounder, Victor Franco, articulated similar views and described community arts as "a tool for social change" that produced "the spiritual uplifting of the people." Franco affirmed that "the goal [of community arts] is to awaken [people] spiritually to the point where they can become politically conscious of their environment and what's happening to them and their lifestyle and hopefully to stimulate them to do something about their condition."[56]

Clearly articulating what Shifra M. Goldman had identified as "a totally noncommercial" and non-elitist attitude and expectation, the silk-screen program—and Mechicano's arts programming in general—was an important strategy for creating new images and communicating and collaborating across the Mexican American neighborhoods of Los Angeles.[57] The grants allowed Mechicano to pay artists without charging fees for printmaking, a noncommercial policy that also operated at Goez, where the founders told people, "Just come and paint here, everything is on the house."[58] Using public funds, Mechicano would repeat this economic model to finance the murals created at Ramona Gardens and elsewhere.[59] When coupled with the unequal distribution of public financial support among arts institutions, this generosity meant that for-profit status did not easily translate into actual financial gain.

The arts classes at Goez and Mechicano were equally important as spaces for producing a politicized identity. Though the classes were largely conventional in content, the instructors of the studio classes embodied a critical consciousness and made use of the location of the courses as a tool for social change—that is, the spatial location of arts education allowed for a new epistemology, a new way of conceiving and embodying community authority, subjectivity, and aesthetic value. As Castellanos states about Mechicano and its courses in drawing, painting, graphic art, photography, silk-screen, and mural production, the arts center functioned as "an alternate educational vehicle . . . because we're fulfilling needs that schools and universities aren't."[60] The East Los Angeles School of Mexican-American Fine Arts, a nonprofit institution housed at Goez, also determined that arts training in local schools and universities was insufficient for Chicana/o artists. The school taught painting, drawing, and mural production to anyone who walked in the door, operating on minimal public funds. As at Mechicano, the classes proposed new understandings of Mexican art and culture as well as East LA barrio aesthetics. Mechicano and Goez offered an alternative education because they provided new information about Chicana/o art, and they exposed and challenged the hierarchies of value within the art world by elevating vernacular visual culture and Mexican aesthetic styles. Furthermore, a studio art class taught by a Chicano artist was itself a new method of engagement. The Chicano instructors embodied aesthetic authority, and their classes bypassed the local schools and universities, which largely employed Euro-American males.

Both institutions had a flexible understanding of commerce and the arts. Mechicano operated in East Los Angeles as a nonprofit organization, but Franco, Bright, and Castellanos continued throughout the 1970s to forge networks with and sponsor productions within the emerging establishment of the Los Angeles art market.[61] As Reina Prado argues, Mechicano's mobility throughout the LA area underscored the founders' "self-awareness" about the organization's impact and their ability to build on the momentum of the civil rights movement and the artistic proliferation that was occurring throughout Southern California.[62] Franco sought financial support from the entertainment industry, other businesses, and the arts establishment, and this strategy was duplicated at Goez. Although José Luis and Juan Gonzalez focused on neighborhood businesses such as the First Street Store in East Los Angeles, Goez also contracted with national companies, including 7UP, Anheuser-Busch, Atlantic Richfield, Dewar's, Disney, and Vidal Sassoon. Similar to other small businesses in Chicana/o communities of the Southwest, Franco and the Gonzalez brothers had difficulty obtaining market-rate loans to cover initial capital expenses.[63] Collaborations with the Westside art establishment, Euro-American philanthropists, and national corporations were essential to the survival of Chicana/o arts organizations, and the attempt to solicit a broad range of constituents was a strategic response to institutional racism and market hierarchies.

Mechicano found solid purchase on the affluent Westside for "Chicano MAD"—"Music, Art, Dance"—an event that raised funds for Plaza de la Raza's capital campaign. The festival, which was held at the Hollywood Palladium on July 26, 1970, included performances by groups such as El Chicano, which became one of the most popular bands for the Eastside sound. The event drew six thousand people.[64] This tremendous success allowed Mechicano to produce a second benefit, "El Mundo Chicano," at the Ash Grove in September 1971. The Ash Grove was a legendary Los Angeles music club that featured masters of blues, bluegrass, jazz, gospel, folk, and international music. The Ash Grove's founder, Ed Pearl, had grown up in the Boyle Heights section of the city. Pearl supported socially and politically conscious theater, comedy, poetry readings, and lectures, and activists converged at the Ash Grove. He met with women's rights and civil rights organizers and with activists protesting the Vietnam War, and El Teatro Campesino, which supported the farmworkers movement, performed at Pearl's invitation in September 1968 and several times subsequently.[65] In this spirit, the weeklong collaboration between Mechicano Art Center and the Ash Grove suited both institutions' interest in the coffeehouse tradition of music, poetry, theater, and politics. A reviewer noted that "'El Mundo Chicano' opened with a few reminders of the Mexican American presence in Southern California" and that the emcee had calculated the politics of demography for the "Anglo" audience, pointing out that "one out of six individuals in Los Angeles is a Chicano; by 1978, that figure will be one in four." The reviewer observed that "no sycophantic attempts are made to assuage Anglo sensibilities" and that the performances by Teatro de la Tierra and Teatro Barrio Ensemble, as well as the musical contributions by Willie G and God's Children and Junior and the Preludes, were seamlessly interwoven into a weeklong "crash course for Anglos."[66] The benefit also included a panel discussion by Chicana/o activists and a screening of Jesús Treviño's 1969 documentary about the high school walkouts in 1968, *¡Ya Basta!*[67] Mechicano's screening of this free-form film suggests a pedagogical strategy to immerse non-Chicano audiences in the contemporary vernacular experiences of Mexican Americans in Los Angeles.

The collaborations between Mechicano and Westside institutions have been buried, censured, or dismissed by Chicana/o commentators whose concept of culture and community is untenable. Even if Franco and Castellanos intended to turn a profit for Plaza de la Raza through "El Mundo Chicano," they did not aim to sell out Chicana/o culture through appeasement, obsequious behavior, or opportunism. Mechicano's contribution to the Los Angeles art scene, which was defined in large part by its links to other local and national arts establishments, was significant. These collaborative efforts were also important for Goez.

## Heritage Tourism as Critical Pedagogy

The promotion of public art as the subject of heritage tourism strategically transformed urban, working-class Mexican American neighborhoods into aesthetic sites of value. Heritage tourism should be distinguished from cultural tourism, a form of capitalist appropriation that commercializes and promotes a supposedly authentic cultural experience of a people or place. For example, Christine Sterling's invention of Olvera Street as an "authentic Mexican shopping street" for tourists was driven by economic, social, and political motivations. As the conceptual architect and manager of Olvera Street, she devised a romantic vision of Mexico and Mexicans that required ridding the area of crime and "filth"—or any reference to actual Mexicans.[68] Her dream came to fruition with the help of Harry Chandler, publisher of the *Los Angeles Times*, who set up the for-profit Plaza de Los Angeles Corporation to help fund the project.[69]

Heritage tourism contrasts with vulgar consumerism because it has historicizing claims to authenticity. Unlike the conventional tourist, "who voluntarily visits a place *away from home* for the purpose of experiencing a change," or the cultural tourist, who seeks romantic or exotic experiences of *others*, heritage tourists are local residents who seek depth, expansion, or consolidation of their own heritage.[70] For example, heritage tourism is typically associated with national heritage rather than with the cultural identity of marginalized populations within the nation-state. Goez and Mechicano expanded heritage tourism by aestheticizing Chicana/o culture and "transform[ing] East LA into an outdoor gallery," an intervention that changed the very terms of cultural authority.[71] Events for national and international guests who were invited to visit East Los Angeles retained this alternative orientation. Heritage tourism as practiced by Goez was not invested in US nationalism; instead, it challenged national myths that devalued Mexican and Chicana/o culture, people, and history. While Goez extended this economic model further than Mechicano, both institutions engaged in heritage tourism by promoting tours, festivals, and parades, along with products that could be reproduced and circulated, such as maps, postcards, calendars, prints, and advertisements.[72] The heritage tourism activities of Goez and Mechicano were a new form of commerce that was not distanced from the cultures of East Los Angeles.

Once Mechicano made its home in East Los Angeles, the aestheticization of social space became a major objective. For instance, in 1971 Mechicano organized a bus bench art competition, sponsored by Doctors Hospital, that involved local artists and residents. This project valued the social context of art and the aestheticization of everyday objects. As such, Mechicano advocated a new view of the neighborhood and literally inspired a tour of pride as residents were encouraged to drive along Whittier Boulevard to view the works, which were painted on boards and fastened to the benches, turning the street into an outdoor gallery. Twenty-nine entries were created and installed, and residents were asked to vote for the best one. The ten benches receiving the most votes were displayed at Doctors Hospital, and in 1972, after the contest, the entire collection of paintings and maquettes that had been created for the competition was displayed in Mechicano's gallery.[73] Similar to the murals that Mechicano supported, the bus benches expressed the value of community-based art: it could not be bought by a collector or isolated inside a museum or its storage facility. When one bench was stolen from its street-corner location, Mechicano artists read the vandalism as the highest compliment and an indication of their successful transformation of everyday objects into works of art.

Castellanos was aware of the co-opting effects of beautification projects. Rejecting interpretations of public art that claimed to beautify and thus increase the market value of property, he argued that Mechicano's bus benches and murals represented "more than some glorified antigraffiti campaign."[74] The city's antigraffiti programs relied on the demonization of street artists as well as an aesthetic hierarchy that established murals as a step above graffiti yet below painting and sculpture. Castellanos's comment suggests that he saw these efforts to locate art in the Chicana/o community as articulations of collective empowerment rather than individual autonomy and personal accomplishment. His notion of public art insisted on inclusion and a commitment to social transformation.

Mechicano's most formal expression of heritage tourism was the sponsorship of neighborhood arts festivals. An aspect of what urban geographer and critic David Diaz describes as a pedestrian culture, community arts festivals generate massive gatherings of Chicana/o families and friends who come out to the parks, streets, or other open spaces to view art exhibitions, listen and dance to musical performances, enjoy poetry and street theater, and eat and socialize.[75] These all-encompassing aesthetic experiences breach the disciplinary boundaries of music, visual arts, theater, and dance, and Mechicano did not separate everyday forms of arts practice (such as food preparation and domestic crafts) from the formal arts. At the festivals the visual arts were embedded within the sensual delights of sight, sound, taste, smell, and touch, further aestheticizing Chicana/o culture. In many ways the social and multidisciplinary engagement was a culturally relevant method for contextualizing the visual arts. The numerous festivals and public celebrations sponsored by Mechicano consistently placed the visual arts within a larger social scene involving Mexican cuisine, Chicano rock 'n' roll, Latin sounds, rhythm and blues, *ballet folklórico*, *danzante*, and *teatro*. One example is the March 1972 celebration of Mechicano's second anniversary on Whittier Boulevard. The weeklong open house featured an art exhibition, Mexican folk dancers, and performances by Willie G and God's Children.[76] "Feria de la Raza" at California State University, Los Angeles, was another major public festival that integrated the arts and vernacular expressive culture. Thousands of local residents attended these events.

Similarly, Goez provided residents and visitors with another understanding of the interrelated nature of Chicana/o culture and art with an initiative that sought to revitalize the local business district by increasing pedestrian traffic as well as economic investment. Juan desired "to make

East LA a tourist attraction" through the production of public art.[77] He recognized that Goez could play a role in what Linda K. Richter describes as the "symbolic importance of being represented in heritage sites" by creating art that would contribute to "collective political memory."[78] Envisioning a series of projects in East Los Angeles, Juan imagined that local residents and outsiders would be curious about Chicana/o cultural production and would flock to see the murals and monuments that Goez produced. He planned to instruct residents and visitors about the aesthetic production on the Eastside, and using the orientation of heritage tourism, he would foster an appreciation of spatially and culturally grounded aesthetics. In this way, residents would change how they felt about their community, and national and international tourists would gain respect for an otherwise racialized minority. Juan easily convinced his cofounders to support his idea. Scholars, urban planners, and policy makers had not yet identified heritage tourism as a strategy for urban revitalization or community development, so the founders drew on their intuition when drafting designs for monuments, fountains, and outdoor sculptures; contracting with national corporations and businesses; pushing local businessmen to commission murals; collaborating with Doctors Hospital to produce massive urns that resembled warrior heads from Aztec, Olmec, or Toltec civilizations; promoting tours of Eastside murals; or designing postcards and posters to be sold as collectable items for display in Mexican American households.[79]

Goez's initiative to draw local, regional, and international tourists to East Los Angeles was launched with the creation of a mural, *The Story of Our Struggle* (1974), on the facade of the landmark First Street Store. The massive eighteen-panel mosaic mural was commissioned by First Street Store manager Robert Kemp, designed by Juan Gonzalez and David Botello with assistance from Robert Arenivar, who produced sketches for the project, and fabricated by Mexican ceramist Joel Suro Olivares. José Luis Gonzalez provided technical and managerial support. The mural visually records the cultural and historical heritage of Mexican Americans, depicting the conquest of Mesoamerica, the Mexican War of Independence, the US-Mexico War, and other historical struggles as well as ideological battles such as worker solidarity in breaking the chains of capitalism. *The Story of Our Struggle* brings to public attention the information that the Goez founders and other artists did not receive in school. The mural was to provide inspiration to Mexican American residents about their unacknowledged connection to indigenous Mexico, their historical presence within the geographic boundaries of the United States, and their legacy of struggle against injustice and exclusion, a struggle that predates the contemporary civil rights movement.

Another key project was El Monumento de la Raza, imagined as a pyramid-shaped fountain embellished with icons of Mexico's *mestizaje*, including massive busts of Aztec gods (fig. 3.1).[80] The monument was expected to attract visitors not only to the hilltop site at Indiana and Folsom Streets but also to the entire neighborhood. A related project designed by Botello, Tlalocán Commercial Center (fig. 3.2), would accommodate visitors to El Monumento with its hotels, restaurants, nightclubs, and businesses and stimulate economic empowerment for Chicanas/os living in East Los Angeles.[81] El Monumento and Tlalocán Commercial Center referenced Mexican modernist architecture, reinforcing the contemporary nature of the plans rather than an illusion of timelessness. Although the monument and the commercial center were never realized, Goez's promotion of heritage tourism found success with its fee-based daily bus tours of Eastside murals, which began in 1975.[82] Goez contracted with Gray Line Tours to take local visitors and those from Asia, Africa, and North America on a narrated excursion that included socio-spatial criticism of urban renewal, land use, and freeway construction that had demolished, split, or dispersed working-class Chicana/o communities in Los Angeles. The frequency of the tours forced the cofounders to work from a desk near the front of the gallery rather than from the Spanish-galleon office and to gather other volunteers to assist them with the business, although the financial gain from the bus tours was not significant.[83]

Letters from teachers, school administrators, and students from Central and Southern California document that the Goez tours promoted cultural pride and collective empowerment and gave new value to Mexican and Chicana/o art. As critical education, the tours instructed local youth in the alternative histories of indigenous Mexicans and Mexican Americans. As one educator noted, "You spoke of history, philosophy, math, English—all in relation to ourselves, our families, and always [connecting it] to the people of the world."[84] Goez offered a radically different vision of tourism, one in which the actual community and its artistic accomplishments would be the central focus—not a quaint and distant Mexico, but the contemporary lives of Mexican-descent people living in Los Angeles. Goez used public art to anchor the cultural and aesthetic authority of the barrio, coupling a profit-making enterprise with critical education to produce a complex

3.1 David Botello, *El Monumento de la Raza*, 1970. Black marker and colored pencil on tracing paper, 19 x 24 inches. Photograph by Gil Ortiz of El Sereno Graphics. Reproduced by permission of the artist.

3.2 David Botello, *Tlalocán Commercial Center*, 1972. Watercolor on paper, illustration board approximately 36 x 14 inches. Image courtesy of the artist.

site of alternative knowledge. Goez not only aestheticized Mexican American neighborhoods by creating murals but also enhanced the value of the murals by bringing residents and visitors to witness the cultural authority of the Eastside. The attempt to increase Chicana/o presence in the public sphere in the face of increasing privatization of space is worth noting, particularly for its generative power of resistance and cultural imagination.

## Spatial and Aesthetic Positions

At Goez, heritage tourism was also supported through mapmaking that created new knowledge about East Los Angeles and its residents. Goez produced maps, postcards of murals and other public landmarks, and offset posters as "something that [people] could frame, and something that they could keep with pride," much like the calendars and religious cards that Mexicans and Mexican Americans collected for home display.[85] The Goez maps are significant because they function spatially and symbolically to locate the gallery and its community within a larger context, visually articulating the geographic, political, and aesthetic authority of the gallery and community. Maps are a method for visually coding belonging and cultural authority.

The first maps issued by Goez voiced critical discourse. One map produced in 1975 by David Botello announced, "In Europe all Roads lead to Rome. In Southern California all Freeways lead to East Los Angeles," calling attention to two distinct spatial impositions of power (fig. 3.3).[86] The Roman imperialist expansion relied on roads leading to and from the empire's center, whereas the freeways of Los Angeles were designed to, in the words of Eric Avila, "direct the movement of people and their money toward the suburbs and away from the inner city," especially neighborhoods like East Los Angeles.[87] Both systems imposed power relations through the organization of space. Although the construction of the freeways and their interchanges in East Los Angeles had resulted in a massive displacement of Chicanas/os, by reading the roads as a source of advantage that would bring people *into* the urban core, Goez produced its own "folklore of the freeway" and critically challenged the spatialization of power. This reversal encompassed all of East Los Angeles as a destination with cultural and aesthetic authority. The map precisely illustrates the location "as of April 1, 1975," of "271 individual murals . . . at 107 separate locations" in "East Los Angeles, California, United States of America, Mexico, Aztlan." The last

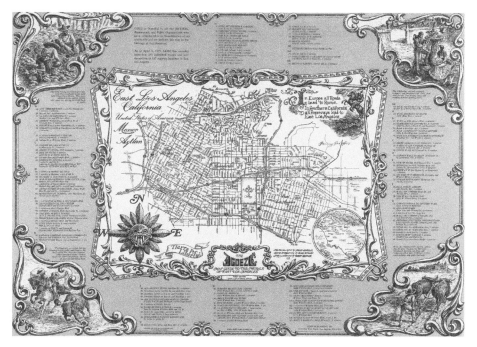

**3.3** David Botello, *The Goez Map Guide to the Murals of East Los Angeles*, 1975. Offset print, 17 1/2 x 23 inches. Photograph by Gil Ortiz of El Sereno Graphics. Reproduced by permission of the artist. © Goez Publishing Company.

phrase further reorders geopolitical spatiality, placing East Los Angeles simultaneously within the boundaries of the United States, Mexico, and the mythical homeland, Aztlán. This alone is a significant political gesture about transnational and transhistorical subjectivity and belonging. The mapmakers used the head of the Aztec god Quetzalcoatl as it is depicted in sculptural form at Teotihuacan to indicate the four cardinal directions. This creates another powerful spatial and temporal allegory, one that links East Los Angeles to an indigenous heritage that serves literally as the compass for contemporary bearings. Centered above the map is a pre-Columbian mask flanked by Mesoamerican step-fret designs and European filigree patterns.[88] To the right of Quetzalcoatl is a revision of the Mexican Revolutionary slogan ("Tierra y Libertad" becomes "Tierra *por* Libertad") that makes a further claim to territorial control. Drawings in each corner by Arenivar illustrate early California history, especially Mexican and Spanish contributions to agriculture, ranching, mining, and leisure.

The radically different contexts—pre-Columbian civilizations and Spanish colonialism, Mexico and the United States—coalesce into a Chicana/o historiography that offers a different reference point for cultural authority. This broad, transhistorical frame or spacio-temporal gesture within Chicana/o cultural production is frequently overlooked by art critics, particularly those who read Chicana/o art as separatist, essential, or parochial. The map offers an alternative: a new vision of space that rejects social hierarchies. The freeways that were intended to vacate the downtown have become channels toward the city center, East Los Angeles. Goez could not "change the course of the freeway, but they could change its meaning."[89] This visual and conceptual reversal of Chicana/o influence is echoed in the fact that some prints are numbered—an indication that Botello likened the map to a limited edition, fine art print.

Mechicano also participated in a widely ranging arts discourse that rearticulated space. Because Franco vigorously supported the civil rights strategies of solidarity building and mobilization, techniques he likely practiced while working as a labor organizer, he established networks across a variety of constituencies. In 1971 he departed Mechicano to form the Los Angeles Community Arts Alliance and to serve as its president. The Community Arts Alliance was a clearinghouse for communities of color that distributed information about local events, arts and urban policy, funding opportunities, employment for artists, and production and exhibition techniques. In his capacity as president, Franco recruited Castellanos and others to the alliance. Mechicano was an active participant in the larger community arts movement in Los Angeles and the nation, collaborating with African American, Asian American, Native American, and Jewish American visual artists, creative writers, performers, and arts advocates. For instance, in 1972 Mechicano played a significant role in the landmark symposium "Community Arts and Community Survival," organized by the American Council for the Arts in Education, which helped launch a national debate about pedagogy, arts curricula, and accountability.

Castellanos recalls, "I became very interested in the concept of developing a central nucleus of information, which we had never had; to advise artists where shows were happening; what was going on where; what festivals were being held; how can art work be shipped."[90] To that end, in 1973 the Community Arts Alliance compiled a directory of fifty-two organizations: neighborhood arts centers, cultural facilities, community arts support groups and networks, galleries, performance groups, sponsors of festivals, artist collectives, media and communications groups, and other institutions located within or established for African American, Asian American, Chicana/o, and Native American communities. The directory was described as an invitation to support dialogue among the participants and supporters of the "community arts movement."[91] I read the directory as a cartography of intercultural and cross-cultural collaborations as well as a foundational document of the community arts movement. Each entry includes the history and origins of the institution, identifies its founders and leaders, states the organization's mission, goals, and programs, and gives its geographic location. The directory thus maps the spatial, ideological, and aesthetic diversity in the community arts movement in Los Angeles. Because several arts advocates were participants in multiple arts organizations, the directory also contains information about solidarity, unity, and mobility. For example, African American artists and organizations of South Central Los Angeles gathered for "The Meeting at Watts Towers," a scheduled monthly event; Amerasia Bookstore served as a site for coalition building within the Asian American arts community; and Mechicano provided a similar space for Chicana/o artist collectives on the Eastside, as it had since 1969.

These coalition-building strategies and spaces in turn laid the groundwork for what the directory calls "a growing social and political awareness of artists, along with an increased awareness of the value of the arts as a tool for social change through education." These artists and arts organizers were not waiting patiently at the gates of the commercial gallery circuit, the Los Angeles Art Association, or so-called public museums; they were agitating and creating their own spaces for dialogue, exhibition, and interpretation of art. By "idea-sharing, work-sharing, [and] information-sharing," the Los Angeles Community Arts Alliance forged inclusive conversations about art, politics, and critical education that crafted a broad coalition across the city.[92] The directory, therefore, maps Mechicano's location within the larger community arts movement. Mechicano was not insular, singular, or parochial in its activity and approach, but was situated among multiple aesthetic movements. One particular copy of the directory illustrates Mechicano's critical location within the LA arts scene. Castellanos owned this copy, and he annotated it with symbols and comments. Each elaboration signifies how and where Castellanos situated Mechicano in the collectively forming notions of art and politics (fig. 3.4).[93] Castellanos also underlined ideological statements about critical arts education and art as a tool for empowerment, as well as statements that challenge racial and economic oppression.

THE BURBAGE THEATRE
Founded: 1969

Director: Sal Romeo

Address: 3789 South Menlo, No. 309
Los Angeles, CA 90007

Telephone: 734-3057

... an experimental theatre company dedicated to developing arts and artists in the community it serves.

The Burbage Theatre Company is an organization created in 1969 to bring new and meaningful socio-theatre into and out to the community in which it exists. The company attempts to do this by performing experimental, classical, musical, original and avant-garde works.

They relate to the community through their works and through workshops in music, dance, movement, acting, awareness and discussion groups where they discuss artistic and community problems, problems which are often the same. The workshops allow them to identify problems and potential solutions which are presented later in theatrical form.

The Burbage has received consistently excellent reviews from major Los Angeles critics. This acclaim has helped make their efforts more acceptable to the public. Public acceptance and support is crucial to their survival as they are supported solely by box office receipts (and occasional loans which must be repaid). "Although the Burbage does not let public acceptance govern the art form, we realize the art form must be at its best to be accepted," says Sal Romeo, director.

Beyond performances and workshops, they have assisted in the formation of a local newspaper, Easy Reader. They started the Hermosa Beach Coalition, a group designed to facilitate communication between the "straight" and "hip" communities there, and several police-community conference group; to foster open dialogue between the two groups.

5

---

\* The Los Angeles Community Arts Alliance has prepared this "Handbook on Community Arts" in the hope that it will serve as the beginning of closer communication between all people interested in the community arts movement.

This is not a complete handbook. We designed it so that new information can be easily inserted from time to time, and old information up-dated.

We are attempting to build links of communication between groups and individuals in this movement. If you belong to a group or know of one that should be included in this handbook, please let us know about it. We will attempt to gather information about it, have it printed in the format we have used here, and send it to those who are on our mailing list.

If you would like to be on the mailing list so that you may receive our newsletter about community arts, please send us your name and address. We ask for your time if you want to become further involved.

The Los Angeles Community Art Alliance
2911 West Temple Street
Los Angeles, California 90026

(213) 487-6422

For more information about the Alliance, see our listing under "Support Groups."

EDITED BY JOHN BLAINE and DECIA BAKER

COORDINATED BY REX and LAINE WAGGONER

PHOTOS BY JOHN BRIGHT

COVER DESIGN BY THERESE HEARN

ii

3.4 Pages from the Community Arts Alliance directory, 1973. Collection of Leonard Castellanos. Image courtesy of California State University Channel Islands, Unique Collection.

They have also begun a theatre coalition of experimental theatre companies in order to share resources and services.

Recently, they began a new program with Studio Watts Workshop to involve artists in the design, construction and management of low-income housing in Watts. The idea is to prevent the rapid deterioration of low-income housing by asking artists from the community how to avoid the conditions which lead to such waste. The Burbage will go directly to the people with its theatre company and through a series of improvisational workshops, will focus on the problems of low-income housing projects. The information gained through this project will be directed to the architects and contractors for the project.

Meanwhile, the company is in search of a home. Several thousand dollars' worth of materials, time, energy and paint were lost recently when what was thought to be the new home for the Burbage Theatre was declared illegal because of zoning and building code laws. (Los Angeles has perhaps the most rigid codes extant because of earthquake potential here. For this reason, probably most community theatre companies are technically operating outside the law.) An experienced administrator could have prevented the problem, but experienced administrators demand salaries. The problem of finance is obviously crucial but has not yet affected the survival of the company. The Burbage has never applied for or accepted any outside funding.

"In order to get funding, one has to define oneself according to criteria the fundor establishes. This puts the artist into a box. Since the artist has only his freedom of expression to offer, he can't allow any fundor to silence or distort his voice and truly survive. Until fundors come to us and find out where we're at and accept us on our own terms, we will not seek funding."

-- Sal Romeo

9

The directory opens with an epigraph by Ananda Coomaraswamy, a Ceylon-born metaphysician who interpreted Eastern culture for the Western world in the early twentieth century. A global scholar and contemporary of Alfred Stieglitz and a participant in New York City's bohemian art scene in the 1920s, Coomaraswamy helped build the Indian and Asian collections at the Museum of Fine Arts, Boston, as well as those at the Freer Gallery of Art in Washington, DC. The epigraph reads, "The basic error in what we have called the illusion of culture is the assumption that art is something to be done by a special kind of man, and particularly that kind of man whom we call a genius. In direct opposition to this is the normal and humane view that art is simply the right way of making things, whether symphonies or aeroplanes."[94] The quotation is from Coomaraswamy's essay "What Is the Use of Art, Anyway?" It challenges the modernist distinction between art and craft and the Western homage to the so-called unique artistic genius. Coomaraswamy proposes that art has meaning only within its original context, not inside museums or galleries that are removed from the artist's environment. Furthermore, each person involved in "making things" is "a genius," not only those who are exhibited, collected, and praised by the dominant art establishment. While I cannot verify that Coomaraswamy's writings were the source for the foundational ideologies of the Chicano arts movement in Los Angeles, I can suggest that a transcultural and cosmopolitan discourse operated within the Los Angeles Community Arts Alliance and inspired Franco and Castellanos to develop an aesthetic vision that exceeded those of European modernism and American art.

## Alternative Modes of Exchange and Agency

Mechicano Art Center and Goez Art Studios and Gallery were founded during the earliest years of the Chicano movement in Los Angeles, and the activities of the two organizations serve as evidence of an interweaving of arts and commerce, an established practice among Los Angeles Chicana/o arts organizations. They also demonstrate the value placed on experimentation, integration, and multiplicity, as well as the influence of diverse aesthetic styles and references on Chicana/o visual production. In addition, these two arts organizations developed a critical pedagogy that would be reflected in postsecondary ethnic studies curricula by the late 1970s and the orientation of the Chicana/o cultural centers that emerged during the 1980s.[95]

The merging of art and economic development continued long after José Luis Gonzalez moved Goez from East First Street to Olympic Boulevard in 1982 and Mechicano permanently closed its doors in 1978. For example, Self Help Graphics & Art's Professional Printmaking Program, which was initiated in 1983 and continues today, was designed as a commercial venture through which artists could independently sell their work. The agreement between the organization and the artist determines the price, the split of the edition, and the conditions of sale. The agreement illustrates a particular capitalist sensibility that avoids exploitation and supports equitable asset accumulation, especially since the signatories are not permitted to undersell each other. Similar to Goez and Mechicano, Self Help Graphics invests in artists.

Arts organizations that emerged in the 1980s and 1990s and at the start of the new millennium engaged the art market without emphasizing profit making. Examples include Galería los Callejeros (1989) and Palmetto Gallery (1988–94), initiated by David Botello and Wayne Alaniz Healy and located in downtown Los Angeles; Aztlan Cultural Arts Foundation (1993–2000), founded by artists Leo Limón and Armando Martinez; Tropico de Nopal Gallery Art-Space, founded in 2002 by Reyes Rodriguez and Marialice Jacob and located west of the civic center on Beverly Boulevard; Avenue 50 Studio in Highland Park, founded in 2000 by Kathy Gallegos; and Tonalli Studio in East Los Angeles, founded in 2012 by an artist collective including Ofelia Esparza. Galería los Callejeros and Palmetto Gallery were commercial ventures that complemented the public art projects of Botello and Healy.[96] Tropico de Nopal and Avenue 50 Studio, both still open, frequently host *mercados*, inviting visual artists, writers, and merchants that normally operate without a storefront location to sell a wide range of products, including fine art, books, clothes, purses, wallets, jewelry, teas, bath salts, skin lotion, herbs, and homemade food. The mercados deliberately blur the lines between fine and folk art, traditional and modern art, and high- and lowbrow art. Most of the vendors operate cottage, organic, or do-it-yourself industries and circulate within the "anti-mall" movement. Practicing and advocating exchange that depends on relationships or shared values, the mercados are an alternative type of commerce that aims to transform how capital is exchanged and how art is contextualized.

Extending this capitalist reformulation in service of the arts, Tropico de Nopal also produces music performances and DJ dance parties, which in turn support collaborations across the creative arts, continuing the legacy of Mechicano, which Rodriguez frequented as a teenager. Tropico de Nopal provides an alternative venue for musicians and audiences and, more critically, offers a stage for LA *latinidad*. Performers include samba bands, Afro-Cuban drummers, spoken word poets, Puerto Rican *bomba* ensembles, and other musicians who bring the Caribbean/Latin American/African sound to the art space. In 2005 Ozomatli, a fusion band that fully subscribes to Chicana/o politics yet is ethnically mixed, took up residency at Tropico de Nopal to write, experiment, and informally record their sessions. The band is known for its blending of hip-hop, salsa, merengue, funk, and other styles, as well as for its participation in mobilizing workers and immigrants. One night during the band's residency visitors were invited to see the installations created by three of the band's members and to dance to improvised music. This live performance and other sessions resulted in *Don't Mess with the Dragon*, the group's 2007 album. When film director Chris Weitz asked Ozomatli to contribute to the soundtrack for his movie *A Better Life* (2011), the band asked Rodriguez to direct the music video of the song, "Jardinero," which was filmed on the roof of the gallery. Later that year, Rodriguez launched an Internet radio show, *Art & Grooves*, in which he interviews artists, writers, and performers about their musical influences, favorite songs, and passions. This creative cross-genre approach to the arts is also seen in Tropico de Nopal's Calavera Fashion Show and Walking Altars (2004–10; revived in 2014). The evening event, which celebrates the Day of the Dead, is formatted like the runway productions of haute couture, but it features cultural *ofrendas* worn as costumes and art installations by artists, actors, and local residents, who perform, dance, or saunter down a catwalk in homage to the dead

In sum, Chicana/o art is alive and thriving in Los Angeles in part because of the legacies of Goez and Mechicano. Both organizations worked to revise how art and commerce are understood by reformulating for-profit ventures as nonexploitative relationships. Both refuted the practices of hegemonic institutions that require artists of color to ignore how they "are fed and inspired by connections and through reference with living communities," as Arlene Dávila notes.[97] Both Dávila and I point to alternative criteria for assessing legitimacy, particularly because the histories and experiences of racialized artists are frequently used to service myths of meritocracy, individualism, and the promise of reward for hard work.[98]

The rhetoric of social integration depends upon a logic of transcendence (of culture or race) in which the racialized population rises out of its so-called traditional, backward, or parochial heritage and matches or acquires the preeminent cultural values of whiteness—especially economic and political power; in so doing, it is divorced from subjectivities of difference and is, therefore, free to enter the mainstream. But social integration is a fable on at least two levels. The rhetoric of integration functions to further entrench whiteness without deconstructing its unearned power and authority. More to the point, as Dávila demonstrates in her analysis of Latino art and representation, the concept of integration depends upon insufficient conceptions of racial and cultural difference: nonwhite communities are inherently separatist or confined and unable to generate their own transformation.

Although Mechicano and Goez did experience moments when their work briefly registered in the dominant art world, Chicana/o arts organizations have not had a lasting impact on mainstream discourses, institutions, or epistemologies. The critical discourse of Chicana/o errata exhibitions has been significant (as I show in chapter 2), but Chicana/o art will continue to remain invisible, truncated, or co-opted as another form of American exceptionalism unless the spaces of Eurocentric cultural authority—museums, galleries, and so on—comprehend their investment in essentialism as well as white privilege and its unearned cultural authority. This omission of Chicana/o art affects the economic stability of arts organizations and artists. Mechicano closed permanently in the late 1970s, as did dozens of other ethnic cultural centers. On a national scale, the DeVos Institute of Arts Management found that the twenty largest arts organizations of color "are much less secure and far smaller than their mainstream counterparts. In fact, the median budget size of the 20 largest arts organizations of color surveyed in this paper is more than 90 percent smaller than that of the largest mainstream organizations in their industries."[99] Fiscal instability within the arts institutions also impacts the bottom line for artists. The National Association of Latino Arts and Cultures reported in 2009 that nearly half of the surveyed Latino artists were living at poverty level and that a majority had seen a decrease in income from the previous year.[100] The same decade witnessed the enactment of laws against public art and the aggressive prosecution of graffiti artists, creating an "anesthetized" landscape devoid of Latino aesthetics and presence.[101]

This history of Goez and Mechicano exposes the misinterpretation of Chicana/o art as static, rigid, and exclusive. It also suggests new frameworks. In establishing arts organizations and collectives, Chicana and Chicano artists "offered both a societal critique and an alternative social vision."[102] Notably, their "hybridity as the ground of agency" was "balanced with a sense of responsibility," a point José Aranda makes about Chicana feminist writer Cherríe Moraga that is also relevant to Chicana/o arts organizations.[103] This hybridity, with its constituent call for collective accountability, points to important continuities within Chicana/o art history that bridge the prevailing dualities of representational versus conceptual and ethnic-specific versus postethnic. Chicana/o centers of cultural production were consistently attentive to larger social, historical, and aesthetic sources, but they also created new forms of validation for the art attributed to Chicanas/os, indigenous populations of the Americas, and Mexicans. Goez and Mechicano produced a generative visual culture that claimed legitimacy as it transformed social space. In the next chapter I document how artists individually followed multiple international routes to aesthetic production, and I continue to expand the ways Chicana/o art is historicized and interpreted.

# TOURS OF INFLUENCE

## Chicana/o Artists in Europe and Asia

In his second journal of his travels in Italy in the early eighteenth century, George Berkeley remarks in stream-of-consciousness style on his observations of the art and architecture of Lecce, a southern Italian city.

27 [May 1717]
Lecce . . . every church as in Rome adorned in frontispiece with columns, statues, bas reliefs etc, stone hardening in the air. . . . Inhabitants now 9000. . . . Function on Corpus Christi day Holy Thursday rather in Lecce, standards, images, streamers, host, rich habits of priests, ecclesiastics of all sorts, confraternities, militia, guns, squibs, crackers, new cloaths. Piazza in it an ancient Corinthian pillar sustaining the bronze statue of S: Orontius, protexi & protegam, marble statue on horseback of Charles the 5th, another on horseback of a King of Spain on the top of a fountain adorned with many bad statues; Jesuites college most magnificent / fine buildings of hewn stone, ornamented windows, pilasters &c large streets divers piazzas, façades of churches &c / . . . / took particular notice of the Jesuites church that of the Dominicans, nunnerie of S: Teresa, convent of the Benedictines, of ye Carmelites, nunnerie of S. Chiara. These & many more deserved attention / most of 'em crouded with ornaments in themselves neat but injudiciously huddled together / The façades of the church and convent of the Jesuites noble and unaffected, the air & appearance wonderfully grand, two rows of pilasters, first composite, 2d or upper Ionic with mezzoninos above the second row of windows / . . . *Nothing in*

*my travels more amazing* than the infinite profusion of altorelievo and that so well done. there is not surely the like rich architecture in the world.[1]

In describing this portion of his four-year Grand Tour of Europe, the Anglo-Irish priest and philosopher documents his inability to articulate beyond brief phrases what he sees and feels.[2] The entire day in Lecce is an aesthetic experience; his senses are overwhelmed. He recounts the Jesuit church and convent with the same rambling prose as he does the secular statues and relates the celebration of Corpus Christi with the same staccato as he does the ornamented structures. As long noted by other European travelers, the Grand Tour left many men simply awestruck. For Berkeley, his experiences with art and architecture in Italy and elsewhere confirmed his own theories of vision, perception, and materiality, which had been published in 1709; his treatise on the limitations of human sight argues that materiality occurs in the mind. Ironically, Berkeley's "subjectivist theory of perception" could not serve him as he wrote about what he saw and how he perceived the aesthetic qualities of Lecce.[3] The journal's style illustrates that the aesthetic experience is somewhat beyond language. The observations induced by Berkeley's gaze upon the art and architecture of Lecce reveal only part of his perception and understanding. They trickle out in the brief phrases about the low-relief sculptures in Lecce, which are "more amazing" than anything else in the world.

George Berkeley's journal entry is a useful introduction to the aesthetic experience and pedagogical lesson embedded in the corporeal act of seeing art in person. As art historian Bryan Jay Wolf argues, "perception is neither merely optical nor entirely 'natural' in its operations. It is rather, like all facets of human experience, profoundly social."[4] An embodied perception, or way of seeing, developed during the sixteenth century. It achieved canonical status with the term "Grand Tour" and was the authentic method for knowing and understanding art and architecture in the Western world. Its relational qualities profoundly influenced how travelers came to appreciate what they encountered abroad, whether they were on a Grand Tour of Western Europe, traveling in the Near East, or venturing to more distant parts of Asia.[5]

Berkeley journeyed from Dublin to England and then to Italy as tutor to St. George Ashe, son and heir of the Bishop of Clogher. Then thirty-one years old, Berkeley was charged with overseeing the educational aspects of the young man's Grand Tour, which was undertaken, as all Grand

Tours were, with a specific itinerary and pedagogical intention—to see and know art and architecture, primarily in Italy. Beginning in the sixteenth century and continuing more systematically from the latter half of the seventeenth century through the eighteenth century, young men of substantial wealth journeyed for several years to gain exposure to classical antiquity and, by the eighteenth century, Renaissance art.[6] Accompanied by cooks and valets, tutors and guides, these privileged travelers visited a standard list of places that were expected to provide the most enlightenment and enrichment.[7] They also commissioned paintings—frequently portraits of themselves staged among antiquities and treasured objects that depicted their status and the "classical virtues that visitors to Italy [and elsewhere] sought to revive and imitate."[8] Along with the portraits, the Grand Tourists bought items that would demonstrate their cosmopolitan wealth and knowledge, collecting "antiquities, paintings, casts, and sculpture" to fill their country houses.[9] The Grand Tour provided a curriculum of ambassadorship, social refinement, cosmopolitan living, and imperial vision.

### "Holy Shit, I've Been Assigned to Europe!"

The contours of the Grand Tour—its pedagogical and aesthetic intentions—correspond to the grand trips taken by several Los Angeles–based Chicana/o artists: Chaz Bojórquez, David Botello, Eduardo Carrillo, Ernesto de la Loza, Roberto "Tito" Delgado, Juan "Johnny" Gonzalez, Leo Limón, Gilbert "Magu" Sánchez Luján, and Linda Vallejo. Unlike the Grand Tourists of earlier centuries, these artists were not trying to establish their social authority and political power, which I acknowledge by using the lowercase phrase "grand tours" to refer to their travels. They embarked on grand tours of Europe and beyond because they valued seeing art in person. This pedagogical impulse to discern the tangible components of European art influenced how Chicana/o artists approached their work back home in Los Angeles. Their experiences with European art, like Berkeley's, were awe-inspiring, although their reactions registered in a different vernacular, as signaled by Delgado's excited exclamation when he learned that the military would post him to Europe: "Holy shit, I've been assigned to Europe! I don't want to miss that!"[10] The grand tour provided opportunities for these Chicana/o artists to make penetrating artistic observations, and their ventures throughout Europe and beyond informed their philosophical outlook, deepened their artistic commitment, influenced their style and composition, enhanced their technique, and solidified their approach to art.

Art historians and critics have only recently begun to account for the ways Chicana/o artists found artistic inspiration in European aesthetic traditions. Chon A. Noriega observes that Mel Casas directly engages Marcel Duchamp; Ruben Ochoa and Marco Rios quote from René Magritte; Rupert García considers the art and politics of Courbet; Juan Capistrán quotes Frank Stella and minimalism; Carlee Fernandez literally places herself within the artistic lineage of modernism; and César Martínez playfully enters the long creative genealogy of avant-garde artists who refigure Leonardo da Vinci's *Mona Lisa*.[11] The exhibition *Asco: Elite of the Obscure, A Retrospective, 1972–1987*, curated by C. Ondine Chavoya and Rita Gonzalez, integrated Asco into Dadaism and conceptualism as well as happenings. Roberto Tejada positions Celia Alvarez Muñoz within minimalism and installation art. My own analysis of Yolanda M. López documents her conceptual and semiotic approach to portraiture. Terezita Romo illustrates how Eduardo Carrillo's work fits within surrealism, a style that occupied the artist for over a decade after he studied in Spain, and she documents specific compositional references to "Hieronymus Bosch, Diego Velázquez, and El Greco [as well as to] the work of Giorgio de Chirico."[12]

In 1973 Jacinto Quirarte was the first to acknowledge the influence of European art on Chicana/o artists, but his methodological design intentionally bracketed Chicana/o art, implying that only artists of the earlier Mexican American generation were capable of finding aesthetic inspiration outside Mexico and barrio experience. Indeed, the overwhelming trend in Chicana/o art history has been to trace influences from vernacular barrio aesthetics, Catholic iconography, Mexican muralists, ancient Mesoamerican or indigenous civilizations, and the Chicano movement.[13] Chicana/o artists' engagement with European styles, aesthetic traditions, or specific artists has not been a systematic topic of study in Chicana/o art history. Given the contentious relationship between art and identity within American visual studies, it is not surprising that the field of American art history has also ignored the multiple references that inform Chicana/o art. However, this lacuna is largely maintained by presumptions of racial neutrality in artistic production and interpretation. As Amelia Jones argues, aspects of identity, particularly race, gender, and sexuality, have been used to delegitimize nonwhite, women, and queer artists, but this dismissal and interpretive strategy emerges from an equally problematic assumption that whiteness, masculinity, and heterosexuality are not raced, gendered, or sexed but instead are normative and present universal legibility.[14] Even those working within a framework of difference and identity frequently presume that culture is unmediated and transparent, and they present Chicana/o art as a regional aesthetic style. Chicana/o art is seen as an anachronism in a race-neutral context, emerging from and narrowly focused on its own subjectivity. It is almost never interpreted as part of an international art form.

My analysis strengthens the recent observations by documenting the ways that Chicana/o artists made a direct study of European artists and of the social and historical value of the arts throughout the continent. This chapter challenges the conventional view of Chicana/o art by presenting intercontinental travel as a source of aesthetic inspiration and influence for Chicana/o artists. I am interested in both subtle and overt influences of European art. My goal is not simply to record these pedagogical ventures abroad, but to illustrate how artists returned to Los Angeles with new ideas and approaches to art, new techniques and styles, and how they blended observations gained abroad with those made at home. This previously untried methodological approach to the study of Chicana/o art begins with a recounting of artists' experiences and a consideration of their informal and formal educational training in multiple settings. It avoids the anxiety over European influence that emerges from narrow expectations about assimilation and authenticity as well as static notions of culture and identity. It relies on borderlands theory, particularly Chicana feminist notions of mestizaje, third space, and differential consciousness.[15] These processes and ways of knowing anticipate and create hybridity and complexity, multiplicity and fragmentation, mobility and emplacement. Borderlands theory imagines codetermination, a concept akin to intersectionality, but one that conceptualizes the multiplicities and simultaneity of race, gender, sexuality, and other categories of identity.[16] Influence is neither unilateral nor unidirectional, and the hybrid mixing of two or more artistic influences does not produce a homogenized third aesthetic, since contact zones are continuously remade. I acknowledge that analyses of European and Asian influences suit dominant interpretative strategies and contributory models in American visual arts and conclude that this discourse has resulted in the invisibility and visibility of Chicana/o art without challenging the hegemonic ideologies that produce value and taste.

This chapter draws on oral history interviews with twelve artists. It focuses on those artists who "came of age during the Chicano movement," a phrase used to establish the artists' generation and to imply that they participated in a particular style of art. Unfortunately, within Chicana/o art history this phrase has structured our methodological inquiry to the extent that we look to *el movimiento* as the dominant aesthetic resource and source of identity consciousness, artistic intent, and community solidarity. While I do not deny a fundamental relationship between the Chicano movement and Chicana/o art, the oral histories reveal that the movement was not the sole source of inspiration for these artists. I focus on artists of the Chicana/o generation because I wish to expose and challenge not only the limits of a methodology that assumes culture is unmediated but also the interpretive frame that privileges the Chicano movement as the sole aesthetic springboard.[17]

The chapter is organized into three sections. The first documents how touring deepened artists' commitment to their profession, informed their style and composition, enhanced their technique, and solidified their approach to art. This section examines the experiences of several artists who were prompted by their pedagogical interest in seeing art in Europe. The second section describes how various artists were inspired to produce public art after their touring. The third section turns first to three artists, Vallejo, Botello, and Bojórquez, as case studies of intercontinental compositional influence, a phenomenon of critical mestizaje in which the "straddling of two or more cultures . . . break[s] down the subject-object duality."[18] This methodology is attentive to artists' lives and their testimonies and reflections about their experiences, and therefore it offers new insights about the artists and their work. I then extend the method to two artists, John Valadez and Yolanda Gonzalez, who ventured outside the United States after the 1960s and 1970s, briefly noting how Valadez's residency in France and Gonzalez's in Japan dramatically influenced the direction of their work. I offer this as preliminary evidence that this methodology has application beyond the early stages of artists' careers.

The chapter concludes with a discussion of the paradigm shift that is required once information about non–North American influences on Chicana/o art is taken into account. This chapter is the first systematic analysis devoted to direct European and Asian influences on Chicana/o artists, a phenomenon that extends beyond the cases explored here.[19] The displacement, omission, and erasure of these influences attest to the cultural hegemony that constrains the interpretation of Chicana/o art and the work of other artists of color. Therefore, I conclude by speculating about the uses and abuses of this methodology as a way to understand the visibility and invisibility of Chicana/o visual arts practices.

## A Desire for Phenomenological Pedagogy: Seeing Art in Person

While serving in the military during the Vietnam War, Botello, Delgado, Limón, and Magu were stationed in Europe, and they took every opportunity to visit the continent's great monuments, museums, and architectural sites. Magu enlisted in the air force and Limón enlisted in the army because they promised to provide opportunities to travel and to see art.[20] Similarly, other artists, including Bojórquez, Carrillo, Gonzalez, de la Loza, and Vallejo, traveled to Europe and beyond to witness the treasures of ancient civilizations and the foundations of Western heritage. Vallejo lived for two years at a boarding high school in Spain, traveled throughout Europe when on school holiday, and upon graduation in 1975 studied lithography for one year at the University of Madrid. Carrillo also studied in Madrid, taking up drawing at the Círculo de Bellas Artes from 1960 to 1961. At the age of twenty-six, Gonzalez fulfilled a childhood dream of seeing the world when he drove a Volkswagen Beetle across the European continent between October 1969 and January 1970. This tour inspired his work at Goez Art Studios and Gallery and the East Los Angeles School of Mexican-American Fine Arts. De la Loza traveled extensively through Europe as well as Mexico and the United States during the early 1970s, and Bojórquez, whose global circumnavigation began in the Pacific Islands, took an eighteen-month tour of thirty-five countries from east to west, starting in the late 1970s. All the artists in this study understood these adventures as pedagogical intentions and as a rite of passage into the profession. Seeing the work at nose length, they perceived what Western philosophers from Plato to Walter Benjamin describe as the aura of the work, its "presence in time and space," its social situatedness, its local authenticity.[21] The combination of contextualized viewing and the direct experience of the object solidified for several artists their commitment to art for the people and to public art.

Leo Limón's foray to see European art is an excellent introduction because it illustrates a theme that is common among the artists interviewed for this project. Born in 1952 in Boyle Heights, Limón was immersed in the cultural politics of the Chicano movement and participated in the development of Chicana/o visual imagery. He was a student at Lincoln High School, where Sal Castro, the educator and activist known for his leadership during the East Los Angeles student walkouts in 1968, was his guidance counselor. In high school, Limón attended meetings of MEChA (Movimiento Estudiantil Chicano de Aztlán), enrolled in the first courses at Lincoln to offer Chicano studies curricula, and contributed a poster of Emiliano Zapata for the walkouts at Lincoln. Although he had been tracked into a blue-collar career and was taking shop classes, an art instructor recognized Limón's artistic talent and encouraged him to enter a contest for weekend classes at Otis Art Institute (now Otis College of Art and Design). At Otis, Limón studied with Charles White and Joseph Mugnaini, taking courses in design, advertising, life drawing, and art history. Before Limón's high school graduation in 1971, his friend Frank Hernández introduced him to Mechicano Art Center (and, later, to Self Help Graphics & Art). Carlos Almaraz suggested that Limón consider illustration, since he was reading books about *New Yorker* cartoonist Saul Steinberg. Limón pursued this career in the early 1970s, landing a job illustrating four interior pages of *The Frank Zappa Songbook*, volume 1, and creating the cholo for Zappa's 1972 album *Just Another Band from L.A.*[22] He also found work with *El Malcriado*, the farmworker newspaper, when he followed Almaraz to Delano, California. Nonetheless, Limón did not decide on a career in the arts until he was stationed in Frankfurt, Germany, and witnessed the integration of art and everyday life. It was his European tour that solidified his personal investment in art in public spaces and art for the people.

Limón realized during his high school years that he enjoyed the visual arts, but he was not satisfied with reproductions. While attending a college art history course, he vowed, "I'm going to go to Europe and see it face-front." When he enlisted for military service in 1973, he requested to be an illustrator. Instead, the army offered him training in photography. Although not his original choice, it was "a guarantee of where you'd be stationed."[23] Based initially in New Jersey, he took every chance to visit Atlantic City, New York City, Philadelphia, and Washington, DC. He was then sent to Höchst, a small town outside Frankfurt, Germany.

From there he explored the medieval and Gothic architecture of the city. He was drawn to the ornate buildings, particularly the gabled houses on the Römerberg, but not to the Bauhaus architecture and its disdain of decoration. When he ventured into museums he discovered art that he had seen "in the books," and these observations helped him articulate a critique of the Eurocentric focus of art history curricula in the United States. It was the displays of sacred Mesoamerican artifacts in European museums as well as the anti-imperialist graffiti that he saw in the streets, however, that inspired a profound attention to a decolonial imaginary. He was determined to return home and study native cultures in order to incorporate them into his art.[24]

Juan Gonzalez made a grand tour to understand the aesthetic development of European art. He journeyed from Southampton, England, to the Netherlands, Germany, Denmark, Sweden, Austria, Liechtenstein, Switzerland, Italy, France, Spain, and Portugal. Initially traveling with a friend in a Volkswagen Beetle that they purchased in Germany, Gonzalez drove the length of Italy, stopping in Turin, Milan, Venice, Rome, Florence, and Pisa; ventured along the coast of France; and eventually stayed in Spain for two months, visiting every major city as well as smaller towns from his base in Benidorm, where he rented an apartment.[25] The four-month grand tour was made at a rapid pace, in part because of the cold and Gonzalez's asthma. He saw most places from the window of his car, observing the cultural monuments and historical landmarks in the streets of Europe.

Roberto "Tito" Delgado followed the same pedagogical impulse to study European art in person, and like Limón and Gonzalez, he also found inspiration in the European use of public space (a point to which I return below).[26] Stationed for three years in Vicenza, Italy, he traveled to Venice, Verona, and Florence, and frequently by bike to Padua. Delgado planned day trips, immersive experiences through which he sought a somatic engagement with art.

> Mostly I just went by myself and looked around places. Verona . . . take a train in the morning on the weekend, sign out, and . . . come back . . . for check-in. So [I would] have a whole day of Verona. What do you do in Verona? [*laughter*] . . . [If] you go to a museum, it's almost anticlimactic. . . . You are walking toward the museum and . . . [you realize] the whole place is a museum.[27]

In Verona, Delgado enjoyed looking at the Arena, the Roman amphitheater built in the first century; Porta Borsari, the ancient Roman gate; Piazza dei Signori, the historic town square of Verona; the medieval streets; and Romanesque, Gothic, and Renaissance architecture, including the cathedral, the Basilica di San Zeno, and Castelvecchio. In Florence he studied the sculptural decorations of the cathedral, the *contrapposto* statues found throughout the city, and the low-relief panels created for the Battistero di San Giovanni, particularly those that employ linear perspective. He was fascinated by dome architecture, from Byzantine to Renaissance styles, which he traced throughout Italy. After his military discharge, Delgado continued this phenomenological investigation as the primary method for comprehending technique and the historicized meaning of art. He entered two schools, one in Venice and one in Rome, but quickly became frustrated by art history lessons that were dependent upon slide reproductions. Nothing could match his experiential learning when he had been "this close"—the distance of a few inches—to the paintings, in which he could "see those brushstrokes."

The desire for a pedagogy that would put him face to face with European art also spurred Ernesto de la Loza's travels throughout the continent in the early 1970s. Born in 1949 in Boyle Heights, de la Loza was "yearning for the classics" when, at the age of twenty-four, he organized a tour of Europe with his cousin. They began in Iceland and traveled to Luxembourg, Belgium, and Amsterdam, and then by bicycle they followed the Rhine through Germany. He also ventured to France and Spain before returning to the United States. He then continued his tour in Mexico, traveling by bike for two years and carrying only ten pounds of essential supplies. In Europe he "sought out museums," but he recognized, as did Delgado, that visiting them "wasn't necessary" to comprehend the aesthetic contributions of the continent.[28]

## Public Art and Art Embedded within the Social Milieu

Finding art everywhere was a profound experience for Chicana/o artists. They learned that "the history, the architecture, . . . the vitality, the design of the towns, the antiquity" was a part of everyday life and that "people lived with the art in their midst," as de la Loza noted. Their encounters with art that participated in a specific social and historical context framed their engagement with their profession. Bojórquez,

**4.1** Ernesto de la Loza, *Organic Stimulus*, 1975. Restored 2012. Mural, 32 x 24 feet. Photograph by Ian Robertson-Salt. Image courtesy of Mural Conservancy of Los Angeles. © 1975 Ernesto de la Loza.

Botello, de la Loza, Delgado, Gonzalez, Limón, and Vallejo were amazed by the way that art inhabited and composed public space. What these artists saw in Germany, Spain, Italy, and France, and what Bojórquez also saw throughout the Pacific Islands and South Asia, deeply shaped their subsequent views about art—namely, the desire to situate art in space and time and an understanding that the value of art emerges from a contextualized viewing of and living with art.

The value of a historicized art, one that does not forgo cultural identity and memory, informed de la Loza's work. When he returned to Los Angeles, he joined the group of painter-muralists working at Estrada Courts, a housing project in East Los Angeles, where he created *Organic Stimulus* (1975; restored 2012) (fig. 4.1). The production of this public work of art and his compositional strategy are direct results of his travels and the aesthetic insights achieved during his journey. According to his sister, Sandra de la Loza, the mural blends futuristic and mythological landscapes, organic forms, and color fields as well as multiple vantage points and horizons. The organic shapes within the mural morph into new forms, and "the wall destabilizes," allowing for multiple readings of the mural: one sees human figures emerging from landscape and clouds changing into snow-capped mountain ranges as the image "give[s] way to pure color, space, and form."[29] *Organic Stimulus* is a compositional quotation of the architectural monuments that the artist witnessed while traveling in Europe, especially the cathedral of Cologne, which dominates the skyline and the city square. It also communicates his spiritual journey to "power spots," places of physical elevation such as the Pyrenees, which supported his quest to connect with the natural world.

Yet, as Sandra de la Loza observes, the deliberate grounding of *Organic Stimulus* in the physical environment of Estrada Courts—the way the shrubbery (present when the mural was painted) was incorporated into the mural's composition—gestures to the artist's coalescence of the surrealism that he studied in Spain with the realities of the housing project's low-cost architecture and monochromatic color design.[30] *Organic Stimulus* shows not only the artist's transnational influences but also his determination to avoid denying the materiality of the mural's location. The mural incorporates Western visual traditions, but these aesthetics are recontextualized for the low-income, Mexican American residents of Estrada Courts, a housing development whose design was intended to inspire compliance through uniformity. De la Loza's use of color and composition challenges the dull conformity of public space and the tacit agreement to acquiesce to power.

Bojórquez, Botello, Delgado, Gonzalez, Limón, and Vallejo were also deeply impressed by European public spaces and the ways art was fully integrated into the social milieu. They transplanted to Los Angeles this spatial, historical, and social approach to art. Indeed, for many artists the grand tour solidified their commitment to a career in the arts that advocates an art for the people. It was their penetrating artistic observations in Europe and beyond, rather than the Chicano movement, that primarily motivated them to champion public art and endorse the relationship between art and life. Through their grand tours, which included Mexico for Bojórquez, Botello, de la Loza, Gonzalez, and Vallejo, the twelve artists developed the conviction that there is no art outside history, culture, and identity. This point is worth restating. Whereas the Chicano movement offered a political context and motivation for artistic expression in the name of social transformation, liberation, and equality, traveling abroad—for some an experience that *preceded* the spark of the Chicano movement—reinforced the decision to become artists and to produce public works or art for the people. Their approach to art was codetermined by the visual traditions of the United States, Europe, and Mexico. For example, Bojórquez realized that he could migrate the visual vocabulary of graffiti into fine arts practice after he ventured around the globe. While he lived in the coastal town of Benidorm, Gonzalez learned to value Mexican cultural expression and vowed to explore his heritage through art and urban design as a strategy of reclamation and affirmation. For Delgado, Italian public space narrated the history and aesthetic contributions of the culture. He determined that art must be attached to place and should visually articulate people's memories or experiences of their location.

After his tour of Europe, Gonzalez dreamed of transforming all of East Los Angeles into a cultural site for tourists and also for residents, who, he believed, would come to understand the value of their heritage by living with cultural monuments, murals, and sculptures that publicly celebrate Mexican indigenous civilizations and contemporary people (as discussed in chapter 3). Arriving in New York from Europe, he thought that a cross-country bus ride back to East Los Angeles would provide a pedagogical lesson, as Europe had. By the time he reached home, however, it was painfully clear to him that "the United States is a cultural desert" whose physical appearance reveals "no history, no monuments, no public art."[31] This observation reinforced his desire to re-create what he had witnessed in Europe, confident that public art in his community would resolve Mexican American cultural inferiority and also dissipate anti-Mexican racism.

Working closely with Botello, Gonzalez designed El Monumento de la Raza as the physical center and catalyst of a revitalization project for East Los Angeles. Proposing a new social geography, the monument, with its "revivalist buildings and markers," sought an "alternate vision for East Los Angeles."[32] For Gonzalez, El Monumento would interrupt a central strategy of urban planning: the demolition of ornamentation, the rejection of historical references, and the use of standardized blueprints for strip malls, shopping centers, and housing. The design of El Monumento would signify more than cultural history: it would indicate an alternative social hierarchy. In the design, stairways flank either side of a fountain that flows from the top of a scaled version of the Pyramid of the Sun. Each level of the fountain holds a sculptural reference to pre-colonial civilizations, such as an Aztec calendar or Cuauhtemoc, the last emperor of the Mexica (see fig. 3.1). Gonzalez envisioned the demise of the assimilationist aesthetic and its neutralization of public space.

This type of project, while not unfamiliar, illuminates the value of using a wide lens when examining aesthetic influences within Chicana/o visual arts. Although the design of El Monumento echoed Mexican modernism and indigenist revivalism, it also drew inspiration from the grand public stairways in Italy, notably Rome's Spanish Steps. The classical European use of public space is fundamental to the alternative urban design Gonzalez and Botello envisioned for the monument, as well as for the Tlalocán Commercial Center and other land use projects conceived by Goez. In this way, Gonzalez, like other Chicana/o artists of his generation, fused European spatial impulses with a transborder and transhistorical cultural identity. Although it was never built, the monument suggests that the appropriated national and regional symbols reclaimed by residents of East Los Angeles were staging new aesthetic conversations that reenvisioned Mexico, Mexican America, the United States, *and* Europe as internationally linked spaces of cultural production. In short, the steps of El Monumento de la Raza figuratively rise from la Raza renaissance and the European social production of publicly accessible and valued art. Because aesthetic components of both are intertwined in its design, the monument gestures forward and back.[33]

Working from a similar analysis of public space and art, Limón sought to produce socially integrated art when he returned to Los Angeles. His vision for civic engagement through art continues to be informed by the European use of space and socially relevant aesthetics. His images of and designs for urban space signal cultural affirmation and a larger sense of belonging that acknowledges political representation and justice, environmental sustainability, and residents' relationship to the land. As Sybil Venegas argues, Limón depicts transformative landscapes of Los Angeles. His paintings, prints, and drawings, such as *Los Muertos* (1998), *Tlaloc's Beauty* (1995), and *Downstream Uprising* (2005), illustrate a "Mexicacentric LA, LA/Aztlan, the pre-invasion Cemanahuac." It is a place "surrounded by water, or in other words, the earth plane or that which sustains us. It is LA reconfigured, grounded in a central Mexican cosmology."[34] In *Downstream Uprising*, Limón visualizes new social spaces that draw on hemispheric signs but also serve a local sense of belonging and historicized identity through civic engagement. Evidence of the code-termined and hybrid inspiration for this approach to art is found in the way Limón advocates for public waterways, public art, and citizenship, insights he developed while observing German uses of public space and appreciation for art in the 1970s. For three decades, he has worked to preserve the habitat of the Los Angeles River and to transform it into open space with public art. His series L.A. River Catz is part of this long-term involvement.[35]

The "underground urban plan" that Venegas identifies in Limón's paintings, drawings, and prints finds three-dimensional articulation in his proposal for Art Peace Park, a project to expand green space along the Los Angeles River. Limón had discovered the river as a teenager, and the concrete tributary created by the US Army Corps of Engineers contrasted with the urban waterway he later explored in Frankfurt. His revision of the Los Angeles landscape and its forgotten and neglected waterway echoes the preservation of the Main River and its graceful integration with public space. Limón first developed the concept when he read about Japan's Hiroshima Peace Memorial Park during visits to the library at the military base. Art Peace Park, which has yet to be built, is a conceptual echo and a spatial quotation of Frankfurt's waterfront that recalls its green spaces, public access, and public art. At the center of his proposal for the riverside park is an environmentally sustainable building for neighborhood city council meetings, surrounded by a low circular wall intended for public art. The wall would provide space for vernacular urban practices and works spontaneously produced by youth, such as graffiti, street art, and murals.[36] The building design calls for large bilingual panels displaying the basic information that residents need for civic engagement: the US Constitution, descriptions of the three branches of government, information about voter registration, and location maps that identify city, county, state, and federal offices. Limón's intention to join urban green space with civic participation recalls the municipal and social position of the Römer, the city hall and site of social gatherings in Frankfurt. Inspired by this use of public space, Limón developed an alternative notion of riverfront conservation that links ecological, aesthetic, and civic practices. His attention to the lived reality of monolingual English-speaking and Spanish-speaking Los Angeles residents, as well as those who are bilingual, further evidences his expansive vision of public space as the site from which participation in the political process can emerge.

When these Chicana/o artists returned to Los Angeles, their encounters with European art—and in the case of Bojórquez, Asian art—directly informed their compositional strategies, styles, media, color palette, and techniques. Their experiences on their grand tours also convinced them that art is fundamentally relational and culturally grounded and, thus, accessible because of its integration into public life. Their study of art and aesthetics while they traveled abroad directly inspired their work and their development as Chicana/o artists. To understand how Chicana/o artists fit specifically within the trajectory of European art history, I explore in greater detail the experiences of Vallejo, Bojórquez, and Botello.

## Linda Vallejo: Line, Composition, and Color

According to Sybil Venegas, Linda Vallejo's indigenous spirituality guides and informs her artistic production. The artist's "life experiences and spiritual sensibilities coalesced" in the 1970s, "when not only her art but also her spiritual life became immersed in the Red Road, Sweat Lodge circles, indigenous *danza* and both ancient and contemporary indigenous philosophy, spiritual practice and community."[37] Her oeuvre, therefore, both utilizes and offers indigenous epistemology as a source of healing, empowerment, unity, and collective strength. The indigenous sensibility and aesthetic that guide Vallejo's visual project are significant. Her body of work rests upon a conceptual understanding of nature and of humanity's relationship with the life force of the natural world. European artists also directly inspire her work, and she has frequently made visual quotations of what she saw in Spain and Italy. Therefore, my analysis builds on Venegas's interpretation but understands Vallejo's indigenous epistemology as the foundation that permits a blending of multiple visual and cultural influences.

Vallejo, who traveled all over Spain, Portugal, Italy, and France while attending a boarding high school in Madrid, enjoyed museums throughout Europe for their ability to produce an aesthetic experience. Her father's military service took the family to Spain, and because of her parents' interest in art, architecture, and history as well as her own explorations in visual culture, Vallejo visited "all the major museums of Europe, many of them as a very young girl."[38] She saw the Roman catacombs and the ancient architecture and Catholic monuments in several countries. Family vacations while living overseas reinforced the pedagogical value of her European experience.

This physical engagement with art defined Vallejo's practice and approach to the study of art. From her adolescence forward, direct experience with art, not reproductions, became her major pedagogical technique. These lessons were both intentional and unplanned. For example, for three years beginning with her junior year of high school, Vallejo had the opportunity to study a major collection of the works of Hieronymus Bosch and other Flemish painters at the Museo Nacional del Prado. Vallejo was enthralled by the observations and revelations that become available when one witnesses art in person. At the time of her stay in Madrid, Vallejo related, the bottom floor of the Prado was "a repository for hundreds of Byzantine works of religious art. I spent a great deal of time studying, memorizing, and being moved by this work."[39] In Italy, she deliberately sought out Michelangelo's frescos in the Sistine Chapel to study his use of color. She recalls that the first time she visited the chapel, "the first thing I did was to sit down on one of the benches to memorize the blue. I said, 'I'm not leaving this room until I memorize the blue.' I have the blue in my head, I know what color it is, I can [reproduce] it." This particular blue illuminates her skyscapes and landscapes, a major focus for the artist since the 1990s. Several works, including *Self-Portrait, Day* (2006), *Standing Elders* (2003), and *Topanga Skyline I* (2002), contain the blue that she saw in the Sistine Chapel.[40]

Although she valued the experiential lesson of witnessing art in person, she could not always anticipate her response to what she saw. Knowing that the Prado held the largest collection of art by Francisco de Goya, she took every opportunity to see the Spanish artist's work. She was initially unprepared for its emotional lesson.

> I went to the Prado and I went to see Goya's paintings. I looked [at *The Third of May 1808 in Madrid: The Executions on Príncipe Pío Hill*, from the Disasters of War series] from across the room . . . and it's devastating. And I walked right up to [it] and one of the faces of horror—it's made with three strokes. The paintbrush is just, basically, a dot, an eye; dot, an eye; swirl, a nose and a mouth. It's just like that, boom, boom, pow. And there's the whole face.

In this late baroque painting from 1814, which documents Napoleon's invasion of Spain and the savage repression of the Spanish "populace [that] rose against the French," Goya used simple brushstrokes to

4.2 Francisco de Goya y Lucientes, *The Third of May 1808 in Madrid*, 1814. Oil on canvas, 2.68 x 3.47 m. Collection of Museo Nacional del Prado, Madrid. Image © Museo Nacional del Prado/Art Resource, NY.

compose the faces (fig. 4.2).[41] Vallejo was overwhelmed by the charge of the emotion behind the brushstrokes and the technical skill that rendered a face with minimal paint. Viewing this work freed her to explore expressionism as well as realism in her compositions.

Goya's ability to put emotion into simple forms has inspired Vallejo to keep returning to expansive skyscapes. She is influenced by the sweeping skies in many of Goya's cartoons—paintings created as templates for tapestries. Among these works are *The Straw Manikin (El Pelele)* (1791–92), *The Picnic* (1776), *The Parasol* (1777), and *The Grape Harvest* (1786–77), which Vallejo studied at the Prado. The soft skies and dreamy clouds, which fill nearly half the canvas in several of the cartoons, express the gentleness and playfulness of Goya's scenes. Art historian Enriqueta Harris observes that these works were Goya's "first opportunity to use those national subjects for which he was later so famous," and they also inspired Vallejo to break away from urban subjects and work within non-figurative and indigenist spirituality by painting realistic, imaginary, and surreal landscapes, some of which include larger-than-life human figures.[42] Vallejo fills her canvas with sky, leaving a small portion of the bottom register for a landscape that grounds the work in a specific geography. Whereas Goya anchored the tapestries to Spain through references to regional customs and costumes, Vallejo employed the landscape to anchor the paintings to indigenous sites and memories. Her skyscapes emerge from her observations of Goya's works and from her experiences in Los Angeles as a participant in *ceremonia*.

The revelations that Vallejo experienced as a result of studying Goya's masterpieces directly inform Los Cielos/The Heavens (1996–2007), a series of skyscapes inhabited by celestial figures. Vallejo referenced Goya's brushstrokes, his compositional strategies that merge landscapes and figures, and the emotional quality of his work—all derived from seeing Goya's art in person. For instance, Vallejo used the palette of Goya's tapestry cartoons and a later work, *The Milkmaid of Bordeaux* (c. 1827), which are lighter in tone than most templates. In Los Cielos, Vallejo employed a free-form technique and the careful handling of light and shade to depict human female figures and faces emerging from expressionistic clouds and shadows. The luminous figures in Vallejo's *Full Moon in Daylight* and *Los Cielos* (fig. 4.3) evoke the menacing and melancholy figure in *Colossus*, another painting that Vallejo studied. Originally attributed to Goya, the work, which depicts a giant torso rising out of clouds, has been described as "the most moving and eloquent record that [Goya] made of the war."[43] Vallejo's celestial bodies are sweeping forms full of strength and lightness; both evaporating mist and felt presence, they produce a tension that is also felt in *Colossus*. The Los Cielos paintings also draw on the "penetrating, sombre, melancholy" mood of Goya's later works.[44] Dark heavens that threaten and humble those on the earthly plane fill several works in the series, including *Struck by Lightning* and *Thunder, Lightning & Rain* (fig. 4.4). Other paintings in Los Cielos depict delicate air and vapor.

When Vallejo studied Michelangelo, she experienced a heightened state of perception. In the Sistine Chapel she moved as close to the *Last Judgment* as security guards would allow, examining Michelangelo's modeling of the figures. She noticed that the Italian artist, like Goya, used bold modeling to create human forms. A dark line was visible around

**4.3** Linda Vallejo, *Los Cielos*, from the Los Cielos series, 1996. Acrylic on canvas, 48 x 60 inches. From the Durón Family Collection. Image courtesy of the artist.

the figures, but it disappeared when she stepped away from the altar. "It was just this immediate sort of cartoon line that reads as a human being with a serious emotional intent," she said. The revelation overwhelmed her senses and nearly left her speechless: "My God, they're cartoons. And yet they look so alive."[45] Inspired by Michelangelo as well as Goya, Vallejo frequently renders the body through simple lines, as seen in the series Woman of Love and Integrity (1990–94), Spirit of Nature (2000–07), and Los Cielos.

Vallejo's European travels allowed for a penetrating study of art, which continued to guide her artistic investigation after those first moments that she identified as devastation and revelation. After college, she continued her experiential method of study and made regular trips to European and North American museums. In the first decade of the twenty-first century she expanded her lessons to include Asian art and ventured to Tokyo for an aesthetic education.

Vallejo merges European visual traditions with Los Angeles Chicana and Native American indigenous ceremony, using the techniques and styles of European masters in her explorations of earth, water, fire, and air—the elemental and natural properties that ground her indigenous spirituality and her practice of *ceremonia*. European art is often her inspiration for celestial compositions, style, and color, but it is her indigenous worldview that places Vallejo's work squarely within Chicana/o visual arts. The holistic epistemology and ontology of Native American philosophy, particularly the concept of interconnectedness, support her fusion of various and seemingly disparate aesthetics. Goya's enigmatic forms

4.4 Linda Vallejo, *Thunder, Lightning & Rain*, 2006. Oil on linen, 48 x 48 inches. Image courtesy of the artist.

offered Vallejo a strategy for painting nonrealistic expressions of the spiritual and cultural heritage that drive her life and work. This focus on her European grand tour brings to light the rich and complex resources that inform her paintings and that provide a strategy for contextualizing her work—especially the landscapes, skyscapes, and ethereal figures—within multiple aesthetic trajectories.

## Chaz Bojórquez: Graffiti as History

Like Vallejo and the other artists discussed in this chapter, Chaz Bojórquez made a deliberate study of art outside the United States. Unlike his contemporaries, however, Bojórquez made equal efforts to understand Western and Eastern aesthetic traditions, and he traveled to Southeast Asia and the Pacific Islands as well as Europe. His formal training, which began in high school, could not offer him the somatic and experiential lessons he sought, so he embarked on a global tour that was informed by previous trips made to Mexico during his youth. Born Charles Bojórquez, the artist was given the name "Chaz" by his peers at Chouinard Art Institute, where he studied ceramics on scholarship for two years starting in 1967 or 1968.[46] The nickname stuck because it suggested the hip cultural scene to which he and his parents belonged. By 1969 it had replaced his street name, "Chingaso," and had become his professional identity. Yet adopting the name "Chaz" was not a gesture of cultural denial; it signaled a childhood experience of blending multiple interests and influences.

Bojórquez has immersed himself in the graffiti tradition of East Los Angeles since the 1960s and is recognized around the world for his role in developing a West Coast calligraphic style. The tag known as *Señor Suerte* (Mr. Lucky), drawn in 1969 on a spiral staircase near the 110 Freeway, evidences his openness to a variety of aesthetic influences. The figure of Señor Suerte, a skull sporting a fur collar and large hat, draws on Día de los Muertos iconography (the skull), horror movies (especially the baron's grimace in *Mr. Sardonicus*), and the black male fashion made popular in movies such as *Super Fly* and *Shaft*. Bojórquez knew members of the Black Panthers as well as Students for a Democratic Society and had seen the "black suits and thin black ties" of his contemporaries involved in the civil rights movement.[47] The fur collar and the large hat registered with black youth, and Bojórquez was invited to create the image at a Black Panther fundraiser and other events. For these invitations, Bojórquez considered audience reception and the social weight of his work. "The original drawing," he notes, had fingers holding "a joint up by his mouth. . . . Curlicue stars [were] coming out. . . . But . . . I was not going to put a symbol about drugs in the street at all. That's where I would not cross the line. So I crossed its fingers" into a sign of luck. The figure has been reproduced numerous times—it appears in a Hollywood film, on posters, and as an icon in several of Bojórquez's paintings—and it is imitated by the fashion industry and popular culture.[48] Prior to its appropriation by grunge, skate, and punk clothing manufacturers, it became a symbol of salvation among incarcerated Latinos, who used a tattoo of Señor Suerte as a form of protection in prison and as a reminder of their hope for redemption.

Bojórquez's imagery and style are influenced by his adolescent years in "the avenues"—the northeastern streets of Los Angeles that cut through the neighborhoods of Cypress Park, Mt. Washington, and Highland Park—but he is also inspired by calligraphy from around the world. While in high school, he studied with master calligrapher Yun Chung Chiang at the Pacific Asia Museum in Pasadena, California, and this investigation of script continued during his employment as a graphic artist. In the late 1970s Bojórquez and his companion, Kathy, circled the globe, starting in the South Pacific Islands, then moving west to Southeast Asia, New Zealand, and Europe, visiting thirty-five countries in total. Before this circumnavigation of the earth, he had journeyed to Mexico and Central America. Everywhere he went he studied the landscape and the script. "I started collecting all these newspapers" in different languages, he recalls. "In Tahiti, in French, and in Fiji, it would be Hindu . . . Sanskrit, Tagalog, Filipino. Even though I could not read [them], I could tell . . . by the size of the headlines, by the pictures, by the formatting" what stories were international or important. His observations of writing forms and layout drove further explorations of composition and form.[49]

Some of this interest in script and the design of text emerged from his successful career in commercial art and graphic design, in which "headline, body copy, logo" were his bread and butter. It was this work in graphic production that provided the financial wherewithal to travel around the world for eighteen months. He developed a "huge knowledge of how type was set, the spacing of type, what bed types look like and how to rearrange type from newspapers for outdoor boards. This [job] was [his] first introduction to composition and layout." Bojórquez's work in graphic arts also alerted him to the similarities between advertising and graffiti. He realized that both make use of public space to announce affiliations, place, and identity, and both are successful when local viewers comprehend the larger message. The most critical revelation for the artist was that both advertising and graffiti require the viewer to read intertextually—between image and word.

Bojórquez has been drawn to calligraphy for additional reasons. His global tour allowed him to explore the anthropology of writing systems and how text reflects and produces cultural meaning. Devoted to matters beyond layout, Bojórquez seeks and sees humanity within the shape, cut, and composition of letters and glyphs, and he draws cultural insights from the line or curves of a script. By positioning urban calligraphy within writing systems from throughout the world, Bojórquez repositions graffiti as he weaves together calligraphic styles from China, East Los Angeles, Fiji, and India. He visually imagines how words and letters can come together on the page, the canvas, or the wall as a method of cultural healing, dignity, solidarity, and empowerment. He makes interconnected gestures of human solidarity through intertextual works of art.

The global tour allowed Bojórquez to witness a universal structure for human communication and to contextualize graffiti within a larger history of language and the visual presentation of ideas. In an interview, he reflects on his investigation of script, particularly ancient writing.

> I found . . . a universal structure. . . . I think as human beings that we have [a structure] of how we interpret language, of how it was laid out. Because when it was laid out in the clay tablets from the Sumerians [of Mesopotamia] they're very much the same layout as now. Because when I saw those clay tablets, there was a headline. . . . Headline, body copy flush left, flush right, indentation, paragraphs, [with the king's signature like a logo].

For Bojórquez, the ancient Sumerian clay tablets resembled a format he knew from mass media and graffiti in East Los Angeles. For example, Bojórquez recognized the linear layout of a tablet sent by the high priest Lu'enna to the king of Lagash, which informed the king of his son's death in combat. The wedge-shaped strokes of Sumerian clay tablets felt familiar and urgent to the artist. At the same time, the aesthetic practices in the South Pacific Islands, Southeast Asia, and the Mediterranean affirmed his belief that art emerges from ritual and that it has meaning because of the artist's social proprioception. He discovered that aesthetic autonomy—the view that art should be considered without reference to the context of its production or its audience—is a myth of the West. This observation freed him to pursue the cultural referents and styles from his childhood neighborhood of Highland Park and to merge his public work—graffiti—with his work on canvas. "When I returned to Los Angeles from traveling around the world, my mind had changed; I wanted to do graffiti, but about much more complex issues." He put into practice formats and styles that had universal legibility with culturally specific references meant to locate the artist and the work.

*Placa/Rollcall* (1980) realizes the artist's impulse to weave together a vernacular style and fine art. Unlike New York–style graffiti and its focus on the individual tag, the calligraphy of Bojórquez's youth emphasized collective identity, either by listing all members of a gang in a roll call or by signing the gang's name to the built landscape. In this large-format work he reproduces this West Coast style on canvas by itemizing the names of his friends: Connie, Tony, Knite, Fernando, Tommy, Kathy, and Kelly. The lettering echoes the Sumerian cuneiform script as well as the graphic style he had used on the streets of Highland Park (fig. 4.5). By deploying a system of barrio communication within a fine arts context, the artist reformulates graffiti to convey the cultural heritage of a specific place and simultaneously participate in the global practice of written communication.

As he traveled from island to island in the South Pacific, Bojórquez observed the human tendency to memorialize a culture in stone or other enduring media. "I started seeing a lot of temples with engravings," he noted, "that were thousands of years old." The link between the medium and the message conveyed both permanence and value. This revelation further supported his reconceptualization of graffiti as art: the urban calligraphic form, although lacking a lasting presence, was produced in public spaces where it proclaimed a truth about territory, presence, or belonging. Bojórquez realized he could create permanence for the message through fine art production. To maintain the graffiti aesthetic, he began to experiment with materials that might simulate the concrete environment of the Arroyo Seco River, the northeastern branch of the Los Angeles River that runs through Highland Park. He found that Zolatone,

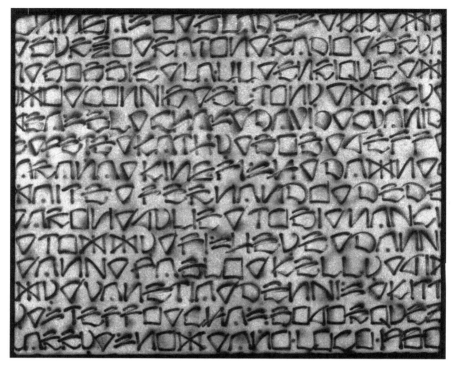

**4.5** Charles "Chaz" Bojórquez, *Placa/Rollcall*, 1980. Acrylic on canvas, 69 x 82 x 2 inches. Collection of Smithsonian American Art Museum; gift of the artist. Image courtesy of Smithsonian American Art Museum. Reproduced by permission of the artist.

the paint used in the entertainment industry to imitate rock or asphalt, produced warm and cool gray colors. It is the undercoat in several paintings, including *Two Talk* (1986), *14th September 1991* (1991), *Graffititext* (1993), and *Eddie's Lament* (1994). Zolatone signifies both the permanence and the value of the intertextual message.

His interest in the human tradition of proclamation easily led to other investigations of script and its accompanying practices. For example, while traveling through the South Pacific, he discovered that tattoos not only functioned as a tag, or *placa*, but also shared the same form. "They are line work, black and white." Bojórquez made a study of the tattooing styles of the Marquesans, the Tahitians, the Samoans, and the Fijians, and he was fascinated by the way tattoos were integrated into ritual and conveyed one's spirituality. His "aesthetic investigation" in "Nepal and

India . . . Malaysia and Indonesia" turned to "wood carvers, spirits" and the ways art is connected to cultural identity, social activity, a sense of place, and heritage. He observed that "culture [is] alive." That presence, of "a living culture," was more powerful than anything he had witnessed. When he returned to Los Angeles, his global investigations legitimated his decision to portray his cultural heritage and social position through his art. His grand tour had taught him that art was relevant only as social expression.

The large painting titled *Eddie's Lament* characterizes an approach to art that crystallized during Bojórquez's grand tour (fig. 4.6). The work draws from "Eddie's Lament," a poem written by a young man Bojórquez only knows as Playboy Eddie. Sentenced to five years for carjacking, Playboy Eddie expressed his grief and pain in the poem, which he sent to Bojórquez from prison. The words of the poem are placed at a slight angle and bleed off the canvas, and some are placed in a diagonal shadow that cuts the canvas nearly in two. Although Bojórquez has mixed figures and text in a few paintings, such as *Golden Boy* (1997) and the works with Señor Suerte, in *Eddie's Lament* the subject is the script. This is a

**4.6** Charles "Chaz" Bojórquez, *Eddie's Lament*, 1994. Mixed media, 41 x 60 x 3 inches. Collection of Mr. Tommy Marron.

style that Bojórquez frequently employs and one that reconfirms his fascination with writing. The text in the bottom register is Playboy Eddie's inmate number. It has a three-dimensional quality, mimicking chiseled stone, and it floats above the poem, which is written in stylized Old-English type, according to Bojórquez, or what other artists refer to as cholo-style graffiti script. The combination of typefaces announces the cultural and geographic origins of the poem and underscores the positionality narrated in the painting.

Eddie's poem ends with a question—"and what have I become?"—but Bojórquez omitted the interrogative punctuation. The painting does not ask what has become of the man. The present perfect tense—"what have I become"—expresses an action that began in the past and continues into the viewer's present. In this way, the painting mourns the loss of Eddie's humanity, dignity, and freedom while it declares that his degraded condition continues, making it a true statement with which viewers must reckon. The shadow that moves across the canvas is a dynamic compositional strategy that Bojórquez frequently employs in his text-based art. It suggests that the door is closing on the man's life, but since Playboy Eddie was placed in solitary confinement for years, it more likely represents a cell door as it sweeps shut and locks out light, fresh air, and sound. *Eddie's Lament* also signals a larger social tragedy. The poem is partially reproduced, words slide off the canvas, lines begin in mid-phrase, and letters are truncated. By representing the poem and not reproducing it exactly as composed by Playboy Eddie, the work signifies a narrative beyond and yet inclusive of the poet's dehumanized state. The painting references the plight of Latino youth, who are disproportionately incarcerated, and the way hegemonic institutions strip them of their social, cultural, and individual identity.

Bojórquez's aesthetic experiences outside North America clarified his relational understanding of himself and his cultural heritage. The revelation of one event provided a sense of belonging that allowed him to return home with a revised sense of place, identity, and purpose. As he and his companion flew from Katmandu to their next destination, the pilot allowed Bojórquez into the cockpit as they approached Mount Everest.

And we were up there at least twenty thousand, twenty-five thousand feet. And it was incredible. . . . By traveling in the world, I got a sense of my place, of what it felt like to be on the other side of the world from

Los Angeles, as far away as I could get from the Chicano culture and still remember it and reminisce and see similarities. . . . And I also felt . . . totally self-reliant, self-sufficient. . . . I felt safe. I felt the similarity in humanity. I started feeling that I was not meeting cultures, but I was meeting aunts and uncles, and *tías* and *tíos*, and brothers and sisters, and that extended family started blurring. Those lines were broken. . . . And I started getting the feeling that I wanted to come home, by continuing my trip.

The last phrase reveals Bojórquez's ability to locate himself in the world and at home without contradiction, which is an aspect of mestiza consciousness. This profound understanding of one's place within the universe and a simultaneous awareness of one's independence and cultural belonging created a sense of security that allowed the artist to return home to Los Angeles while feeling at home anywhere in the world. His connection to a universal humanity did not come at the cost of his cultural identity. The global tour became the anchoring source for his wide-ranging but highly local aesthetic style and approach to art.

## David Botello: Public Art for the People

An interest in local and universal concerns also inspires the work of David Botello. As in the case of Bojórquez, Botello's approach to art places his work within multiple contexts and traditions, and historicizing the work beyond *el barrio* allows new meanings to emerge. I am particularly interested in the ways that classical European art informed Botello's mural compositions and how he turned to a career in the arts because of his travels. Although his teachers, his Aunt Gloria, and others fostered and supported Botello's creativity and interest in the arts, the Los Angeles–born artist did not consider art as a profession until his grand tour of Europe.

Botello was born in 1946. Most of the schools that he attended were parochial schools, where he developed a strong sense of discovery and imagination. His extended, nurturing family also reinforced his penchant for learning and creative expression. His favorite aunt, Gloria, shared her appreciation for classical music and gave young David his first set of oil paints. Her own watercolor paintings delighted him. At the evening dinner table, Botello's father, a member of the cabinetmakers' union, made a game out of reading from an almanac, encyclopedia, or newspaper and then asking his children questions. The playful competition inspired Botello to read dictionaries and reference books, and he also enjoyed copying the illustrations. Other lessons came outside the home. A neighbor allowed Botello to borrow his tools to make a go-cart and to restore a bike with fancy rims and decorations. A friend's mother took Botello to LACMA to see the major exhibition of the 1963 winter season, *Master Works of Mexican Art*, an international traveling exhibition (discussed in chapter 6). His parents instilled a sense of discovery and love for the natural world by taking their children to the Natural History Museum of Los Angeles County. His mother took them to the Whittier Narrows Recreation Area to fish on Legg Lake, reminding them to protect the environment by carrying out their trash. As a child, Botello followed the news about Project Mercury and read about the galaxy and the solar system. This fascination with space would later establish him as a leading practitioner of Chicanafuturism, the term Catherine S. Ramírez coined to describe the conceptual "ways that [artists employ] new and everyday technologies . . . [to] transform Mexican American life and culture."[50]

Because he was assigned to the college preparatory track at Salesian High School, Botello had few opportunities to enroll in art courses. However, the encouragement he received from his only art teacher, Father Ilio, motivated him to enroll in several art courses at California State University, Los Angeles, upon graduation. He received excellent grades in art, but Botello left the college after one year because he floundered for the first time in the sciences and math. He was distracted by a fundamental question: "I was [wondering], what is life all about? My only thing was art. That really was valuable to me. Then, [I was] going to have to start a family. Once that's going to happen, you've got to have a career. But then I dropped out, and I went to the service."[51] He believed that a bachelor's degree in studio art would not lead to full-time employment, which conflicted with his image of masculinity and family. Without college deferment to protect him, Botello was drafted in 1966.

Botello's army unit immediately noticed his artistic skills, and he was put to work painting murals and signs and designing the company logo. His creative talent helped him advance rapidly to the rank of buck sergeant. "I was the top artist in my [military] company, and I think I started getting the inkling then [that] 'yeah, I can do this as a living.'" It was the art and architecture of Europe, however, that defined the role of art in society and made it possible for him to consider a career in the arts. He traveled to Spain and Italy and throughout Germany, where he was stationed. During his travels Botello marveled that "people living here [in Europe], they grow up among all this [art and architecture], they live in it." Residents of Rome, he speculated, understood the intrinsic connection between art and society: art was not just integrated into the urban core, but was at the center of social and civic engagement. "It sort of opened up the window. . . . I saw all this history in Europe, and I saw, again, my value of being an artist." Looking at European art and architecture taught him "firsthand" the social and historical worth of the visual arts, and this understanding gave him license to identify as an artist. The combination of his army unit's support for his creative skills and his frequent encounters with art in public spaces in Europe galvanized him, as it did Leo Limón, Tito Delgado, and Eduardo Carrillo.

After his discharge from the military and his return home, he immediately joined Juan Gonzalez and his brother José Luis Gonzalez to found Goez Art Studios and Gallery. He helped Juan develop plans for public monuments and art in East Los Angeles, and together they envisioned an alternative urban design for the city. In 1975 Botello departed Goez and formed Los Dos Streetscapers (1975–80) with Wayne Alaniz Healy. The pair renamed the public art studio East Los Streetscapers when new members joined them in 1980.

As one of the most important muralists in the city, David Botello serves as an ideal case study for revising Chicana/o art discourse. To show how an examination of Chicana/o artists' engagement with European aesthetic traditions provides new understanding of their work, I consider the profound influence that European art had on the murals that Botello produced during the height of the Chicano movement. My goal is to make use of Botello's experiences with Renaissance art as a foundation for a new analysis of his muralism, particularly how it foregrounds his criticism of patriarchy and heteronormativity. The discussion will also provide another reading of the collaborative revivalist architectural restaging of East Los Angeles by Botello and Juan Gonzalez. This remixing will consider Botello's murals and his contribution to indigenist urban space and will challenge the narrative of art historians and critics who misinterpret his murals as expressing regressive cultural politics.

Botello's work, including murals produced independently, such as *Dreams of Flight* (1973–78), and those produced with Healy, such as *Chi-*

*cano Time Trip* (1977), is considered emblematic of Chicana/o indigenous aesthetics and futurism.[52] While I do not challenge the visual expression of indigenous aesthetics and its Mexican and Chicana/o sources, I aim to document how his appreciation for site-specific public art developed in Europe during his military service. Because his commitment to public art begins in Europe and therefore predates the debates among Chicana/o artists about a people's art, it suggests a new understanding of the compositional strategies and content of his murals, even those created with Healy. I use this formal approach to support an alternative reading of *Chicano Time Trip*, one of the most widely circulated and reproduced images by East Los Streetscapers.

The result of Botello and Healy's first collaboration, *Chicano Time Trip* is a monumental mural of five panels on the exterior wall of a bank at the intersection of North Broadway and Daly Street (fig. 4.7). The panels depict "various figures that represent the numerous components of Chicana/o identity"—El Indígeno, La Española, El Hacendado, and La Soldadera—and culminate in the "representation of the archetypal Chicana/o family" in the largest panel, a critical point for feminist and queer scholars.[53] However, I suggest that the mural directly reflects the compositional strategies of the early Renaissance and includes several quotations from Renaissance visual vocabulary. The epic grandeur of the frescos found in churches throughout Italy finds expression in the five panels of the mural, and the six scenes that surround the heterosexual family portrait in the largest panel recall the technique of continuous narrative. Just as Renaissance artists delighted in rediscoveries of past achievements and sought to establish a thread running from the past into the present, Botello and Healy incorporated indigenous references for contemporary Chicanas/os who lack access to the political significance of their heritage.

Finally, *Chicano Time Trip* employs the allegorical mode of Renaissance art by presenting "larger-than-life figures as the direct ancestors of the contemporary Chicano community." In her analysis of the work, Guisela Latorre points out that the panel featuring La Soldadera restages Agustín Víctor Casasola's photograph of a woman who served in the revolutionary army during the Mexican Revolution. The panel with El Indígeno contains background scenes depicting Olmec artists carving one of the colossal heads found at either La Venta or Tres Zapotes, "an aerial view of the ancient city of Tenochtitlán," a Maya temple, and the Danza de los

**4.7** Wayne Alaniz Healy and David Botello, *Chicano Time Trip*, 1977. Acrylic on stucco, 19 x 90 feet. Mural in Lincoln Heights. Reproduced by permission of the artists (East Los Streetscapers).

Voladores, the ancient ceremonial pole dance.[54] The text in the mural, which appears in the top register of the largest panel, further supports a Renaissance reading as it paraphrases the lesson that Botello took away from Europe: "Our heritage is the foundation of our destiny. The power of our desires and imagination will determine our future." Interpreted from the perspective of Renaissance humanism *as it was pressed into service* during the social upheaval of the 1970s, the mural's heterosexual portrait can tacitly suggest other family arrangements. Furthering the argument that "Botello and Healy engage Chicanos' Mexican past not as a form of historical determinism but as a way of thinking actively about the present," I offer another interpretation of the mural.[55] Certainly, the largest panel portrays the compulsory heteronormativity of the Chicano movement, as both Latorre and Richard T. Rodríguez critically note.[56] But while the mural visualizes the heteronormative family arrangement, the text suggests that Chicanas/os are in control of their destiny, not bound by religious authority, cultural nationalism, or other hegemonic ideologies. Therefore, they have the potential to develop new and expanded forms of household and family through social engagement and commitment to action. If read through the lens of Renaissance humanism, the text—positioned at the apex of the largest panel and composed in saturated colors, a formal strategy that further embeds the message within the image—suggests that multiple familial configurations may emerge from "the power of our desires and imagination."

This blending of text and image resists a linear and causal narrative, and it can suggest expanded present relations, experiences, and institutions in the consideration of future possibilities, thereby placing the mural within Chicanafuturism. The mural's quotation of compositional techniques used in the Renaissance designates Chicana/o desires and imaginations as the potential site for the creation of new familial forms, social relations, and cultural cartographies (the last, a point to which I return). As Colin Gunckel argues, the mural functions as a "public family photo album" but also as much more, as it "proposes a relationship between a fluid temporality and Chicano identity" and represents "an archive of imagery upon which the future will be built."[57] Such a reading of the mural demonstrates that it is less about heteronormativity and more about future possibility. The speculative future "articulates," as Catherine Ramírez notes about Chicanafuturism, "colonial and postcolonial histories of 'indigenismo,' 'mestizaje,' hegemony, and survival."[58] It anticipates Botello's 1996 restoration of *Dreams of Flight*, in which he pointedly painted pigtails onto the child holding a biplane and repainted the central figure, originally a boy, as an androgynous youth (fig. 4.8).

Contextualization in Renaissance art and Chicanafuturism also illuminates the feminist critique within *Read between the Lines*, a mural produced in 1975 while Botello was still with Goez (fig. 4.9). His social criticism focuses on multiple aspects of hegemony, especially patriarchy, capitalism, and the promise of assimilation. The mural's three scenes are united compositionally by the technological instruments that span its width. At the right is a Chicano family living room in which two children and the father watch a massive television whose screen shows an image that reinforces American consumerism, patriotism, male hero-worship, and military power. The television image also conveys the Mexican American obsession with whiteness, symbolically depicted by a Cesar Romero–type Latin lover embracing a blonde woman. Botello has explained that the scene registers Chicana/o complacency: the father

4.8 David Botello, *Dreams of Flight*, 1973. Restored 1996. Acrylic on stucco, 17 x 31 feet. Mural at Estrada Courts, Los Angeles. Image courtesy of Social and Public Art Resource Center (SPARC). Reproduced by permission of the artist.

drinks a Coors beer and his six-pack rests on a crate of grapes, two items that were boycotted at the time, while the daughter, her hand to her mouth as if to suppress a yelp of joy, delights in the TV romance, suggesting that the dark-skinned Chicana youth identifies with the blonde actress. Similarly, the mother, who is held "captive to the kitchen" by culture and technology, enters the scene with a tray of drinks and food, signifying her subservient role. Above the kitchen oven is a large electrical outlet for the cable that connects the surveillance devices in the top register of the mural. The same cable becomes a snake that ensnares the man in the scene at the far left, indicating that the Chicano household is powered by "contracts" for consumerism and the financial oligarchy that supports American capitalism, which Botello notes is represented by "mortgages, loans, insurance, Wall Street, business, corporations, partners, bankruptcy, lawyers." By placing "mortgages" first on the list, Botello registers his suspicion regarding homeownership, a key element of the American Dream. The mural literally warns the "amigos" who might sign the contract.

4.9 David Botello, *Read between the Lines*, 1975. Acrylic on fiberglass mesh on stucco, 20 x 10 feet. Mural. Photograph by Isabel Rojas-Williams, art historian. Image courtesy of the artist.

The middle scene expresses potential and hope. It illustrates how knowledge and indigenous culture, represented by a history book and the god Quetzalcoatl, can break the hold of consumer culture and the American Dream. The anthropomorphized feathered god cuts through cables that connect to the cameras above the living room and the medical laboratory in the left-hand scene. This break ends the cycle of brainwashing that forces Chicanas/os to shed their cultural heritage, critical consciousness, and dignity. Quetzalcoatl gestures to a reading boy, the younger version of the man in the left register, and cautions him about his future. By linking Mesoamerican culture to contemporary Chicana/o salvation, the artist has issued a counterhegemonic call to resist consumption and other forms of spiritual and social entrapment.[59] The mural depicts the evil that results from not only the institution of patriarchy but also the myth of assimilation.

*Chicano Time Trip* and *Read between the Lines* evidence both the modernist impulse to appropriate a work from its spatial and temporal context and the Renaissance desire to employ past achievements as cultural legacies that inform the present.[60] While Botello was working on the murals, he and Juan Gonzalez initiated a larger project to create an alternative urban plan for all of East Los Angeles. The architectural innovations that Botello and Gonzalez envisioned were influenced by indigenous revivalism as well as the spatial design of European cities. The wide boulevards, monuments, prestigious buildings, and use of vast perspectives and open spaces that they planned echoed the urban scenarios of Europe, especially Haussmann's restructuring of Paris. Thus, Mexican modernism and indigenous revivalism were blended with European use of space, but the design maintained direct references to East Los Angeles.

Similarly, in *Read between the Lines*, Quetzalcoatl is not presented as a static pre-Columbian icon; rather, the mural invokes the mythical figure's powers of renewal, a quality that finds form in Christian imagery as the god descends from above, surrounded by a halo of light. Evocative of Michelangelo's iconic portrayal of God extending his hand to give life to Adam, *Read between the Lines* depicts the reading boy's acquisition of critical consciousness, signified by his gesturing hand and outward gaze. This new awareness allows for the healing of psychic wounds from cultural and historic trauma. The work proposes an alternative social and cultural strategy: one need not accept the contract that hangs at the left; other meanings beyond the most apparent are possible. This fresh analysis of *Read between the Lines* and *Chicano Time Trip* offers new interpretations that do not see indigenous references as retrograde, but as prospective.

Rather than reinforce the dominant method in art history, which assumes that early childhood experiences determine the artistic expression of adults, I next explore the experiences of two artists, Yolanda Gonzalez and John Valadez, who traveled abroad after their formal training in the arts and after they had established careers. My analysis suggests the need for a biographic methodology that begins with the premise that an artist's ethnic identity is not predetermined by her culture. Scholars must examine an artist's entire life and not rely exclusively on experiences that occur in childhood or while "coming of age" during the Chicano movement.

## John Valadez: European Allegory

John Valadez's willingness to explore beyond the bounds of East Los Angeles began, by necessity, in childhood. His mother insisted that he and his brother stay clear of gangs in the neighborhood. She moved the family from the Geraghty Loma community, where John was born in 1951, and later from Estrada Courts to prevent her two young boys from joining local gangs. She also enrolled Valadez in Huntington Park High School in South Los Angeles, another tactic to protect him from gang activity.[61] Valadez's youth was filled with explorations of jazz music and movies; comic books and model cars, especially the work of Ed "Big Daddy" Roth; drawing and contemporary literature; and out-door adventures on a homemade skateboard or refurbished bike or on foot. He often biked to Roth's shop in Maywood, California, carpooled with classmates to art and film classes at Barnsdall Park, took a bus to see movies or concerts, or hitched a ride from East Los Angeles to the beach, where he bodysurfed. One adventure took him to the Los Angeles County Museum of Art with his mother to see Edward Kienholz's *Back Seat Dodge '38* (1964).[62]

After high school Valadez entered East Los Angeles College with the goal of becoming an artist. He enrolled in the studio art program, which was led by notable artist-instructors and contemporaries of Eduardo Carrillo, such as Roberto Chavez and Louis Lunetta. Later, in 1972, he studied at Long Beach State College with Maxwell Hendler. During this period Valadez immersed himself in the cultural milieu and radical politics of the early 1970s. His interest in the arts was expansive, and he collected record albums of jazz and rock 'n' roll. He also performed with Teatro Corazon, a theater troupe at East Los Angeles College that staged Chicana/o works such as *I Am Joaquin* by Corky Gonzales, and he worked with the Chicano Moratorium Committee. His reading included politics (*The Black Panther* party newspaper and *Soledad Brother* by George Jackson), social criticism (Lenny Bruce and Hunter S. Thompson), and literature (Kurt Vonnegut and Beat poets). He saw foreign films by directors Federico Fellini, Michelangelo Antonioni, and Sergei Mikhailovich Eisenstein at the Vagabond Theatre, and he continued to study realism in drawing and photography. His political consciousness flourished and blended into his interest in the arts, an experience that many Chicana/o artists report. Valadez recalls that "the music and the politics and the whole art thing for me, it all kind of became one [form of] expression at that time."[63]

Valadez enjoyed a rich arts education, yet it was a grand tour of Europe that transformed what he had seen in art history courses and books into a personal understanding. Valadez traveled to Europe with his partner, Sandra, more than a decade after completing his bachelor of fine arts degree at California State University, Long Beach, in 1975. In 1987, at the age of thirty-six, he received a ten-week artist residency at Château de La Napoule, France, through La Napoule Art Foundation. He was profoundly moved by the art he witnessed. As he notes, "It wasn't really until I went to Europe and saw these paintings and saw all of the art [that I understood the trends]." His years of artistic training and exploration could not equal the experience of seeing European art of the fifteenth, sixteenth, and seventeenth centuries. His pedagogical strategy was to tour the museums that he could reach by train from Mandelieu-La Napoule, the village in southeastern France where he was based.

> We were able to go to Barcelona. [We] saw the Dalí Museum. We went to Paris. We got as far as Florence. . . . We went to Pisa and Florence. But we mostly stayed around Nice and Cannes. . . . You would see it in art history [classes], but to see these places was very moving. To go see the Uffizi [Gallery in Florence]. I spent two days at the Uffizi, ending with Caravaggio, the *Medusa*. We saw the Botticellis. I'm a pretty emotional person. If that doesn't make you cry, you must be crazy.

Valadez's investment in the physical experience of seeing the European works, his emotional vulnerability and exhilaration, and his ability to integrate his responses into his own art inspired a deeply surrealist and allegorical trend in his work.

When he returned from his residency in France, his interest in allegory and his experimentation with composition intensified. Before departing for Europe, Valadez had been working on *Battle of Culture* (1987), a large-scale pastel drawing on paper that depicts in one field a battalion of Spanish conquistadors pursuing indigenous warriors who are plainly clad and outfitted with spears (fig. 4.10). The energy of the battle is conveyed in the turbulent and fiery sky, swirled with clouds whose soft pink and orange hues belie their violence. Cherubs and a winged angel descend as if attending the earthly gods who are at battle, reinforcing the otherworldliness of the scene. Rising at the far right is the Basílica de la Sagrada Família of Barcelona, designed by Catalan architect Antoni Gaudí, with its blend of Gothic and curvilinear art nouveau styles. After Valadez returned to Los Angeles the edifice became a compositional medley of sculptural forms taken from his collection of slides, photographs, and postcards. In the drawing, it appears as if the conquistadors

4.10 John Valadez, *Battle of Culture*, 1987. Pastel on paper, 50 x 90 inches. Collection of Grafton Tanquary III. Image courtesy of Museum of Contemporary Art San Diego. © John Valadez.

are defending the bricolage, a compositional strategy that turns colonial history on its head, since the Spanish occupied indigenous temples and cities and the battles were fought on American soil. The work depicts a speculative fiction, a surreal scene, or an allegory. Just as various architects added their own interpretations to Gaudí's plans for La Sagrada Família, history is made and remade by the colonizer and the colonized in *Battle of Culture*.

*Europa #1* (1988) also presents a conglomeration of European architectural elements—columns with Corinthian capitals, a pier, arches, and a stone monument that supports a sculpture of Europa in rapture or dismay (fig. 4.11).[64] Here Valadez pushed the boundaries of perspective and composition. The sculpture rests on a platform above a tent designed after those found in Spanish marketplaces. Valadez captured the yards of canvas in realistic detail, evoking the style of sixteenth- and seventeenth-century paintings. The sculpture and tent occupy the foreground, while the columns and the arches that support them appear to float in the background, as if to imply both the symbolic weight of European visual tradition and its mobility: European art travels the globe as the unmarked universal standard. The images that make up the composition were drawn from the artist's collection of slides, photographs, and postcards.

Valadez extended his experimentation with the bending of time and space in *Fall of Babel* (1989), a pastel drawing that depicts fire and clouds,

TOURS OF INFLUENCE

4.11 John Valadez, *Europa #1*, 1988. Pastel on paper, 64 x 50 inches. Private collection. Digital image by Miyo Stevens-Gandara. © John Valadez.

4.12 John Valadez, *The Chase*, 1989. Pastel on paper (diptych), 50 x 112 inches. Private collection. Digital image by Miyo Stevens-Gandara. © John Valadez.

one of many technical challenges that he explored after his residency in France. White clouds roll over two figures, a nude female is engulfed in flames but shows no pain, and steps of an ancient pyramid rise to meet the clouds in the left register. Valadez was inspired by the compositional strategies of European masters, especially their use of obscure symbols that may or may not convey meaning to viewers. By merging Caravaggio's use of chiaroscuro and Botticelli's allegorical style in this work, Valadez produced one of his most dramatic and surreal stagings of ecstasy, tragedy, and the unknown.[65]

The artist's experiences in Europe influenced several works of the 1980s. In *The Chase* (1989), quotations from Peter Paul Rubens occupy the left side of the diptych (fig. 4.12). Five nudes evoke human sensuality in their dynamic and rotund forms and in their expressions of ecstasy and surprise.[66] The quotations are countered by the contemporary scene in the right register, which is taken from photographs Valadez shot in Los Angeles. A group of fully clothed men occupy the cramped field, apparently fleeing an unknown pursuer outside the frame, as suggested by the figure at the far right who glances over his shoulder. The composition is united not only by the vivid magenta of this man's jacket and the similarly hued cloth clutched by the most prominent Rubenesque female but also by texture and modeling. Valadez's treatment of flesh and textile—with the nudes' musculature echoing the deep folds of the men's clothing—and the contortions of the bodies unite the composition and suggest a deep level of human struggle.

Other works express a turn toward the surreal as well as European influences; these include *Picnic* (1989) and *Resbalado* (1989), the deeply cryptic *Revelations* (1989), and works depicting the ocean, such as *Queen's Harvest* (2007) and *Sea Monsters and Freight* (2007). These works also squarely reflect Valadez's observations of the American Southwest, as the landscapes portray the deserts of the borderlands between Mexico and the United States or the beaches of Southern California. Valadez shows a powerful ability to meld the disparate qualities, colors, compositional strategies, allegories, and aesthetics of Europe and Chicana/o culture.

I focus on Valadez in my remixing of Chicana/o art history precisely because he was widely active within the Chicano movement and was recognized as instrumental to the development of Chicana/o visual production. His life and work, as well as that of the other artists discussed here, reveal the fallacies surrounding Chicana/o art history and the narrow approach to culture and influence, aesthetics and subjectivity, that it has employed. Valadez is known for his iconic portraits of urban residents, especially those executed as large-scale realist pencil-on-paper drawings, and for his murals. Yet he continued to integrate his responses to European art as he produced Chicana/o art in the late 1980s, the 1990s, and into the new millennium. His life and work suggest a mestiza consciousness, particularly the agency that Chicana feminists attribute to *nepantleras*.[67] Rather than assimilating, Valadez draws from the aesthetics of his immediate surroundings in Los Angeles as well as the Western visual tradition.

### Color and Line: The Affective Journey of Yolanda Gonzalez

The artistic heritage of Yolanda Gonzalez dates back to 1877, and she and her family have been long engaged with the roots and routes of the Western visual tradition. Her great-grandfather was an artist; her grandmother, Margarita Lopez, was a pianist and painter; her father made a career as an interior designer; and one of her older sisters studied art.[68] Her fascination with the arts began when she was a toddler and her older sister received a set of watercolors. She recalls being captivated by the silver tubes and wanting to possess them. When the artist was approximately eight years old, her grandmother sat her down to compose with oil paints. Together they created a painting of "two ladies" who carried baskets on their heads as they walked on a country road. Gonzalez recalls that her childhood was full of imagination: "I was creating in my head, in my heart, and in my soul." She recounts that she "can still smell the oils."

Although immersed in a creative environment that offered aesthetic inspiration, she did not begin to practice her craft until her junior year in high school, when she was gently pushed by her art teacher, Dixie Bowman. Bowman had instructed her students to create a tree, but having forgotten about the homework assignment, Gonzalez hastily drew a stick tree during lunch. It was the only drawing in the entire class that lacked integrity, effort, and sincerity. When Bowman asked, "Who drew the stick tree?," she did not intend to shame or punish her student, but simply wanted to encourage her to access her visual world. She asked Gonzalez to resubmit the assignment. "I want you to [go home]," Bowman instructed, and "draw a tree and draw exactly what you see." Gonzalez returned the next day with a beautiful tree, and from then on they worked together. Bowman created a special private class for Gonzalez, an amazing accomplishment in the 1980s, when arts funding in California public schools was severely cut.

Bowman was so impressed with her student that she secretly entered Gonzalez's work in an art contest. Gonzalez was surprised and delighted when she won first place and a scholarship that allowed her to attend the Art Center College of Design in Pasadena. When she walked through the doors of the Art Center, she immediately felt at home: "It was the first time in my life that I belonged somewhere." At the Art Center she studied drawing and painting with Peter Liashkov, who taught the European color palette. Ironically, the training under Liashkov freed Gonzalez to explore primary colors, even though she could not at the time name the source for this aesthetic inspiration. Her personal style reflected youth culture, and only one color was important to her: she cultivated a heavy metal look with black hair, black lip liner, and black platform shoes.

To support herself while studying at the Art Center, Gonzalez worked as a hair stylist, and through this work she met Arturo Urista. In the early 1980s he introduced her to Self Help Graphics & Art, the second arts institution that would change her life. There she took classes from Yreina D. Cervántez (watercolor), Eloy Torrez (life drawing), and Patssi Valdez (painting), but she recalls that everyone, including Leo Limón, Margaret Garcia, and Michael Amescua, treated her like their younger sister, mentoring her in the profession. The welcoming artistic environment was a magnet for Gonzalez: "I was there constantly—I was there nonstop." After her premier exhibition at Self Help Graphics & Art in 1989, prominent collectors such as Cheech Marin and Armando Durón sought her work, and her career "took off."

After working for nearly a decade as an artist, Gonzalez began enjoying professional success. She traveled to Japan for a residency at Art Studio Itsukaichi in 1993, the inaugural year of the artist-in-residence program, which was initiated as part of TAMA Life 21, an event held to commemorate the one hundredth anniversary of the Tama area adjoining Tokyo. Gonzalez lived for six months with three other artists, including Brazilian artist Magda De Jose, sharing a home and an expansive studio located in an old residential town, Itsukaichi, then west of Tokyo and now within the city limits of Akiruno. The solitude of the rural environment and the freedom to explore printmaking, the medium for which the Japan Foundation had offered the residency, allowed Gonzalez to think about herself and her work in new ways. Inspired by the isolation, beautiful scenery, and quiet, she initiated the Monster Series, a portfolio of etchings composed of repulsive faces. Her goal was to "put a face on mental realities, the monsters in our head" and to see "their beauty through their grotesqueness." The Monster Series was as much a technical exploration as it was a psychological investigation. In these works chiaroscuro produces a haunting quality that is echoed in the multilayered twisting and unraveling lines that split and suture the composition.

When she returned to Los Angeles, the lessons she learned in the calm of Itsukaichi remained with her. Prompted by the beauty and simplicity of Japanese calligraphy, Gonzalez asked herself, "What happens when I drop the color?" This question has been asked by other Chicana/o artists, although for different reasons. For instance, Diane Gamboa and Judithe Hernández regarded it as a technical challenge. Gamboa showed a series of black and white works in her 2004 exhibition *Bruja-Ha* at Tropico de Nopal Gallery Art-Space, and Hernández used white oil stick on black paper for pastel drawings that she created for the

2012–13 City of Los Angeles (COLA) Individual Artist Fellowship. These works challenge art world expectations of Latina/o art that were articulated by Livingston and Beardsley in *Hispanic Art* and have been revived consistently by curators and art historians. For Gonzalez, the black and white of Japanese calligraphy inspired a series titled Metamorphosis. In these works Gonzalez depicted women with a near absence of color. Just as monsters could reveal beauty, so could black and white disclose the rich interior of the self and one's sense of belonging and cultural heritage. The first painting in the series, *Metamorphosis Nude Woman* (1994), portrays a torso confined to a space that is only two feet wide, a compositional strategy that presses the body forward as it simultaneously recedes (fig. 4.13). The nude's closed eye reinforces the modest yet alluring quality of the portrait. It communicates not so much a wink as a concentrated stare in which the gaze of one eye is knowingly withheld while the other eye looks directly at the viewer. The portrait is the allegory for an identity that is withheld. The weighted brushstrokes, especially the half circles in the left register, mimic the calligrapher's effort to choreograph each stroke with a beginning, middle, and end. The purposeful gestures contrast with the black acrylic paint that saturates the canvas and, uncharacteristic of a master calligrapher's hand, drips down the side of the torso. The oversaturation of the paint alludes to the art historical overemphasis on color, identity, and cultural essence. As in the Monster Series, chiaroscuro invokes the specter of a mutilated form, and in this case it references an imposed realist and political style of Chicana/o art.

The second portrait created for the series, *Metamorphosis Nude with Red* (1994), extends several elements of *Metamorphosis Nude Woman*. Both paintings are cubist in style, and in both the artist used purposeful brushstrokes and oversaturation that produced streaks of dripping paint. *Metamorphosis Nude with Red* repeats the intense gaze of *Metamorphosis Nude Woman*, but it is magnified in *Metamorphosis Nude with Red* because the woman is in profile, yet her eye turns toward the viewer. The major distinction, as indicated by the title, is the addition of color, which was teasingly applied to the right register of the painting and to the artist's signature, but not to the female figure. Gonzalez played with small additions of color throughout the series, tantalizingly offering and withdrawing an element that is expected in Chicana/o art (fig. 4.14).

**4.13** Yolanda Gonzalez, *Metamorphosis Nude Woman*, 1994. Acrylic on canvas, 60 x 24 inches. Image courtesy of the artist. © Yolanda Gonzalez.

4.14 Yolanda Gonzalez, *Metamorphosis Nude with Red*, 1994. Acrylic on canvas, 36 x 48 inches. Image courtesy of the artist. © Yolanda Gonzalez.

Yolanda Gonzalez finally and fully returned to the use of color in her series Sueños, initiated in 1999. Works at the start of the series depict trios of men and women in black or gray clothes with streaks of black paint that layer the images. Throughout the series, and particularly in the later works, where clothing of various colors replaces the black and gray costumes, Gonzalez used black primarily to outline the images. The borders at the perimeter of the paintings draw the viewer's attention to the social construction of the work, just as photographers introduce the frame to deliberately draw the viewer's attention to the author and thus avoid any illusion of naturalism or realism. In this case, the black frame denaturalizes the essence and obligatory aesthetics attributed to Chicana/o art. The experiment with black and white inspired by her residency in Japan released Gonzalez from any preconceptions about her work and pushed her to reconsider the palette from which she had been intuitively working since her formal training began. Throughout the series and in subsequent explorations, Gonzalez successfully reclaims color but withholds an essentialized interpretation.

## Remix or Apocrypha?

The relatively uncharted space between Chicana/o and European as well as Asian aesthetics requires new frameworks to make sense of the international dynamic of Chicana/o art. The grand tours that have been related in this chapter force a reanimation of our understanding of Chicana/o, Mexican, European, and Asian art history. Each of these national or regional or ethnic categories may be obliged to cultural or geographic contexts, but ideas and aesthetics also travel. Scholarship need not reproduce the ideological impulse to narrowly define art production as an identifier of a nonwhite artist's nationality, cultural heritage, ethnicity, or race. Whether walking along the narrow streets of Italian, French, German, and Spanish towns and cities, viewing the architecture, traveling through the countryside of Japan, Italy, Spain, and Germany, or strolling along the galleries of the Uffizi, the Louvre, or the Prado, viewing the paintings, sculptures, maps, and documents of Western and Asian civilizations, Chicana/o artists found meaning in the places where art resides, in its specific historical and anthropological position and context. They developed a penetrating awareness of their place and identity *through* their engagement with art produced and located elsewhere. The witnessing of public monuments, artifacts, and art "clos[ed] the distance in time" between the object (a painting, sculpture, building, ruin, ancient book, or monument) and "one's own act of looking at it."[69]

It was seeing art outside the United States that provided a penetrating awareness of the self and of the relationships between the self and others and between art and society. The interpretation of art as socially connected to a place and its residents crystallized the historical consciousness of the artists discussed here, which they transplanted to Chicana/o communities upon their return to Los Angeles. Their grand tours reinforced a social approach to art rather than a modernist approach rooted in aesthetic autonomy. They created new forms and meanings for their work without forgoing their social proprioception. I do not dispute that Maoist, Leninist, and Mexican principles of cultural production informed Chicana/o art and influenced muralism and other public forms as well as representational styles, but these touring artists also learned to perceive the "profoundly social" nature of art as they gazed on it abroad.[70] The spirit of humanism, the European use of public space, South Pacific and Southeast Asian script and ritual, the aura of antiquities, and the techniques of European and Japanese artists inspired these artists. Their experiences abroad shaped their commitment and approach to art, placing their visual production within global contexts.

Chicana/o critical consciousness and subjectivity did not prohibit artists from seeking an aesthetic experience beyond North America. They simultaneously valued European artistic practices and productions and formulated a criticism of American art for its Eurocentrism, coloniality, and male privilege. Their experiences in Europe, the perceptions they developed, and the ways that these informed or transformed their art challenge the dualism between assimilation and segregation, a form of essentialism. The Chicano movement's call for public art and accessibility was strikingly in tune with the observations that these Chicana/o artists made in Europe and Asia. Radical politics and conventional views of art informed their decisions to paint murals, create posters, or volunteer their time with the United Farm Workers and other organizations working to transform workers' rights, education, and health care. They formulated another modernism, not one defined by the rejection of tradition but a complex commitment to the historical context and social embeddedness of art as a strategy to critically engage the present and future.

Impressed by the accessibility of public art that is integrated into the urban landscape and cultural milieu of European cities, the artists returned to Los Angeles to create murals, monuments, and public sculpture for Chicana/o residents and to promote the full integration of visual arts into public life. For Chaz Bojórquez, the aesthetic practices in the South Pacific Islands, Southeast Asia, and the Mediterranean affirmed how art emerges from ritual and symbolic meaning and how this embedded cultural significance produces accessibility. The observation freed him to pursue the cultural referents and styles from his childhood neighborhood of Highland Park and to merge his public work—graffiti—with his work on canvas. Civic spaces in Europe and Asia integrate ancient architecture and art and through this convergence of past and present proclaim the value of a nation's cultural heritage—this is what inspired several Chicana/o artists to produce public art. For decades, Tito Delgado traveled between Chiapas, Mexico, and Los Angeles to create public monuments and massive murals that contain coded criticisms of inequalities that structure each location while also visualizing the connections across the border. Artists such as Leo Limón, David Botello, Ernesto de la Loza, and Juan Gonzalez also imagined alternative urban landscapes for Los Angeles, merging their experiences of European public space with the realities of Chicana/o communities. Linda Vallejo's ongoing pedagogical explorations allowed her to apply the revelations she had in the Sistine Chapel and the Prado as a student to her work years later. A focus on these artists' experiences during the early stages of their careers and an examination of moments that *precede or are concurrent with* the Chicano movement can extend how we evaluate aesthetic influences on Chicana/o art and artists. Remixing the record also reveals that Chicana/o artists did not separate art from society, endorsing the antimodernist attitude emerging among California conceptual artists in the 1970s, but that experiences abroad informed this position.[71]

I also examine aesthetic influences on Yolanda Gonzalez and John Valadez, who traveled later in their careers, because of the problematic tendency in art history to focus on childhood and youth at the expense of other experiences. It is important to analyze what inspires artists of color after their formative years. The methodological overemphasis on early life experiences has had the effect of reducing or essentializing artists of color, since nonwhite people are presumed to have unmediated, coherent, and transparent identities, cultures, and aspirations.

Can this new information about European and Asian influences, particularly those authorizing Western aesthetic traditions, avoid servicing assimilationist or integrationist desires? I worry that the hegemonic model of cultural contact—assimilation and acculturation—will fold Chicana/o artists into the categories of European and European American art without challenging the insufficiencies of these categories. I realize that this documentation of international influence can serve to interpolate Chicano and Chicana artists into the political hegemony of US exceptionalism and the ideal of the assimilating immigrant, even as I suggest that their work interrogates and exposes the ruse of assimilation and universal modernism. I worry that Chicana/o art becomes legible only when it is read within the matrix of the European tradition.

As LACMA curator Ilona Katzew observes, "context *is* important and *does* inform an artist's work."[72] Certainly, the sociopolitical context is difficult for American art historians to confront, as the field has attempted to maintain a stance that separates art and politics as well as art and identity. Katzew draws attention to the ways art historical categories are political fields, not neutral taxonomies of analysis. She makes an important observation that I also apply to Chicana/o art: "How we present Latin American art in an encyclopedic museum remains contested territory." Her observations come from years of serving as a curator at LACMA and reflect the persistent question of how to place Latin American art within the museum. The gallery dedicated to Latin American art, she suggests, allows for the specific context of the work to remain visible, particularly because the category of Latin American art is itself still "uncomfortably between categories (local vs. international; high art vs. low art; original vs. derivative)." The Latin American art gallery does not mitigate "the liminal position that the field continues to occupy within encyclopedic museums and the art historical canon in general," but it does permit its historical specificity to remain at the forefront of the analysis.

Unfortunately, Katzew employs a strategy common in the art world. She fails to question the role of those who have the power to decide how Latin American art is presented, declining to ask how those individuals come into power and how the museum and art worlds define authority. She states, "At the end of the day the decision is entirely subjective and made by those who at the moment can (i.e., museum professionals and scholars)." But the decision is not simply subjective, as she implies. Those holding the stewardship of cultural production must interrogate their assumptions, tastes, biases, investments, and privileges. They must be attuned to how and why they make decisions or "genealogical fabrications." Their subjectivities must be open to scrutiny, and they must be sensitive to the ways politics is embedded in the display and interpretation of art. We cannot hide behind a gesture of surrender and futility—"Ah, what is one to do?"—without acknowledging that context (race, class, gender, sexuality, nationality, and more) informs our work and our privilege. Museum professionals and scholars must determine how power and privilege at social and individual levels shape their curatorial selections, interpretative strategies, methodologies, and research.

The analysis of European influences requires a decolonial methodology—a methodology that is not traumatized by colonial oppression. This methodology acknowledges the generative qualities of hybridity, contradiction, and domination, and it opens a third space in which multiple histories can be lived outside of and yet be connected to European aesthetic heritage. It avoids the anxiety of influence because it restages power dynamics, and it employs the reappropriation of Western concepts and aesthetics as a strategy of inversion. Similarly, reappropriation acknowledges that which has been appropriated or destroyed under the historic trauma of colonialism and imperialism. The decolonial method requires an awareness of one's context and social location.

My goal, therefore, in exploring histories and experiences that previously had not been permitted to surface is to force a reevaluation of value, the methods of valuation, and the processes of taste making. I would like this work to expose how art history maintains its own hierarchies of authority. Likewise, the strategies of cultural coherence have shifted since the 1980s, when US Third World feminists offered new paradigms of belonging that depended not upon singularity and sameness but on complexity, ambiguity, creativity, and openness to multiple positions and codeterminations. The analysis presented here reveals the ways artists successfully blend their aesthetic experiences and influences and employ the postmodern tactic of multiplicity. We recognize their ability to engage contradictory elements—in this case, cultural specificity and modernism, which resulted from imperialism and colonialism, the very social systems that Chicanas/os challenged during the 1960s and 1970s—and to make European aesthetic and visual traditions serve social transformation in Los Angeles. In short, this discussion and the documentation that supports it are evidence that the artistic hybridity of these artists did not displace their history, identity, or culture. This chapter illustrates how artistic hybridity that is grounded in identity can engage the transformative spaces of visual art—an important new understanding of Chicana/o art.

# CHICANA/O ART COLLECTORS

## Critical Witness to Invisibility and Emplacement

M ariana Williamson Coronel and Antonio F. Coronel were the first Mexican American collectors of the nineteenth century, and their efforts to safeguard the region's cultural history are an instructive introduction to this chapter about contemporary Chicana/o art collectors. The Coronels were invested in cultural preservation and in notions of belonging in a context of political and social disenfranchisement, and they sought to establish a city museum to perpetuate their vision of inclusion and historical memory.

> [The Coronels] had gathered, during the course of many years, the largest and most valuable collection of historical materials relating to this section [of California] and to this coast, in the country. [They hoped to cooperate with other citizens of means] to aid in preserving and safely guarding the materials of local history which they and their fathers and mothers have helped to make, and at the same time manifest to the world by their acts the fact that they recognize the obligations they owe to the community in which and off of which they have made their wealth.[1]

This passage recognizes the moment in 1900 that the collection became public. The widowed Mariana agreed to donate the massive trove to the Los Angeles Chamber of Commerce with the understanding that when a local museum opened, it would be gifted to that institution. The collection was displayed in the Chamber of Commerce building and then moved to the nascent Los Angeles Museum of History, Science and Art in 1913, the year that the museum opened in Exposition Park. The Antonio F. Coronel Collection was formally donated to the county museum in 1958.[2]

Contemporary Chicana/o art collectors in the Los Angeles metropolitan area echo the Coronels' desire to protect the cultural heritage of the region, but they operate in a very different context. Whereas the Coronels assumed that a public museum would enthusiastically share their appreciation of Mexican art and culture, contemporary Chicana/o art collectors are skeptical of the county museum and other authoritative institutions. Their private collections function both as restitution for past failures and ongoing exclusions and as an interrogation of the terms by which authorized arts institutions collect the cultural production of the region and nation. Because the exhibition record and collection practices of authorizing museums are uneven, Chicana/o art collectors have reservations about the capacity and long-term interest of the region's arts institutions. Whereas the Coronels were engaged with a politics of memory, Chicana/o art collectors enact a politics of reclamation and visibility, using preservation and collecting as a form of critical witnessing. Chicana/o art collectors of the late twentieth and early twenty-first centuries amass works of art because the Los Angeles County Museum of Art (LACMA), which was established in the late 1950s to house the county's art holdings, functions within a discourse of racial and national cultural hegemony that overlooks the heritage that the Coronels worked to safeguard. The treatment of the Coronels and their collection is emblematic of the county museum's mechanisms of verticality. Today they are largely unrecognized as founding contributors, and their collection is largely unacknowledged.

Antonio Coronel and his wife were Californio residents who witnessed the transformation of the region after the close of the US-Mexico War (1846–48).[3] In some ways they were like many other elite Mexicans in California who negotiated their status to preserve their wealth and power. They owned and managed "seventy-five acres of fruitful land lying in the valley of the Los Angeles River, on the southern outskirts of the city" and lived comfortably, first in the adobe hacienda El Recreo, built in 1834, and eventually in a Victorian manor.[4] Deeply invested in suturing together the social fabrics of Mexico and the United States, they organized festivals to celebrate Mexican culture and independence, supported beautification projects in the city, opened "the city's first English-speaking theater" in their home on July 4, 1848, and served as founding members of the Historical Society of Southern California in 1883. They also played a prominent role in civic and political life, with Don Antonio holding several public offices, including the fourth mayorship of Los Angeles under the US flag. Elected in 1853, he was the city's first Mexican American mayor.[5] The Coronels collected the history, art, and culture of the region for fifty years.

Encompassing a variety of materials largely produced between 1830 and 1900, the Coronel Collection evidences the complexities of the borderlands experience—its contradictions and tensions, its creative responses and critical consciousness. The collection reflects the history of colonial settlers who reconciled their subordination of and injury to indigenous people through a sentimentalism that attempted to salvage pieces of the culture they sought to displace and control. Several samples from the collection convey romanticism and contradiction as well as a critical response to disenfranchisement. For instance, correspondence between the Coronels and Helen Hunt Jackson, author of the 1884 novel *Ramona*, reveals their sympathies for indigenous people as well as their desire to "protect" Native American lands and rights through the establishment of a reservation system in California.[6]

The oldest objects in the collection are implements associated with Spanish colonization: a lance (c. 1780), a Spanish flintlock musket (c. 1770), a Spanish sword (c. 1769), and a Spanish salute cannon (c. 1750), the last two apparently brought to Alta California by Father Junípero Serra and used in the founding of missions.[7] The collection also reveals the Coronels' concern about the shifting position of elite Californios. Don Antonio's efforts to maintain Mexican land titles is documented in the collection, including his 1857 trip to Mexico to secure legal papers and political support for "several [Mexican] claims around the San Francisco area."[8] The abundance of portraits created and reproduced through various photographic and printing processes signals the Coronels' overall strategy of encyclopedic preservation and collection of Mexican and Native American life and culture.

Although the Coronel Collection was initially described as focusing on the "dress, diversions, sports, dances, customs, and manners of early California," it also records the political transformations of the region.[9] A principal part of the collection consists of civic, government, and legal documents, including correspondence between Mexican officials and military personnel during the US-Mexico War. There are ephemera from political campaigns before and after the war and from landmark dedications, parades, and religious ceremonies. The political restructuring of California is evinced in the subsequent invisibility of the collection and the erasure of the Coronels' significant role in the region's cultural production. Consistent with national interests in preservation and education, the Coronels viewed their collection as a civic duty and public service, and they actively pursued the formation of a museum dedicated to Los Angeles and Southern California history, culture, and arts. Antonio held leadership positions in the Historical Society of Southern California, and Mariana managed and augmented the couple's collection.[10] In her letter of instruction to the Los Angeles Chamber of Commerce that accompanied the donation, Mariana indicated that "it was [Antonio's] desire that this Collection should be so located as to be of general value, alike for the instruction as for the entertainment of the people."[11] When the collection was first displayed at the Chamber of Commerce in 1901, a local reviewer stated that it was expected to form "the nucleus for a magnificent California museum." This regard began to lag after the collection was transferred to the county museum, and by midcentury the importance of the collection had faded.[12]

In 1958, when the Antonio F. Coronel Collection was officially donated to the county museum, plans were under way for building a new facility in Hancock Park for the museum's fine art holdings. The original facility in Exposition Park, renamed the Natural History Museum of Los Angeles, would house the balance of the county's collections. Historian Ruth Mahood acknowledged the importance of the Coronel Collection to the reconfigured museum, observing that "the Coronels understood very well the value that their collection would have in bringing about an understanding of life in early California. They loved their California heritage and they were willing to do the most painstaking research and careful documentation in order that this heritage might be passed on to future generations."[13] Indeed, exhibitions on California history have consistently relied on the collection, although often without attribution to the Coronels. Notably, the collection's photographs of daily life on the rancho became studies for museum dioramas created in the 1930s, but the connection was not specified for museum visitors or for readers of the county museum's publications. These three-dimensional visual nar-

5.1 Mariana Williamson Coronel in her parlor, 1896. Image courtesy of History Collections, Los Angeles County Museum of Natural History.

Perhaps the most eloquent document of her relationship to the collection is a photograph taken in her parlor two years after Antonio's death. It records the range of items in the collection and shows how the Coronels lived with the objects (fig. 5.1). The photograph is a long shot of two rooms. Items in the collection dominate both living spaces in a dense yet controlled arrangement of textiles, framed works of art, and miniatures. Paintings, lithography, and feather work by Mexican Indians hang salon-style from the three visible walls. Pottery and a Victorian bell jar sit atop a small table draped with *rebozos*. Textiles with diamond patterns cover the Victorian settee and hand-woven rugs are scattered across the carpet. A small figure on a horse, enclosed within a glass case, is visible on the right. It is likely a wax figure created by Mariana, who appears seated at a piano in the background, almost as if she is also on display. Certainly, her presence does not upstage the collection that she and Antonio had acquired; her demeanor is diminished, almost melancholic.

Because of the composition of the photograph, it could not be mistaken for a portrait, unless it is compared to the portraits made during seventeenth- and eighteenth-century Grand Tours. Travelers often commissioned portraits of themselves along with the objects they had acquired during their journey. In Grand Tour portraits, the travelers tend to dominate the images. Mariana, in contrast, seems almost an afterthought to the photographer. In the US context, the photograph is akin to Charles Willson Peale's self-portrait titled *The Artist in His Museum* (1822), as both images document a collector among a dense arrangement of objects that are presented to inspire and educate.[23] Although seven decades separate the two images, in both images the objects are allowed to dominate the composition. The eye shifts to the collection and only briefly to the collector.

## Collecting Chicana/o Art

This chapter brings attention to the larger social implications of the private practice of collecting Chicana/o art.[24] Since the late twentieth century, Chicanas and Chicanos have been accumulating objects attributed to Mexican-origin artists in order to rescue the art and the artists from art historical and sociopolitical oblivion, a strategy that appears to have driven the Coronels in their time. The collectors resist dominant narratives about Mexicans and Mexican Americans through a politics of reclamation. By collecting, they challenge the authority of public holdings and a discursive understanding of American art. The collection—or, more precisely, the act of collecting and the occasional presentation of the collection—prevents the object, the self, and the community from being discarded, degraded, or rendered invisible; it claims social space in the name of the community. It is a type of emplacement or reclamation for the collector, who is also otherwise displaced and invisible. Thus, collecting Chicana/o art functions as a critical act of witness to the historic and ongoing institutional violence that continues to push Mexicans and Mexican Americans into marginalized social positions.

Here I borrow from the work of Tiffany Ana López and her analysis of Latina/o creative writers. She persuasively argues that Latina/o writers "view trauma as critically, politically, and personally generative," thereby rejecting the "predictable" rhetoric of "evil perpetrators and forsaken victims." As López observes, "to be a critical witness entails more than just documenting, repeating, or otherwise telling a story or event. Rather, critical witnessing works from conveying a story's impact as a means of spotlighting the conditions that brought the story into being." In this case, collectors spotlight the narrowness of the American and Latin American aesthetic, the subsequent neglect of Chicana/o art, and the ongoing mishandling of Chicana/o cultural production. Some collectors point to the larger historic traumas of colonization, Manifest Destiny, and institutionalized racism and sexism. The private collections tell a story that "instructs in order to reconstruct" the self and the community. The focus is on the "work enacted" by the collection. In this way, the collections are a "transformative force of love in the healing of personal and cultural [or collective] wounds" of a people.[25] As with other forms of cultural production, Chicana/o art collections embody a poetics and politics of love and rescue.

This chapter is based largely on structured, open-ended interviews with a dozen Chicana/o art collectors who live in Southern California and on fourteen years of observation and informal conversations with various collectors, artists, and arts advocates. Following a brief review of relevant scholarship, I describe the coparticipatory methods by which I gathered information about Chicana/o art collectors at public events and forums. This section allows me to introduce the collectors who shared their stories, which appear prominently in the latter part of the chapter. In short, I approach Chicana/o art collecting from the perspective of critical cultural studies, feminist scholarship, and ethnic studies.[26] I do not evaluate the practice of collecting in terms of consumerism—thereby avoiding a Marxist trend in Chicana/o and cultural studies—because consumption is not the frame used by collectors.[27] Collector Rosalie Gonzalez explains that collections of Chicana/o art respond to emotional and ethical—not financial—logic:

> It's personal fulfillment; it's supporting the artists. I don't go out and protest a lot but I am furthering the cause by supporting the arts. . . . I am the first in [my] family to go to college, and first Chicana from Garfield High School to go to MIT [Massachusetts Institute of Technology], so I always felt this responsibility to my community, to do well, and work hard, as my migrant farmworker grandparents did. I felt a responsibility to take advantage of those opportunities and give back to the community, and collecting is part of it.[28]

Gonzalez voices the perspective of the overwhelming majority of Chicana/o art collectors who have been active in Los Angeles in the late twentieth and early twenty-first centuries. They are not "in it for investment purposes," and several are uncomfortable with the word *collector* because of its colonial origins and capitalist connotations. Like Gonzalez, they acquire art because they "appreciate the work and like to support our community, to support artists."

Gonzalez admits that she did not consider herself a collector during her college years, when she hung posters in her dorm room at MIT. Nor did she consider herself a collector when she and her husband, artist Ramon Ramirez, frequented Galería de la Raza in the San Francisco Mission District and the walls of their small apartment in Berkeley filled with art. The idea began to emerge when she "realized" she was buying art from Westside and Eastside galleries in Los Angeles and municipal arts organizations in Southern California such as the Pico Rivera Centre for the Arts. Developing an identity as a collector, Ramirez explains, was "a learned process" for both of them that slowly took hold over two decades. Although ambivalent about this identity, Gonzalez consistently seeks works of art that express her family history and the "fighting spirit" of her mother and grandmother or that provide "personal fulfillment." She has developed a specific aesthetic and conviction to "further the cause by supporting the arts." This conviction is a major focus of this chapter.

I privilege the perspective of the collectors because consumer analysis typically overshadows the interpretation of art acquisition by people who do not conceive of their purchases as commodities. In the words of collector Anita Miranda, the collection "is not for the purposes of making a profit from it."[29] Although Cheech Marin, the actor, collector, and arts advocate, pragmatically suggests that Mexican American collectors should sell their collections to authorizing museums to gain access to museum infrastructure, he is simply encouraging Mexican American collectors and philanthropists to reproduce the method used by "Theodore Roosevelt, Jr., J. P. Morgan, Cornelius Vanderbilt, Russell Sage, John D. Rockefeller, Morris K. Jesup, and William Sloan," as well as other elite capitalists from the 1880s through the 1930s to build the public collections of museums.[30] Marin's ultimate interest is in creating a strategy for visibility and authority.[31]

## Rethinking Collecting

Chicana/o art collecting requires a reading of space that blurs the long-defunct dichotomy between public and private spheres. As Chon A. Noriega argues about Chicano Art Collectors Anonymous (CACA), an irreverent group of Los Angeles professionals who enjoy the scatological humor of the acronym and the pathological implication of their activity, the home becomes a "charged meeting ground between the private and the public" when personal possessions outgrow the limitations of one's domestic space.[32] A spatial analysis informed by the notion of critical witnessing allows us to understand the actions of collectors such as Rosalie Gonzalez as a form of community making rather than a practice that is limited to the physical places in which the art resides. A spatial analysis draws their activity into social or public domains of meaning.

Although individual collectors typically purchase pieces for their artistic qualities and not as political statements, these assemblages as a whole and, I would add, the combined activities of Chicanas/os who acquire art "[bear] the weight of a social function."[33] This partial definition of collecting is consistent with scholarship that allows for a motivation broader than selfish materialism.[34] My interpretation of Chicana/o art collectors is not an examination of individuated collectors, a major methodological focus in art historical scholarship. It departs from studies that view collecting as a psychological perversion or individualization, and it builds on scholarly attention to collectors as custodians.[35] This chapter looks at the function of art collections developed by women and men in a historically specific traumatic moment after imperialism and especially considers the veiling of inequalities in contemporary Los Angeles and other sites of América Latina organized by and through the legacies of colonialism. Attention to the ways an accumulation of objects is assigned communal significance and can "sustain identity" answers some questions about the various meanings of collecting for a population that is separated from the normative citizen.[36]

Artist and scholar David Driskell encourages us to look at collectors of color as social agents whose activities are part of a larger experience within or on behalf of racialized, silenced, or erased communities.[37] Their collections challenge the dominating framework of American art history and function to emplace and protect the culture and history of the group. Chicana/o art collectors, influenced by systematic practices of racial, ethnic, gendered, and material exclusions, are making purchases that signify belonging in a larger group beyond their immediate kin group or household. The practice of collecting and the set of objects becomes a strategy of intervention, a tactic identified by decolonial and feminist writers.[38] As Mary K. Coffey argues about collectors of Mexican folk art, "the forms of subjectivity [that collecting] creates and the social affinities it cultivates contain the potential for more radical forms of cultural identification and citizenship."[39]

Chicana/o art collectors are acquiring images that reflect their own lived experiences, and the images with which they surround themselves are necessary for self-fashioning. Ariana Guerrera, a collector with over two hundred examples of Chicana/o art, Mexican folk art, and religious artifacts, notes that she places works on her walls in order to "displace what I grew up with."[40] Olivia Sanchez-Brown explains that she has purchased paintings, sculptures, textiles, and drawings that depict women of subtle strength because they convey the same indirectness and delicateness that she used in the 1970s to negotiate between the feminism she found at the Woman's Building and the contrasting gender roles of her Mexican family.[41] Terry Muñoz has selected paintings that "remind me of my lifetime."[42] The purchasing of Chicana/o art is a social practice, contextualized and contingent upon the raced, gendered, and sexed histories of Mexican-origin populations in the United States. Just as Guerrera, Sanchez-Brown, and Muñoz surround themselves with works that reinforce life choices and bring comfort, other collectors, such as David Diaz, feel a "sense of responsibility" to their community.[43] For Chicana/o art collectors, the community is not only embodied in the artwork but also in the passion or desire that the collectors have for preservation and presentation. The ethos of love and rescue expressed through the consistent purchasing of Chicana/o art challenges the hate and exclusion manifest in racism, sexism, xenophobia, and nationalism. The words and actions of these collectors tell of a social commitment made on behalf of a larger population—a community—of Mexican-origin people.

## A Coparticipatory Method

The legacy of possession, domination, and appropriation associated with the term *collector* made it difficult for some people to speak with me about the art in their homes as collections. Indeed, half a dozen people were entirely uncomfortable with the term and would not grant me an interview. While these individuals own art attributed to women and men of Mexican descent, they told me that they are not collectors. As one Chicana stated, "The word 'collecting' imperializes it." Chicana artist Delilah Montoya notes this troubling history in her exhibition statement for *From the West: Chicano Narrative Photography*: "Collecting generates a communion with the object, not the culture."[44] Montoya refers to the imperialist collectors of non-Western cultural artifacts who, in the early nineteenth century, destroyed the very cultures they hoped to preserve. Her assessment clarifies precisely why some Chicanas/os would not describe themselves as collectors: unlike imperialists, they have an intimate relationship with "the culture" and it is through "the object" that this connection is reinforced. More critically, their notion of "the culture" is not static but dynamic and negotiated.

This tension required my coparticipatory immersion into the practice of collecting in order to build rapport and understanding. Although I had been collecting art for a decade or more, in 2000 I was introduced to the larger community of collectors when Chon A. Noriega invited me to contribute a catalog essay for the exhibition *East of the River: Chicano Art Collectors Anonymous*. My involvement with the show drew me into a significant group of Los Angeles collectors that included Anita Miranda, Mary Salinas Durón and Armando Durón, Esperanza Valverde, Martha Abeytia Canales and Charles Canales, and David Serrano and Robert Willson. Active since the 1980s, CACA was an informal group that at one time exceeded a hundred women and men, including Ricardo Valverde before his death and Sanchez-Brown before she left the group in the 1990s to reclaim her original intention of selecting art in order to, in her words, "hold onto a memory." The members of CACA "shared a similar history as participants and/or beneficiaries of the civil rights struggles of the 1960s and 1970s. Most were first-generation college-educated professionals who still maintained a working class and community-based ethos."[45] While the informal meetings at one another's homes helped create a common social experience for the group's members, their goal of cultural preservation was not unique, as I soon learned when I expanded my investigation to include collectors outside CACA.

Another Los Angeles–area collecting group, Chicano Art Federation, formed in 2006 because its members shared a vision to "preserve and foster Chicano art," but not merely as an investment. In this case, an artist recommended that I speak with the group. The federation consists of five young professionals, including Rosalie Gonzalez, who have known one another since childhood. Individually, they have been collecting art since the late 1990s and early 2000s, and it is their hope that collecting "will both preserve the culture for coming generations and encourage artists to continue to engage the activity of making art."[46]

I met several collectors, such as Domingo Rodriguez and Terry and Ricardo Muñoz, at events designed to cultivate collectors among the growing Chicana/o professional class. Sponsored by Self Help Graphics & Art or Avenue 50 Studio, these events took several forms, but most involved discussions of art and collecting, tours of a collector's home, and public presentations by collectors. Some events concluded with an art auction.[47] When gatherings were held in a collector's home, such as the fundraiser events that the Muñozes hosted for Avenue 50 Studio, dozens of people would attend, including the artists whose work was up for auction. The artists' presence helped create an atmosphere of aesthetic and cultural value rather than one of capital investment, and most collectors were more than a little uncomfortable talking about their acquisitions as economic speculation. Conversations with collectors at these events were informal but nonetheless informative because I was often able to corroborate information I had gathered from formal interviews.

It was usually in these spaces that I would meet colleagues who purchased art but refused the category of "collector." Their perspective underscores the complex position of Chicana/o professionals who question vertical hierarchies as well as forms of appropriation, yet who enjoy luxury purchasing. The informal and formal conversations reveal that art acquisition is more than a personal, ego-based activity. Cheech Marin sees his collection as serving a greater purpose. "I travel extensively," he informed me during an interview. "I have seen the growth [of the Latino population] throughout my career. I have seen the growth in every state, [in] Montana or South Carolina. [It's] mostly Mexican, about 85 percent, and under twenty-five [years old]. Simultaneously in every state . . . we are the mainstream. We are going to be the majority."[48] His collecting practices and advocacy for Chicana/o art bear critical witness to Mexican American demographic and cultural authority as it unfolds across the nation.

Several collectors spoke about acquiring art when asset accumulation allowed for purchases beyond basic necessities. A few, such as Gonzalez,

Diaz, and John Sanchez, began to purchase art before they had wealth. Gonzalez bought a woodblock print a few years out of college. Diaz gathered posters and prints as early as the 1970s, while he was attending college in the San Francisco Bay Area. Similar to Marin, who collected marbles and baseball cards as a child, Sanchez collected items as a teenager, arranging categories for his collection of concert posters, albums, and concert T-shirts. Nevertheless, the passion for collecting Chicana/o art developed once Marin and Sanchez had established careers. The majority of the collectors are homeowners and college-educated professionals with working-class backgrounds, which I understand as one factor that informs their ambivalent responses to questions about bequeathing their collections. Asset accumulation is not part of their family history or experience. Several were exposed to art at an early age. Diaz and Sanchez-Brown attended arts festivals in Laguna Beach. Generally, Chicana/o art collectors focus on artists from their own region, one factor in the collecting process as a demonstration of place and belonging.

All of the collections have outgrown the rooms and walls of the collectors' homes, spilling into offices and in some cases into museum-quality storage facilities. Although individual collectors classify their acquisitions in distinct ways that I will address below, acquisitions number from about thirty objects to hundreds of items, as in the case of Marin, whose collection contains over seven hundred works, mostly paintings. Collectors demonstrate their passion for art by quickly filling empty spots on their walls when objects are loaned for an exhibition or by rotating the collection so that items come out of storage and into the home or office.

## Generating Self-in-Community

Chicana/o collectors are social agents of change because they are engaged in the process George Lipsitz describes as "art-based community making" or what José Esteban Muñoz refers to as "worldmaking."[49] While normative views of Mexicans and Mexican Americans assume criminality, illegality, and shiftiness, Chicana/o art collectors resist these narrow portraits by "making communities" and defining "community" in ways that confound mainstream conceptions of nationhood and belonging. Their actions work against national narratives of "citizen" and "foreigner" and complicate the history of collecting as it has developed in conjunction with public museums in the United States. In short, their actions place

Chicanas/os within a contemporary and historical landscape, imagining belonging for indigenous and marginalized populations that have been created and/or injured by diaspora and colonization processes. Their agency is rooted in the transformative experience that the art provides. For example, the Chicana art collectors with whom I spoke identify the art of Diane Gamboa as empowering. They describe her paintings, drawings, and serigraphs as "powerful," "feminist," and "beautiful." Her glamorous and androgynous characters—typically clothed only in tattoos, body piercings, jewelry, a headdress, or chains—appear to release men and women from gender constraints. Chicana art collectors enjoy the ways androgyny empowers women and expands their gendered and sexual options.

Collectors are also drawn to content that records family history, even when the artist did not intend the work to be biographical. Terry Muñoz purchased a simple watercolor, *La Planchadora*, by Ramses Noriega because the image of a woman ironing clothes reminded her of her mother and aunt, who would press the vestments of priests at their family's Catholic parish. She selected a portrait by Yolanda Gonzalez because it reminded her of her sister, who also has green eyes and red hair. Other works in the collection symbolically represent Terry's children and remind her of her children's lives, careers, or interests. As Anita Miranda states about the hundreds of paintings, prints, sculptures, photographs, and drawings in her own home, items are collected because the artists have recorded Chicana/o collective experiences: "Generally, [the collection] has to do with my own culture," a phrase that presupposes a transnational sense of belonging in the United States and Mexico. For example, a photograph by Christina Fernandez, a Los Angeles–based artist, that captures the social and physical landscapes of downtown and East Lost Angeles illustrates Miranda's family memories. In addition, Miranda is drawn to the matrilineal narrative in the work because it echoes her own childhood and tells her family's story. She views the work as a depiction of her own biography.

This inclusive vision, one central to Chicana/o cultural politics, resonates with other collectors even as it challenges master narratives about belonging in the United States. Members of CACA not only engage in collecting to preserve a cultural patrimony, they also organize and sponsor exhibitions. Exhibitions are the spaces in which collectors call others to engage in critical witness against the dominant museum practices—

collecting, exhibiting, preserving, and interpreting—that censor Chicana/o art and artists. In addition, the exhibitions from private holdings generate, as do errata exhibitions, a critical lens for understanding Chicana/o art. Marin has produced four international shows of items from his collection: *Chicano Visions: American Painters on the Verge* (2001), *The Chicano Collection/La Colección Chicana: Fine Art Prints by Modern Multiples* (2005), *Chicanitas: Small Paintings from the Cheech Marin Collection* (2011), and *Chicano Dream: Chicano Artists from the Cheech Marin Collection, 1980–2010* (2014). Each is a challenge to particular invisibilities within American art. Los Angeles–based collectors have also worked individually and collectively to push mainstream institutions to reconsider their politics; for example, Armando Durón urged the Museum of Latin American Art in Long Beach to collect US-born Mexican American artists, Marin urged LACMA to value Chicana/o art, and Miranda urged the Women's Caucus for Art to include Latinas in its leadership and programming.

Collectors also design exhibitions in their own homes in order to introduce emerging artists or to balance the art historical record. Marin, for example, arranged for collectors to see the work of Yolanda Gonzalez by hosting a salon in his home. In 2005 the Duróns culled for a private exhibition thirty-three works by Chicanas from their collection of five hundred works of art and over twenty-five hundred ephemeral items from exhibitions, such as postcards, flyers, and other announcements from galleries, museums, and art centers. Titled *Beyond Beauty and Impulse*, it evidenced the presence and influence of Chicana artists in the region, offering another view of Los Angeles art history. Similar private displays of works from the Durón Family Collection are not conceived for viewing by the public or even a select group of friends and associates, but Armando prepares an essay and a description of the staging, which he shares with his family. It is for "my own pleasure," he states. The essay for *Beyond Beauty and Impulse* calls for a comprehensive exhibition and catalog of Chicana art; in this way the Duróns' private exhibition was a reprimand to the art establishment. Private collections and the exhibitions drawn from them function as a critical witness to the injuries enacted by authorizing museums.

Most collectors in this study articulated a sense of place, identity, and comfort created by the collection or the act of collecting. Speaking of the spiritual and feminist power generated by works in her collection,

Sanchez-Brown observes that several images of women possess a "quiet strength." None are "following someone to the mountain," a phrase that alludes to the Chicano movement and the masculine charge to storm up the mountain. One image remains on the same wall even when Sanchez-Brown rotates the collection because it has a special meaning for her and continues to offer her feminist inspiration. Ricardo Muñoz states that his collecting practices are motivated by "self-identity and personal philosophy" about the "profound loneliness that is held by each individual" and our desire to "transcend [our] separateness." He gathers works that convey something about the artists' "own sense of their being." A painting by Carlos Bueno, for instance, depicts a middle-aged prostitute sitting at a table with her head in her hands. This painting is part of the series Virgenes de Media Noche and the image of "desolation . . . serves as an example of self reflection."[50] Muñoz's sense of identity and place may stem from his heritage and activism, but his notion of belonging is grounded in existentialist philosophy about human nature.

Guerrera finds refuge in certain works and hangs them on specific walls in her home. Unlike Miranda and Marin, whose bedrooms are the spaces in which they create serenity through the display of specific works of art, Guerrera enjoys viewing the art in her living room: "They are my blanket of comfort. I lie on my couch and look at my art." After a strategic pause she added, "It's a political statement," as if to summarize the entire act of collecting and joyfully viewing art objects that portray healthy, egalitarian relationships between women and men. When she gazes at images that match her vision, the art functions as a cure for the pain Guerrera endured as a child growing up in a predominantly European American neighborhood, where isolation and rejection were common. Diaz keeps works in his office that function as "inspirational muse," motivating his writing as well as offering sustenance when his direct expression is inhibited. The works tell him "don't hold back," and they allow him to pursue his "political voice," particularly through his publications, which challenge urban development and policies that ignore working-class and poor Latino residents. This type of engagement with art and sentiment is a form of art-based community making. Chicana/o art collectors surround themselves with objects that reconfigure the normative images of Mexican-origin people as a method of visualizing themselves and their communities as whole.

While an entire collection bears critical witness to the complexity and brilliance of Chicana/o communities, collectors spoke about specific works of art that illuminate the depth of this sentiment. For instance, when they enter their home, the Duróns open their front door to an expansive oil painting of a mysterious and luminous sky. While the walls are regularly transformed by new arrangements of the collection as items are lent for exhibitions or returned to storage, this massive painting by Linda Vallejo rarely moves. It has become the family's touchstone, a source of inspiration, tranquility, and permission to dream. The charged simplicity of the canvas suggests an indigenous spirituality that the Duróns regard as part of their family heritage. Armando felt compelled to acquire the painting because of its depth: as the light on the canvas changes, Mesoamerican symbols of creation are exposed. The Duróns enjoy the painting's ability to represent their cultural heritage as well as its universal beauty.

The Muñozes have a hallway filled with images of women. When I asked whether the art was arranged in a particular way to display themes or areas of concentration in the collection, Ricardo replied, "The hallway is all women," and Terry immediately finished the thought, saying, "It is deliberate." Both Ricardo and Terry come from activist families with empowered women: Terry's parents helped mobilize farmworkers in the 1960s and 1970s, and Ricardo's parents led political efforts in Los Angeles. Although Terry describes herself as a private person and a "typical Mexican homemaker," she is an assertive and self-possessed woman who, after retirement from a full-time career in municipal finance, stabilized the leadership at LA Plaza de Cultura y Artes while the new organization sought to hire a permanent executive director. The work displayed in the hallway is a testament to the family's generations of strong, resilient, and dignified women.

Similarly, Miranda is mindful of the art in the entryway to her home because she wants to experience the pedagogical lessons of the art as she enters the house. Portraits of close friends and of people unknown to her are placed near the entrance so that "family" greets her when she comes home: "So if I'm coming home I can immediately see friends who support me and . . . like a welcome . . . They are like my family." Her ability to make family from scratch, to paraphrase Cherríe Moraga, articulates a position in which Miranda is neither "a mother, [nor] a future wife/mother" to those on her wall, suggesting new definitions of womanhood and gender.[51]

Although this interpretation of collecting is speculative, several collectors reaffirm family bonds through their collections. Sanchez gave his brother a vintage Cantinflas movie poster because the brother expressed appreciation for it. The gift held symbolic meaning for their relationship and strengthened their obligations to each other, as French social analyst Marcel Mauss argues in his book about exchange in nonmonetary societies. The work is a metonym for their shared cultural heritage. The vintage Mexican poster and its passage from one brother to another traversed and created a social landscape of Chicana/o culture as it reaffirmed what they came to share and appreciate from "the old country," a phrase Sanchez uses to express his social, familial, and cultural connection to Mexico as a homeland.[52]

Sanchez-Brown recalls that her daughter was eight years old when she made her first purchase of art. Her daughter deliberately studied all the sculptures at artist Michael Amescua's studio before carefully selecting a piece. Her desire to buy a work of art was, for Sanchez-Brown, evidence of her daughter's connection to their home and the collection it displays, as well as to a way of life and aesthetic sensibility that Sanchez-Brown hoped to instill in her child. Rosalie Gonzalez expressed similar emotions of parental pride when her son asked why his name did not appear on the label that identified his parents as the owners of *Queen of Denial* (2005), a large mixed-media work on canvas by Gronk that was being exhibited at the Vincent Price Art Museum. She realized that her son could recognize several works in the collection, and he asked to pick one for his bedroom. She was delighted that he held a visual image of the works in his mind's eye and was developing his own aesthetic taste.

The Muñozes' adult children continue to construct multiple meanings from their parents' collection and its cultural weight. Even after moving out of the family home, they enjoy the works their parents have acquired by displaying pieces in their newly established households. Ricardo and Terry are both very proud of their children's desire to continue to live with the collection. It is an indication, they say, that the children know their Chicano heritage and are proud to be Chicanos. In these cases, the act of collecting Chicana/o art reinforces the connections within and between individual households and forges communal identity.

## Acquisition: A Poetics of Love and Rescue

General discussions about acquisition and criteria for collecting also conveyed a sense of community, history, and identity. David Diaz joined the growing art scene of East Los Angeles in the 1970s and was attending events and openings long before he identified as a collector. During the

Chicano movement he was "not focused on art," but "the appreciation of culture led [him] into the art community." In the 1990s he had "an epiphany" when he saw John Valadez's exhibition on Skid Row in Los Angeles. The work displayed from Valadez's early period consisted of portraits of cholas and cholos and a monumental pastel drawing, *Getting Them Out of the Car* (1984), now part of the Cheech Marin Collection. "That changed me," Diaz reports, and he determined to plan for multiple acquisitions of Chicana/o art each year. It was the moment when he realized that art was an "extension" of Chicana/o political activism and that "the whole movement was an extension of the artist's work." His relationship to the solidarity movement and other social movements increasingly informed his collecting practices and sense of belonging in those communities of advocacy and agency. He would often acquire works through auctions hosted to benefit a community-based organization, such as the Coalition for Humane Immigrant Rights of Los Angeles (CHIRLA) or the Central American Resource Center (CARECEN-LA).

Several collectors are aware that their childhood households inspired an appreciation for art. This recognition refutes the stereotype of intellectual and aesthetic poverty associated with Mexican and Mexican American households. Terry Muñoz's mother could crochet, knit, and create finely detailed embroidery, some of which was provided to a local Catholic church to adorn the vestments. Ricardo Muñoz's uncles were trained artists who worked in graphic design and interior decoration. The Muñozes valued everyday creative expressions and brought their appreciation for color and composition to their collecting practices. Terry favors minimalist drawings and deep hues, while Ricardo favors expressionistic works that match his interest in existential philosophy. The important point is that they easily and without conflict merge a working-class and women-centered aesthetic with fine arts, a sensibility shared by Diaz, who "was exposed to art from my mother and to fine art at Laguna Beach from an early age of ten or eleven years old." The papier-mâché and other crafts that Diaz's mother would make at home established an aesthetic sensibility derived from domestic arts, Mexican *arte popular* (a term that replaces "folk art" and its inherent hierarchy), and fine arts.

Such a broad introduction to the arts produces expansive collections that include a variety of styles, media, themes, and approaches. Diaz collects works produced by homeless women and hangs them alongside works by Mexican artist Lucille de Hoyos. Olivia Sanchez-Brown and the

Muñozes display whimsical ceramic pieces or children's drawings alongside masterpieces by established artists. John Sanchez hangs in the same space geometric works by Victor Vasarely and his own art that is in visual conversation with the Hungarian French artist, along with lenticular art and paintings by Jaime "Germs" Zacarias.

Ariana Guerrera selects paintings, fine art prints, and even posters that represent and affirm her identity and spirituality. "I choose them because they represent spirituality and relationships between men and women, romantic or funny, or I choose those to surround myself with that sense of presence and to affirm me culturally and affirm me as a woman." The works created by Chicanas/os, perhaps more than thirty items in the collection, provide Guerrera with a sense of self and emplacement. The art with which she surrounds herself represents who she is as a person; it is this physical extension of her own image that provides her with a sense of being. For instance, she collects the art of Yreina D. Cervántez, a Los Angeles artist known for her indigenous imagery and feminist messages, because the spiritual symbols and religious icons affirm Guerrera's spiritual beliefs. But this notion of the self is not separate from her sense of a collective experience among Mexican Americans and women. More important, the art in her collection affirms an identity in relationship with others, both men and women, including, as she noted in a follow-up interview, relationships between women.

Guerrera and others are not interested only in art that decorates their walls with "something beautiful." They also acquire objects that bear witness to death, suffering, and injustice, documenting a fuller history and experience of Chicanas/os. Some pieces frighten or disturb visitors and family members. Anita Miranda is careful about what she places in the guest room. Sometimes visitors or family members question the collectors' choices, but this has not deterred collectors from purchasing nudes or images depicting fragile human lives, trauma, or self-destruction. They are inspired by the images that document lived realities, particularly those that bear critical witness to indigenous, Chicana/o, or Mexican suffering, as Ricardo Muñoz notes about the image of an older prostitute. Their criteria for inclusion, therefore, extend outward from self to self-in-community.

Santa Ana Salvo's criteria for inclusion are duplication, reproduction, and surplus. As a collector of images of la Virgen de Guadalupe in all media and styles, such as pop art, fine art, functional religious objects, and commercial items, Salvo appears to express and reproduce her sense of empowerment through excess. The ubiquitous nature of Our Lady of Guadalupe is a sign of the community's presence: Chicanas/os are everywhere, and the cultural and religious icon is proof of their physical and cultural saturation across geopolitical borders and social boundaries. Furthermore, Salvo notes that the brown-skinned woman who appeared at Tepeyac to an indigenous man in 1531 suggests that a female goddess, such as Tonantzin, the Aztec goddess of earth and life, is central not only to Nahua civilization but also to contemporary experience. Salvo's interpretation of Guadalupe is part of a major social phenomenon that can be seen in Chicana creative literary and visual arts as well as Latina feminist theology. This reconfiguration of Guadalupe and Tonantzin emerged in the 1970s with the works of Ester Hernandez, Yolanda M. López, and Patssi Valdez, and subsequent decades witnessed important developments by novelists Sandra Cisneros and Carla Trujillo, by visual artists such as Alma López and Isabel Martínez, and by performance artists and collectives such as Paulina Sahagun and Mujeres de Maiz. Surrounded at home and work by hundreds of images of Our Lady, Salvo fashions a life of feminist agency. Many Chicana art collectors participate in the feminist reconstruction of Guadalupe and, like Salvo, purchase more than one of the prints, posters, or mixed-media assemblages by Ester Hernandez, Alma López, Yolanda M. López, Judithe Hernández, Margaret "Quica" Alarcón, or Gina Aparicio. Some collectors seek queer representations of Guadalupe. The reconstruction of Our Lady of Guadalupe into a powerful feminist icon transforms and ultimately leaves behind the conventional expectation that la Virgen is passive, selfless, and deferential.[53]

The Duróns state that their motivation to collect art began when they noticed that "the buyers were not Latino and we wanted our own patrimony."[54] Their collection is a form of critical witness against appropriation, a topic that continues to animate discussions at Self Help Graphics & Art's annual print sales. Preservation for the larger Chicana/o community inspired and motivated John Sanchez to collect his first work of art. When he found Willie Herrón III's painting *El Barrio* (1971) collecting dust and spiderwebs in a garage, he knew he had to rescue the work for the public good. The environmental conditions of the garage weren't "doing it any justice," and he quickly made the purchase. In his own words of love and rescue, he states,

To me, it's an important piece. It belongs in an important institution. . . . It's an important piece because it depicts the movement. Willie incorporated graffiti into the background. . . . It was a milestone. It was important not to delete those items from the piece because they were very much part of the community as they are today and it gave a lot of integrity to the piece. . . . I think this painting is larger than me, and should not be in a private home. It should be shared.

At the end of the interview, when I asked Sanchez whether he had any final comments, he stated, "Children bring life to a home. Art gives the home soul."

His belief in art's philosophical and affective purpose resonates with the views of several collectors. Some even understand art as the essence or the legacy of societies. Terry Muñoz asked, "Over all the centuries, what really remains? It is always the art, and [sadly], it is the thing people think is expendable." The poetics of love and rescue inform the actions of these collectors. With a desire to preserve their art and culture, they join a larger movement, one that strives for equity, identity, and self-determination and that is framed against a backdrop of social injustice, from the US imperial invasion of Mexico in the nineteenth century through the disenfranchisement of Mexican American citizens after 1848 to today's anti-immigrant hostility.

Some collectors, such as the Duróns, Diaz, and Marin, are also arts advocates, and they have worked to make local institutions accountable to the growing population of Mexican-origin residents. Notably, they have financially supported exhibitions, publications, and access to Chicana/o art. Similar to the Coronels, who in the late nineteenth century acquired exhibition catalogs, the Duróns define their collection as more than works of art. The Durón Family Collection includes ephemera from exhibitions, books, and other material culture documenting the display and interpretation of Chicana/o art. The flyers, broadsheets, catalogs, postcards, and exhibition announcements are not only content but also context for the collection. These are items that public museums and libraries have yet to systematically acquire, although two institutions in Southern California and one in Texas have been building collections of artists' papers, publications, and ephemera.[55] Another Southern California collector claimed that she accumulates posters, clippings, and books because "somebody had to do it."

This attitude of social obligation, cultural rescue, and urgency drove art historian Shifra M. Goldman to acquire over seven thousand books, hundreds of slides of Mexican, Chicana/o, and Latin American art, and over eighteen linear feet of newspaper clippings, exhibition announcements, and other ephemera on Chicana/o artists, organizations, and institutions before her death in 2010. Goldman's sense of a social contract supported not only her own research but also the research for dozens of dissertations and scholarly publications (my own included). Goldman started to collect as a student precisely because public library and archival holdings were insufficient. Although the California Ethnic and Multicultural Archives at the University of California, Santa Barbara, acquired Goldman's papers in 2008, the continuing and larger vacancy within authorizing institutions remains a pressing problem that Chicana/o collectors, scholars, and curators acknowledge.

For instance, Terezita Romo, independent curator and art historian, found that museum collections could not assist her in locating and identifying early Mexican American artists for the exhibition *Art along the Hyphen: The Mexican-American Generation* (2011). Few institutions had acquired the work of Eduardo Carrillo (1937–97), Roberto Chavez (b. 1932), Domingo Ulloa (1919–97), or Alberto Valdés (1918–98), although the works of Hernando G. Villa (1881–1952) and Dora de Larios (b. 1933) had entered a few institutional collections and several private collections outside the family. Romo describes her curatorial work as a "reclamation process," identifying one of the motivations for Chicana/o art collectors. Her call for a "paradigm shift" within arts institutions also echoes the transformative direction that Chicana/o art collectors take in their acquisition of art and their desire for a future that will bring Chicana/o art and artists into focus.[56] Marin felt the same urgency to shift the paradigm when the director of LACMA "stonewalled Chicanos out of the museum" and initially rejected Marin's traveling exhibition *Chicano Painters*. Even though the county museum eventually exhibited works from his collection, it was the last museum to host the show. "You'd think that LACMA would be the first museum" to host the exhibition, said Marin, given the demography and history of the region.[57] Collectors recognize that a "paradigm shift" may not occur in their lifetime and, therefore, that private holdings are critically important for Latin American and American art history.

Not only do Chicana/o art collectors house an archive of and for their community, their actions produce a community that resists normative and patriarchal notions of Mexican heritage and culture, particularly the heteropatriarchal visions of womanhood. The majority of the works collected by Chicanas include those by artists such as Barbara Carrasco, Yreina D. Cervántez, Christina Fernandez, Elsa Flores, Diane Gamboa, Margaret Garcia, Yolanda Gonzalez, Dolores Guerrero, Ester Hernandez, Alma López, Delilah Montoya, Patssi Valdez, and Linda Vallejo—all artists who are known for their specifically feminist representations of women and of heterosexual and queer relationships. As noted above, the Muñozes own several works that represent empowered women, and these images were created by both men and women. Anita Miranda "started collecting very specifically only women," and this was "a political decision" that reinforced her feminist views and work. As she explains, "I have a strong commitment to support women artists, particularly artists of color, and to promote and encourage their representation in the exhibition arenas. My impulsiveness for collecting art falls in accord with my philosophy about my reason for creating art and the search for the past, present, and future life. I relish discovery, creativity and innovation."[58] By purchasing and caring for art by Chicanas and other women, Miranda attempts to balance the art historical record. Moreover, her private sensibilities carry over into the public social order, and like other collectors, she is an advocate for gender equity in the arts. Ariana Guerrera prefers to collect fine art by and about Chicanas: "The images in the pieces tend to be women; [there are] no men in the pieces" in her collection. Although it was not deliberate, the Duróns have created a collection that is balanced in terms of male and female artists, a point they proudly acknowledge because it challenges male privilege. In this sense, these collectors invest in women's empowerment by constructing a community free of sexism.

## Bearing Critical Witness

Collecting Chicana/o art is a stand against social injustice. It promotes a new way of seeing oneself, one's cultural community, and the cultural production of that community. By collecting images of Chicanas/os that match their memories, the Muñozes defy exclusion and historical amnesia. "They remind me of my lifetime" and of the family, said Terry. The unspoken emphasis for Terry and other collectors is that the figures with brown or red hair, dark skin, and brown or green eyes look like them, disputing the media and popular representations of Mexicans and Mexican

Americans as well as indigenous communities. The Chicana/o act of collecting, therefore, is an act of critical witness that generates a space of recognition and documents a vision of self and community.

According to assimilationist rhetoric, the Chicana/o art collector should service capital and exalt the values associated with a meritocracy: individualism, hard work, thrift, ingenuity, and self-reliance.[59] From this view, the Chicana/o art collector is seen as a contributor to the nation by virtue of her wealth and calculated investments. Yet even though Chicana/o collectors draw objects of art near to them and acquire, as a group, thousands of works for the national patrimony, they have not, as a community, been granted access to museum boards, curatorial planning meetings, or the private luncheons reserved for philanthropists and capitalists who continue to outfit Southern California museums. A few individuals have been part of museum programming and policy, such as Chon A. Noriega, Armando Durón, and Richard Duardo, and each has contributed to policy shifts at LACMA over the past twenty-five years. However, even Marín, the most visible Chicana/o art collector, did not accumulate sufficient cultural capital to sway authorizing museums in the same way that Eli Broad, businessman and collector, swayed two local museums during the early twenty-first century.[60] In short, Chicanas/os have not gained systematic access to the arts institutions and sites of cultural authority because the prevailing racial contract prohibits the accumulation of value by people of Mexican heritage.

Chicana/o art collectors operate elsewhere and for another purpose. They recognize their social exclusion, and they break out of this "uncomfortable suspension" through the act of collecting.[61] In Mary Salinas Durón's words, collecting is a strategy for survival, visibility, and accountability: "Being Chicano is about making sure our cultural heritage is not left out. . . . We have ownership in what is collected and what *isn't* left out."[62] According to Mary, the act of collecting allows her and Armando to participate in the process of making history and community. She creates the archival record through her preservation and accumulation; it is ownership in the interest of the public good. The Duróns are custodians of culture, acting precisely because local and national authorities have not done so.

The object, then, does not "lie outside" the subject—the individual collector—as museum studies scholar Susan Pearce suggests. Nor is the object torn from its "context of origin," as Susan Stewart argues in her assessment of collecting as appropriation.[63] Rather, through the act of collecting, that very context—history, demography, aesthetics—is further constructed, embellished, and performed. The accumulated objects produce a picture of Chicanas/os as a collective, not just as individuals. The object does not completely cross the "threshold from the outside to the inwardness of collection" but enjoys liminality between public and private.[64]

By exceeding the categories of public and private, the object is repositioned within the historical legacy of colonization, conquest, and racism as well as the memories and experiences of contemporary injustices, such as massive deportations of Latinos, English-only laws and schooling that deny Spanish speakers their language, or anti-union legislation that limits the collective bargaining power of service, domestic, and other workers. The act of collecting is a form of critical witness, attentiveness, and responsibility that extends beyond the individual. As the personal property of a Chicana or Chicano, the object is seen with the eyes of one who shares cultural space with the artist. Since the object and subject are similarly positioned, possession is not appropriation but the acquisition of something already located within the realm of the collective. "These attachments matter," posits Coffey, "and they are never entirely contained or controlled by the forces of capital."[65] It is a spiritual intervention, a politics of reclamation, a memory about and for one's cultural community or ancestors.

This repositioning takes place when Chicana/o art collectors escape the surveillance of racial objectification, with its roots in colonial and imperial gazing, and acquire and care for objects attributed to Chicanas/os. Not only do Chicana/o art collectors position themselves as agents in history, in the present and for the future, their actions also serve as a critique of the current racial hegemony in the United States. Chicana/o art collectors do not follow the increasingly codified rule that Mexicans must shed their culture and race in order to integrate into the United States. Their wealth indicates that they have achieved financial success, but they have refused the first part of the assimilationist equation: denial of heritage. Moreover, the objects they possess are positioned to preserve, validate, and in turn create the culture they are supposed to have forgotten.

Even in moments of so-called middle-class arrival, when their names are displayed on the walls of an exhibition, Chicana/o art collectors continue to resist their co-optation. Most showed obvious discomfort when I asked how they felt about seeing their names on an exhibition label or being approached to lend works to an exhibition. They were somewhat uncomfortable with their own pride in seeing their names announced in print as collectors. With an embarrassed smile, John Sanchez states, "I should be more humble." Referring to the public announcement that he was the owner of Willie Herrón III's painting *El Barrio* (1971), he admits, "It was a great feeling. . . . I shouldn't think of it in that way, [because] it is like tooting my own horn." However, the sheepish grin quickly fades as Sanchez explains, "I had a piece that I was able to share. All art should be shared. . . . It should be back into the public eye." His discomfort and humor suggest that he is not relying on a rhetoric of individual investment. He finds satisfaction in his ability to preserve the work for the public good and sees his act of collecting *and* sharing as a form of community accountability. His name on the didactic label is a symbolic intervention against the authorizing institutions that have yet to collect and preserve Chicana/o art. Like Marin and other collectors who have loaned their privately held art for traveling exhibitions, Sanchez gestures his willingness to act for a larger public.

As this book aims to illustrate, and the work of Romo confirms, public institutions in the Los Angeles area exhibit and collect Chicana/o art only sporadically. Given this vacancy in authorizing museums, I have suggested that private collections become part of public space when the process of purchasing works is a form of critical witness. I also posit that the Chicana/o art collectors in this study are functionally located within public space because they have accumulated more paintings, prints, drawings, sculpture, mixed-media assemblages, and printed material of Chicana/o art than they can display on the walls or shelves of their homes or offices. They are acquiring more than their private spaces can accommodate because they are considering their community, a social contract not yet realized by institutions charged with preserving the aesthetic heritage of the region or nation. Because of the invisibility and relative absence of Chicana/o art in municipal, state, and federal institutions, the collectors' activity becomes a public engagement.

Spiritual, political, and social work is performed when art collections are created to preserve cultural memory in the face of systematic national amnesia or the "willful neglect" of museums, as identified by the Smithsonian Institution Task Force on Latino Issues in 1994.[66] This is a neglect that Antonio F. and Mariana Coronel did not live to see but unknowingly anticipated in their comprehensive desire to collect the art and life of Mexico and California and to create a museum for the collection. Furthermore, the failure of authorizing museums to collect and preserve Chicana/o art and culture must be understood in the context of ongoing efforts to deny belonging. These include contemporary challenges to the legal and resident status of Mexicans in the United States by anti-immigrant hate groups such as Save Our State and the Minutemen, who illegally patrol the southern border with Mexico; by cities and states attempting to regulate immigration, voting rights, and education of Mexican-origin people; by police and sheriff's departments that racially profile Mexican-origin people, often detaining or injuring them; and by the federal government, through deportation that separates families and endangers the lives of political refugees.

In the state of California, the historical context, well known to the Coronels, includes the disenfranchisement of indigenous and Mexican American residents, who lost land, legal status, and economic viability within decades of annexation. Indeed, the historical moment from which California museums emerged depended fully upon the displacement of Californios and their control of the state. From this perspective, it is no accident that the county museum eventually misrecognized its connection to the Coronel Collection in establishing itself as a comprehensive arts institution of the West. The following chapter remixes the exhibition record in Los Angeles at the turn of the millennium to illuminate the visibility and invisibility of Chicana/o art.

# REMIXING

Tracing the Limitations of Art History in Los Angeles

I n October 1963, at the end of a long European tour, *Master Works of Mexican Art from Pre-Columbian Times to the Present* opened at the Los Angeles County Museum of Art. Fernando Gamboa, art historian, curator, and the director of the exhibition, had organized the international exhibition to serve as an introduction to "Mexican life since its first beginnings."[1] The traveling exhibition had not originally been scheduled for a North American stop, but when LACMA director Richard F. Brown viewed the exhibition in Paris, he decided that the show "had to be seen in Los Angeles" because "very few people [in the United States] . . . had anything near a complete knowledge or accurate conception of Mexican art and its history." The exhibition, which contained ancient artifacts, colonial art, folk art, and twentieth-century graphic arts, as well as modern art by Diego Rivera, José Clemente Orozco, and David Alfaro Siqueiros, would "make what had been fragmentary a whole experience."[2] Museum administrators and cultural ambassadors of the United States and Mexico agreed to extend the international tour, even securing sponsorship from presidents John F. Kennedy and Adolfo López Mateos. Gamboa added a single US city, Los Angeles, to the exhibition's tour as *Master Works of Mexican Art* made its way back to Mexico.

Brown successfully argued that the exhibition should come to the county museum because California and Mexico had "centuries of common historical association" and the city was home to the second-largest population of Mexicans "outside of Mexico itself."[3] (Brown of course did not address the basis for this "common historical association"—the US occupation of Mexico beginning in the 1830s, the annexation of Mexico's northern territories in 1848, and the bilateral agreements starting in 1942 that brought thousands of Mexican braceros across the border to labor in the fields and factories.) The city's inhabitants responded enthusiastically, and within two weeks, twenty-five thousand people had seen the exhibition.[4] The volume of ticket sales caught the museum by surprise, but it responded emphatically by extending the exhibition run for two months and by remaining open until ten o'clock at night to accommodate the record-breaking crowds.[5] Perhaps the advertisements placed in the *Herald-American*, a regional paper published in Spanish and English that circulated among Mexican Americans who lived mainly east of the Los Angeles River, was successful in reaching working-class residents previously unacknowledged by the museum. Gamboa presented a lecture series *in Spanish* on Mexican art and culture, which strongly suggests that the museum understood the lived reality of the newcomers who were crossing its threshold in unprecedented numbers.[6]

*Master Works of Mexican Art* offers important lessons about the possibilities for inclusion at a comprehensive public art museum in Los Angeles County. LACMA acknowledged and temporarily institutionalized the presence and cultural history of the Mexican American and Spanish-speaking residents of Southern California well before Chicana/o activists began their broad mobilization to demand access and equity. The exhibition did not emerge from cultural movements, public demands for the democratic inclusion of Mexican Americans in civic and cultural institutions, or charges of aesthetic exclusion; indeed, the Chicano movement did not become active in Los Angeles until two years later. Brown was motivated by a desire to remedy art historical ignorance, by the quality of the work, and by the historical linkages between Mexico and Los Angeles, even if he resorted to euphemisms that obscured Spanish colonialism and US imperialism in the region. Still, in light of what happened (and did not happen) at LACMA in the ensuing decades, *Master Works of Mexican Art* inaugurated a paradox: moments of inclusion were followed by erasure. In this chapter, I try to make sense of this, not as an attack on specific curators or administrators, but to understand LACMA's institutional limitations. My aim is to remix the exhibition record of Los Angeles to bring visibility to illegible and forgotten aspects of Chicana/o art history.

A perusal of LACMA's exhibition history reveals that the efforts the museum undertook in 1963 to reach the fastest-growing population in the state were an anomaly. Between 1965 and the end of the millennium—three decades in which Chicana/o art appeared on Los Angeles streets and walls, in high school and college classrooms, and was created through numerous art centers and artist collectives—the mainline museum would only sporadically exhibit "Mexican art and its history" or make an attempt to include Chicana/o audiences. Moreover, Brown's observation of the "common historical association" between Mexico and Mexican Americans in Los Angeles did not drive the collection policy at LACMA even as Chicana/o visual culture flourished outside its doors. In 2004 the UCLA Chicano Studies Research Center forged a partnership with LACMA to launch the Latino Arts Initiative, an effort that was designed to "capitalize on the strengths of both institutions to create a greater understanding of Chicano and Latino arts and cultures for the wider public." Although this historic collaboration allowed a leading Chicano scholar, Chon A. Noriega, to advocate within the museum, my analysis suggests that the very "strengths" of LACMA also produced some inconsistencies in its attempt to "create a greater understanding of Chicano and Latino arts and cultures."[7] The art institution that billed itself as the largest comprehensive museum in the Western United States could not see how *Master Works of Mexican Art* had repositioned what had been a peripheral concern of Eurocentric art history or that the art attributed to Chicanas/os expanded the restrictive categories of "American" and "Mexican" art. The museum has continued to adhere to established disciplinary boundaries and preferences despite the success of *Master Works of Mexican Art* and subsequent exhibitions at LACMA. "A greater understanding of Chicano and Latino arts and cultures" remains elusive.

## Terms of Visibility

This chapter remixes art history in Los Angeles to discuss the paradoxical conditions of visibility and illegibility. I begin with *Master Works of Mexican Art* to convey the fragile nature of visibility. While I frame this exhibition as a narrative of arrival, subsequent events at LACMA illustrate that the international traveling show was a quirk because its tremendous success did not leverage lasting institutional change. As Jennifer A. González observes, mainstream institutions like LACMA have

demonstrated "a general ambivalence toward an influx of new paradigms, cultural differences and aesthetic vocabularies."[8] Exhibitions of
Mexican art, which were sporadic between 1963 and 2004, have become
a seasonal staple, with one nearly every year in the new millennium. Yet
Chicana/o art has not enjoyed the same institutionalization, and when
LACMA did make important advances in the interpretation and framing
of Chicana/o art, it quickly abandoned them. It wasn't until 2005, with
the help of the UCLA Chicano Studies Research Center and the Getty
Foundation's Pacific Standard Time initiative, that Chicana/o art started
receiving sustained attention.[9] The long-term and broader effects on collections, publications, and criticism are unknown, although the newest
installation of Pacific Standard Time: LA/LA (for Los Angeles and Latin
America), which is supporting three proposed exhibitions at LACMA in
2017, registers the transnational orientation that artists and scholars
have been using in Chicana/o art history and practice since the 1960s.

To understand the unfortunate erasure of Chicana/o art that originated within LACMA, I devote considerable attention to the museum's
reproduction of conventional policies and practices. This concern can be
applied to most public museums: How can an institution founded on the
disciplinary conventions of art history support, exhibit, collect, and interpret art that exceeds, complicates, or challenges them? I delve deeply
into LACMA's exhibition history to illuminate its paradoxical treatment
of Chicana/o art, not to attack a local institution that by other measures
is making important strides (the Latino Arts Initiative is one example),
but to understand the difficult conditions of inclusion if institutions
retain conventional categories and methodologies. By focusing on the
exhibition record, I expose fallacious claims made by the museum, and I
explore their meaning to show the historical linkages that are suggested
by the museum's rhetoric and to ponder what is or is not accomplished
by those connections.

During the years of the Chicano movement, LACMA hosted four exhibitions that conveyed the cultural and artistic heritage of Mexican
Americans: *Sculpture of Ancient West Mexico* (1970), *Los Four: Almaraz/
de la Rocha/Lujan/Romero* (1974), *Chicanismo en el Arte* (1975), and *Treasures of Mexico from the Mexican National Museums* (1978). Over a decade
passed before LACMA again presented art with cultural ties to the county's Mexican American residents. The first of these exhibitions, *Hispanic
Art in the United States: Thirty Contemporary Painters and Sculptors* (1989),

drew thirty thousand visitors in the first four weeks. Reservations for school tours for five thousand students were filled three weeks prior to the opening, and the museum began opening early on Wednesday to accommodate the tours.[10] The absence of political art, political realism, murals, and prints meant that the exhibition was not well received by scholars of Chicana/o art and cultural history (as I observe in chapter 2), but it nonetheless inspired Cheech Marin to collect and champion Chicana/o art. Two years later, *Mexico: Splendors of Thirty Centuries* mobilized a vast network of Chicana/o arts organizations that provided over a hundred supplemental programs during the exhibition's run and increased the Latino audience at LACMA. The museum failed to recognize the value of these developments and did not leverage or institutionalize the newly created network, reach out to the new audiences, or cultivate individual Chicana/o arts advocates.[11] These two exhibitions were followed by *A Tribute to Carlos Almaraz: Selections from the Permanent Collection* in 1992 and *¡Gronk! A Living Survey, 1973–1993* in 1994.

The county museum collaborated with other arts institutions, but it did not anticipate, lead, or advance public interest or scholarly endeavor in Chicana/o art. Of the four exhibitions in the 1980s and 1990s, three originated at other institutions and traveled to LACMA. The fourth, *A Tribute to Carlos Almaraz*, was a condition of a donation made by Almaraz's widow. LACMA did not create an infrastructure of curators, collectors, and donors that could have established a dynamic relationship between the museum and Chicana/o art. Is it unfair to expect a comprehensive museum in the county of Los Angeles to have an infrastructure that values Chicana/o art, its advocates, and its audiences?

*Master Works of Mexican Art*, the first exhibition to attract a significant Mexican American audience, is my starting point for investigating LACMA's engagement with Chicana/o art.[12] Between 1963, when the show opened at LACMA, and the turn of the millennium, social and civil rights movements transformed Mexican Americans into "Chicanas" and "Chicanos" and identified US expansion as an imperialist occupation. This dramatic moment of civic engagement and social unrest was followed by massive growth in the Mexican-heritage population and then, in the twenty-first century, by a new immigration reform movement. These events supported a critical consciousness that reimagined the temporal and spatial homeland of Mexican-heritage peoples and generated a profound transformation. Three decades of Chicana/o critical thought and action changed education, politics, health care, and labor relations in Southern California and beyond and positioned Chicana/o cultural production as something other than a national Mexican *or* American art. The exhibition of Chicana/o art in the Los Angeles area during this time produced new paradigms—namely, borderlands theory—and aesthetic vocabularies that are in wide circulation among Chicana/o artists and scholars (as I note in previous chapters). Nevertheless, LACMA has yet to alter its practices or policies to account for them.

This chapter remixes the exhibition record and art criticism with an emphasis on the early twenty-first century. The first section spotlights the ambivalent relationship that authorizing institutions have with Chicana/o art and artists. My analysis begins with *The Road to Aztlan: Art from a Mythic Homeland* (2001) because this exhibition exemplifies how LACMA battles its own historical and institutional context. Although *The Road to Aztlan* relied on new epistemologies and methods, it only temporarily influenced LACMA. Similar to *Master Works of Mexican Art* in 1963, *The Road to Aztlan* created a sense of inclusion for Chicana/o audiences and artists, but its success was not sufficient to establish an institutional track record for Chicana/o art at LACMA. An examination of the discourse surrounding *Phantom Sightings* in 2008—specifically, the language used to characterize the exhibition—shows that the innovations of *The Road to Aztlan* were soon forgotten.

The second section takes a closer look at the historical record, excavating new information about two exhibitions from the 1970s, *Los Four: Almaraz/de la Rocha/Lujan/Romero* and *Chicanismo en el Arte*, in order to understand LACMA's initial engagements with Chicana/o art. The museum's early productions reveal how and why a long silence ensued and the tacitly conveyed meaning in the new millennium when the art institution ventured into Chicana/o art exhibitions. I also remix the art criticism generated by *Asco: Elite of the Obscure* (2011) to bring attention to the erasure of LACMA's art historical accomplishments and the fragility of the visibility and legibility of Chicana/o art. The chapter ends with a consideration of *Los Four* in relation to a much earlier and largely undocumented exhibition, *4 Chicano Artists*. This remix proposes a new understanding of Chicana/o art. Like a sound engineer who returns to original master recordings to produce a clearer rendition of a song, I use remixing to bring new information to light, enabling a deeper and more accurate understanding of the art historical record.

Road Show

While chapter 2 provides a critical analysis of the shortsightedness of *The Road to Aztlan*, which opened at LACMA in 2001, here I remix the analysis to point to what the exhibition was able to accomplish and how it brought Chicana/o art into view using methodologies or frameworks long familiar in Chicana/o art history and exhibition practices.[13] A remix of *The Road to Aztlan* brings to the forefront Chicana critical thought—namely, the concepts of diaspora and *nepantla*. The historically and geographically comprehensive exhibition, which was curated by Virginia M. Fields and Victor Zamudio-Taylor, deserves additional attention because it was widely appreciated. Approximately 140,000 people saw the show, breaking exhibition attendance records.[14] Fields was largely responsible for pressuring the county museum to acknowledge the linguistic realities of local residents, and LACMA produced bilingual explanatory labels, free brochures, and other materials, just as it had for *Master Works of Mexican Art*.

Chapter 2 described how *The Road to Aztlan* traced an aesthetic tradition across national borders and temporal periods. This curatorial strategy required a dramatic departure from dominant art historical interpretations of Latin American, Chicana/o, and American art.[15] *The Road to Aztlan* was a crucial moment that promised a revision of art criticism because it reproduced important characteristics of Chicana/o art historiography. Sidestepping art historical conventions that are region- and nation-specific, or universalist, the curators employed the phenomenon of diaspora as a framework for concurrently presenting Mexican art (normally associated with Latin American art) and Chicana/o art (normally excluded from both Latin American and American art). In this way, *The Road to Aztlan* advanced the pedagogical concerns that had prompted Brown to bring *Master Works of Mexican Art* to Los Angeles. Both exhibitions acknowledged the dispersal of Mexican art and culture across national borders.[16] The "quest for Aztlan" represented in *The Road to Aztlan* also refused the binary distinctions between art and artifact, modern and ancient, and fine art and folk art. While these boundaries had been recognized and questioned in Mexican art history and were referenced in *Master Works of Mexican Art* by the presentation of historical artifacts, colonial art, folk art, twentieth-century graphic arts, and modern art, it was not until the 1970s that Chicana/o art critics and other scholars of subaltern aesthetics pointed out that the distinction between art and artifact, or between folk and modern art, is rooted in colonialism and racism.[17]

The Chicana/o art historical method was formalized in 1975, with the opening of the Mexican Museum of San Francisco. The museum abandoned the method of classifying art according to Western categories—designations that originate with colonialism.[18] The inaugural exhibition contained objects on loan as well as objects from the museum's permanent collection. Toys, ceramics, masks, and skeletons made in Mexico, some produced for tourism and others for community rituals, were displayed alongside colonial art and artifacts from the Spanish viceregal period (1521–1821) and paintings by contemporary Mexican and Chicano artists Robert Gonzales, Raoul Mora, Manuel Neri, Gustavo Rivera, Esteban Villa, and Manuel Villamor. The curatorial decision to display so-called unrefined, tourist, or traditional art (also known as lowbrow or folk art) with objects of the so-called approved styles—techniques and media in contemporary art that are accepted by art markets, curators, and critics—was groundbreaking. The Mexican Museum developed this new vision of Mexican and American art and institutionalized this new paradigm by structuring its permanent collection in the same way, classifying the art of pre-Columbian civilizations, colonial Mexico, contemporary Mexico, Chicanas/os, and *arte popular* within the heritage of Mexican America.[19] In the following decade, the National Museum of Mexican Art in Chicago initiated its permanent collection with nearly the same considerations, bringing objects from Mesoamerica together with art from colonial Mexico, contemporary Mexico, and US-based Chicana/o experience, as well as *arte popular* from multiple time periods.[20] These two accredited Chicana/o museums developed an infrastructure and a methodology for Chicana/o art history that were broad in scope, extending beyond national boundaries and time periods and resisting the distinction between folk and fine art by valuing objects produced with various intentions.

*The Road to Aztlan* worked to challenge the racializing effects of the categories "art" and "artifact" by exhibiting a range of objects that documented "the persistence and revival of native cultural practices throughout the Southwest."[21] For instance, one section titled "Survival and Translation: Contemporary Concepts of Aztlan" presented Rupert García's poster *Festival del Sexto Sol* (1974), two fiber basket trays from

Arizona (c. 1920), John Valadez's pastel *The Border* (panel 2, 1991–93), a ceramic bowl (c. 1925) by New Mexican artist Maria Martínez, and Yreina D. Cervántez's *The Nepantla Triptych* (1995), which is composed of three conceptual lithographs.[22] Together these objects staged the centrality of place and origin. Multiples (the poster and the lithographs) were placed alongside unique fiber baskets, unsigned works shared gallery space with authored ones, and Valadez's massive surreal drawing was exhibited with Maria Martínez's pottery. Absent were the hierarchal formulas that suggest a fixed social order, as well as the temporal classificatory schemes that separate contemporary art (post-1945), Chicano art (1965–75), and so-called commercial or conceptual art by Chicanas/os (post-1975).

I remix the curation of *The Road to Aztlan* to spotlight an approach to art history that developed outside LACMA because I wish to document the transformation within LACMA. For decades, cultural institutions to the east of LACMA had articulated a transhistorical and transnational sense of belonging in the Americas that reflects Anzaldúan borderlands theory and the concept of nepantleras—persons or practices that facilitate passages between worlds (see chapters 2 and 3).[23] Curators and art historians who consider artistic production through the lens of borderlands theory embrace a range of works (paintings, sculpture, pottery, prints), a full temporal and spatial scope (from ancient Mesoamerica to twenty-first-century America), and multiple artistic orientations (ritual specialists, colonial chroniclers, modern artists, to name a few).[24] Eurocentric art historical conventions, vocabularies, and paradigms were unsuitable for *The Road to Aztlan*. Although the exhibition followed a chronological path and promoted an evolutionary framework (see chapter 2), the design of the exhibition also indicated transhistorical and transnational depth, shifting art historical conventions that begin and end with national boundaries or collapse ethnic and racial differences. That is, *The Road to Aztlan* discursively announced and made visible new aesthetic vocabularies and paradigms through *Chicana/o* art.

My remix brings to the forefront the art historical scholarship of Constance Cortez. Drawing on the metaphor of nepantla because it engenders and supports multiple subjectivities without disavowing an artist's origins, Cortez shifts our attention to negotiation, transformation, and hybridity, characteristics that can more fully explain the transnational lives and aesthetics of the artists represented in *The Road to Aztlan*. If we follow the Anzaldúan framework offered by Cortez in "The New Aztlan: Nepantla (and Other Sites of Transmogrification)," her essay for the exhibition catalog, we see that *The Road to Aztlan* is much more than a visual exploration of the cultural production that emerged from the American Southwest and parts of Mexico. The border is a site of complex and creative tensions that strengthen resilience and the ability to live with cultural ambiguity and multiplicity. In this way, Chicana/o cultural production is constitutive, hybrid, and complex, an interpretation that directly challenges the view that Chicana/o art is inherently derivative, uniform, separate from larger social spheres, or anachronistic in its aesthetics. As Cortez makes clear, Chicana/o art finds inspiration in the Chicano movement, but the movement is not the only touchstone. "Intracultural diversity and personal visions" also inform aesthetic production.[25] This framework allows art historians, critics, and curators to acknowledge, and even anticipate, European or Asian influences on Chicana/o art (as I do in chapter 4) while retaining the category "Chicana/o art."

Perhaps in an effort to rethink the standard for identifying artists, Fields and Zamudio-Taylor state that Silvia Gruner and Javier de la Garza were born and raised in Mexico, Rubén Ortiz-Torres was born in Mexico but was educated in the United States, Thomas Glassford was born in the United States and is active in Mexico, and Roberto Gil de Montes, Enrique Chagoya, and the late Carlos Almaraz were born in Mexico and were (or still are) active in the United States. Several artists, such as Frida Kahlo, Ortiz-Torres, and David Avalos, were active in both countries.[26] By documenting the mobility of artists, the curators disturb nationalist sensibilities and shift the focus from Aztlán as a homeland to Aztlán as a transnational in-betweenness. Certainly, art historians and critics have grappled with artistic mobility for decades, but it is typically described at the individual level, as evidenced by France's claim to Pablo Picasso and Spain's rejection of the Andalusian artist during Franco's fascist regime. It is rare within art history to understand this diasporic movement as a social phenomenon, and it is unique for a mainstream arts institution to join aesthetic projects, specifically Mexican and Mexican American ones, across transnational space.

Nepantla can even enhance our understanding of migrational flows of people and aesthetics during earlier periods of cultural production. Discussions of an object's authenticity and purity can recede as an awareness of mutuality and reciprocity surface. More critically, nepantla can neutralize the homogenizing impulse of Aztlán, which "obscures or even ignores intracultural differences and differences within the community that are based on class and gender," as Cortez and other Chicana feminists have observed for decades. Cortez finds that "nepantla fulfills [the] need" to register gender and class as well as anticolonialism in the work of Santa Barraza, Yreina D. Cervántez, James Luna, and Armando Rascón.[27] The practice of nepantla exposes colonial racism and vertical social ordering, sex-gender privileging, and nationalism.[28] Finally, nepantla is a "site of transformation," and because of this, "the result of transformation is always secondary to the act."[29] Nepantla is foremost an engagement with potentiality; it is the attention to process that makes agency visible. Nepantla activates possibilities in a way that notions of Aztlán cannot, since the quest for the homeland is deeply tied to normative and nationalist expectations. This expectation is precisely what limits the work of Fields and Zamudio-Taylor: the visibility of Chicana/o art in *The Road to Aztlan* was dependent on their ranking it below Mexican art. Nepantla refocuses art criticism on hybridity, which blends hegemonic forms and processes with agency. Nepantla can therefore account for ambiguity, complexity, and contradiction—even the modernist impulse to foreground continuity with the past through a reinterpretation of aesthetic styles and approaches—in ways that nationalist or universalist art histories cannot.

The narrow conception of Chicana/o art that was presented in *The Road to Aztlan* was likely due to long-standing disciplinary boundaries. The exhibition originated with Fields, a curator of pre-Columbian art at LACMA and a leading scholar of Mesoamerican art and archeology; at the time of her death she was senior curator of art of the ancient Americas. For her co-curator, Fields was encouraged to invite Zamudio-Taylor, who at the time was an independent curator of Mexican art. Methodological and epistemological conventions of their respective fields do not consider Chicana/o art as subject. Their specific training would make it difficult to see how Chicana/o art exceeds conventional categories and boundaries in American and Latin American art. Despite this limitation, *The Road to Aztlan* was a vital intervention that brought Chicana/o art to critical attention as well as a huge audience.

With so much accomplished, it is curious that LACMA could not recall or activate the exhibition's contributions to art criticism several years later. This dismissal of a Chicana/o art historiography was produced by the rhetoric used to define *Phantom Sightings: Art after the Chicano Move-*

*ment*, which opened at LACMA in 2008. In contrast to *The Road to Aztlan*, *Phantom Sightings* was developed in LACMA's contemporary art department, and it was a collaborative effort of three curators: Rita Gonzalez, a performer, filmmaker, scholar of film studies, and assistant curator of special exhibitions at LACMA; Howard Fox, a curator of contemporary art at LACMA; and Chon A. Noriega, an interdisciplinary scholar of visual culture, curator, and advocate for Chicana/o art. Presented in multiple cities and conceived for multiple audiences, *Phantom Sightings* was described as the museum's "*first* comprehensive consideration of Chicano art in almost two decades and the *first* such effort at the Los Angeles County Museum of Art since the end of the Chicano movement of the 1960s and 1970s."[30] This claim was made in the press release and the introduction to the catalog, and it was emblazoned on the wall. It greeted museum visitors as they entered the exhibition. The proclamation has the effect of overlooking *The Road to Aztlan* and the curators' groundbreaking strategy of presenting contemporary Chicana/o, Mexican, and ancient Mesoamerican art together. The transformative contribution of the 2001 exhibition vanished. Why does *The Road to Aztlan* not count as "comprehensive"? The accolade for *Phantom Sightings* limited the borderlands paradigm to contemporary art "after the Chicano movement."[31]

LACMA appeared to be confounding its own message about Chicana/o cultural production. Even as it presented art that resonated with Chicana/o audiences, even as leading scholars and advocates joined its ranks as employees, even as it added a few works to its collection, and even as it attracted attention from a range of art critics, LACMA failed to fully acknowledge the existence and viability of a Chicana/o art and the ways it exceeds categories of "American" and "Mexican" art. The contested phrases "first comprehensive consideration" and "first such effort" may be celebratory terms for marketing or subtle points of critique, but the effect is devastating to the accomplishments of *The Road to Aztlan*. I do not argue that *Phantom Sightings* should have included work from various time periods. I am simply curious about the omission and the inability to account for nepantla aesthetics and experiences. For me, it makes a point about institutional boundaries and conventions and reveals what has typically been disqualified from the category of Chicana/o art.[32]

Perhaps these claims should be dismissed as simple marketing tools, since the catalog's foreword by chief executive director Michael Govan takes the expected celebratory tone and states that LACMA has hosted a number of notable exhibitions—including *Los Four* in 1974 . . . as well as *Hispanic Art in the United States: Thirty Contemporary Painters and Sculptors* (1989), *A Tribute to Carlos Almaraz* (1992), *Gronk! A Living Survey, 1973–1993* (1994), *The Road to Aztlan: Art from a Mythic Homeland* (2001), *Selections from the Cheech Marin Collection* (2008), and others.[33]

The marketing strategy does little to illuminate the museum's discursive or interpretive record regarding Chicana/o art. Nevertheless, it feels like window dressing because the record indicates minimal institutional change, even though Govan mentions *The Road to Aztlan*.

### Excavation of "Firsts"

Remixing is also fruitful when we look closely at the exhibitions that were tacitly proposed as precedents to *Phantom Sightings*. A closer look reveals that LACMA was ambivalent in its promotion of Chicana/o art of the movement. Two of the shows implicated in the introduction, *Los Four: Almaraz/de la Rocha/Lujan/Romero* (1974) and *Chicanismo en el Arte* (1975), originated elsewhere and the welcome mat was not completely unfurled.

LACMA curators did not organize an exhibition of Chicana/o art at the museum until 1992, with *A Tribute to Carlos Almaraz: Selections from the Permanent Collection*, and this exhibition resulted from circumstances rather than an institutional decision or vision to showcase Chicana/o art. Elsa Flores, Almaraz's wife and the executor of his estate, offered to donate seventy paintings, drawings, prints, and etchings to the museum and made the exhibition a condition of the gift.[34] No catalog was created for *A Tribute to Carlos Almaraz*, and the exhibition has become art world ephemera. A forthcoming retrospective funded by the Getty Foundation Pacific Standard Time: LA/LA initiative received media attention because of the gaps in the collection. The headline read: "The late Chicano artist Carlos Almaraz will get his biggest exposure at a 2017 LACMA exhibit, yet many of his *key works remain missing*."[35] Why does the curator, Howard Fox, need to track down the key works? Because comprehensive museums like LACMA have not been acquiring them. The donation and 1992 exhibition did little to change the institution.

The *Los Four* exhibition at LACMA also involved messy circumstances. It's the favorite "first" Chicano show in a mainstream museum, and this accolade is marketed consistently as LACMA's leadership. Yet *Los Four* was the result of a collaboration initiated in 1973 by Hal Glicksman, director of the University Art Gallery at the University of California, Irvine, who invited Gilbert "Magu" Sánchez Luján to curate an exhibition of Chicana/o art. The team that brought *Los Four* from Irvine and to LACMA's attention has not received sufficient acknowledgment, and their collaboration is consistently overshadowed by the triumphant declaration that LACMA premiered Chicano art. In the 1970s, alliances among regional colleges and universities flourished, and several institutions of higher education in California continue to be major venues for promoting Chicana/o art.[36] The focus on mainstream arts institutions undermines our understanding of venues outside the arts that have long-term relationships with Chicana/o art production.

After its run in Irvine the exhibition moved to LACMA, opening in February 1974 and including some additional works.[37] It is not an overstatement to declare that *Los Four* was a watershed moment in American art. It attracted twenty-eight thousand visitors to LACMA, a blockbuster at the time, and LACMA has been rightly credited with launching the success of the four credited artists—Carlos Almaraz, Roberto "Beto" de la Rocha, Gilbert "Magu" Sánchez Luján, and Frank Romero—as well as the uncredited fifth artist, Judithe Hernández, and John Valadez, who joined after the exhibition. They were subsequently invited to exhibit collectively and individually at museums and galleries throughout the 1970s and 1980s, and they found representation at several commercial galleries, including Daniel Saxon and B1, operated by Robert Berman. The success of the exhibition has been well documented.

The history that is not widely known, however, provides some cautionary notes. The exhibition arrived at LACMA after serious negotiation about its location and budget, and LACMA was not an ideal host. The exhibition was crowded into Lytton Hall of the Frances and Armand Hammer Wing, and resources for hanging the show were scarce. In fact, after requests for financial support to pay for an opening reception were ignored, the artists contacted a lawyer to pressure the museum for sufficient funds. California Law Center's Monroe Price, whose wife had been one of Almaraz's instructors at Otis, wrote to Jane Livingston, curator of modern art at LACMA, and explained the art collective's demands for equitable treatment and for bilingual educational programs, tours, and announcements for the show.[38] Linguistic relevance and educational programming were hallmarks of emerging Chicano arts institutions, and Los Four's insistence on these signature efforts indicate the artists' attention to the factors that distinguish Chicana/o arts from mainstream conventions. Los Four may have arrived at the county museum, but they were not welcomed into the institution as legitimate artists. The celebratory claims about *Los Four* overshadow the conflictive relationship LACMA had with the artists of Los Four even as they were admitted into its hallowed halls.

The history of *Chicanismo en el Arte*, the other proposed historical precedent for *Phantom Sightings*, also reveals LACMA's uneasy attitude toward Chicana/o art. *Chicanismo en el Arte* was a massive exhibition of more than two hundred works that originated at the Vincent Price Art Museum at East Los Angeles College. Thomas Silliman, curator and director of the museum, initiated the institutional collaboration that resulted in the exhibition. He was fully aware of the critical, urgent, and oppositional position of the Chicano movement and the radical desire of Chicanas/os for self-determination and liberation, and this was a fundamental premise of *Chicanismo en el Arte*. Silliman positioned the exhibition as a launch for Chicana/o aesthetics and as an effort to bring attention to artistic activity in East Los Angeles, particularly at Goez Art Studios and Gallery and Mechicano Art Center. Silliman had been in contact with Mechicano cofounder Leonard Castellanos since 1971, and Castellanos was a member of the curatorial team.[39]

After its premier at the Vincent Price Art Museum, *Chicanismo en al Arte* made its way to LACMA, but it was greatly reduced in size—now only seventy works of art—and very different in tone. While the original design of *Chicanismo en el Arte* embraced ethnic-specific art and politics, the county museum described the exhibition differently. Whereas Silliman drew on discourses of relevance, accountability, and quality, LACMA promoted the art for art's sake and disavowed the ethnic referent. A press release quotes Jeanne D'Andrea, the coordinator of exhibitions and publications at LACMA, who was part of the curatorial committee and author of the catalog essay. She states that "as a whole, these works by Chicano student artists not only demonstrate a high degree of vitality and technical accomplishment, but they frequently manifest involved attitudes toward 'lo Chicano' that avoid many of the visual clichés often associated with social commentary or protest in twentieth century art."[40] This claim positioned the exhibition as evidence that political or representational styles were passé precisely at the moment that they were developing among Mexican American communities. The rush to dismiss "social commentary or protest" as it was unfolding was unfortunate for the Chicano movement and its artists. It was as if Chicana/o art, at least the political type, never had a chance.

## Remixing Asco

A remix of LACMA's exhibition history requires attention to one of the most successful presentations of Chicana/o art, *Asco: Elite of the Obscure, A Retrospective, 1972–1987*, which opened at LACMA in September 2011. Folded into the Getty Foundation's Pacific Standard Time initiative, the retrospective presented over 170 works that represented the range of Asco's work: video, sculpture, painting, collage, correspondence art, performance and exhibition ephemera, and photography, some of which "double[d] as documentation and art."[41] The exhibition also explored the development of the group's aesthetic and the individual ventures of Asco core members Patssi Valdez, Harry Gamboa Jr., Gronk, and Willie Herrón III, as well as some of the fluid group of artists who joined the collective in the 1980s for one or more projects, including Barbara Carrasco, Diane Gamboa, and Marisela Norte. Curators Rita Gonzalez of LACMA and C. Ondine Chavoya, scholar of art history and Latino studies at Williams College, offered a critical orientation—namely, the aesthetics of poverty—to interpret the work of Asco and its use of vernacular materials and "make-do" tactics.[42] As critic Annie Buckley observed, the show captured "Asco's wide-ranging work: the simultaneous humor and seriousness, the costumes pieced together from what was on hand, the drama and the bravado, and perhaps most important, the layering of social, political, cultural and personal agendas into one exuberant and idiosyncratic event."[43]

Deliberately employing the display conventions of fine art exhibition, the curators hung elegantly framed photographs of Asco performances with generous space between the images. Indeed, the photographs in *Asco: Elite of the Obscure* were received as fine art. A wide range of reviewers praised the exhibition and the abbreviated traveling shows that developed from it, with art criticism appearing in local, national, and international venues in English, Spanish, and Italian. While some of the reviewers focused on Asco's style—the hair, boots, makeup, and funky costumes—allowing an admiration for fashion to masquerade as art criticism, most critics paid serious attention to the exhibition. It was named "Best in [Los Angeles] Art, 2011" by *Los Angeles Times* critic Christopher Knight, and it received the same ranking in *Artforum*'s annual review of international highlights by critic and independent curator Michael Ned Holte. The exhibition and the praise were long overdue.

A closer look at the criticism, however, suggests that Chicana/o art was dismissed even as Asco was praised. As with *The Road to Aztlan* and *Phantom Sightings*, the discourse surrounding *Asco: Elite of the Obscure* both expresses triumphalism and effects erasures, adding up to a compromised visibility for Chicana/o art. After an examination of the accomplishments of *Asco: Elite of the Obscure*, I remix the discussion surrounding the exhibition by focusing my analysis on the befuddled critics. Art criticism is an important barometer for assessing the reception of Chicana/o art, and the critics' responses to *Asco: Elite of the Obscure* reveal that they had only a patchy understanding of the art they were sent to review. More important, the remix suggests that broader hegemonic forces are at play in art historical discourse. The miscomprehension of Chicana/o art is systemic; it is not simply an error found at LACMA or perpetuated by specific individuals. The methodological limitations of American art history and criticism as well as museum structures make it difficult to see Chicana/o art as "art" and as "Chicana/o."

As Rita Gonzalez tells it, the making of the Asco retrospective took ten to fifteen years. She did not mean that the two curators had spent more than a decade planning the exhibition (although they had been working together for several years).[44] The proposal for *Asco: Elite of the Obscure* had been folded into the county museum's exhibition schedule shortly after LACMA hired Gonzalez in 2004. Her comment locates the show within a web of interests and events that made the exhibition possible: the growing number of art historians conducting research on Chicana/o art, the archival initiatives at several universities and public institutions, and a new focus on contemporary art, particularly as expressed by the Pacific Standard Time initiative, which supported research, exhibitions, and art criticism, and the development of new art histories, about cultural production in Los Angeles.[45] Her comment was also an oblique reference to the quiet pressure generated by the growing number of Chicana/o artists, scholars, and arts advocates, which had captured LACMA's attention in the new millennium. The backlash against mul-

ticulturalism that had developed at LACMA in the 1980s and its con-
comitant defense of artistic "quality" as well as the rejection of outreach
programming for Mexican Americans were administrative decisions that
were becoming more and more untenable. In response, LACMA made
some calculated gestures toward change by hiring Gonzalez and com-
mitting to the multiyear collaboration with the UCLA Chicano Studies
Research Center that produced the Latino Arts Initiative.

By their own account, Gonzalez and Chavoya presented *Asco: Elite of
the Obscure* as a compensatory practice inside a mainstream museum.
The show was intended to "make Asco more well known," as Gonzalez
stated during tours of the exhibition, and to illustrate the group's contribution to American and European art, particularly to the avant-garde
movements in New York and Zurich and Dadaist uses of photography,
performance, and ready-mades. This corrective to the archive, popular
knowledge, and the art historical canon, particularly the conventional indexes of Chicana/o art, allowed buried or unrecognized arts to surface
and come into view. Although compensatory visibility is laudable, by reinforcing similarity over difference it typically reinforces the status quo
and can obscure important contributions. Gonzalez and Chavoya accomplished much more. By highlighting the anti-homophobic and anti-sexist
practice and politics of Asco, orientations that are frequently overlooked
by compensatory scholarship, they introduced a major rethinking of
Chicana/o art. The exhibition documented the queer aesthetics and interventions of Gronk and his collaborators Cyclona, Jerry Dreva, and Mundo
Meza, and the ways that Patssi Valdez and other women who joined Asco
for certain projects—Barbara Carrasco, Teresa Covarrubias, Diane Gamboa, and others—performed multiple challenges to patriarchy and gender
norms. *Asco: Elite of the Obscure* was simultaneously an introduction to
the collective's work and a significant revision of Chicana/o art history,
at least for artists, scholars, and advocates of Chicana/o art. Nearly sixty-
two thousand visitors witnessed this new analysis of Asco, although it is
unknown how many understood the exhibition's importance because the
backstory is largely undocumented. Several art critics apparently missed
the main point, since they never mentioned it in their reviews.

Chavoya and Gonzalez offered a substantial reinterpretation of Asco's
art. As they note in the introduction to the catalog, "The reception of
Asco's work has circulated more as rumor than as documented historical account."[46] Within Los Angeles Chicana/o communities, the group

has been widely described as an artist group that was not sufficiently Chicano in style or attitude and whose work was irrelevant to cultural politics and communities because of its avant-garde aesthetics. Two interviews reproduced in the catalog document the uneasy relationship between Asco and muralists, particularly those associated with Mechicano.[47] The interviews also suggest that Asco's style was inaccessible or immaterial to Mexican American residents of Los Angeles, particularly during the height of the Chicano movement. Yet the exhibition brilliantly argued that the work, while cutting-edge, is not removed, inaccessible, or unimportant to Mexican American residents. The curators convincingly situated the collective's artistic practice as a deliberate engagement with the Chicano movement. This reinterpretation of Asco's production was integral to the exhibition's design and was a central argument in the catalog essays.

Asco used avant-garde art forms such as conceptual and performance art to call for redressing the minoritized and racialized status of Chicanas/os. To illustrate this, the curators hung photographs of the group's performances throughout the exhibition. Several images of *Stations of the Cross* (1971) were displayed in the first gallery, introducing audiences at the outset to Asco's "ritual of remembrance and resistance against the deaths in Vietnam."[48] *Stations of the Cross* had ended with the artists' effort to blockade the door to the Marine Corps recruitment center in East Los Angeles, evidence of the group's political engagement with the Chicano movement in Los Angeles. My own introduction to their revisionist approach came during Gonzalez's tour of the exhibition, in which she explained in detail Asco's political activism and critical consciousness, recounting specific performances and how each articulated central issues of the Chicano movement.

More radically, the curators argued that Asco's public performances were not simply political interventions but alternative methods of mobilizing residents of East Los Angeles to protest not only the disproportionate numbers of Mexican Americans dying on the frontlines in Vietnam but also the normalization of police brutality and the harassment of East Los Angeles residents, the undereducation of Chicana/o youth, gang violence, and other forms of community destruction. Another major issue concerned claims to public space, which Asco addressed in *Walking Mural*. Performed in 1972, the piece was a response to the city's decision to cancel the annual East Los Angeles Christmas parade as part of a clampdown on public assembly following the Chicano Moratorium. *Walking Mural* was "the group's effort to bring a parade back to Whittier Boulevard."[49]

*Three Causes of Death* (1976), whose photo documentation appeared in the second gallery, offers a fine example of how art and politics were inextricably linked for Asco (fig. 6.1). In 1976 the collective used the public celebration of Día de los Muertos to bring attention to violence within Chicana/o communities. The annual procession organized by Self Help Graphics & Art became a vehicle to provoke the residents of East Los Angeles to account for community self-destruction. Asco members joined the procession costumed as "a switch blade, a pharmaceutical drug, and a hypodermic needle," and they were accompanied by a "collection of young boys roped together and made up to look like zombie Cholos."[50]

Similarly, the curators reframed Asco's No Movies—works that combined performance and documentation—within the Chicano movement's "overall project of self-representation," including muralism. No Movies, which "crystallized in 1973" and continued into the 1980s, criticized institutions (particularly the Hollywood film industry) that excluded Chicanas/os.[51] To their documentation of Asco's political activism, the catalog essayists added analyses of Patssi Valdez's and Gronk's anti-patriarchy along with Gronk's and Humberto Sandoval's cross-dressing as a challenge to heteronormativity. (Sandoval, an occasional member, was noted for his customized platform boots.)[52] The exhibition incontrovertibly described Asco's work as political art. This view also pushes against the conventional reading of conceptual art as an art form that exists outside social affairs.

*Asco: Elite of the Obscure* serves as an important critique of postethnic art exhibition. The retrospective corrected, as Harry Gamboa Jr. notes, the limitations implied by "Art after the Chicano Movement"—the subtitle to *Phantom Sightings*—by reinserting "Chicano" as a modifier into the discourse about art during a moment of intense anti-Mexican sentiment.[53] This was of course a grand triumph over the established practice of using normative criteria to develop collections and exhibitions, a tactic that has made Chicana/o art invisible. But it is the use of the term *Chicano* as grounds for visibility that makes the intervention so significant for art criticism. The members of Asco fully embraced their "Chicano" identification as an aesthetic practice and strategy. Their politically charged conceptual and performance art constitutes a historicizing

**6.1** Ricardo Valverde, *Three Causes of Death*, 1976. Color slide. Esperanza Valverde and Christopher J. Valverde Collection. Image by El Sereno Graphics. Reproduced by permission of the Valverde Estate.

project in which "Chicano"—the descriptor—no longer represents an essentialist position. Rather, it describes connected aesthetic phenomena in Mexico and Los Angeles (and even New York, the apparent center of the American avant-garde art); interweaves gender, sexuality, and class; and reveals racial containment as a ruse of power, not democracy. As Arlene Dávila notes, "Manifestations of ethnicity and cultural difference within a given state are never entirely free of its dominant ideological canons."[54] Artists who came of age during the Chicano movement had been cast as cultural producers whose works were predetermined expressions of a binding heritage. They were presented as either incapable of cultural synthesis or stuck in a bygone era in which interests were focused on parochial or regional concerns. With *Asco: Elite of the Obscure*, engagement with European movements and contemporary avant-garde trends in California and New York appeared not as selling out but as a mobilization that willingly hybridized the resources at hand.

I continue this remix by spotlighting Jesse Lerner, who subtly changes the discourse about Asco's relationship to muralism in his essay for the

*Asco* exhibition catalog. As Gonzalez notes in the exhibition catalog, the rumors or undocumented art history of Asco portray the collective as opposed to muralism in Los Angeles, ignoring the fact that three of the four original members created murals. Lerner cogently argues that "muralism is not simply a straw man for the founders of Asco" and brilliantly demonstrates that "muralism inhabits a contradictory position for these artists." In many of their performance pieces, he notes, Asco members "situate themselves within" muralism even as they offer criticism about the content of Chicano murals. Performances such as *Walking Mural* (1972) and *Instant Mural* (1974) are "haunted" by muralism. Lerner observes that this "point of reference" is also evident in Asco's Super-8 films, where the moving images become an alternative to muralism. Lerner's analysis reveals the "filmic response to and activation of muralism" and highlights the public accessibility that Asco found relevant in murals. Lerner concludes that "Asco did in fact work in the street and in plain daylight, though the strategies they chose were very different" from those who painted murals on the Eastside. Rather than rejecting the public art form, Asco circulated it in the streets of Los Angeles. The artists' willingness to situate themselves within the history, practice, and method of muralism, especially in relation to its public accessibility, forces a reconsideration of the art criticism that states that Asco opposed the form even though its members are on record for their critique only of the content of LA murals. In Lerner's hands, the "restrictive binaries that stultify"—the dichotomous interpretations of Asco's performances— fade into a nuanced placement that does not require pitting the collective against everyone else—or, at least, the older muralist set.[55]

Lerner's perspective also prompts us to reconsider the range of exhibitions that have depended upon a binary interpretation of Chicana/o art. Essentialist rhetoric, which insists on a distinction between authentic subalterns and postethnic assimilated artists, cannot account for the ways that Chicana/o artists are trained and how they are collected and exhibited within authorizing arts institutions. In his foreword to the exhibition catalog, LACMA director Michael Govan notes that even if Asco were to be "institutionalized or neutralized" by the exhibition, as some might argue, that condition would not diminish the group's innovations or influence.[56] In fact, Asco's institutional critique and the institutionalization of its work have always been simultaneous. Harry Gamboa Jr. did not go to LACMA to inquire, for instance, about the exhibition of

Chicana/o art in 1972 simply because he wanted to spray-paint the museum's exterior; he was primarily interested in inclusion inside its walls.

The critical rereading of Asco presented in the exhibition and the catalog was not sustained in the initial reviews. Perhaps I cannot legitimately lament the fact that this major revision of Chicana/o art history was lost on the art critics who were unaware of Asco's largely undocumented designation as "not Chicano enough." The authorizing arts institutions in the region had not kept current with the developments in Chicana/o cultural production, and art critics would have had to dig deeply for primary material about Asco, although the catalog includes reproductions and reprints of several interviews from the 1970s. Nevertheless, the effect was disturbing because these critics overlooked the history of Chicana/o art and, worse, Asco's political interventions were used to celebrate the collective at the expense of all other Chicana/o artists.

Christopher Knight's review in the *Los Angeles Times* is a prime example, one that follows a current trend in American art history that finds politics and identity distasteful. While praising Asco, he used his review as a platform to dismiss the Chicano art movement and ethnic-identified art in general. He accomplished this by admiring

one great feature of the group's early years, . . . [namely,] how assertively stylish the artists are in the abundant photo-documentation. Posing like bored fashion models around a grungy Malibu . . . drainpipe [as seen in *Ascozilla/Asshole Mural* (1975)], Asco put the chic in Chicano. Some of it comes from turning up the heat on clichés of Hollywood glamour; some from post-Pachuco wardrobes; some from the mannered codes of gay drag and punk and more.[57]

Calling this a "savvy" strategy, Knight interprets Asco's "high-style attentiveness to fashionable presentation" as "healthy artistic ambivalence" toward not only the Chicano movement but also "socially engaged Chicano artists in the politically minded 1970s" and "any organized campaign" of art. By calling Asco's style "healthy," he shows his disapproval of "organized" Chicana/o art and its "politically minded" strategy or aesthetic. Knight used Asco's work to legitimate his attack against ethnic-specific art, political art (or art of politics), and the critical "campaigns" that Chicana/o artists used to intervene against the art museum system.[58] For Knight, Asco's choice to dress up put it at odds with the

Chicano social movement and its cultural politics. He positioned Asco's style as an expression of discontent with the mobilization and solidarity tactics of Chicana/o artists and activists who were calling for public accountability, representation, and inclusion within the museum and art gallery establishment.

In the review Knight notes that Asco's style allowed the collective to avoid the "limitations" of the Chicano art movement, which, "like any other" mobilization, inevitably formed "idealized self-perceptions, claims for legitimacy and [a] creed of acceptable and unacceptable aesthetic propositions." This repurposing of Asco high fashion functions as a warning to other artists who dare to consider claims for legitimacy and subjectivity. "Asco's artistic queasiness was partly directed toward those limitations [of the Chicano art movement], as well as toward easier objections about the larger culture."[59] In narrowing the terms of visibility for Chicano art, Knight successfully neutralized the case for Asco's radical politics that is so cogently argued by Lerner.

My point is that the terms of visibility are so tenuous that structural gains within authorizing spaces such as museums are difficult to achieve. Yes, Asco has been presented in new ways within American as well as Chicana/o art history, but the advances are very easily bruised or brushed aside by the cultural hegemony that drives American art criticism. I wonder how many serious studies—Knight described the exhibition catalog as an "academic slog"—will be needed to gain the attention of curators, critics, and scholars across the nation.[60] Since mainstream arts institutions are already decades behind in the area of Chicana/o art criticism, museums such as LACMA must double their research efforts and continue to partner with institutions and collectives that are already constructing and debating Chicana/o art scholarship. If groundbreaking advances are overlooked by reviewers or curators who have not done their homework or who are unwilling to reconsider their Eurocentric epistemologies, then where and how can we expect change? Curators must rethink the disciplinary assumptions that further support the bracketing of their own methods as primary without giving due acknowledgment to others. LACMA's inability to institutionalize the advances of *The Road to Aztlan* is a clear example of the tenuous relationship between Chicana/o art and mainstream museums.

When I asked Harry Gamboa Jr. in 2011 about the media and curatorial attention to Asco, he quoted an observation he had made in 1999 about his experience as an artist in an elitist system: "I look at that carrot and it looks a little spoiled to me. I'm not exactly allergic to carrots but the way it's dangling. It just—it doesn't look right. It should be at least on a plate."[61] The allegory of the carrot in an anemic state suggests that Gamboa has not lived a life of luxury, or even economic sufficiency, even as he has received international attention generated by the success of *Asco: Elite of the Obscure* and *Phantom Sightings*. Since 2008, he has been invited to lecture or exhibit his work in France, Mexico, England, Belgium, and Switzerland, and his work has been reviewed in regional media outlets in Los Angeles, New York, London, Paris, Mexico City, and Milan, as well as national outlets in Spain, Italy, and the United States. In 2013 Gamboa was invited to lecture in Nottingham, England, in conjunction with the opening of *Asco: No Movies* at the Nottingham Contemporary.[62] Despite the international acclaim, Gamboa continues to teach at California State University, Northridge, and serve as codirector of the photography and media program for California Institute of the Arts. The exhibiting museums, LACMA included, have not collected his work.[63]

Likely mindful of this paradox as it unfolded during the Getty Foundation's Pacific Standard Time initiative, Gamboa exposed and challenged the art historical attachment to authenticity as well as the co-optation of his work through a deft intervention against LACMA and the Getty. He approved two versions of his photograph of *Instant Mural* (1974), a performance in which Gronk taped Patssi Valdez (and later Humberto Sandoval) to a wall. One version portrays Valdez facing left and the other depicts her facing right. The Getty Foundation received the image with Valdez facing right for its massive Pacific Standard Time marketing campaign and reproduced it in advertising that appeared across the region on buses, ATM terminals, and placards, and in its media release and exquisitely designed VIP announcements. Meanwhile, LACMA presented Valdez facing left for the exhibition.

When curators pursued the question of the original, Gamboa claimed that it had been lost or destroyed; whether print, slide, or negative, it was no longer in his personal archive. Gamboa sidestepped every attempt to establish one version as original, claiming he could no longer recall how he took the shot. Shrugging, he noted in the language of art history that what the curators considered a problem was simply a consequence of working with reproductions. By refusing to participate in the effort to establish authenticity, Gamboa subverted notions of value and legitimacy—hallmarks of curatorial practice. More relevant to the artist were intention, style, and process. Gamboa's irreverence for authenticity was an intervention that affected LACMA's representation of Chicana/o art.[64]

## Coda: 4 Chicano Artists and a Remix of Los Four

When we remix the exhibition record of Chicana/o art in Los Angeles, another art history comes into view, one that has the potential to reconfigure Chicana/o art criticism. Toward that end, I offer a final reshuffling of the exhibition record, this time at a distance somewhat removed from LACMA. This reconsideration demonstrates the benefits of remixing. It is a methodology that changes our orientation, allowing us to achieve a new understanding of Chicana/o cultural production.

In 1970 Josine Ianco organized 4 Chicano Artists, one of the first Chicano art exhibitions on a Southern California college campus. It opened at the Fine Arts Gallery at California State University, Los Angeles, in 1970, moved in 1971 to California State University, Dominguez Hills, and then returned to Cal State LA later that year.[65] Ianco, who was then the director of the Cal State LA gallery, brought together the work of Carlos Almaraz, Leonard Castellanos, Robert Gómez, and James Gutiérrez.[66] An iconoclastic curator, Ianco selected works that for the most part fit squarely within the West Coast minimalism, finish fetish, and light and space movements. The artwork expressed the artists' interest in abstract forms and sensory perception, particularly through the use of reflective finishes and illumination. Ianco demonstrated the artists' connection to regional styles, but she did so without forgoing the term Chicano, as she seemed to understand the ways these nonwhite artists maneuvered among multiple identities and aesthetics.

The exhibition secured significant reviews and media attention (fig. 6.2). Some commentators, however, missed the point.[67] Art critic William Wilson could only see "urban Latin ghettos" as the influence for Gutiérrez's "cast polyester and lucite sculpture" with its "arrangement of clear geometric solids clearly abstract-optical in tone" or Castellanos's "colored sculptural cubes."[68] They were not examples of the light and space movement in Los Angeles. He could not place Castellanos in the context of his teacher, Conner Everts, whose decomposing forms and deconstructive style likely influenced Castellanos's drawings of "black

# Chicano Art Show Opens On Campus

The works of four Chicano artists are on exhibit in the Cal State L.A. Fine Arts Gallery. The exhibit, which opened Sunday, will continue through Nov. 26.

The artists are Leonard Castellanos, a graduate of CSLA who gave direction and advisement on the exhibition, Robert Gomez, also a CSLA graduate, Charles Almaraz, who once attended CSLA, and James Gutierrez.

A reception for the artists and special guests, Nov. 1, will officially open the exhibit.

"This show is not going to be the typical Mexican girl with a flower in her hair," said Josine Ianco, gallery director. "These are all artists. It doesn't matter what their ethnic origins are."

The artists are expressing their background but not in a stereotyped way, Miss Ianco said.

Two of the artists will display more than one period in their development, said the director.

"I think the artist, as he develops, goes through stages, and I see these stages as waves," commented Miss Ianco. "An artist pursues an interest up to a point and then tires of it."

She said that even an unsuccessful wave, or phase, contributes to the artist's development, for he uses the knowledge gained in exploring the next "wave."

The works can be seen Monday-Thursday, 10 a.m.-4 p.m. and Sundays 1-5 p.m.

## Season Tickets For Playhouse Available

CHICANO ART---This untitled work by Leonard Castellanos is currently being displayed at the Cal State Fine Arts Gallery together with the work of three other Chicano artists. The exhibit, opened Sunday and will run through Nov. 26.
(C.T. Photo by Tad Swida)

6.2 1970 campus newspaper review of *4 Chicano Artists*, with detail of untitled work by Leonard Castellanos. Image courtesy of John F. Kennedy Memorial Library, Special Collections, California State University, Los Angeles.

geometric shapes on white grounds . . . suggesting worms, sperm, offal and clouds."[69] In contrast, Mildred Monteverde recognized Castellanos's Los Angeles sensibility. In a scholarly essay on Chicana/o art that included an analysis of the exhibition, she noted how the artist "juxtaposes abstract images, often gorgeously bright figures against ominous heavy forms in a special environment."[70] Gómez's "complex, box-like forms," constructed from photo-engraved glass, had images that "merge, mirror, or disappear."[71] Monteverde also found contrast in the works by Almaraz: although two earlier canvases were "in the character of the minimalist school," his later work registered "an abrupt change of style and iconography." In this work, he "fill[ed] the composition with animated figures and graffiti-like forms, with no consideration for illusionistic scale."[72] The textual gestures and figures of this work resonated with Dadaism in a negation of the regional styles shown in the other works in the exhibition. Largely forgotten by art historians, *4 Chicano Artists* demonstrated not only that Chicana/o art was engaged with contemporary regional (and national) trends but also that Chicana/o artists were pushing beyond those interests.

Permitting *4 Chicano Artists* to serve as a new index for Chicana/o art offers opportunities for reassessment that can reveal aspects of Chicana/o art history that have been hidden. In this remix, the early exhibition replaces *Los Four*, which for some time has provided the baseline by which Chicana/o art has been evaluated. Applying the new index to *Chicanarte*, another exhibition curated by Ianco, is illustrative. *Chicanarte* was a major exhibition of over a hundred artists that was presented at the Los Angeles Municipal Art Gallery in 1975, after Ianco became the gallery's curator. Although it is frequently referenced as foundational for establishing the political aesthetic as the so-called obligatory style of Chicana/o art, another aspect of the exhibition comes into view when it is considered in light of *4 Chicano Artists*. The works in *Chicanarte* incorporated diverse styles and eclectic approaches, as reviewer Frank Sotomayor observed: "A wide spectrum of painting is included, from classical to contemporary and abstract. In some, the Chicano stamp is heavy, in others subtle."[73] A small sample of works suggests that the art was not predictable. According to Gamboa, Jack Vargas exhibited an intertextual piece that engaged conceptual concerns about difference and belonging. Using a Rolodex file, Vargas invited viewers to perform different identities, including a queer and a Chicano, by reading prepared texts printed on index cards.[74] Gamboa's *Colonial Failure Kit* was a minimalist installation of two chained chairs and cinematically arranged photographs. Yreina D. Cervántez's watercolor *La Muerte de Artemio Cruz* was a collage of images without a horizon or a continuous narrative. Teddy Sandoval's *Dear Ted*, a color intaglio of a woman resting against a larger-than-life phallus and testes with an orchid, aimed for the erotic, a style that continues to be silenced within Chicano art history. Carlos Bueno's *El Chicano*, a portrait in ink on mat board, had psychedelic flourishes in the background and foreground. Similar to Sandra de la Loza's *Action Portraits* (2011), which makes visible a range of mural aesthetics, my remixing of the exhibition record and bringing *4 Chicano Artists* to the foreground allows a range of styles within *Chicanarte* to surface.

Using *4 Chicano Artists* as an index for Chicana/o art also allows for a rereading of *Los Four* that considers it in terms of conceptual and abstract art. This revision enriches the usual narrative of the exhibition as iconographic, an interpretation that relies solely on the figurative and narrative works that were displayed, or as an unmediated cultural reflection presented within a mainstream art museum. In this new view, the urban calligraphy—graffiti—that appears in the exhibition might be a reflection of gestural art, Dadaism, abstract expressionism, or pop art. This is not a stretch, since Almaraz was included in both exhibitions and the artists of Los Four trained at local colleges and universities and worked in graphic design.

More to the point, the exhibition catalog for *Los Four* serves as an example of the artists' ease with a wide aesthetic range. A simple accordion-style booklet designed by Frank Romero, it is closer to an artist book than the usual exhibition catalog (fig. 6.3). Its content evokes postmodern techniques of sampling and remixing, and it participates in the antinarrative stance of conceptual and Dadaist art since it contains no essays and no captions; apart from the title, date, and location of the exhibition and short biographies of the artists, it has no text. On monochromatic pages, each printed in one of four colors, Romero arranged a collage of family photographs mixed with snapshots of the collective's art. The catalog's emphasis on saturated color recalls color-field painting and depicts the colorist style of the group. It also recognizes the intentions of Dada: "to destroy visual and textual homogeneity, to emphasize the materiality of the signifier over a presumed universal legibility of either the textual or iconic signified." This rupture with the "very fabric of legibility," when voiced by the explicitly racialized Chicano artists, extends the Dadaist principle to their work and implies a critique of Eurocentric notions of a universal aesthetic and the role of museums in fostering the myth.[75] When the index shifts to Ianco's exhibition, the *Los Four* catalog resonates less as a work of documentation, representation, and figuration and more as a modernist and postmodernist reexamination of aesthetic traditions of the West. This assessment is particularly valid when we consider the avant-garde printmaking techniques that produced the folio.

The new index also remixes how art historians have assessed *Los Four*. The exhibition featured two collaborative murals on canvas and art by the individual artists. Among these were works on paper, canvas, and tortillas; woodcuts and lithographs; and assemblages. The artists designed the installation of the art, and they modeled the space in a salon style, echoing the history of museum display and vernacular modes found in Chicana/o households. They also collaborated on altar-like assemblages, using ready-made objects and their own art. The eclectic presentation was dense and energetic, and it undermined the value modernism assigns to the unique genius, even as the art and its installation drew upon impressionism, abstraction, figuration, and surrealism. One of Magu's works, titled *Lowrider's Regime* in the exhibition checklist, is burned

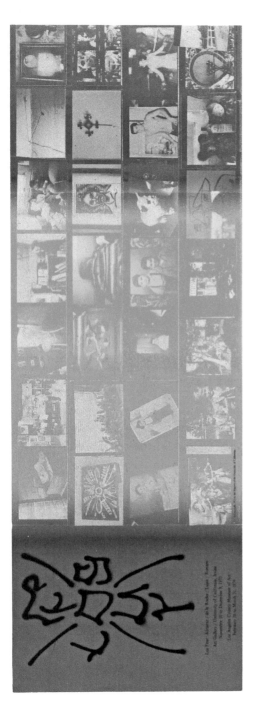

Figure 6.3
*Los Four*
catalog,
designed
by Frank
Romero,
1974.

into my memory. The front end of a Chevy lowrider was surrounded by an arrangement of everyday objects, including Mexican masks and religious statues, and the wall behind was inscribed with spray-painted graffiti.[76] Magu's blending of aesthetic forms—pop, folk, and lowbrow art—challenged the Western tastes that degrade such things. The analyses that followed *Los Four* and the favoritism that was subsequently showered on the members of the collective resulted in an overly limited aesthetic that became widely known as "Chicano art," even though multiple styles were present in the exhibition and continued to surface in the work of Chicana/o artists.[77] Using *4 Chicano Artists* as a new point of reference for Chicana/o art exposes not only the biases of LACMA but also those of Chicana/o art history.

# CONCLUSION

## Chicana/o Day at the Museum

W hen exposing and interrogating the discourse on Chicana/o art, it is difficult to shift to closure: the methodology of remixing the discursive and historical record supports exploration and reconstruction. It requires intellectual nimbleness, as remixing shifts one's methods across disciplines, and it invites new investigations. Similarly, borderlands theory works against fixedness and prescription. Sandra de la Loza participates in this practice of exploration and even refusal of the definitive image of Chicana/o art, and she reminds us of Tomás Ybarra-Frausto's discussion of rasquachismo, "to name this sensibility, to draw its contours . . . is to risk its betrayal."[1] Something must be withheld to avoid the appropriation of Chicana/o art, specifically because the category "Chicana/o" is both monolithically defined and held in doubt by some scholars and curators at this particular moment. The paradox of its supposed existence and its narrow construction is lost on its critics, who tend to codify difference. This final chapter is an experimental effort to refuse codification and to reaffirm the rethinking that I have proposed as a new methodology. This methodology requires us to continually modify the terrain of the field not only by returning to the archive of Chicana/o art but also by expanding it. It is a vibrant methodology that emerges from the art practice itself and that asks us to rethink the questions and reorient the findings that have traditionally animated the fields of art history and Chicana/o studies. We must seek ongoing reexamination in order to bring to the surface that which has been rendered invisible within American, Latin American, and Chicana/o art histories. As Sandra de la Loza conveys through *Action Portraits* (2011), we must see the process of remixing the archive as a critical act.

At the same time, it is important to reiterate in these closing pages that remixing emerges from a decolonial imaginary. I have not reconsidered Chicana/o art discourse simply to make it suit the conventions that have been employed in American, Latin American, and Chicana/o art historiographies and methodologies; rather, remixing is a tactic for accounting for the historical context of Chicana/o art while dislodging hegemonic notions of art and identity, especially those that have done little to bring Chicana/o art into focus. I have argued that it is untenable to imagine a moment when visual art will move beyond issues of identification. However, this position does not assume that every visual expression is an explicit focus on identity: artists withhold and obfuscate social signifiers, but they also intertwine them. This intermixing complicates the normative view of artists of color as prescribed, unmediated, and nearly without agency. I have turned to an intellectual genealogy of borderlands theory and decolonial imaginaries rather than American art history or visual cultural studies to argue that nonwhite artists, specifically Chicanas/os, and the art attributed to them are complex and multidimensional. Binary thinking cannot account for this complexity.[2] By remixing the archive and excavating new information, I question the social and cultural dimensions of American art history—specifically its unnamed cultural codes, privileging of whiteness, masculinity, and European heritage. Indeed, the making of history—the formation of a new historiography that shelves the Eurocentrism of American art history—affords us the pleasure of agency.

I offer three tales to support a call for art histories and epistemologies that move beyond hegemonic concepts of nation and the racist, sexist, homophobic, and materialist impositions of modernity. Scholars in other fields have referred to these alternate endeavors with the terms *trans-American studies*, *transmodernism*, and *trans-Americanity*. From Gloria Anzaldúa we have learned that they spring from "mestiza consciousness" and "borderlands theory." They appear when the subject of Chicana/o art is historicized. To shift our perspective, I begin with a remix of Graciela Iturbide's 2007 exhibition at the Getty Center, an account grounded in the pleasure of viewing East Los Angeles cultural production. Next is a story about another type of "day at the museum," one that occurred at

Avenue 50 Studio and that evidences the increasing cultural authority among Chicana/o artists and advocates. I end with a remix of the Getty Foundation's Pacific Standard Time initiative that looks at other spaces of unprecedented, yet relatively unrecognized, activity in Chicana/o art. While it may appear that I am having a bit of fun at the expense of the Getty, my aim is to outline another art history, one that is expansive, inclusive, and allows for a "convergence of extremely diverse modes of cultural production."[3]

## Chicana/o Art Smuggled into the Getty!

In December 2007 the Getty Center presented a survey exhibition of more than thirty years of photography by Mexican artist Graciela Iturbide. *The Goat's Dance: Photographs by Graciela Iturbide* displayed the artist's major series of photographs, which were taken in Mexico and the United States. These series included La Frontera (The Border); Juchitán; La Matanza de la Cabras (The Slaughter of the Goats); and East L.A. The last one in particular held the attention of Chicana/o Los Angeles.

The East L.A. series was originally produced for the book *A Day in the Life of America*, an initiative of the Kodak Corporation. In 1986 Kodak invited two hundred international photographers to document the quotidian of US experience. Kodak provided film and travel expenses and required the photographers to work within the same twenty-four-hour period—hence, a day in the life—to capture in specific towns and cities across the country what the book identified as a typical American day. Even in 1986 such a claim was loaded with expectations about "America," and the project produced a paradoxical space that both supported the status quo and embraced a new citizen-subject through a large-format photography book.

Breaking two rules specified by Kodak, Iturbide spent four days taking photos rather than one, and she chose East Los Angeles, a neighborhood location rather than a city or town. Determined to push boundaries, she photographed a community of deaf Chicana/o youth who lived in an area known as White Fence because it was the territory of the White Fence gang. Her ability to reach and photograph this particular community was facilitated by Chicana artist Margaret Garcia, who was asked by several parties to assist Iturbide in selecting and gaining entrance into a Chicana/o community. At the time, Garcia was working at the Los Angeles Photo Center and was identified by Self Help Graphics cofounder Sister Karen Boccalero and others as the ideal liaison for the Mexican photographer. Once Garcia agreed to help, she knew immediately where she would send Iturbide and to whom she would introduce the photographer. Garcia appreciated Iturbide's "compassionate eye" and knew she would see the youth "as human beings, not just as models or subjects." Iturbide could be trusted not to reproduce the "method of photojournalism. . . . They shoot from their car, sort of like a drive-by!"[4] It was Garcia, therefore, who conceptualized a project about East Los Angeles deaf youth who sign as a method of communication and not simply as gang affiliation. She negotiated the introductions for Iturbide and implicitly supported the photographer's exploration of the White Fence gang and their Chicana/o community for the Kodak project.

The portraits by Iturbide express her unique photographic eye through their high contrast and intense compositional focus. They struck a chord with LA Chicana/o residents, who flocked to the exhibition at the Getty Center. Even without knowing Garcia's role in the project, audiences appear to have understood the transnational triangulation that connected the Mexican photographer, the Chicana artist, and the Chicana/o neighborhood.[5] Facilitating the transnational visual exchange were the photographs that included well-known murals in East Los Angeles. Although the murals were backdrops to Iturbide's iconic portraits of the White Fence members, a major contingent of visitors to the Getty exhibition viewed the murals not as background but as subject. Indeed, during the exhibition, audiences familiar with Chicana/o art and culture congregated around the photographs that included the murals and community landmarks.

Returning to the gallery over several days, I witnessed an energy in the room. As I listened to visitors conversing in Chicano English, Spanish, and Spanglish, it became apparent that from the perspective of these men and women, who announced their Chicana/o identification with East Los Angeles by recognizing its landmarks, the exhibition was not simply the work of a Mexican photographer: it was a display of Chicana/o art. Chicana/o museum goers congregated in the gallery presenting the series East L.A., commented on and debated the images—and created headaches for the docents and security guards by gesturing or looking too closely at the photographs. These viewers not only shifted their bodies in ways that signaled a breach of protocol to museum security, they

**7.1** Graciela Iturbide, *Cholos, Harpys, East L.A.*, negative 1986; print 1990. Gelatin silver print, 29.8 x 41.9 cm. (image), 40.6 x 50.8 cm. (sheet). The J. Paul Getty Museum, Los Angeles. Gift of Susan Steinhauser and Daniel Greenberg. Image courtesy of ROSEGALLERY. © Graciela Iturbide.

also shifted the perspective that had been conceived by the curator and the museum. They came to witness Chicana/o art.

The freestanding wall placed just inside the entrance to the gallery containing the East L.A. series featured *Cholas, White Fence, East L.A.* (negative 1986, print late 1990s), a photograph of four women and a baby signifying before a mural of Emiliano Zapata, Pancho Villa, and Miguel Hidalgo y Costilla. It became an energizing space of critical contemplation, autohistoria, and counterhegemony.[6] Other works in the gallery also generated intense discussion and alternative interpretations of the place and people. *Cholos, Harpys, East L.A.* (1986, print 1990) is a mural-like composition that captures the shadows of four young men as they raise their hands above their heads, making ambiguous gestures that fall between American Sign Language and the street signals of gang affiliation (fig. 7.1). The shadows hug the walls in the same type of linear figurative composition frequently used in early Chicano murals. Another photograph showed a young man standing before an unfinished mural of

Guadalupe; her iconic outline appears to hover over him as he rests gently against the wall. The composition is familiar to tattoo artists as well as to residents of Chicana/o Los Angeles, who understand that a portrait of Guadalupe is tattooed on one's back to provide protection. For visitors to the exhibition, however, the Guadalupan image behind the young man had additional meaning: it is a celebrated Chicana/o mural.

Several of the images on display portrayed White Fence residents positioned in front of murals, but one in particular invites a remixing of Iturbide's work as Chicana/o art. *Cholos, White Fence, East L.A.* not only mimics mural figuration but strategically places residents of East Los Angeles within the mural composition (fig. 7.2). The photograph depicts a group of men and women and one child in a tight cluster, arms interlocking and hands joining in sign. Iturbide tricks the eye, however: what appears to be a group of seven is in reality a group of five standing in front of a mural. This photograph was the focus of intense discussion and visual scrutiny. Visitors challenged each other to identify the artifice. I observed how people approached the photograph for closer inspection, and I watched their pleasure in discovering that the two men at the back of the group are painted figures. Iturbide also incorporated two other elements from the mural into the photograph: a classic lowrider car and a second group of figures, all blended seamlessly into her composition. With the help of Margaret Garcia, Graciela Iturbide had smuggled Chicana/o art into the Getty.

As an audience, we were elated and empowered by our presence inside the museum. In the gallery of East L.A. images, strangers chatted with strangers, and crowds formed near each photograph that included a mural. Families urged their young children to look closely at the photographs, identifying buildings and other architectural features. It was their home, their neighborhood, and their cultural community captured in black and white photographs and mounted on the walls of one of the most prestigious institutions in the region. An alternative and perhaps oppositional gaze was engaged the moment the viewers recognized the murals as Chicana/o art. This engagement was not accomplished by the Getty Center, which had yet to recognize Eastside murals as any kind of art. The viewers' pleasure was based on a remixing of art history that shifted the focus of the photographs and on the fact that Iturbide was, at least by extension, a Chicana photographer. It was a profound, affective response to historical amnesia and the critical erasure of Chicana/o art.

7.2 Graciela Iturbide, *Cholos, White Fence, East L.A.*, negative 1986; print 1990. Gelatin silver print, 11 2/3 x 17 1/3 inches. Image courtesy of ROSEGALLERY. © Graciela Iturbide.

We kept coming back to the exhibition, according to one tour guide, and we hung around those photographs of East LA murals.

This clandestine accomplishment was underscored and reinforced as an active revision of art history during the Getty Center's supplemental events for the exhibition. At each of the presentations designed to complement the exhibition, the audience appeared to be overwhelmingly composed of Mexican American residents of Los Angeles, judging from the number of people I recognized and the way the audience responded to Chicano English, Spanish, and Spanglish. The first event, held in the Harold M. Williams Auditorium on January 8, 2008, was an interview with the photographer conducted by poet, art historian, and curator Roberto Tejada. As a colleague of Iturbide's, Tejada skillfully directed a lively conversation in Spanish before a packed house of Chicana/o residents, some of whom made use of the simultaneous translation to English. Margaret Garcia and her niece, who had been photographed in 1986 by Iturbide, were in attendance, as were many people affiliated with the arts and scholarship of Chicana/o cultural production in Southern California.[7]

Each event felt like a special celebration designed specifically for us. The feeling of inclusion reminded me of the occasions in my childhood when Disneyland was reserved for Dodger fans or Los Angeles County employees. With the theme park closed to others, we had the entire place to ourselves. It was not simply that the lines were shorter or that we did not have to navigate thick crowds; it was the pleasure of knowing that the whole place was exclusively for us. For this reason, I use the phrase "Chicana/o Day at the Museum" to refer to the experience at the Getty, because it reminds me of the excitement we felt when we were designated as special recipients of an experience, when our sense of belonging was made more solid by a claim to space. It was a physical and spiritual emplacement.[8] The experience at the Getty was "accompanied by an important affective element": everyone was proud of Chicana/o Day at the Museum—Chicanas and Chicanos and the Getty alike.[9]

The triangulation that linked the Mexican photographer-cum-Chicana artist with the East LA murals and the exhibition produced a relational position that allowed visitors to gaze on the photographs of East Los Angeles *as* Chicana/o art. In this way, the photographs were visual records of Greater Mexico, the transnational and transhistorical space that embraces the wide-ranging cultural sensibilities of the Americas, extending in this case to Los Angeles. The visitors who came to Chicana/o Day at the Museum embodied, through their gazing, their pleasure in gazing, and their presence, the transnational and transhistorical subjectivity so eloquently described by Gloria Anzaldúa as mestiza consciousness. They looked at Chicana/o art as a form of cultural production that does "much more than illustrate the agenda of a social protest movement." They saw the photographs as also "push[ing] in other directions, mak[ing] other connections, and participat[ing] in other worlds."[10] The photographs embodied what "Chicana/o" has meant for the artists, curators, collectors, and advocates who are at the heart of this book.

I wish to emphasize, however, the more practical border crossing to which mainline museums must be attentive. My intention in retelling this tale is to alert mainstream museums to the preparations that they must undertake if they are to thrive in the twenty-first century as the Chicana/o population continues to grow. The success of Chicana/o Day at the Museum signals that we are not attached to our exclusion, victimization, or loss, although critics of identity politics propose that we are.[11] The Getty Center and other arts institutions in the region must not only allow Mexican Americans to cross into the sanctuary of interpretation, they must invite their participation. An infrastructure of art historians, curators, critics, publishers, and funding agencies is necessary to support the growing interpretive power of Chicana/o residents. As I witnessed at the exhibition of Iturbide's photographs, Chicana/o audiences will make Chicana/o art visible in ways that the conventions of American art history cannot imagine.

## Cultural Authority and Horizontal Inclusion

Another story is worth noting especially because it records demographic shifts in the audience as well as conceptual discernment and cultural authority among Chicana/o arts institutions. Two exhibitions, *Resurrected Histories: Voices from the Chicano Arts Collectives of Highland Park* (2012) and its counterpart, *Mapping Another L.A.: The Chicano Art Movement* (2011), provide evidence of the closing gap between cultural resource and cultural authority. In most cases, Chicanas/os and Latinas/os have been incorporated into exhibition development as a cultural resource: Chicana/o artists and scholars are invited to the table as consultants for specific projects within mainstream museums and arts institutions, or Latinas/os are hired within the education and outreach departments to increase membership at mainstream museums. But this limited investment does not change the methods and practices that perpetuate the invisibility of Chicana/o art. Produced by Avenue 50 Studio, *Resurrected Histories* was in conversation with *Mapping Another L.A.*, an exhibition at UCLA's Fowler Museum and one of four components of *L.A. Xicano*, which was developed by the UCLA Chicano Studies Research Center and funded by the Getty Foundation's Pacific Standard Time initiative. Artists, cultural workers, and scholars were invited to collaborate on *L.A. Xicano*, including Sybil Venegas, curator of *Resurrected Histories*, and me. *Resurrected Histories* and *Mapping Another L.A.* were equally invested in cultural resources, and it was the presence of people such as Venegas in both spaces—a public university and a community-based art gallery— that indicates the rising cultural capital of Chicana/o arts centers and the critical force of the errata exhibition in generating new sites of cultural authority in Los Angeles.

*Resurrected Histories* opened on January 14, 2012, and ran concurrently with *Mapping Another L.A.* during the final weeks of the Fowler show. Venegas chose a title that would indicate the exhibition's restorative position. *Resurrected Histories*, a retrospective exhibition, was a form of critical witness presented in paintings, drawings, graphic arts, photography, publications, archival documents, and ephemera produced at Mechicano Art Center and Centro de Arte Público. The two shows pointed to the growing critical discourse and cultural authority generated by Chicana/o arts institutions. Various people participated in the formation of *Mapping Another L.A.*: artists such as David Botello, Barbara Carrasco, Richard Duardo, Judithe Hernández, Kathy Gallegos, Joe Rodriguez, and Reyes Rodriguez; arts advocates such as Armando Durón and Gallegos, director of Avenue 50 Studio; and intellectuals who had participated in the Chicano movement, such as Margarita Nieto and Sybil Venegas. Their experiences and perspectives, particularly their private archives and oral histories, were essential to the exhibition's formation. The conversations between the curators, staff, and participants of the two shows reveal how the terms of visibility and an investment in social change articulated by errata exhibitions since the 1970s had entered public space—or at least the space of the local public university.

*Resurrected Histories* and *Mapping Another L.A.* shared a curatorial strategy—to collaborate with artists and arts advocates—and told similar stories. The Fowler exhibition surveyed "artifacts and artworks from nine Chicano arts groups active between 1969 and 1980," and *Resurrected Histories* focused specifically on those in Highland Park.[12] Crucially, both exhibitions recorded the multiple collaborations among Chicana/o artists. This information challenged the long-held assumption within Chicana/o art history that groups such as Asco and Los Four were antagonistic simply because their styles were different. The exhibitions illustrated the lively cross-generational network of artists and the fluid membership of the arts centers and collectives. Both exhibitions valued documentation, bringing to the forefront the forgotten or underrecognized parts of the archive.

The social, political, personal, and aesthetic networks in Highland Park were vividly portrayed at Avenue 50 Studio in *Resurrected Histories: Voices from the Chicano Arts Collectives of Highland Park*, a video documentary directed by Abel Mora Alejandre, and in the installation *Highland Park, Late 1970s: Web of Connections* (fig. 7.3). The video and the three-dimensional interactive installation created by Alejandre and Venegas visually registered "the connections between East Los Angeles and

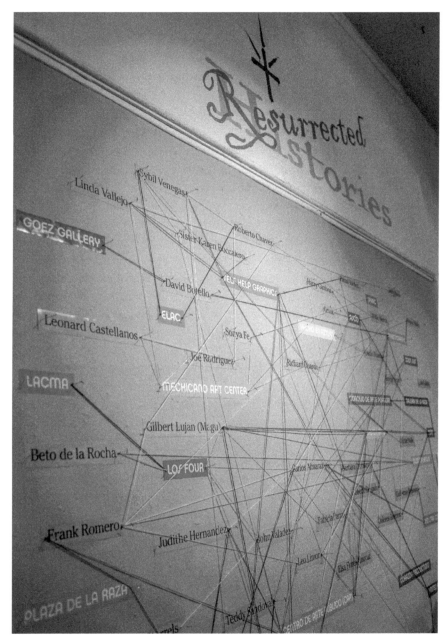

**7.3** Sybil Venegas and Abel Mora Alejandre, *Highland Park, Late 1970s: Web of Connections* (detail), 2012. Installation for the exhibition *Resurrected Histories: Voices from the Chicano Arts Collectives of Highland Park*, Avenue 50 Studio, Los Angeles, January 14–February 5, 2012. Image courtesy of the artists.

Northeast Los Angeles Chicano art centers, art collectives, and artists . . . to document the social and professional interactions among Chicana and Chicano artists working in this genre in the late 1970s." Color-coded yarn linked individual artists, such as Carlos Almaraz, David Botello, Barbara Carrasco, Leonard Castellanos, Roberto Chavez, Roberto "Tito" Delgado, Richard Duardo, Sonya Fe, Elsa Flores, Dolores Guerrero, Judithe Hernández, Leo Limón, Patricia Parra, and John Valadez, to groups and organizations such as Asco, Centro de Arte Público, East Los Streetscapers, Mechicano Art Center, Self Help Graphics & Art, and SPARC, as well as to largely undocumented Highland Park groups such as Aldama House, Chisme Arte, Corazon Productions, and Hecho en Aztlán. The chart also included arts administrators, art historians (such as Shifra M. Goldman), and writers (such as William Bejarano), as well as "intellectuals involved with this community."[13] Additionally, the artists' connections to California State University, Los Angeles City College, Otis College of Art and Design, United Farm Workers, and other California arts organizations were chronicled. This complex network deepened during the course of the exhibition, as visitors added new lines of yarn to trace relationships.

The web at Avenue 50 Studio functioned as an erratum to similar maps created to tell the history of art in Los Angeles for Pacific Standard Time.[14] The gap in received LA history was most apparent in the Getty Map posted on the official PST website, which gave the impression that Chicana/o artists, institutions, collectives, and studios did not exist (fig. 7.4). Although numerous flags on the west and north sides of Los Angeles signaled the locations of artist studios, collectives, organizations, and happenings of the 1940s through the 1970s, nothing appeared on this map for East Los Angeles. The tragedy is that the Getty Foundation funded *Mapping Another L.A.*, which resurrected the work of Goez Art Studios and Gallery and Mechicano Art Center, among others, from archival records and oral histories. Information that had been excavated because of Getty financing did not translate into public education and knowledge production designed by the Getty. In this case, conventional art historical and museum practices caused the erasure of the very subject that funders elected to investigate.

The victory for Chicana/o cultural production was realized in the dialogue and collaboration that shifted an exclusive claim to cultural authority to a form of horizontal inclusion. Public museums maintain their cultural capital by keeping community-based arts organizations at bay

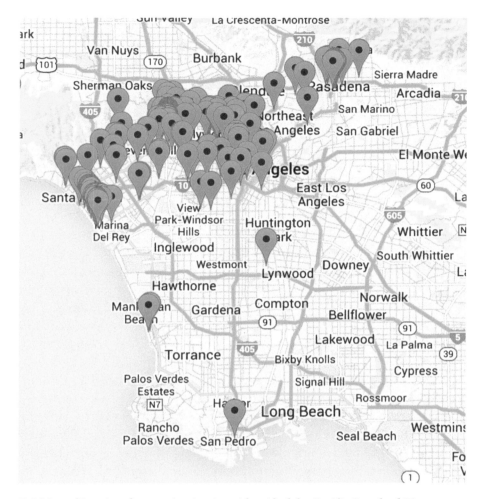

7.4 Map of Los Angeles arts institutions identified for Pacific Standard Time initiative. "*Pacific Standard Time* at the Getty." Map data © 2014 Google, INEGI.

through circulation, reproduction, and the staging of racial differences. *Resurrected Histories* and *Mapping Another L.A.* collapsed this fable of cultural authority as each exhibition attracted a similar Chicana/o audience, articulated a similar message about the rich collaborations among artists, reinterpreted the contributions of Chicana/o art, and valued both artistic production and archival material.

Furthermore, the two exhibitions staged the artists' use of a historicizing frame that theorizes resurrection and documentation as structurally and materially informed. A historicizing paradigm is most vividly portrayed in the documentary *Resurrected Histories*. Director Alejandre allowed the speakers to turn again and again to the contemporary moment as they recounted the past. As several artists noted, their current and past resistance to the onset of gentrification in Highland Park is part of their lives as artists: politics and art are intertwined and cannot be separated. They also connected the long moratorium on murals (1992–2013) in the city of Los Angeles and the current graffiti abatement program of the county of Los Angeles to the censorship and rejection they faced in the 1970s. The whitewashing and obliteration of public art was interpreted as an ongoing strategy against Chicana/o expressive culture and its claims to belonging. The artists engaged in social proprioception: always aware of the relative location of art and their art-making community, they insisted on their social location. What Alejandre documents in the video is the way that artists demanded a historicized interpretation of their strategy for making Chicana/o art and making art visible. Their historicizing frame recognizes a politics of aesthetics. In short, the two exhibitions, *Resurrected Histories* and *Mapping Another L.A.*, demonstrate that Chicana/o artistic agency, not the work's appearance or its intent, is a vital framework for understanding the art.

Throughout this book I remix the archive of Chicana/o art and, by extension, reconstruct American, Latin American, and Chicana/o art histories. I recognize that it is difficult to understand the visibility of a body of work that is disputed, and therefore I explore the conditions of visibility that emerge from Chicana/o cultural centers and the strategies of position taking that are available to racialized artists on the margins of critical discourse and art historiography. The strategies and criticism of Chicana/o art are largely formulated through errata exhibitions—sites that critically document, represent, and give witness to polymorphic aesthetics rather than predetermined and rigid notions of art, culture, and identity. Errata exhibitions are oppositional spaces that intervene in arts discourse by reimagining the field and openly reconsidering the structures of representation while subverting Western aims of representation. The errata exhibition is fundamentally aware of the context of racial invisibility and misrepresentation.[15]

Correcting our theoretical and empirical blind spots is an ambitious project. It looks to arts institutions for a radical reconsideration of commerce and art. It takes seriously the aesthetic influences of Europe and Asia on Chicana/o artists as well as the collecting practices in private Chicana/o homes, suggesting that these experiences articulate a transnational and transhistorical sensibility. It remixes the accomplishments of major institutions like LACMA and finds that Chicana/o art criticism has a precarious position within these places. In short, it tacitly implies a rethinking of Latin American and American art history.

Anzaldúan epistemology, I suggest, is central within Chicana/o art historiography because it allows from the outset the possibility of polyvalence, complexity, and hybridity. It emphasizes process and relationality so that meaning can emerge from engagement and can transform over time and space. Operating as a counternarrative to modernist thought, Anzaldúan epistemology is not anxious about its origins or authenticity as it transforms and crosses new cultural spaces. Therefore, this epistemology operates historically; it is historically contingent without apology, to borrow a phrase from Chicana feminist Edén Torres. This is its most useful lesson. It does not obligate the artist or the work to forgo its name even as the terms of visibility account for the conditions that gave rise to its invisibility.

As I wrote this book, the apparatus that orchestrates interpretations of Chicana/o art—the terms of visibility and invisibility—frequently immobilized me. The epistemic strategy to discredit identity politics disavows the question "What is Chicana/o art?" It is also difficult to leave behind the hegemonic hold and convincing force of the bifurcating categories of Western thought; I feared I would slip unknowingly into binary thinking. The disavowal of identity, as Linda Martín Alcoff notes, illogically assumes that identity creates the reification problem (which results in obligatory categories for art) and creates racial thinking. Normative racial thinking presumes that no one with a marked identity—whether that is nonwhite, nonmale, non-Christian, and/or nonheterosexual—can think rationally. Alcoff observes that these assumptions do not "correspond" to lived experience. There is nothing within the "real epistemic and political implications" of identity that creates the problems of reification or irrationality.[16] However, by focusing on identity as the problem, as the source that supposedly prohibits aesthetic transcendence or relevance, the art world can dismiss its own culpability in the omission of Chicana/o art and other artists with subaltern identities. Mainstream museums, curators, art historians, and critics—the infrastructure of the American art world—may not have been signatories to the "racial contract," to borrow Charles W. Mills's term for racial stratification in the United States, but they have been beneficiaries of it.[17]

As cultural anthropologist Arlene Dávila observes, the tenets of nationalism and racialization maintain that any position other than assimilation and acculturation results in disharmony and disunity in the nation, and therefore those who are not fully integrated pose a national threat. Difference threatens the core myths of American homogeneity, exceptionalism, authenticity, and security. The demands for the termination of identity frameworks cannot be reconciled with the rights-based strategies of belonging that guide democracy. In this way, the American ideology of assimilation provides within the idiom of culture a strategy of political stability and containment. From this perspective, visual production is merely the deliberate activity of individual artists who work unfettered by historical processes. Any insertion into the historical moment, such as the naming of Chicana/o art, or feminist or black art for that matter, is compared with the unexamined universal aesthetic and classified as "difference." The apparatus for the terms of visibility requires the hegemonic view that culture is unmediated for those who are classified as Other. Within this apparatus, Chicana/o art can never be considered as American art, and, ironically, it is this difference that disqualifies its insertion into the category of Latin American art. Therefore I turn, with several others in fields as diverse as literature and anthropology, to borderlands studies, arguing that through this lens, the terms of visibility are not dismissed, but are manifest, acknowledged, and critically engaged as sites, spaces, and practices of Chicana/o art that negotiate between and against nations in a third space or a decolonial imaginary.

In the fifty-year period I examine, Chicana/o artists, arts organizers, and collectors have tirelessly invented strategies for making Chicana/o art visible. I share one final story to further illustrate the terms of visibility and the vibrancy of Chicana/o art. This story is about the recent historic exhibitions of Chicana/o art in Los Angeles and how they convey terms of visibility that reflect a decolonial subjectivity and criticality. I do not refer to the six exhibitions that were part of the Pacific Standard Time initiative. While no other city could boast such a rich and well-funded exhibition season of Chicana/o art within mainstream institutions, these recent historic presentations of Chicana/o art were generated *and* maintained elsewhere. I posit that Chicano-landia had been making history long before PST and will continue to do so long after the artistic and economic stimulus package of PST has faded.

I point to a historic moment in Chicana/o art when the Vincent Price Art Museum (VPAM) at East Los Angeles College opened its fall 2013 season with three solo exhibitions of Chicana/o artists: *When You Sleep: A Survey of Shizu Saldamando*, curated by Karen Rapp; *La Luz de Germs*, a site-specific installation by Germs (Jaime Zacarias); and the traveling exhibition *Santa Ana Condition: John Valadez*, which originated at the Museum of Contemporary Art San Diego in La Jolla. The moment is unprecedented for multiple reasons. First, it is significant that VPAM had the gallery space, curatorial expertise on staff, and budget to produce three solo exhibitions of Chicana/o art in one season. It is likely the only institution in the region able to do so.[18] Not even *L.A. Xicano* could claim so much real estate at the Fowler Museum in 2011.

Second, the shows were solo presentations of individual artists, not a survey—the most common method in Chicana/o art exhibition practice. The quantitative and qualitative aesthetic force necessary to present a solo exhibition is significant, requiring a consistently powerful oeuvre from which to select a focus for the curatorial exploration. That VPAM presented two emerging artists and one midcareer artist is a testament to the vibrancy of the local arts community and its aesthetic accomplishments.

Third, VPAM staff produced two of the shows, not a team of consulting experts who were paid modest commissions to produce essays and exhibition designs, as with PST. Even though *Santa Ana Condition* did not originate at VPAM (its only Los Angeles stop), Karen Rapp and museum manager Victor Parra were able to significantly redesign the exhibition to fit spatial constraints. Their important changes tightened the focus of the exhibition on the artist's photography and on car shows as source material. At VPAM the exhibition emphasized the artist's process, not art historical categories or a chronological presentation of his work, as in La Jolla. Fourth, each show was accompanied by a catalog, ensuring its presence in the art historical record and etching a path in the long-term memory of scholarly discourse.

Finally, the works on display were overwhelmingly borrowed from private collections. Although Rapp and Parra wished to avoid presenting works that were owned privately—an art museum convention intended to separate scholarship from the market—it was difficult to do so with the work of Valadez and Saldamando. For the refit of *Santa Ana Condition*, several drawings and photographs were omitted, but building a visual narrative required the addition of drawings and paintings owned by Cheech Marin and other collectors. The Saldamando show also relied on works from private collections. Because the artist had recently emerged onto the art scene and had been participating in group exhibitions since 2000, more than half of her works were from private collections. Even the installation by Jaime Zacarias included recent works already acquired by private collectors.

These exhibitions are witness to the importance of private collections in the face of institutional disregard. Private collections are the main source of Chicana/o visual arts preservation (as I argue in chapter 5). In addition, the number of works from private collections evidence that the art scene has entered new territory, especially when these three exhibitions are compared to the major exhibitions of the twentieth century. *Chicano Art: Resistance and Affirmation, 1965–1985*, for example, largely displayed works that had been lent by the artists. *When You Sleep* also documented the roots of and routes to Chicana/o art collections. Most of the works in the exhibition had already been acquired by private collectors through Tropico de Nopal Gallery Art-Space, which had presented Saldamando's solo exhibition in 2007. Chicana/o arts institutions are essential to the infrastructure of Chicana/o art production, circulation, and marketing (as I posit in chapters 2 and 3), and these historic exhibitions further underscore this observation.

The three exhibitions—*When You Sleep, La Luz de Germs*, and *Santa Ana Condition*—anticipate the Getty Foundation's initiative for PST, LA/LA (Los Angeles/Latin America). Although the plans are still unfolding as this book is being written in late 2015, the Getty proposes that this new round of PST will explore "the artistic connections between Los Angeles and Latin America, the relationships between Latin America and the rest of the world, the history of exchange among Latin American countries, [or] the Latin American diaspora."[19] The call appears a bit belated, as the transhistorical and transnational art historiography has been registered through Chicana/o art exhibition since the late 1960s and VPAM has been presenting such work since the 1970s. The solo exhibitions discussed above each demonstrate different types of connections between Los Angeles and Latin America: Valadez conceptualizes a form of magical realism identified with Latin American literature; Germs incorporates Mexican and Chicano popular iconography; and Saldamando embraces her own mestizaje, a cultural mode made evident by Mexican philosophers, artists, and critics, but revised by Chicana feminists such as Saldamando. The Getty seemed to have a limited understanding of this transnational discourse when it kicked off the new initiative with a symposium on the topic and its speakers were all East Coast Latin Americanists and art historians from Latin America. Only one local Latino scholar, Chon A. Noriega, made it onto the panel, and he was invited to introduce the event, not present his research. As several artists and arts advocates noted, the symposium could have taken place anywhere. The "Los Angeles" in the LA/LA dyad was missing.

As curator and independent scholar Terezita Romo argues in her assessment of the first Getty initiative of 2011, the producers of art historical knowledge can no longer hide behind universality:

> In this era of Obama and the "post-race" discourse, many would like to believe that we have moved beyond the need for the identity politics of the 1990s, which they equate with an art that sacrificed aesthetics and quality for the sake of political statements. I would argue that all art has *always* been—and still is—about identity politics, but it has been hidden behind notions of aesthetic universality and artistic purity, otherwise known as "art for art's sake."[20]

Since the 1960s, Chicana/o visual art has evidenced a hybridity that is historicized. I join Romo in calling for systematic reflection about the terms of visibility within art history. Without a sustained effort, its methods, paradigms, and theories will be exposed simply as taste, or as the essential qualities of what "makes" "America" "great" for Donald Trump, which values but does not name white supremacy.

*Chicana/o Remix: Art and Errata since the Sixties* calls for an infrastructure that is fundamentally an interrogation of art history, but it is an infrastructure that can sustain transformation at all levels. It advocates a remixing and rethinking of archives, exhibitions, collections, and museum practices. It calls for new curators, trained in new ways, who can publish their interrogations, insights, and expansions of art history in journals, books, encyclopedias, community media, and global outlets that value identity-based art. It demands conferences and other public venues that support debate even as Chicana/o art withholds its name. These venues must be able to sustain our efforts as we grapple with ambiguity, obfuscation, and complexity—the most generative aspects of Chicana/o cultural production.

PREFACE

1 The oral history method created a gap in my research because my selection of artists privileged those who had been active within an arts organization, allowing me to corroborate personal memories with institutional histories.

2 The Smithsonian Institution has a significant archive of interviews, but the individual interviews with Chicana/o artists focus on specific questions and time periods, and the process of transcribing the interviews did not include collaboration with the artists. The CSRC Oral Histories Series was designed to archive an enormous amount of information that could support future scholarship, curation, and acquisition of Chicana/o art. A fragment of that information is used in this book, and thus I invite scholars and students to access the oral histories at the UCLA CSRC Library, www.chicano.ucla.edu.

3 See Peña, *Performing Piety*; and Foley et al., *From Peones to Politicos*.

4 Shifra M. Goldman was the originator of *Arte Chicano*. See the Shifra Goldman Papers, CEMA 119, California Ethnic and Multicultural Archives, Special Collections Department, Davidson Library, University of California, Santa Barbara (hereafter cited as Shifra Goldman Papers). The unprocessed papers with relevant evidence of Goldman's preliminary work on the bibliography can be found in the folders "Arte Chicano: Bibliography" and "Bibliography 4 of 11," which contains the certificate of copyright registration, October 30, 1978; folder "Bibliography 6 of 11," which contains correspondence from Francisco Garcia-Ayvens to Dr. Shifra M. Goldman, October 23, 1984; folder "Bibliography 10 of 11," which contains "Preliminary Bibliography of Chicano Art and Related Readings (Southwest and Mid-West)" by Shifra M. Goldman, 1978; and folder "Bibliography 11 of 11," which contains "Preliminary Bibliography of Chicano Art and Related Readings (Southwest and Mid-West)" by Tomás Ybarra-Frausto, 1979.

5 Tomás Ybarra-Frausto's papers were acquired by the Smithsonian American Art Museum in 1997, and Shifra M. Goldman's papers were acquired by CEMA at the University

of California, Santa Barbara, in 2008. According to her records, Goldman permitted dozens of students and scholars, including me, to make use of her archive prior to its deposit at CEMA. Her private collection supported nearly every dissertation, thesis, and major publication on Chicana/o art in the mid- to late twentieth century.

6  Diaz, "Flying under the Radar with the Royal Chicano Air Force," 80, 114–15.

7  Although the artists' experiences and memories are the invaluable and living archive, preserving fragile institutional papers is a parallel concern. Some documents are housed in basements and garages of individuals. See Grimm, *Identifying and Preserving the History of the Latino Visual Arts*.

8  This record of exhibitions is largely based on the ephemera in the Durón Family Collection. My calculations include exhibitions specifically focused on Chicana/o art and exhibitions that include Chicana/o artists, although somewhat conservatively defined. For example, an exhibition of Mexican artists at a commercial gallery is not included, but one of Frida Kahlo at Plaza de la Raza is, because of the location and her time in the United States. My calculations do not include exhibitions of Chicana/o art at restaurants and cafés, even though these have become important sites in the new millennium, particularly with the opening by writer Luis Rodriguez of Tia Chucha's Centro Cultural in Sylmar, California. Mexican art exhibitions are also part of the ephemera, but this project does not analyze the exhibitions of Francisco Toledo, Rufino Tamayo, José Luis Cuevas, and others who were regularly presented in Los Angeles since the 1940s. Two galleries stand out in this respect: Iturralde Gallery and Latin American Contemporary Art Gallery. These galleries presented Latin American but not Chicana/o art, with the Museum of Latin American Art in Long Beach following the same pattern until 2011 (it changed course after the death of the founder).

9  Armando Durón curated a fifth exhibition at the UCLA Chicano Studies Research Center Library.

## CHAPTER 1. INTRODUCTION

1  For a bruising account of the undocumented nature of Latino art history, see Rita Gonzalez, *An Undocumented History*. I also wish to acknowledge Ella Maria Diaz for her own recovery project that focuses on the Royal Chicano Air Force. Her work helped me recognize that Chicana/o art history is on a parallel path with the literary recovery project. Diaz, "The Necessary Theater of the Royal Chicano Air Force."

2  Mercer, "Black Art and the Burden of Representation," 240. This book joins current scholarship that recognizes "merit" as a euphemism for white racial primacy. See Fernandez-Sacco, "Check Your Baggage." The burden of representation is also recognized in the area of Chicana/o literature. As literary scholar Silvio Torres-Saillant describes, the "compulsion to bear witness" was most urgent during the earliest years, when writers of the "Recovering the US Hispanic Literary Heritage" project were "particularly anxious to show that a vast corpus of texts written by authors of Hispanic descent actually existed." Torres-Saillant, "Introduction: Inscribing Latinos in the National Discourse," 1.

3  Part of my attachment to the burden could stem from the very different contexts in which Kobena Mercer and I speak about art. Black visibility appears in the context of

over 150 African American museums in the United States, whereas only two accredited museums in the country are devoted to artists of Mexican heritage. Nevertheless, the moral burden is mine alone, not a critique of others.

4 Torres-Saillant, "Introduction: Inscribing Latinos in the National Discourse," 2. For instance, my compulsion to carefully document the history of Goez Art Studios and Gallery, one of the first Chicana/o galleries in Los Angeles, was urgently felt because its story was buried twice: once under the conventions of Chicana/o cultural politics, and a second time, as were nearly all Chicana/o visual artists, under the weight of historical amnesia and the Eurocentric education that erased the aesthetic production of Mexican-descent populations living in the United States.

5 The expansion of the intellectual discourse community has not kept pace with the growth of Chicana/o art production. Scholars with advanced degrees in art history who focus on Chicana/o art number just over a dozen, and this number increases to thirty-five if we include scholars like me who are trained in other disciplines but consistently participate in Chicana/o art history. These art historians include Holly Barnet-Sánchez, Charlene Villaseñor Black, C. Ondine Chavoya, Ruben C. Cordova, Constance Cortez, Ellen Fernandez-Sacco, Shifra M. Goldman, Judith Huacuja, Guisela Latorre, Ann Marie Leimer, Amelia Malagamba, Dylan A. T. Miner, Mario Ontiveros, Victor Sorell, and Sybil Venegas, one of the first to write about Chicana art. Scholars outside art history include Max Benavidez, Cary Cordova, Ella Diaz, Ramón García, Alicia Gaspar de Alba, Jennifer A. González, Rita Gonzalez, Colin Gunckel, Robb Hernandez, Gary Keller, Jesse Lerner, Amalia Mesa-Bains, Margarita Nieto, Chon A. Noriega, Laura E. Pérez, Maria Ochoa, Roberto Tejada, George Vargas, Tomás Ybarra-Frausto, and me. Carlos F. Jackson holds an advanced degree in the fine arts. Malagamba's doctorate is a multidisciplinary emphasis on sociology, art history, and anthropology.

6 Johnson, "They're Chicanos and Artists"; and Caroline A. Miranda, "How Chicano Is It?"

7 Jennifer A. González, *Subject to Display*. Miwon Kwon points out that "reductivism and counterreductivism" in art criticism have produced rather static and homogeneous images of artists of color and their communities of origin; see Kwon, *One Place after Another*, 144–45. Kate Mondloch also addresses the "reliance on a troubled taxonomy" to understand feminist art; see Mondloch, "The *Difference* Problem," 25. See also Jones, *Seeing Differently*.

8 Jennifer A. González, *Subject to Display*, 11. See also Jones, *Seeing Differently*.

9 For a recent review that reinforces expectations about identity and nonwhite artists, see Kennicott, "Art Review: 'Our America' at the Smithsonian."

10 For the first record of this periodization, see Goldman and Ybarra-Frausto, introduction to *Arte Chicano*. Since these two scholars clearly understood the range of Chicana/o art as they traveled around the country gathering material for their bibliography, I propose that they published this periodization as a formal admonition to those who were perceived as turning away from community accountability. Unfortunately, it eventually functioned to solidify expectations about Chicana/o art. For scholarship that relies on this methodological binary, see Griswold del Castillo, McKenna, and Yarbro-Bejarano, *Chicano Art*; Jackson, *Chicana and Chicano Art*; Mesa-Bains, "Art of the Other Mexico"; Romo, "Points of Convergence"; and Zamudio-Taylor, "Inventing Tradition, Negotiating Modernism."

11  Goldman, *Dimensions of the Americas*, 162.

12  Ybarra-Frausto, "The Chicano Movement/The Movement of Chicano Art." Victor Zamudio-Taylor also claims that "artistic expressions" in the second period, which he argues extend to the early 1990s, were "no longer directly linked to a political and ideological agenda," and artists "articulate[d] issues and themes that go beyond frameworks of identity and deal with more hybrid global concerns." Zamudio-Taylor, "Inventing Tradition, Negotiating Modernism," 350, 355. See also Vargas, *Contemporary Chican@ Art*.

13  Ybarra-Frausto, "Post-Movimiento."

14  The Montoyas' call for an art of politics is misread as a specific style, but they do not advocate for a particular style, form, or media.

15  Romo, *Malaquias Montoya*, 80; Goldman, "Response"; and Montoya and Salkowitz-Montoya, "A Critical Perspective on the State of Chicano Art." In *Exhibiting Mestizaje*, I incorrectly assess the dialogue between the Montoyas and Goldman as a debate, as if they stood on opposite shores. Here I recant that claim. Although Goldman assumes a stance of opposition against the Montoyas, her argument depends upon the culture of resistance for which the Montoyas call. Unfortunately, in making this error I reinforced the periodization without looking more deeply into the structure of their arguments, as Romo does. Davalos, *Exhibiting Mestizaje*.

16  Noriega, "The Orphans of Modernism," 30, 44 n. 24.

17  In terms of Chicana/o literature, José F. Aranda Jr. identifies a similar polarity when he notes that resistance theory categorizes creative writing as either resistant or assimilationist. Aranda, *When We Arrive*, xxi.

18  Mondloch, "*Difference* Problem," 19, 26. Mondloch's analysis of a taxonomy that governed feminist art criticism came at an important moment in my writing, and I acknowledge her skilled handling of intellectual entrenchment. See also Colin Gunckel's analysis of Oscar Castillo's photographs, which simultaneously "bridge conventional boundaries" between documentation and aesthetic objects. Gunckel, "'I Was Participating and Documenting,'" 1–3.

19  In some ways this case study is idiosyncratic because it emerges in part from my employment in Los Angeles, which provided me with extensive access to a complex city's cultural production.

20  The first drafts of this book claimed that Los Angeles was "unique" in the historic exhibition season with several mainstream institutions presenting Chicana/o art, but in 2016 Chicago witnessed collaborations across nearly sixty institutions to present sixty-five exhibitions of Latina/o art. Spring of Latino Art (SOLA) was produced without the financial support of a major foundation. SOLA is unprecedented, and not simply because of extensive, nonfinancial investments that made it possible.

21  Nonmuseum institutions proved critically important to PST. The Center for the Study of Political Graphics (CSPG) made possible the presence of Chicana/o posters in multiple PST exhibitions. CSPG was invaluable in providing accurate information about the works, and without Carol Wells, executive director and founder of CSPG, several curators would have been unable to complete their research. Yet something is askew when a nonprofit organization, CSPG, as well as the UCLA Chicano Studies Research Center,

acquired more Chicana/o art in the last ten years than LACMA, the Getty Center, the Museum of Latin American Art, and the Museum of Contemporary Art combined.

22  Sandra de la Loza also does not disguise her affection for the past and for the archive. With each sample of a vanished mural, we sense de la Loza's love for the public art of her childhood. Novelist and law professor Yxta Maya Murray observes that the portraits are "valentines for the sitter." The affective qualities of the work require further research, and I credit Murray for bringing to my attention how affect functions in *Action Portraits*. During the exhibition's run, we exchanged ideas by e-mail. Her first communication exclaimed, "Naked Painting! Reinscriptions! Xicana artistic interventions!"—a phrase that informed my analysis. Murray, personal communication with author, January 2012.

23  The Nancy Tovar Murals of East Los Angeles Slide Collection (hereafter cited as Tovar Collection) is housed at the UCLA Chicano Studies Research Center Library. The archive contains more than six hundred color slides of East Los Angeles murals created in the 1970s.

24  Sandra de la Loza, interview by Davalos. Unless otherwise noted, all Sandra de la Loza quotations in this chapter come from this interview.

25  With technical assistance from Santarromana, de la Loza employed "an old video technique, called green-screening." The muralists painted their bodies with green paint, an action that de la Loza captured in digital media. The green color was then digitally removed and images from the Tovar Collection were dropped into those spaces.

26  Because Sandra de la Loza deliberately produced a work of art about murals when she learned that the Getty Foundation initiative Pacific Standard Time would not focus on Chicana/o muralism, I interpret the muralist's gesture as an indictment of the county of Los Angeles and its failure to support youth programs and arts in the schools while it annually spends $52 million to eliminate graffiti by painting over it with a blend of the cheapest colors of paint. The abatement program does not distinguish between street art, urban calligraphy, and commissioned murals, and the county offers no legal mechanism and no physical barrier to protect public art. Instead the county abatement policy directs workers to obliterate with brown-out paint any form of writing, even if it appears in a mural. In addition, the city established a moratorium on murals between 2002 and late 2013 to avoid legal challenges from corporations claiming that massive multistory advertisements are protected by free speech. The mural moratorium prevented artists and private owners from creating murals in the city. Ironically, these policies against public art are concurrent with a booming arts development in the downtown area: one museum recently opened and another is under expansion. See Sandra de la Loza, "Mural Remix."

27  When the exhibition was restaged in other settings, de la Loza changed the three-channel video configuration. Viewers in Boyle Heights, a community east of downtown Los Angeles, did not witness the same triptych as did viewers at LACMA. A continuous recombination of images crafted a larger visual record and theoretical frame, and this effort to make the work living rather than static supports a Chicana feminist view of multiple subjectivities. See Gloria Anzaldúa, *Borderlands/La Frontera*;

and Anzaldúa, *Interviews/Entrevistas*. Richard J. Powell reminds us that bodies are not the same as embodiments. See Powell, "The Deep."

28 The muralists' names appear on the identification label for the work, but unless the viewer is familiar with East Los Angeles muralists, he or she cannot attach the names to specific portraits. Moreover, the artist known as Timoi, an acronym for Trapped in My Own Imagination, completely withholds her name.

29 I follow scholars who argue that "ethnic identity has been racialized," and thus I investigate Chicanas/os as a phenomenon of both racial and ethnic construction. Alcoff, *Visible Identities*, 21. See also Schiller, "Editor's Foreword," iii–iv.

30 Jones, *Seeing Differently*, 151.

31 Wolf, *Vermeer and the Invention of Seeing*, 5, 6 (emphasis in original).

32 Sandoval, *Methodology of the Oppressed*.

33 Pérez, *The Decolonial Imaginary*.

34 Lorde, "The Master's Tools." Lorde criticized the feminist movement for its exclusion of women of color and its perpetuation of patriarchy, stating that the "master's tools . . . will never enable us to bring about genuine change" (112).

35 Wald, "American Studies and the Politics of Life," 192.

36 Eng, "The Civil and the Human," 210.

37 I am not the first to claim that American art history is generally inattentive to practices associated with race, gender, and politics. For scholars working in similar ways, see Mondloch, "*Difference* Problem," 18–31; Jennifer A. González, *Subject to Display*; Selz, *Art of Engagement*; and Jones, *Seeing Differently*.

38 Saldívar, *Trans-Americanity*, 9. Also see Cockcroft, "From Barrio to Mainstream," 192.

39 Marin, remarks in panel discussion of *Artifex* exhibition.

40 Palumbo-Liu, "Introduction: Unhabituated Habituses," 19. For mestiza consciousness, see Anzaldúa, *Borderlands/La Frontera*.

41 This pedagogical lesson is provided by Sandoval's *Methodology of the Oppressed* and Saldívar's *Trans-Americanity*. Both authors presume intracultural flows and dynamics rather than cultural stasis, national containment, homogeneity, or essentialism, the mainstays of American art history.

42 See Jones, *Seeing Differently*, for a thorough discussion of essentialist interpretations of artists of color.

43 Sandoval, *Methodology of the Oppressed*.

44 Keating, "Introduction: Reading Gloria Anzaldúa."

45 Latorre, *Walls of Empowerment*; also see Lippard, *Mixed Blessings*, 152.

46 Davalos, "'All Roads Lead to East L.A.'"

47 Luján, oral history interview by Rangel. The artist took numerous pictures of art and architectural sites in Europe, suggesting that Luján most certainly studied the aesthetic traditions of Europe. The images are part of his estate.

48 López, "'Stunned into Being.'"

CHAPTER 2. ERRATA EXHIBITIONS

1 *Hispanic Art* portrayed an art historiography that few scholars and artists in the field found credible. Art historians Shifra M. Goldman, Tomás Ybarra-Frausto, Mari

Carmen Ramírez, Eva Cockcroft, Amalia Mesa-Bains, and others characterized
Chicana/o art as situated within a matrix of historical contexts, particularly race,
ethnicity, class, and gender in the United States, but also within US-Mexico relations. See Goldman and Ybarra-Frausto, "The Political and Social Contexts of Chicano
Art"; Mari Carmen Ramírez, "Beyond 'the Fantastic'"; Cockcroft, "From Barrio to
Mainstream"; and Mesa-Bains, "El Mundo Feminino." For a comprehensive review
of the criticism of *Hispanic Art*, see Chavoya, "Orphans of Modernism." Even artists
included in the exhibition were suspicious of its ability to improve their access to the
art world. Rather than celebrate their visibility in *Hispanic Art*, Los Angeles Chicano
artists Gronk, Carlos Almaraz, and Frank Romero called to public attention LACMA's
consistent silence on Chicano art. Almaraz viewed the traveling exhibition as an act
intended to "appease the peasants . . . for another 15 years." But "the peasants" did
not remain silent, and LACMA was pressured to exhibit the work of Carlos Almaraz
in 1992, a few years after his death. A major survey exhibition of Chicana/o art did
not appear until the twenty-first century. See Venant, "On-the-Wall Latino Art at
LACMA."

2  Jane Livingston and John Beardsley of the Corcoran Gallery of Art originally organized *Hispanic Art* for the Museum of Fine Arts, Houston. It premiered in 1987 and
traveled two years later to Los Angeles.

3  Beardsley and Livingston, "Preface and Acknowledgments," 10.

4  Honoring the contributions of Armando and Mary Salinas Durón and their children,
the SPARC Gallery was officially renamed the Durón Gallery in late 2012.

5  Baca, *Judy Baca*, interview by Davalos, 146. Unless otherwise noted, all Judy Baca
quotations in this chapter come from this interview.

6  Padilla, interview by Davalos. Examples of exhibitions at the SPARC Gallery that
expanded critical consciousness include *Elect This!* (October–November 2000, closing
on election day); *Hijas de Juarez* (October–November 2002); *MaquiL.A.* (March 2007);
and *Death of the Bush Era: What Next?* (November–December 2008, opening on Election Day).

7  Davalos, "'All Roads Lead to East L.A.'"

8  I invite other scholars to situate the errata exhibitions I explore within the larger field
of contestation.

9  When contextualized within the broader field of art criticism, the errata exhibition
is especially relevant given the minimal presence of Chicana/o art within American
art criticism. Rita Gonzalez has documented the lacuna produced by the hegemonic
forces at work within American art history that leave the work of Latina and Latino
artists, including Chicanas/os, relatively unexplained, unexamined, and under-
theorized. Gonzalez searched for citations on a sample of ninety-three established
Latina and Latino artists. Using the primary search engines of art history, such as
Art Abstracts, Art Index Retrospective, and the Getty Research Institute's Union List
of Artist Names, as well as six major teaching texts for twentieth-century American
art history, she found that "few artists on [the sample] list had more than one article
published about their work; and more often than not the few articles published
consisted of brief exhibition reviews. In comparison, searching for one hundred of

the most exhibited non-Hispanic White artists would yield thousands of entries."
The indexes record minor attention to Mexican American men: thirty works on Luis
Jiménez, twenty-two on Anthony Hernandez, eighteen on Carlos Almaraz, fourteen
on Gronk, twelve on Rupert García, and eleven on John Valadez. Chicana artists fared
especially poorly: thirteen works on Amalia Mesa-Bains, eleven on Carmen Lomas
Garza, seven each on Diane Gamboa and Patssi Valdez, six on Judith Baca, five on
Barbara Carrasco, one each on Celia Alvarez Muñoz, Yolanda M. López, Ester Hernan-
dez, and Kathy Vargas, and none on Santa Barraza or Yreina D. Cervántez. Gonzalez,
*Undocumented History*, 1–8. After the report was published, and in part to address the
lacuna it revealed, A Ver: Revisioning Art History, a series of the UCLA CSRC Press,
was launched and completed its first volume. To date, the series has published books
on Chicana/o artists Gronk, Yolanda M. López, Carmen Lomas Garza, Malaquias
Montoya, Celia Alvarez Muñoz, and Ricardo Valverde, as well as Latina/o artists
María Brito, Rafael Ferrer, Pepón Osorio, and Luis Cruz Azaceta.

10  Jennifer A. González, *Subject to Display*, 1.

11  Corrin, "*Mining the Museum*: Artists Look at Museums," 5, 7.

12  Jennifer A. González, *Subject to Display*, 15.

13  Noriega, "Conceptual Graffiti and the Public Art Museum," 260, 256–57. It bears noting
that Asco's critical intervention against LACMA came on the heels of the museum's
first two exhibitions of African American art. The museum's curator of prints and drawings organized the first show, and the Black Arts Council curated the second. See Cooks,
*Exhibiting Blackness*, 95. Other interventions outside the museum structure include Internet broadcasts by Harry Gamboa Jr., who since the late 1990s has displayed his work
via e-mail listserv, attachments, and web links. These curatorial projects are announced
to an "A-list" of e-mail recipients. The subject line of his e-mail message, "A-list," is a
sardonic nod to the structures of power within the art market.

14  In chapter 3 I take up the formation and mission of *centros culturales*, but at this point
it is important to briefly touch on the art-based community-making processes and
practices of these arts centers. Since their founding, Self Help Graphics & Art, Plaza
de la Raza, and SPARC, three arts organizations that emerged from the Chicano
movement, have regularly and intentionally produced errata exhibitions and have
consistently offered new interpretations about the intersection of life and art. For
art-based community making, see Lipsitz, "Not Just Another Social Movement." See
also Davalos, *Exhibiting Mestizaje*.

15  Davalos, *Exhibiting Mestizaje*.

16  Mondloch, "*Difference* Problem," 26.

17  Other errata exhibitions deserve future attention. *Arts of Mexico: Its North American
Variant* (1991), organized by Self Help Graphics & Art, was part of the local festival
Artes de Mexico, and it functioned as an erratum to the traveling exhibition *Mexico:
Splendors of Thirty Centuries* (1991) at LACMA. *Reminders outside the Circle* (2005),
organized by Tropico de Nopal, was an erratum to *Leaving Aztlan: Redux*, a version
of an exhibition curated by Kaytie Johnson for the Center for Visual Art in Denver,
Colorado, and presented at Arena 1, a gallery in Santa Monica, California.

18  Zabala, "*Chicanarte*: A Cultural Statement."

19  It is instructive to compare how ELAC and LACMA, the two sites that presented *Chicanismo en el Arte*, differently interpret Chicana/o art. Preliminary analysis of the exhibition catalog suggests that *Chicanismo en el Arte* reveals the college museum's embrace of ethnic-specific art and the county museum's desire for postethnic aesthetics. Whereas ELAC drew on discourses of relevance, accountability, and quality, LACMA confined itself to the logic of art for art's sake and disavowed rights-based claims to inclusion. In this way, the exhibition documents paradoxical conditions of visibility. The director of ELAC's museum, Tom Silliman, envisioned the exhibition as a collaboration, and he worked in partnership with Chicano arts organizations, anticipating the collective process that would drive Chicana/o exhibition in the late twentieth century and beyond.

20  Zabala, "*Chicanarte*: A Cultural Statement." As early as 1968, public and private colleges and universities in Southern California consistently exhibited Chicana/o art, sometimes using an exhibition to spur advocacy on behalf of Chicana/o artists. I leave this topic for future analysis, but it is important to briefly note that throughout the 1970s and 1980s the public and private institutions of higher education in the Los Angeles metropolitan region supported dozens of exhibitions of Chicana/o art. For instance, during Barbara Carrasco's legal battle with the Los Angeles Community Redevelopment Agency, which had decommissioned and censored her mural *L.A. History: A Mexican Perspective* (1981), Loyola Marymount University exhibited her drawings, paintings, and posters. Organized by Robert Andrade and with assistance from faculty members Francisco Vasquez and Rudolfo Torres, the exhibition mobilized support for the artist as she tried to establish her copyright status. See Department of Archives and Special Collections, Library, Loyola Marymount University, Group 4, Library Publications and Exhibits, 1980, folder "Displays 1980–, Announcement and Invitation, Application Form." The UCLA Chicano Studies Research Center has been part of Chicano visual art production since the inaugural publication of *Aztlán: A Journal of Chicano Studies*. Founding editors, such as Reynaldo Macias, Juan Gómez-Quiñones, and Teresa McKenna, published and promoted Chicana/o art on the journal's cover or inside pages.

21  *Chicanismo en el Arte* was originally an art contest for advanced high school and college students; this eliminated two Chicana artists, Judith Baca and Judithe Hernández, who had already completed degrees by 1975. More than eleven thousand visitors attended the exhibition during its three-week presentation, a major accomplishment for the East Los Angeles campus, and the show received considerable media coverage. "Vincent and Mary Price Gallery, 18 Apr 75 Chicanismo en el Arte," news clipping, folder "Chicanismo en el Arte," Vincent Price Art Museum Archive, East Los Angeles College. The founding members of Asco—Patssi Valdez, Harry Gamboa Jr., Gronk, and Willie Herrón III—had several works among the over two hundred items on display at ELAC, including one collaborative piece. Gronk presented under the pseudonym Jetter Letter. Harry Gamboa Jr., personal communication with author, March 28, 2011. See also *Chicanismo en el Arte*, exh. cat.

22  Hernández, interview by Davalos. Unless otherwise noted, all Judithe Hernández quotations in this chapter come from this interview.

23  Ibid. Hernández reports a third installment of *Las Chicanas* at Mechicano Art Center. Michelle Moravec reports that Quezada's installation first appeared at Mechicano, and the Woman's Building secured funding to bring the exhibition to its location. Moravec, "Historicizing the Chicana."

24  Hernández, interview by Davalos.

25  Moravec, "The Past Put into Chicanismo Perspective."

26  See, for example, Aldana, review of *L.A. Xicano* and *Asco*. Aldana contrasts Judith Baca with Asco even as she observes that the exhibitions *Mapping Another L.A.* and *Asco: Elite of the Obscure* require us to reconsider dualist assumptions about Asco and Chicano art.

27  Hernández, interview by Davalos.

28  Santillano, "Asco," 118.

29  Moravec, "Judithe Hernández's Altar." According to the artist, the installation was not titled; Hernández, interview by Davalos.

30  Davalos, *Yolanda M. López*.

31  Jennifer A. González, *Subject to Display*, 7–10.

32  Baca, *Judy Baca*, interview by Davalos, 106. This interpretation of *Las Tres Marias* differs from Alicia Gaspar de Alba's interpretation, which is based on the 1990 installation at *Chicano Art: Resistance and Affirmation, 1965–1985*. Baca notes that the 1990 installation lacks the performance and the vanity table, which changes how audiences understand the title. The Three Marias are conventionally associated with the virgin/mother/whore paradigm.

33  Moraga, *The Last Generation*, 71 (emphasis in original).

34  The first quotation is from Venegas, *Image and Identity*, under "Diane Gamboa" and "Dolores Guerrero Cruz." The catalog is unpaginated. The second is from hooks, "Homeplace: A Site of Resistance."

35  Carrasco, *Barbara Carrasco*, interview by Davalos.

36  Venegas, introduction to *Image and Identity*, ii.

37  See Moraga and Anzaldúa, *This Bridge Called My Back*.

38  Fields and Zamudio-Taylor, "Aztlan," 40, 75. This section benefits from an interview that Virginia Fields granted me on January 23, 2002. Her untimely death in July 2011 prevented me from sharing my analysis with her. I return to the LACMA exhibition in chapter 6 for a deeper consideration of its place in American art history.

39  As artistic director of SPARC, Judy Baca plays an important role in exhibitions, but her dedication to a collaborative method means that she involves others in producing, designing, and conceptualizing exhibitions. I did not pinpoint or second-guess who made decisions for the errata exhibition as it was shared among SPARC leadership and Armando Durón, the show's lead curator.

40  Davalos, "The Mexican Museum of San Francisco."

41  Fields, interview by Davalos. Constance Cortez brilliantly argues in her catalog essay how and why nepantla proves more useful than Aztlán as a central metaphor for understanding the visual arts. Cortez, "The New Aztlan."

42  Fields and Zamudio-Taylor, "Aztlan," 68–69 (emphasis added). Although it may seem snarky, I am fascinated by the way their comparative model evokes the refrains of

popular contemporary songs—such as Andrea True Connection's disco tune, "More, more, more—how do you like it?" and Billy Idol's punk song "Rebel Yell," which intones, "in the midnight hour, she cried more, more, more."

43 Fields and Zamudio-Taylor's comparative enlargement of Mexican artists unfortunately gets coupled with the grossly erroneous statement that appears in the catalog. Zamudio-Taylor states that "first-generation" Chicana/o artists "did not have a well-rounded academic training" and "lack a formal rigor," making them appear as untrained naïve geniuses who are incapable of the type of complex intellectual thought and visual production attributed to Mexican artists and a "second generation" of Chicana/o artists. However, it is unclear precisely who is included in this "first generation." As he acknowledges, the artists in *The Road to Aztlan*, such as Luis Jiménez (b. 1940), Gilbert "Magu" Sánchez Luján (b. 1940), Yolanda M. López (b. 1942), Santa C. Barraza (b. 1951), John Valadez (b. 1951), and Yreina D. Cervántez (b. 1952), were trained at colleges and universities, completing bachelor's and master's degrees in fine arts. Zamudio-Taylor, "Inventing Tradition, Negotiating Modernism," 343, 351. Terezita Romo documents that two artists not included in the exhibition but born in the 1930s, Roberto Chavez and Eduardo Carrillo, both received MFA degrees from UCLA. Romo, "Mexican Heritage, American Art."

44 As I discuss in chapter 6, the exhibition labels apply another strategy, capturing the diasporic phenomena among Mexican-heritage people who crisscross the US-Mexico border, a point raised in the errata exhibition. The final gallery identified the artists' place of birth as well as the site of their artistic activity—that is, the labels did not match art historical conventions and focus on the nationality of the artist as method of classification. The spectator could not map the curators' description of Mexican or Chicana/o artists to all of the objects on display. For example, Thomas Glassford, born (1963) in a "bilingual household in Laredo, Texas," was active in Mexico since 1990; is he classified as a Mexican or Chicano artist? Fields and Zamudio-Taylor, "Aztlan: Destination and Point of Departure," 73.

45 Zamudio-Taylor, "Inventing Tradition, Negotiating Modernism," 355.

46 Amelia Jones brilliantly discusses how the field of art history misuses identification of nonwhite artists. Jones, *Seeing Differently*.

47 Armando Durón, "Other Footprints to Aztlan," in *Other Footprints to Aztlan*, exh. cat. The catalog is unpaginated.

48 "SPARC Continues Its 25th Year with Other Footprints to Aztlan," SPARC press release, September 21, 2001.

49 Durón, "Other Footprints to Aztlan."

50 Magu's retelling of the colonial past links the work to Chicanafuturism, especially the aspect of Chicanafuturism that "articulates colonial and postcolonial theories of *indigenismo*, *mestizaje*, hegemony, and survival." Catherine S. Ramírez, "Afrofuturism/Chicanafuturism," 187.

51 Durón, "Other Footprints to Aztlan."

52 Durón is quoted in "SPARC Continues Its 25th Year with Other Footprints to Aztlan."

53 My interpretation draws on the artist's statement and discussion of her creative process, which begins with symbolic meaning, narrative, character, or emotion. No-

tably, this painting accomplished its critical commentary on belonging and resistance through abstract art. See Pagel, "Monique Prieto."

54 Armando Durón, "The Works in the Exhibition," in *Other Footprints to Aztlan*.

55 Huacuja, "Borderlands Critical Subjectivity in Recent Chicana Art." Although Huacuja is discussing López's *Ixta* (1999), a digital print, the two works contain an identical portrait of the lesbian lovers.

56 Reyes Rodriguez, personal communication with author, November 8, 2013.

57 I encourage readers to systematically analyze the catalog, since my exploration is limited. For me, the essays serve as documents of the ethnographic information I gathered—the unsolicited comments, the long but unrecorded conversations, the facial expressions, and whispers of dozens of people—at the exhibition's formal opening, programmatic events, and at other local galleries in 2008.

58 Gonzalez, Fox, and Noriega, introduction to *Phantom Sightings*, 13.

59 Ibid.

60 Ibid., 14 (first quotation) and 13 (second quotation).

61 Ibid., 13.

62 Reyes Rodriguez made these comments at "Keeping It Real: An Open Roundtable Discussion."

63 Amelia Jones makes a similar observation about Freestyle. The exhibition, which originated at the Studio Museum of Harlem and traveled to the Santa Monica Museum of Art in 2001, was described as "post-black." Jones, *Seeing Differently*, 141.

64 Noriega, "The Orphans of Modernism," 20. Chicana feminists made similar assessments during the movement as they called for recognition of gender differences within the Mexican American community.

65 Ibid., 30 (first quotation), 24 (second quotation).

66 Rita Gonzalez, "Phantom Sites: The Official, the Unofficial, and the Orificial," 48 (emphasis added).

67 Fox, "Theater of the Inauthentic," 78.

68 Ibid., 98.

69 For criticism of *Phantom Sightings*, see Mendoza, "Deciphering the Decoy"; Shaked, "Event Review: Phantom Sightings"; Sandra de la Loza, "Mural Remix"; and "Keeping It Real."

70 Although artists in *Phantom Sightings* likely also articulate the same complex positioning that I find in Linda Arreola's work, my point is that the many spectators with whom I spoke did not perceive this aspect of the work because the binary debate ruled local discussion.

71 See Alarcón, "The Theoretical Subject(s) of *This Bridge Called My Back*"; Alarcón, "Chicana Feminism"; Anzaldúa, *Borderlands/La Frontera*; and Moraga and Anzaldúa, *This Bridge Called My Back*.

72 Elsewhere I make a similar argument about the work of Diane Gamboa. My project here is to illustrate how Chicana feminist artists intervene against Chicano art historiography and have been doing so since the 1970s. See Davalos, "The Art of Place."

73 Arreola, "Vaguely Chicana," 7.

74 Laura E. Pérez, "The Poetry of Embodiment."

75  McWhorter, *Racism and Sexual Oppression in Anglo-America*, 14–15.

76  Hames-García, *Identity Complex*, 6 (emphasis in original).

77  Aranda, *When We Arrive*, 30.

78  Jones, "'Traitor Prophets.'" Jones argues that Asco "has also been excluded [from the hegemonic art world] precisely because their work was in between" (108). I extend her argument to the work addressed here.

79  Huacuja, "Borderlands Critical Subjectivity," 111.

80  Anzaldúa, "Chicana Artists."

CHAPTER 3. LOOKING AT THE ARCHIVE

1  Castellanos, *Leonard Castellanos*, interview by Davalos, 1.

2  Emerson Woelffer described himself as an abstract surrealist, while critics labeled him an abstract expressionist. See Muchnic, "Emerson Woelffer, 88."

3  Castellanos, *Leonard Castellanos*, interview by Davalos, 4.

4  Ibid., 4–5.

5  Although the show was announced in the Calendar section of the *Los Angeles Times*, the title was not indicated.

6  Two reviews document the works featured in this exhibition, and both journalists provided descriptions and interpretations of Carlos Almaraz's work. "Mechicano Art Center Works on Display at Junior Art Center," *Eastside Journal/Belvedere Citizen*, May 31, 1973, is the source of the first quotation; and William Wilson, "30 Works from the Grass Roots," *Los Angeles Times*, June 4, 1973, I2, is the source of the second.

7  I do not address Goez's continued venture under the direction of José Luis (Joe) Gonzalez, who specializes in restoration, conservation, and restaurant interior design. Joe moved Goez to Olympic Boulevard and then to the City of Commerce, in southeast Los Angeles County, where he continues to operate as of 2015.

8  The founders of Goez Art Studios and Gallery operated several companies on First Street, each supporting a particular activity. Originally, Goez Imports and Fine Arts opened to sell Mexican furniture, Spanish imports, *arte popular*, tourist art, and reproductions of Mexican and European masterworks. With an inaugural exhibition in December 1971, the commercial venture focused on fine arts, and the founders changed the name to Goez Art Studios and Gallery. This is the institution at the center of my analysis, which I also refer to as "Goez." Near the end of the 1970s, Goez Institute of Murals and Fine Arts was also functioning out of the First Street location. It served as a clearinghouse for muralists looking for projects, businesses, community organizations, schools looking for artists, and students seeking arts instruction. The First Street location additionally housed the East Los Angeles School of Mexican-American Fine Arts. See Panicacci, "The History of Goez."

9  Dávila, *Culture Works*, 113.

10  Wilson, "30 Works from the Grass Roots."

11  Martin Berger's analysis of whiteness in late nineteenth- and early twentieth-century genre painting as well as films and landscape photographs depends on artworks that lack obvious "racial themes or tropes" to demonstrate that "a decidedly racialized per-

spective animated even those cultural products most removed from racial concerns."
Martin A. Berger, *Sight Unseen*, 2.

12　Wilson, "30 Works from the Grass Roots." About a year later, he made similar statements in his review of *Los Four: Almaraz/de la Rocha/Lujan/Romero*. Wilson lamented
that LACMA brought only "college-trained artists who, by the very act of leaving
the barrio, ceased to be authentic folk artists." He implied that the county museum
should have given the public "the real article," untrained and unsophisticated natives
who are authentically distinct. In this way, Wilson implied the cause of the "head-
ache" the show gave him: the rupture of the binary model that requires Chicanos and
Chicanas either to remain authentically native and exotic (and thus incapable of high
art) or to become fully integrated Americans of Mexican descent who live as undif-
ferentiated citizen-subjects. Wilson, "'Los Four' a Statement of Chicano Spirit," *Los
Angeles Times*, March 10, 1974, O64.

13　Noriega, "The City of Dreams."

14　Although beyond the scope of this project, my observations resonate with the work
of Arlene Dávila, Linda Martín Alcoff, and Lisa Duggan, who investigate the neoliberal relationship between identity and culture. See Dávila, *Culture Works*; Alcoff,
*Visible Identities*; and Duggan, *The Twilight of Equality?*

15　Shifra M. Goldman states that Mechicano existed for a year on Gallery Row, but she
only details the institution's activities after it relocated to East Los Angeles in 1971.
See Goldman, "How, Why, Where, and When It All Happened," 46; and Goldman, "A
Public Voice," 53.

16 ˌNoriega and Tompkins Rivas, "Chicano Art in the City of Dreams," 91–96.

17　In the 1970s the use of public support was already viewed as unearned privilege, a
rhetorical strategy that discredits the civil rights movement and its reformulation of
the liberal state.

18　For examples of limited narratives, see Kun, "This Is Chicano Art?"; Jackson, *Chicana
and Chicano Art*, 81–82; Keller et al., *Contemporary Chicana and Chicano Art*; and Vargas, *Contemporary Chican@ Art*, 21. Although George Vargas documents artistic production in Michigan and Texas, two areas rarely covered by scholars of Chicana/o art
history, the bulk of the book restages familiar material and arguments about Chicano
art. As I observe in the introduction, Sandra de la Loza visually demonstrates that
Vargas's account of early Chicano murals as figurative and representational collapses
under scrutiny. For a wonderful exception, see McCaughan, *Art and Social Movements*.

19　See Cockcroft, "From Barrio to Mainstream"; Cockcroft and Barnet-Sánchez, *Signs
from the Heart*, 28; Cockcroft, Weber, and Cockcroft, *Toward a People's Art*, 57; Jackson,
*Chicana and Chicano Art*, 81–82; and Latorre, *Walls of Empowerment*, 151. Two sources
acknowledge the varied activities of Goez. See Saavedra, "Arte de 'East Los'"; and Torres, "A Profile of an Hispano Artist."

20　This brief historical account of fourteen arts organizations established in the 1970s
calls for additional research. I relied on the directory of the Los Angeles Community
Arts Alliance (1973); the documentary *Resurrected Histories* (2012), directed by Abel
Mora Alejandre for Avenue 50 Studio; and over a dozen oral history interviews I
conducted on behalf of the UCLA Chicano Studies Research Center's Oral Histories

Series. EastLos Gallery was also invested in the flow and sharing of artistic ideas beyond Southern California. Founded in 1978 by two East Los Angeles College professors, Sybil Venegas and artist Roberto Chavez, the gallery's premier exhibition featured José Montoya and his series Pachuco Art. EastLos Gallery showcased the work of Eduardo Carrillo, Chavez's classmate from UCLA, who had joined the faculty at University of California, Santa Cruz. Although the gallery lasted only a year, it served as a venue for the growing intra-state movement of Chicana/o art. I thank Sybil Venegas for sharing this information with me. See also Davalos, "Centro de Arte Público."

21  CAP was an art collective in Highland Park that operated for approximately three or four years, between 1976 and 1980, but it had an earlier incarnation as Aldama House/Corazon Productions. See Alejandre, *Resurrected Histories*.

22  Kwon, *One Place after Another*, 152. For theories and criticism on the avant-garde, see Bürger, *Theory of the Avant Garde*.

23  Gilbert "Magu" Sánchez Luján clearly understood the value of the artists' colloquy, and he staged Mental Menudos in Fresno in the 1970s and thereafter in Los Angeles until his untimely death in 2011.

24  In my examination of women's involvement in the community arts organizations, I follow the method presented by Ella Diaz in her analysis of the Royal Chicano Air Force. She refuses a feminist discourse that criticizes patriarchy within an organization and yet erases the roles of women. Diaz, "Necessary Theater of the Royal Chicano Air Force."

25  Fe, "Mechicano Art Center: Discovering the Center" and "Mechicano Art Center: Creating Awareness," videotaped interviews available on *Departures*, KCET website.

26  Both articles appeared in "La Mujer," special issue, *Chismearte* 1, no. 4 (1977).

27  "Revista Xhismearte," special issue, *Chismearte*, no. 7 (1981). Carrasco's cover art was untitled.

28  According to Peter Tovar, Sister Karen used a calendar to demonstrate to the staff that November was a time that Self Help Graphics could distinguish itself from other arts institutions. Davalos and Gunckel, "The Early Years," 64.

29  For information about the Barrio Mobile Art Studio, see Guzmán, "Self Help Graphics & Art."

30  Juan Gonzalez, *Johnny Gonzalez, with Irma Núñez*, interview by Davalos; José Luis Gonzalez, interview by Olivares; and "Chicano Art People, Minutes, c. 1971," folder "Saul Solache," Shifra Goldman Papers.

31  Aranda, *When We Arrive*, 11.

32  Leonard Castellanos speaking at panel discussion, "Symposium on the Politics of the Arts: Minorities and the Arts," transcript in *Arts in Society* 10, no. 3 (1973): 70.

33  Juan Gonzalez, *Johnny Gonzalez, with Irma Núñez*, interview by Davalos, 163.

34  Botello, *David Botello*, interview by Davalos.

35  "Ecology and Art Join Forces," *East Los Angeles Brooklyn Belvedere Comet*, June 24, 1971; "Busy Creations" (photo), *Los Angeles Sun*, July 18, 1971, 1; and "Art Center for East Los Angeles," *American Baptist Magazine*, February 1972, personal papers of José Luis Gonzalez. Juan Gonzalez adopted the professional name "Don Juan."

36 Panicacci, "History of Goez."

37 Estrada, *The Los Angeles Plaza*.

38 Loper, "Giving Her All for Mechicano Center"; and "Images of Aztlan at Méchicano."

39 "Califas: Chicano Art and Culture in California," Transcripts Book 4 (archival documents of the Califas Conference held at the Mary Porter Sesnon Gallery, University of California, Santa Cruz, 1982), 7; and "Mechicano Art Center," c. 1971, personal papers of José Luis Gonzalez. Regarding the September 1969 opening, see "Chicano Art Exhibited at Price Gallery," *Los Angeles Times*, December 12, 1971, SE6.

40 "'Man Came This Way' Will Open," *Los Angeles Times*, March 7, 1971, O55.

41 "Califas: Chicano Art and Culture in California," Transcripts Book 4. For the types of classes, see "The Mechicano Historical Experience Outline," c. 1977, personal papers of Joe Rodriguez; "Art Center Celebrates First Year," *Eastside Journal*, March 2, 1972, 3; Franco, oral history interview by Schwartz; and Castellanos, oral history interview by Bassing. Castellanos joined the collective full-time after he quit his position as director of fine arts and cultural affairs at TELACU, a community development agency. For information about Castellanos's employment at TELACU and later at Mechicano, see "Images of Aztlan at Méchicano"; "Califas: Chicano Art and Culture in California"; and "The Mechicano Historical Experience Outline," c. 1977, personal papers of Joe Rodriguez.

42 A collective challenge to patriarchy did not surface among Chicana/o arts organizations until the late 1970s.

43 Blaine and Baker, "Finding Community through the Arts," 132; and "Images of Aztlan at Méchicano."

44 Castellanos, interview by Bassing; and Guerrero, "Chicano Art Center Showcases Minorities."

45 Wilson, "A Distressing Overlap in 'Mechicano'"; and Wilson, "Gallery Shows Chicano Art."

46 Wilson, "A Distressing Overlap."

47 "Latin Art Exhibit Set Today at Goez Center," *Eastside Sun*, December 5, 1971, 1.

48 Haecki, "Goez Art Studios and Gallery KOs Doubters." See Davalos, "Centro de Arte Público" for additional information.

49 Description of box 3, folder 6, Guide to the Harry Gamboa Jr. Papers, 1968–1995, Collection M0753, Department of Special Collections and University Archives, Stanford University Libraries. The folder contains Gamboa's slide of Herrón's work.

50 However, Mechicano did not follow the lead of SPARC, where Judy Baca uses the process of art making as a tool for community organizing and social change. Rather, Mechicano, as well as Goez, relied on the didactic quality of public art to teach cultural awareness and inspire change.

51 Castellanos, "Chicano Centros, Murals, and Art," 39. See also "Background," on the website for the Avenue 50 Studio documentary *Resurrected Histories by Alejandre* (article no longer available).

52 del Olmo, "Murals Changing Face of East L.A."

53 Ibid.

54 "Catholic Group Makes 33 Self-Help Grants," *Los Angeles Times*, January 1, 1972, B18; and Loper, "Giving Her All for Mechicano Art Center."

55  Blaine and Baker, "Finding Community through the Arts," 133.

56  Franco, interview by Schwartz. Franco's view of art as spiritual guide distances him from Marxist thought that distrusts spirituality as a source of subordination, but also from the colonial logic that understands the spirituality of nonwhite people as primitive. Franco reclaims the spirituality of art as a force for critical consciousness. As Laura E. Pérez asserts in her analysis of Chicana art, the political element of spirituality has been overlooked in Chicana/o studies. Pérez, *Chicana Art*.

57  Goldman, *Dimensions of the Americas*, 162.

58  José Luis "Joe" Gonzalez, quoted in Ava Gutierrez-O'Neill, "Cinco de Mayo: Putting the French on the Run," *Los Angeles Herald Examiner*, 1975, 9, personal papers of José Luis Gonzalez.

59  Prado Saldivar, "On Both Sides of the Los Angeles River," 46.

60  Castellanos, interview by Bassing.

61  Ibid.

62  Prado Saldivar, "On Both Sides of the Los Angeles River," 41.

63  For an account of how real estate and banking industry practices affected Chicana/o organizations, see David R. Diaz, "Barrio Logic."

64  "Mixed Media Festival Set by Art Center," *Los Angeles Times*, July 17, 1970, D19; and "Mechicano Art Center," c. 1971, personal papers of Joe Rodriguez.

65  Luis Valdez (founder/director of Teatro Campesino), personal communication with author, February 15, 2011. A fire in 1973, believed to be arson, destroyed the Ash Grove.

66  Kilday, "Chicano Review Opens: Crash Course for Anglos."

67  Chon A. Noriega notes that Treviño's use of "jump cuts, dramatic recreations, and multiple story lines" relies on the audience's firsthand experience of the walkouts. Noriega, *The Ethnic Eye*, 8.

68  Estrada, *Los Angeles Plaza*, 13. Olvera Street opened to the public in 1930. According to Estrada, Sterling's tourist attraction echoed earlier efforts in the 1880s by Charles Lummis and others to prevent "undesirable" groups, including the poor, laborers, and communists, from congregating in the area. Because preservation requires financial support, Sterling invited Chandler to rally local elites who were eager to join a Chandler venture. Redesigning Olvera Street as a tourist site allowed Sterling and her supporters to displace any group or business that did not match their capitalist interests or their quaint image of Mexico and Mexicans. Among those targeted were labor unions, communists, and others who used the plaza to engage in free speech and mobilize constituents. Sterling used a "triumphant Anglo narrative" to inspire boosters, telling how US troops briefly occupied "the old adobe during the final occupation of the city in January 1847" (195). Ironically, the threat of deportation persuaded thousands of actual Mexicans to return to Mexico during the 1930s.

69  Ibid., 190. See also Estrada, *Los Angeles's Olvera Street*, 28.

70  Smith, introduction to *Hosts and Guests*, 1.

71  José Luis Gonzalez, interview by Olivares.

72  Generally, Mechicano does not appear to have described its public art or calendar-like prints in the same language as Goez, but the artist collective integrated art into pub-

lic space to challenge the media representations of Mexicans and the social stigma assigned to Mexican culture.

73 "Bus Bench Art Contest Winners Placed on Exhibit," *Los Angeles Times*, March 28, 1972, C1. See also Eve Simpson, "Chicano Street Murals."

74 Quoted in del Olmo, "Murals Changing Face of East L.A."

75 David R. Diaz, "Open Space and Recreation."

76 "Art Center Celebrates First Year," *Eastside Journal*, March 2, 1972, 3.

77 Juan Gonzalez, *Johnny Gonzalez, with Irma Núñez*, interview by Davalos, 257.

78 Richter, "The Politics of Heritage Tourism Development," 109.

79 For an analysis of the development of heritage tourism, see Jansen-Verbeke and Lievois, "Analyzing Heritage Resources for Urban Tourism in European Cities." For information about Goez cultural tourism initiatives, see Gutierrez-O'Neill, "Oportunidad para el artista," personal papers of José Luis Gonzalez; and Juan Gonzalez, *Johnny Gonzalez, with Irma Núñez*, interview by Davalos. Goez also produced calendars, postcards, and maps as souvenirs for tourists, although some, such as the postcards of murals commissioned by the Victor Clothing Company, were offered free to gallery patrons.

80 Johnny Gonzalez, also known as Don Juan, is credited with the concept and design of El Monumento de la Raza.

81 Botello, *David Botello*, interview by Davalos; and Juan Gonzalez, *Johnny Gonzalez, with Irma Núñez*, interview by Davalos.

82 "The Opening Door," *Career World*, December 1975, 17, personal papers of José Luis Gonzalez. Prior to the mural tours, school groups came to Goez for tours of the gallery.

83 Juan Gonzalez, *Johnny Gonzalez, with Irma Núñez*, interview by Davalos; and José Luis Gonzalez, interview by Olivares. It is not clear when the bus tours ended, but it likely coincided with Juan's decision to leave Goez.

84 Correspondence from Ophelia Flores to John Gonzales [sic], July 6, 1973, personal papers of José Luis Gonzalez.

85 Juan Gonzalez, *Johnny Gonzalez, with Irma Núñez*, interview by Davalos, 286. See also Goldman and Ybarra-Frausto, *Arte Chicano*, 23.

86 Juan "Johnny" Gonzalez coined the phrase, and it was used in his 1970 initiative, "Project: E.L.A. to Tourist Attraction."

87 Avila, "The Folklore of the Freeway," 17. See also Avila, *Popular Culture in the Age of White Flight*.

88 The mask is likely a composite of Aztec and Maya styles. It lacks the flared headdress associated with the Aztecs but includes the ear flares and jade necklace associated with Maya at Copán, as well as scarification found on Teotihuacan masks. I acknowledge Constance Cortez for these observations.

89 Avila, "The Folklore of the Freeway," 25.

90 Castellanos, interview by Bassing.

91 *Community Arts Los Angeles*, ii.

92 Ibid., 51.

93 This copy of the directory, a donation from Denise Lugo, is housed at the California State University Channel Islands Library.

94  Coomaraswamy, *Christian and Oriental Philosophy of Art*, 98.

95  On the methodology and pedagogy of Chicana/o studies, see Chabram-Dernersesian, "Introduction to Part One."

96  Botello, *David Botello*, interview by Davalos.

97  Dávila, *Culture Works*, 134.

98  For examples of the assimilationist interpretation of Goez's success, see "The Opening Door"; and Haecki, "Goez Art Studios and Gallery KOs Doubters."

99  DeVos Institute of Arts Management, "Diversity in the Arts: The Past, Present, and Future of African American and Latino Museums, Dance Companies, and Theater Companies," September 2015, 2.

100 Quoted in Dávila, *Culture Works*, 112.

101 Londoño, "An Aesthetic Belonging."

102 Noriega and Tompkins Rivas, "Chicano Art in the City of Dreams," 92.

103 Aranda, *When We Arrive*, 29.

### CHAPTER 4. TOURS OF INFLUENCE

1  Berkeley, *Journals of Travel in Italy*, 283–85 (emphasis added).

2  Chaney, "George Berkeley's Grand Tours."

3  Ibid., 328. Chaney documents that Berkeley's letter to Sir John Percival describes in more complete detail his observations of Lecce and his response to the Doric and Corinthian aesthetic (346–47).

4  Wolf, *Vermeer and the Invention of Seeing*, 11.

5  John Berger, *Ways of Seeing*; Harvey, *The Condition of Postmodernity*; Wolf, *Vermeer and the Invention of Seeing*.

6  Verstraete, *Tracking Europe*; Black, *The British Abroad*; Black, *Italy and the Grand Tour*; Baram and Rowan, "Archaeology after Nationalism"; Bowron and Kerber, "British Patrons and the Grand Tour"; and Urry, *Consuming Places*.

7  Chaney, *Evolution of the Grand Tour*, 331. Chaney argues, however, that Berkeley broke away from the "stereotyped Grand Tour itinerary" and visited the southern tip of Italy before other northern Europeans (123).

8  Bowron and Kerber, "British Patrons and the Grand Tour," 38.

9  Calaresu, review of *Italy and the Grand Tour*, 180. See also Bowron and Kerber, "British Patrons and the Grand Tour."

10 Delgado, *Roberto "Tito" Delgado*, interview by Davalos, 13.

11 Noriega, "Orphans of Modernism."

12 Romo, "Mexican Heritage, American Art," 22. For works that contextualize Chicana/o art within a larger art history, see also Selz, *Art of Engagement*; and Quirarte, *Mexican American Artists*, xx.

13 Griswold del Castillo, McKenna, and Yarbro-Bejarano, *Chicano Art*; Jackson, *Chicana and Chicano Art*; Mesa-Bains, *Ceremony of Spirit*; Ybarra-Frausto, "Rasquachismo: A Chicano Sensibility"; Goldman and Ybarra-Frausto, *Arte Chicano*; Vargas, *Contemporary Chican@ Art*; and Sorell, "Barrio Murals in Chicago."

14 Jones, *Seeing Differently*.

15 See Davalos, *Exhibiting Mestizaje*; and Pérez-Torres, *Mestizaje*.

16 "Codetermination" is a rethinking of the allegorical method of intersectionality, which may imagine race, class, gender, sexuality, and other subjectivities as distinct axes that cross at a single point.

17 The use of the artist's biography is a common convention in art history. Different this time is the value attributed to the biography of a person of color who under normative views has no individuality, no personal story, but presumably lives the prescribed culture of his or her race or ethnic group.

18 Anzaldúa, *Borderlands/La Frontera*, 80.

19 While conducting research on Los Angeles artists, I learned that other Chicanas/os had traveled abroad, several of them through military deployment. An expanded analysis of non-Mexican artistic influences on Chicana/o artists would consider Oscar Castillo's military deployment to Japan; Judy Baca's travels to Ireland, Finland, and Moscow for the *World Wall*, a traveling mural installation created by an international group of artists; Frank Romero's numerous trips to Paris; Barbara Carrasco's artist collaborations in the Soviet Union in the 1980s; Wayne Alaniz Healy's travels to Ireland starting in 1983, and then to Egypt, Pakistan, Japan, Spain, England, and Scotland; Richard Duardo's collaborations and commissions in Japan; and José Montoya's and Esteban Villa's travels beyond North America.

20 Luján, interview by Rangel.

21 Benjamin, "The Work of Art in the Age of Mechanical Reproduction," 220.

22 *The Frank Zappa Songbook*, vol. 1 (Los Angeles: Frank Zappa Music/Munchkin Music, 1973). Limón joined illustrators Richard E. Brown, Corny Cole, and Gary Lund.

23 Limón, *Leo Limón*, interview by Davalos, 34. Unless otherwise noted, all Leo Limón quotations in this chapter come from this interview.

24 Leo Limón, personal communication with author, August 23, 2013.

25 At one point Gonzalez planned to settle in Benidorm, as he was finding some work as a singer and he felt that he could also support his brother's import business, Goez Imports and Fine Arts.

26 Throughout the Chicano movement, Roberto "Tito" Delgado divided his time between Los Angeles and Chiapas. His mobility meant that curators frequently overlooked his work, even those seeking artists who worked in Mexico and the United States. Future scholars should consider Delgado's political awareness. For example, Delgado's adventures in Europe began in 1966, when he enlisted in the army after a recruiter promised to place him in officer candidate school. Like many Chicano and African American young men who shared information about the war in Vietnam, particularly the mortality rates associated with each recruitment center in the Los Angeles area, Delgado knew that his chances of survival depended upon his assignment or military rank. He did everything he could to avoid an infantry assignment, since he knew that a disproportionate number of African American and Mexican American men were sent to the frontlines and did not come back alive. See Delgado, *Roberto "Tito" Delgado*, interview by Davalos.

27 Ibid., 16. Unless otherwise noted, all Roberto "Tito" Delgado quotations in this chapter come from this interview.

28 Ernesto de la Loza, interview by Davalos, Los Angeles. Unless otherwise noted, all Ernesto de la Loza quotations in this chapter come from this interview.

29  Sandra de la Loza, "La Raza Cósmica," 56.

30  Ibid.

31  Juan Gonzalez, *Johnny Gonzalez, with Irma Núñez*, interview by Davalos, 128.

32  Noriega and Tompkins Rivas, "Chicano Art in the City of Dreams," 83.

33  Although the monument was not built, it was inadvertently copied. In 2004 Los Angeles county supervisor Gloria Molina initiated the East Los Angeles Civic Center Renovation Project, which echoed the proposal. Chicana/o artists Michael Amescua, Linda Arreola, Roberto "Tito" Delgado, and Richard Duffy were commissioned to create public art for the East Los Angeles Civic Center. Their work, along with the exterior renovation of the several buildings designed by José Antonio Aguirre, unified and reflected the very aesthetic that Gonzalez and Botello envisioned. In the three decades since the original proposal for an East Los Angeles public monument, the Chicana/o community had attained political leadership—namely, a mayor, several city council members, and a county supervisor, who rose up through the ranks of community activism and advocacy of the Chicano movement.

34  Venegas, "Mi Corazon/My Sacrifice, Mi Sacrificio/My Heart." Cemanahuac is the name of the Mexican territory before the Spanish conquest.

35  Confirming Leo Limón's role as arts ambassador of the Los Angeles River, in July 2011 the Studio for Southern California History produced a retrospective of his visual art about the river; his public art, the L.A. River Catz; and the Art Peace Park.

36  The wall would be similar to the Graffiti Pit in Venice, California, where street artists have been able to paint legally since 2000 (although permits have been required since 2007).

37  Venegas, "Walking the Road: The Art and Artistry of Linda Vallejo," 102. See also Davalos, "The Visual Art of Linda Vallejo."

38  Vallejo, *Linda Vallejo*, interview by Davalos, 12. Unless otherwise noted, all Linda Vallejo quotations in this chapter come from this interview.

39  Linda Vallejo, personal communication with author, May 18, 2011.

40  Ibid.

41  Harris, *Goya*, 19.

42  Ibid., 7–8.

43  Quotations in this paragraph in ibid., 19, 24. At the time of Vallejo's visits, *Colossus* (1818–25) was attributed to Goya, but research that began in the 1980s has determined that the work is not Goya's and may have been painted by one of his assistants. Geoff Pingree, "More Doubt over Goya's *Colossus*," *Time,* June 30, 2008.

44  Harris, *Goya*, 24.

45  Four decades later, she made a similar observation about the work of Sandro Botticelli. Attending the Florence Biennale in 2005, she went to see Botticelli's *Birth of Venus* (c. 1482) because she had never seen the original, although she had seen it "published a million times." Vallejo recalls, "It looks like a cartoon. Botticelli's *Venus*, when you go up to it, you can literally see that he's taken a terracotta-colored line and literally gone around the entire figure of the form. And when you step back from it, you don't see this cartoon, but when you step up to it . . . there is the line going around the body."

46 Bojórquez, *The Art and Life of Chaz Bojórquez*, 17. See also Bojórquez, *Charles "Chaz" Bojórquez*, interview by Davalos. The artist's curriculum vitae dated 2007 indicates that he started at Chouinard in 1968, after one year of state college.

47 Bojórquez, *Charles "Chaz" Bojórquez*, interview by Davalos, 43. Unless otherwise noted, all Chaz Bojórquez quotations in this chapter come from this interview.

48 Skulls that are dressed and accessorized, as is Señor Suerte, are found throughout popular culture but are largely distinct from the skull icon made popular in the 1970s by London counterculture.

49 Bojórquez's interest in script overshadowed his interest in architecture and in the paintings and sculpture housed in European museums. In Europe he studied maps and ancient manuscripts, such as the Rosetta Stone, for their typeface, layout, and design. However, he did marvel at *The Birth of Venus*, *The Four Seasons*, the unfinished sculptures of Michelangelo, and the work of Vermeer. His landscape-inspired paintings and drawings are documented for the first time in Bojórquez, *Art and Life of Chaz Bojórquez*.

50 Catherine S. Ramírez, "Afrofuturism/Chicanafuturism."

51 Botello, *David Botello*, interview by Davalos, 25. Unless otherwise noted, all David Botello quotations in this chapter come from this interview.

52 Latorre, *Walls of Empowerment*, 84; and Catherine S. Ramírez, "Deus ex Machina."

53 Latorre, *Walls of Empowerment*, 84–85; see also Richard T. Rodríguez, *Next of Kin*.

54 Quotations and description are from Latorre, *Walls of Empowerment*, 84, 87.

55 Noriega and Tompkins Rivas, "Chicano Art in the City of Dreams," 90.

56 Latorre, *Walls of Empowerment*, 85–87; and Richard T. Rodríguez, *Next of Kin*, 41.

57 Gunckel, "It Is the Artist's Function to Act Like a Camera for Society."

58 Catherine S. Ramírez, "Afrofuturism/Chicanafuturism," 187.

59 See Cockcroft and Barnet-Sánchez, *Signs from the Heart*. See also Tiffany Ana López on healing power of cultural production in "'Stunned into Being.'"

60 Urry, *Consuming Places*. Urry claims that modernity permits the "disembedding" or "'lifting out' of social relations from local involvements and their recombination across larger spans of time and space" (143).

61 Although Valadez attended high school in Huntington Park, he was aware of the East Los Angeles walkouts in 1968 and participated in the earliest moratorium marches in 1969 and 1970.

62 Valadez recalls that everyone was going to the county museum to see the work of art that had scandalized the city, and his mother, who took her teenage boys, was simply intrigued by art that was considered notorious. Raised by a young single mother who listened to rock 'n' roll, rhythm and blues, and other dance music, Valadez was exposed to cultural expressions that were forbidden to his peers whose fathers were military veterans and political conservatives.

63 Valadez, *John Valadez*, interview by Davalos, 16. Unless otherwise noted, all John Valadez quotations in this chapter come from this interview.

64 It is possible that Peter Paul Rubens's copy of Titian's *The Rape of Europa* (1562) served as John Valadez's inspiration for the figure. Rubens's painting, *The Rape of Europa* (1628–29), hangs in the Prado. During the 1980s, Valadez was clearly inspired by Rubens's fleshy and rotund bodies.

65 When the traveling exhibition *Santa Ana Condition: John Valadez* reached East Los Angeles in 2013, the organizers of the show, Karen Rapp and Victor Parra of the Vincent Price Art Museum, also observed European influences in the artist's work. As noted in the didactic label, the figure tumbling from the Impala convertible in *Getting Them Out of the Car* (1984) "recalls conversion scenes by the Baroque artist Caravaggio," and the tiled floor in the left register of the iconic pastel drawing resembles a "Renaissance proscenium."

66 The two primary female figures are taken from Rubens's *Diana and Her Nymphs Surprised by Satyrs* (1639–40), which Valadez saw when he toured the Prado. Other works by Rubens that are in the Prado and seem to have inspired Valadez are *The Rape of Proserpina* (1636–38), *The Victory of Truth over Heresy* (c. 1625), and *The Triumph of the Eucharist over Idolatry* (c. 1625).

67 Cortez, "New Aztlan."

68 Yolanda Gonzalez, interview by Davalos. Unless otherwise noted, biographical information and quotations in this section come from this interview, which I conducted at her studio. Gonzalez identifies her mother's aunt, Margarita Lopez, as her grandmother.

69 Berger, *Ways of Seeing*, 31.

70 Latorre, *Walls of Empowerment*, 70; and Goldman, *Contemporary Mexican Painting in a Time of Change*.

71 Lewallen and Moss, *State of Mind*.

72 Katzew, "'Only If It Bothers You.'" Emphasis in original. Unless otherwise noted, quotations in the remainder of this section are from this source.

CHAPTER 5. CHICANA/O ART COLLECTORS

Portions of chapter 5 are adapted from Karen Mary Davalos, "A Poetics of Love and Rescue in the Collection of Chicana/o Art," *Latino Studies* 5 (2007): 76–103, © Palgrave Macmillan Ltd.

1 Barrows, "Antonio F. Coronel." I am grateful to Armando Durón for introducing me to the Antonio F. Coronel Collection.

2 Newmark and Newmark, *Sixty Years in Southern California, 1853–1913, Containing the Reminiscences of Harris Newmark*, 622.

3 According to John P. Schmal, Mariana Williamson was born in San Antonio, Texas, to Nelson Williamson of Maine and Gertrude Roman, "a Mexicano Tejano woman from Los Brazos river area." Nelson Williamson brought his Spanish- and English-speaking daughter to California at age nine. Schmal, "The Four Latino Mayors of Los Angeles." See also *The National Cyclopaedia of American Biography*, s.v. "de Smith, Mariana Coronel (Williamson)," 566.

4 Davis and Alderson, *The True Story of "Ramona,"* 21.

5 Barrows, "Antonio F. Coronel," 80.

6 Correspondence from Antonio Coronel to Helen Hunt Jackson in December 1882 and August 1883, items 404, 405, and 406, Antonio F. Coronel Papers, Seaver Center for Western History Research, Natural History Museum of Los Angeles County (hereafter cited as Antonio F. Coronel Papers). See also Mathes and Bringandi, "Charles C.

Painter, Helen Hunt Jackson," 89. For her novel's characters, plot, and setting, Jackson studied the Coronel collection of pottery, woven baskets, beads, and textiles of Mission Indians. See Woolsey, "Antonio Coronel and Southern California's Romantic Lore, Ramona."

7  Barrows, "Antonio F. Coronel."

8  Woolsey, "Antonio Coronel," 143.

9  Mahood, "Coronel Collection," 4.

10  Barrows, "Antonio F. Coronel." The state of California "had repeatedly sought to acquire this collection for the exhibit of the State Historical Society, and $30,000 had been offered for it; but this and all other offers were declined." Davis and Alderson, *The True Story of "Ramona,"* 56.

11  The letter is included in the booklet that accompanied the first exhibition. See Los Angeles Chamber of Commerce, *Antonio F. Coronel Collection*, 7. The letter, dated June 6, 1900, is also held in the Antonio F. Coronel Papers.

12  Lummis, "Relics of Old Mexico," 115. Lummis wrote the first review of the collection and its exhibition.

13  Mahood, "Coronel Collection," 6.

14  The miniature dioramas were built in the 1930s by a dozen dioramists, model makers, and artists under the direction of Arthur A. Woodward, then curator of history. Mahood, *The 20 Dioramas of California History*, 1. For my personal encounter with these dioramas, see Davalos, *Exhibiting Mestizaje*.

15  Gonzales-Day, *Lynching in the West*, 274 n. 2.

16  Los Angeles Chamber of Commerce, *Antonio F. Coronel Collection*, 8, 16.

17  Correspondence from Henry Y. Sandham to Antonio Coronel, October 7, 1882, item 407, Antonio F. Coronel Papers.

18  Although these works are not in the collection, the Antonio F. Coronel Papers include one Sandham painting that may have been a gift to the artist's benefactors: a delicate watercolor in black, white, and various shades of gray depicts the southern end of the porch at El Recreo, with the Coronel orchard in the background (item GC 1001, box 20V A.110. 58–1664.1). The photographs in the collection include one attributed to C. C. Pierce, a prominent photographer of early Los Angeles urban development (item 1438 P-157, box 3). See also Davis and Alderson, *The True Story of "Ramona,"* 251–52. According to Davis and Alderson, Henry Sandham stayed with the Coronels in Los Angeles and often spent his time making sketches of them, their American Indian servants, and the property.

19  Correspondence from Alex F. Harmer to Mrs. Coronel, May 6, 1894, item 451, Antonio F. Coronel Papers.

20  Los Angeles Chamber of Commerce, *Antonio F. Coronel Collection*, 9. The Antonio F. Coronel Papers include dozens of portraits of unnamed individuals in the Papers and Photographs section; several were gifts to Doña Mariana. A certificate in the collection recognizes "Mary F. Coronel" for an exhibition of art, but her participation in the Los Angeles art scene has not been documented. Several anonymous watercolors and drawings of animals, landscapes, and flowers appear in the collection, and the catalog of the collection's premier at the Chamber of Commerce in 1901 attributes several

works, including the wax figures, to her. During my research, access to the collection was restricted, and thus these observations are strictly preliminary.

21  Davis and Alderson, *The True Story of "Ramona,"* 166.

22  Antonio F. Coronel Photograph Collection, P-157, Natural History Museum of Los Angeles County. The photo collection includes items captioned "Our Alps" and "Sheep by Water," both with the notation "MC Coronel, Mrs. AF 1910."

23  Sacco, "Racial Theory, Museum Practice."

24  In the past I focused on Chicana art collectors in an effort to balance the record, but most of the women I interviewed explained that many decisions to select the art were made with their partners. This study therefore investigates men and women collectors in the Los Angeles area.

25  Quotations in this paragraph are from López, "'Stunned into Being,'" 182, 183, 185, 188.

26  Elsewhere I elaborate on the intellectual utility of this approach in preference to consumption and museum studies, which both emphasize the individual as a unique but socially dysfunctional human being clouded by materialistic desire. See Davalos, "Poetics of Love and Rescue."

27  Although I do not have space to address it here, there is a small secondary market for Chicana/o art and a major discrepancy between auction and gallery prices. I acknowledge Patrick Ela and Armando Durón for pointing this out to me (personal communication, December 2, 2011). They independently offered Carlos Almaraz and John Valadez as examples, noting that the hammer price at auction for these artists' pastel drawings is between $4,500 and $6,000, while the works sell in galleries for $30,000 to $50,000. The discrepancy encourages me to sidestep consumer analysis.

28  Rosalie Gonzalez, in response to the question, "Why do you collect art?" Interview by Davalos. The interview took place in Gonzalez's home, with her partner and son present during some of the conversation. All quotations in this paragraph, as well as information about the Rosalie Gonzalez and Ramon Ramirez Collection, come from this interview.

29  Anita Miranda, interview by Davalos. Unless otherwise noted, all quotations from Anita Miranda in this chapter come from this interview. In a previous article (Davalos, "Poetics of Love and Rescue"), Anita was identified by a pseudonym, Elena Hurtado.

30  Davalos, *Exhibiting Mestizaje*, 41. Los Angeles has seen its own twenty-first-century version of elite capitalists shaping the direction of museums through the efforts of developer and entrepreneur Eli Broad.

31  Marin, remarks in panel discussion of *Artifex* exhibition. See also Marin, interview by Davalos.

32  Noriega, "Collectors Who Happen to Be . . . ," 10.

33  Ibid.

34  Muensterberger, *Collecting: An Unruly Passion*. Scholars of collecting use the term *rescue* for items valued in the past. Discussions of "rescue" are not applied to collectors who gather objects not yet valued. These people are typically classified as "pack rats" or "obsessive." See Belk, *Collecting in a Consumer Society*; and Pearce, *On Collecting*.

For exceptions that explore race, ethnicity, gender, and material inequity, see Codell, "Indian Crafts and Imperial Policy"; Macleod, *Enchanted Lives, Enchanted Objects*; Mary Caroline Simpson, "Modern Art Collecting and Married Women"; Ann Fabian, "The Curious Cabinet of Dr. Morton"; Garvey, "Dreaming in Commerce"; and Kastner, "Collecting Mr. Ayer's Narrative." For an excellent analysis of collecting and sexuality, see Camille and Rifkin, *Other Objects of Desire*.

35  On psychological perversion and individualization, see Pearce, *Interpreting Objects and Collections*; Baekeland, "Psychological Aspects of Art Collecting"; Baudrillard, *Simulacra and Simulation*; Elsner and Cardinal, *The Cultures of Collecting*; Muensterberger, *Collecting*; Stewart, *On Longing*; and Belk, "The Double Nature of Collecting." Belk argues that the image of the noble benefactor is used to rationalize and assuage the guilt of the "self-indulgent" collector. See also Belk, *Collecting in a Consumer Society*, 81.

36  Pearce and Bounia, introduction to *The Collector's Voice*, xiii. As Pearce notes elsewhere, the activities of women fall outside the narrow definitions of collecting. Pearce, *Museums, Objects and Collections*, 60–61. She contends that most scholars do not problematize the social construction of gender and rely instead on pseudo-psychoanalysis to interpret the motivations, meanings, and actions of men collectors (see, for example, Baekeland, "Psychological Aspects of Art Collecting"). Naomi Schor criticizes Jean Baudrillard for assuming that the collector is "unquestionably male" and specifically heterosexual. Schor, "Collecting Paris," 257. For a recent answer to Pearce's charge, see Mary Caroline Simpson, "Modern Art Collecting and Married Women in 1950s Chicago." My contribution to this scholarship on collecting brings into view the gendered and racialized aspects of the practice.

37  For a recent affirmation of Driskell's view of collecting, see Hayes, "On the Cusp." Also see Driskell, *The Other Side of Color*.

38  For important sources, see Moraga, *Loving in the War Years*; Moraga and Anzaldúa, *This Bridge Called My Back*; and Emma Pérez, *Decolonial Imaginary*.

39  Coffey, "Banking on Folk Art," 309.

40  Ariana Guerrera (a pseudonym), interview by Davalos, Tempe, AZ, May 2, 2003, and July 21, 2005. Unless otherwise noted, all quotations from Ariana Guerrera in this chapter come from this interview.

41  Sanchez-Brown, interview by Davalos. Unless otherwise noted, all quotations from Olivia Sanchez-Brown in this chapter come from this interview.

42  Maria Teresa "Terry" and Ricardo Muñoz, interview by Davalos. The interview was conducted at their home in Los Angeles. Unless otherwise noted, all quotations from the Muñozes in this chapter come from this interview.

43  David Diaz, interview by Davalos. The interview was conducted at his home in Los Angeles. Unless otherwise noted, all David Diaz quotations in this chapter come from this interview.

44  Delilah Montoya, exhibition wall text in *From the West: Chicano Narrative Photography*, Mexican Museum, 1995.

45  Noriega, "Collectors Who Happen to Be . . . ," 8.

46  Quotations are from an undated statement circa 2006 and from an interview with four members on June 7, 2006, at a restaurant near Olvera Street in downtown Los Angeles.

47  I attended these types of events between 2003 and 2013.

48  Marin, interview by Davalos.

49  Lipsitz, "Not Just Another Social Movement," 84; and José Esteban Muñoz, *Disidenti-fications*.

50  A few weeks after the interview, Ricardo Muñoz sent me a statement about his moti-vations for collecting. The quotations are taken from this unpublished essay, written around 2010.

51  Alarcón, "Making Familia from Scratch," 221.

52  Sanchez, interview by Davalos. Unless otherwise noted, all John Sanchez quotations in this chapter come from this interview.

53  Román-Odio, *Sacred Iconographies in Chicana Cultural Production*; Jeanette Rodríguez, *Our Lady of Guadalupe*; and Pineda-Madrid, "Notes toward a ChicanaFeminist Episte-mology."

54  Statement made at a public presentation and repeated during interviews with the Duróns in 2002 and 2005.

55  At the University of California, Santa Barbara, Salvador Güereña has been building the California Ethnic and Multicultural Archives since the 1990s. In 2001 the UCLA Chicano Studies Research Center Library and the International Center for the Arts of the Americas, Museum of Fine Arts, Houston, began systematically building col-lections.

56  Romo, "Curating without a Rear View Mirror."

57  Marin, interview by Davalos.

58  Anita Miranda Holguin, "Biography," unpublished artist statement, November 1993.

59  See Pomian, *Collectors and Curiosities*, 95. Mary Coffey made this same observation about folk art. Coffey, "Banking on Folk Art," 309.

60  In 2003 Eli Broad indicated that he would donate his collection to LACMA, but he withdrew the offer in 2008, when he announced that he would retain control of his works through an independent foundation that would loan items to museums. In 2010 he announced plans to locate a new museum for his collection in downtown Los Angeles; the Broad Museum opened in 2015. Edward Wyatt, "To Have and Give Not," *New York Times*, February 10, 2008; Mike Boehm, "Eli Broad, White Knight and Lightning Rod, Gets Ready to Open His Own Museum," *Los Angeles Times*, September 9, 2015; Deborah Vankin and Mike Boehm, "Eli Broad Won't Be MOCA's Lead Funder for Much Longer," *Los Angeles Times*, September 18, 2013. Broad was the primary funder of the Museum of Contemporary Art in the period 2008–2013, and he was engaged with a public campaign to change governance during that time, claiming that he helped found the museum. It was his donations, however, that spoke volumes to the board, which eventually caved in to his demands. Connie Bruck, "The Art of the Billionaire: How Eli Broad Took Over Los Angeles," *New Yorker*, December 6, 2010.

61  Rony, *The Third Eye*, 213.

62  Mary Salinas Durón, presentation at Social and Public Art Resource Center, Venice, CA, October 13, 2001 (emphasis in original).

63  Stewart, *On Longing*, 164.

64  Pearce, *Museums, Objects, and Collections*, 194, 48.

65  Coffey, "Banking on Folk Art," 309.

66  Yzaguirre and Aponte, *Willful Neglect*.

### CHAPTER 6. REMIXING

1  Fernando Gamboa, *Master Works of Mexican Art*, xi.

2  Richard F. Brown, foreword to Gamboa, *Master Works of Mexican Art*, vii. Founded in 1913 as the Museum of History, Science and Art, the institution originally housed art and artifacts, cultural material and archeological specimens, and animal taxidermy. The natural history museum and the art museum split in 1961, but the Los Angeles County Museum of Art did not move to its new location until 1965.

3  Ibid., vii.

4  "Masterworks of Mexican Art," *Los Angeles Times*, October 16, 1963, 1.

5  Schumach, "Mexican Art Seen by Many." It is impossible to determine precisely who came to the museum during the extended hours on Tuesdays, Fridays, and Sundays, but I suspect that the museum was attempting to accommodate a working-class audience.

6  "Lectures Slated," *Herald-American* (Los Angeles), October 17, 1963, clippings folder "Masterworks of Mexican Art," Research Library, Los Angeles County Museum of Art.

7  Press release, October 26, 2004, "UCLA Chicano Studies Research Center, Los Angeles County Museum of Art Forge Partnership and Announce Latino Art Initiative," jointly issued by UCLA and LACMA; "LACMA and UCLA Latino Arts Initiative," *Eastside Sun*, November 4, 2004, 5. Noriega was appointed adjunct curator of Chicano and Latino Art in the Center for the Art of the Americas at LACMA. Rita Gonzalez also joined LACMA as part-time staff in 2004 and in the following year, she was assistant curator of contemporary art. The five-year initiative was "to ensure that Chicano and Latino art play a consistent role in our [LACMA's] encyclopedic program," and it supported three exhibitions already in progress: *Lords of Creation: The Origins of Sacred Maya Kingship*, *Phantom Sightings*, and *Los Angelenos/Chicano Painters of L.A.: Selections from the Cheech Marin Collection*. See also Catherine Wagley, "Rita Gonzalez: LACMA Curator and Defender of Subtlety," *LA Weekly*, May 15, 2013.

8  Jennifer A. González, *Subject to Display*, 14.

9  The exhibitions are *The Road to Aztlan: Art from a Mythic Homeland* (May 13–August 26, 2001), *Inventing Race: Casta Paintings and Eighteenth-Century Mexico* (April 4–August 8, 2004), *Lords of Creation: The Origins of Sacred Maya Kingship* (September 10, 2005–January 2, 2006), *The Arts in Latin America, 1492–1820* (August 5–October 28, 2007), *Olmec: Colossal Masterworks of Ancient Mexico* (October 2, 2010–January 9, 2011), *Contested Visions in the Spanish Colonial World* (November 6, 2011–January 29, 2012), *Children of the Plumed Serpent: The Legacy of Quetzalcoatl in Ancient Mexico* (April 1–July 1, 2012), and *The Painted City: Art from Teotihuacan* (March 29, 2014–January 4, 2015). LACMA hired its first Latin American curator, Ilona Katzew, in 2000.

10  Venant, "Hispanic Art Sparks Ethnic Pride."

11  With Rockefeller Foundation support, Chicano and Chicana arts advocates of Los Angeles, including Armando Durón, created a nonprofit entity, the Artes de Mexico Festival Committee, to solicit, coordinate, and market events to complement *Splen-*

*dors*. Working pro bono for over four thousand hours, with assistance from staff at the University of Southern California, the committee coordinated approximately 230 events at 166 cultural and educational institutions during the presentation of *Splendors* at LACMA. Six months of performing arts, visual arts, and educational programming across the metropolitan area drew over five hundred thousand people to see the art and culture of Mexican America. Because of Artes de Mexico, new audiences were drawn to LACMA, one of the objectives of the Rockefeller Foundation. The county museum "vastly increased the Hispanic audience" at the museum. In the six-month period, an estimated 30 to 40 percent of the 352,854 visitors to the county museum were Latino.

LACMA hoped to recapture the cultural capital of Artes de Mexico when it began program planning for *The Road to Aztlan*. However, the county museum was caught off guard when many of the same committee members rejected the invitation to assist with supplementary programming because it came without financial support. Artes de Mexico had initiated the institutional changes that were needed at LACMA: financial reallocation, bilingual tour guides, and outreach to Latino audiences, but this did not lead to permanent structural changes. For information about Artes de Mexico, I consulted the unprocessed papers at UCLA Chicano Studies Research Center, Artes de Mexico Collection (Armando Durón donation), box Events and Binders II, Artes de Mexico Festival Final Report, submitted by the Artes de Mexico Festival Committee, April 1992. The quotation and the data about audience attendance appear on page 20 of the report.

12  Exhibitions are important, but collections permanently change an institution. This is not a critique of a curator, since one person cannot be expected to mobilize institutional policy. In the past decade, Rita Gonzalez advanced from temporary employee to staff curator of contemporary art, a rare achievement for Latina scholars in a comprehensive public art museum. Nonetheless, the artists for whom she has advocated, such as Gronk and Harry Gamboa Jr., have yet to find substantial representation in the county museum's collection. As I finished this manuscript in 2015, LACMA was celebrating its fiftieth anniversary and leveraging donations from collectors, which might include one or two works by Chicano artists, such as Ken Gonzales-Day and Mario Ybarra Jr.

13  My distinct interpretations of *The Road to Aztlan* emerge from different methodologies. In chapter 2 I begin with ethnographic methods and investigate the perspective of those who crafted the errata exhibition—namely, Armando Durón and the leadership of SPARC—and their response to the curators' comments in the exhibition catalog. Audience reception also drives my analysis. Here I use visual cultural studies methods and focus on the exhibition checklist, design, didactic labels, and another essay in the catalog. However, the two interpretations of this exhibition do not alter the value of the errata exhibition and the paradigm it brings to light.

14  Fields, interview by Davalos.

15  At the time of the exhibition, I publicly inquired how Chicana/o thought had arrived at the public museum. Had I missed the demonstration when Chicanas/os stormed the public museum and took control of the curator's office? Or were non-Chicana/o

scholars finally reading Chicana/o studies scholarship and finding it inspirational and insightful? The actual events that led to the exhibition are much less satisfying than revolutionary desires, and indeed its origins are altogether indicative of Chicana/o positionality within public museums. Virginia Fields writes in her catalog acknowledgments that anthropology professor Karl Taube of the University of California, Riverside, suggested the concept and title for the exhibition in 1991. Taube had been working out the symbolism of wind among the Olmec and Aztec of Mesoamerica and among the Western Pueblo communities of Zuni and Hopi in the geographic area of Aztlán. Thus, while Chicana/o historiography is not named as the framework for the show, it is clearly present within the design, the catalog, and the curators' statements.

16   LACMA unfortunately overstated its role in presenting a transhistorical and transnational argument through the exhibition. The curators mistakenly hailed the exhibition as trailblazing, claiming that "in terms of museum practices, the exhibition *breaks new ground* in looking at the southwestern United States and northern Mexico not as two culturally distinct regions, but as a heterogeneous yet unified cultural area." Fields and Zamudio-Taylor, "Aztlan: Destination and Point of Departure," 75 (emphasis added). This was sadly inaccurate: LACMA was not the first museum to argue for a unified cultural area or to offer this interpretation of space, time, and belonging. See Davalos, "The Mexican Museum of San Francisco."

17   Davalos, "The Mexican Museum of San Francisco." See also Fusco, "The Other History of Intercultural Performance."

18   Davalos, "The Mexican Museum of San Francisco." Certainly, the shortage of funds and space could have determined the exhibition design. But the cultural strategy of rasquachismo, in which "resilience and resourcefulness spring from making do with what is at hand," gave Peter Rodríguez, founder of the Mexican Museum, license to think and act outside the box—or outside the white walls of the conventional gallery design (Ybarra-Frausto, "Rasquachismo: A Chicano Sensibility," 156). The cultural sensibility of rasquachismo matches the oppositional and critical stance that is identified with the museum's exhibition aesthetic and general orientation. See also Yarbro-Bejarano, "The Female Subject in Chicano Theatre."

19   Davalos, "The Mexican Museum of San Francisco."

20   Davalos, *Exhibiting Mestizaje*. The museum opened its doors in 1987.

21   Fields and Zamudio-Taylor, "Aztlan: Destination and Point of Departure," 63.

22   Some references to Valadez's *The Border* use a different title; artists frequently use multiple titles for the same work, which might explain this apparent discrepancy.

23   While this concept of nepantla can be seen to be driving the latest installation for Pacific Standard Time: LA/LA, preliminary analysis indicates that a majority of the forty-six proposed exhibitions focus on Latin American artists, with little or no reference to Los Angeles or US Latino artists. Funding is also favoring Latin American exhibitions at mainstream institutions with little track record or expertise in the areas of Chicana/o critical theory of the borderlands and transnational art of US Latinos.

24   It is curious that Constance Cortez is the only essayist in the exhibition catalog to shift significant interpretive weight toward Chicana feminist thought in her analysis

of the exhibition and the problematic emphasis on Aztlán. My analysis about the exhibition is informed by her expansion of the parameters and theoretical contribution of the exhibition.

25 Cortez, "New Aztlan," 358.

26 This information was noted on wall labels and is part of the "Checklist of the Exhibition" in the catalog, Fields and Zamudio-Taylor, *The Road to Aztlan*, 374–92.

27 Cortez, "New Aztlan," 358. The concept of nepantla resonates with Amelia Jones's notion of queer feminist durationality. Jones, *Seeing Differently*.

28 This view might also have been expressed through the art of *Phantom Sightings*, but the curators make little mention of Chicana feminist thought.

29 Cortez, "New Aztlan," 367.

30 Gonzalez, Fox, and Noriega, introduction to *Phantom Sightings*, 13 (emphasis added).

31 Press release, 2004. Another possible reading of the statement emphasizes the sly form of public shaming of LACMA: it has been *two* decades since the county museum presented a comprehensive exhibition of Chicana/o art.

32 I could also point to another institutional practice that makes it difficult to see Chicana/o art in LACMA: the search engine designed to provide Internet access to the collection does not recognize "Chicano art" as a category. My students make this complaint every year. While searches for "Mexican art" and "African American art" produce results (over six hundred and over one hundred, respectively), a search for "Chicano art" yields only two works because the term "Chicano" appears in the titles. One must know the name of the artist or the work of those in the collection, such as Carlos Almaraz, Chaz Bojórquez, Enrique Chagoya, and Ruben Ortiz-Torres. Searching highlights from the collection, which is organized by media (prints and drawings, for example) and time (contemporary or ancient), also requires this type of foresight. The numerous prints by Chicana/o artists that Richard Duardo convinced the Graphics Arts Council to purchase during his tenure in the early 2000s and the collection of prints from Self Help Graphics & Art are lost or inaccessible within the online infrastructure. In 2016 LACMA announced acquisitions of works by Ken Gonzales-Day and Marrio Ybarra Jr.

33 Michael Govan, foreword to *Phantom Sightings*, 11.

34 Wilson, "The Troubled Gift."

35 Reed Johnson, "Carlos Almaraz's Time Is Coming." Emphasis added.

36 These collaborations are discussed in chapter 2; see note 20.

37 "Supplement to Los Four," *Los Angeles County Museum of Art Members' Calendar* 12, no. 2 (1974), n.p.

38 See the Shifra Goldman Papers. The unprocessed papers with relevant evidence can be found in the folder "Los Four." When I used Goldman's papers in her home in 2004, they contained correspondence, which I copied, from Monroe Price, California Law Center, to Jane Livingston, modern art curator at LACMA. Cecil Ferguson, who had the role of "special curator" for the exhibition, was most likely the person who encouraged the emerging artists to hold the county museum accountable. Ferguson, who died in 2013, was an African American staff member who had worked his way from museum custodian to exhibition preparator and eventually to curatorial staff.

He was a pioneer in the black arts scene and was instrumental in bringing African American art to the county museum. I agree with Roberto Tejada: "There is no overstating [Chicano artists'] indebtedness to Cecil's efforts" to include Chicano art at LACMA after the seminal exhibition *Los Angeles 1972: A Panorama of Black Artists*. Tejada, "Los Angeles Snapshots," 77.

39 Vincent Price Art Museum Archive, folders "Mechicano" and "Chicanismo en el Arte."

40 Press information, LACMA, "Chicanismo en el Arte: Juried Sale Show for Chicano Student Artists," p. 1, Vincent Price Art Museum Archives, Chicanismo en el Arte April–March 1975 folder.

41 Buckley, "Asco Elite of the Obscure."

42 Chavoya and Gonzalez, "Asco and the Politics of Revulsion," 57.

43 Buckley, "Asco Elite of the Obscure."

44 I heard Rita Gonzalez make this claim at several public events, including the one held for faculty at the Chicano Studies Research Center in spring 2011. Given C. Ondine Chavoya's dissertation topic, it is likely that he and Rita Gonzalez were informally discussing the Asco retrospective for a decade. A proposal to the Fellows of Contemporary Art includes a statement that the two had discussed the exhibition prior to their appointments at their respective institutions, around 2002 and 2004 (author's personal files).

45 This is a minor point, but it corrects the inaccurate claim that two Pacific Standard Time exhibitions traveled from Los Angeles because PST was so successful in achieving national attention. From the start, *Asco: Elite of the Obscure* was designed as a traveling exhibition, and thus its installation at Williams College was not an achievement that was due to Pacific Standard Time but the result of long-term planning and collaboration between Chavoya and Gonzalez.

46 Chavoya and Gonzalez, "Elite of the Obscure: An Introduction," 19.

47 Eddie (Edy) Ytuarte, "Chicano Art Lives in East L.A.: 'A True Barrio Art,'" *El Chicano*, December 7, 1972, 9; and Harry Gamboa Jr., "Gronk and Herrón: Muralists." Both are reproduced in the "Documents" section of Chavoya and Gonzalez, *Asco: Elite of the Obscure*, 384–91.

48 Chavoya and Gonzalez, "Asco and the Politics of Revulsion," 48.

49 Romo, "Conceptually Divine," 276.

50 Chavoya and Gonzalez, "Asco and the Politics of Revulsion," 55. In the 1970s in the Southwest, and in the 1980s in the Midwest, Day of the Dead celebrations became a site for revealing the damages and traumas of gang violence and substance abuse.

51 James, "No Movies," 182, 187.

52 Jones, "'Traitor Prophets,'" 107; and Gunckel, "'We Were Drawing and Drawn into Each Other,'" 151.

53 Harry Gamboa Jr., personal communication with author, September 18, 2011. See also "Keeping It Real: An Open Roundtable Discussion." It is also significant that identity politics was one of multiple aesthetic and exhibition strategies available to curators of Chicana/o art.

54 Dávila, *Barrio Dreams*, 10.

55 Lerner, "Asco's Super-8 Cinema," 240, 238, and 244. Amelia Jones, in "'Traitor Prophets,'" also offers a more subtle interpretation of Asco. She takes Chicana feminist

theory as her starting point and thus admits to ambiguities in Asco's aesthetic. This allows her to avoid the dichotomous reading that places Asco against figuration, Chicano representation, and muralism.

56 Govan, foreword to Chavoya and Gonzalez, *Asco: Elite of the Obscure*, 16.

57 Knight, "Art Review." See also Duvernoy, "Asco at LACMA"; and Cheng, "Asco." The attention to Patssi Valdez's fashion sensibility can function as public voyeurism, a sexual perversity apparently permitted among elites looking at racialized and exoticized women.

58 Knight, "Art Review."

59 Ibid.

60 Ibid.

61 Harry Gamboa Jr., personal communication with author, September 18, 2011. The quote appears in Harry Gamboa Jr., oral history interview by Rangel.

62 *Asco: No Movies* opened in October 2013 and ran through January 5, 2014, at the Nottingham Contemporary.

63 In 2015 the Whitney Museum of American Art acquired several Asco photographs by Gamboa, and in 2016 the National Portrait Gallery and the Autry Museum of the Americas acquired for their permanent collections several photographs from Gamboa's series Chicano Male Unbonded. "CSUN Professor's Photographs to Become Part of National Portrait Gallery and Autry Museum Permanent Collections," *CSUN Today*, April 11, 2016.

64 Harry Gamboa Jr., personal communication with author, September 18, 2011. This intervention also represented control of Chicana/o art, the very category mainstream museums had pressured Gamboa to shed if he wanted to achieve critical and financial success. Independently, Willie Herrón III and Diane Gamboa also insisted on engaging the county museum on their own terms. Both artists required a fee for the exhibition of their work. D. Gamboa also demanded clarity on the interpretation of her work with Asco. Although their terms clash with conventions in American art museums, the artists' agency and critical interpretation of the redistribution of wealth constitute significant resistance against decades of aesthetic erasure.

65 The earliest record of such an exhibition on a college campus is *El Arte del Pocho*, which opened at California State University, Long Beach, in 1968 under the leadership of Gilbert "Magu" Sánchez Luján. This Chicano student exhibition included, among others, Roberto de la Rocha, Jesus Gutierrez, Ed Oropeza, Robert Esteban Chavez, and Magu. See the folder "El Arte del Pocho" in the Shifra Goldman Papers. *4 Chicano Artists* was itself a referential gesture toward prior exhibitions of three artists conceptualized as a group, Los Tres Grandes (Diego Rivera, José Clemente Orozco, and David Alfaro Siqueiros).

66 This quartet should not be mistaken for the renowned group known as Los Four, originally made up of Almaraz, Magu, Roberto "Beto" de la Rocha, and Frank Romero, with the later additions of Judithe Hernández and John Valadez.

67 For the reviews, see Monteverde, "Contemporary Chicano Art." Ianco later presented Asco in *Ascozilla* (1975) at the Fine Arts Gallery of California State University, Los

Angeles, and Harry Gamboa Jr. in *Approaches to Xerography* (1979) at the Los Angeles Municipal Art Gallery.

68 Wilson, "Chicano Exhibition 'Cheerfully Angry.'"

69 Ibid.

70 Monteverde, "Contemporary Chicano Art," 60. That same year Castellanos exhibited abstract and colorist work at numerous colleges and universities as Mechicano sought a new home. Mechicano Art Center collaborated with California State University at Long Beach, Compton Junior College, Pasadena College, and the University of California at Santa Barbara in 1970 and 1971. Shows ran concurrently. See Castellanos, interview by Bassing.

71 Monteverde, "Contemporary Chicano Art," 59.

72 Ibid.

73 Sotomayor, "*Chicanarte* Exposition Opening in Barnsdall."

74 Gonzalez, "Frida, Homeboys, and the Butch Gardens School of Fine Art," 319; see also Harry Gamboa Jr., interview by Rangel.

75 Quotations in this paragraph are from a discussion of Dada in Foster et al., *Art since 1900*, 176.

76 The checklist was published in "Supplement to Los Four."

77 With *4 Chicano Artists* as the new index, Mexican American artists such as Domingo Ulloa, Roberto Chavez, Eduardo Carrillo, and Dora de Larios are not only "facilitators" of Chicano art but also participants. *4 Chicano Artists* asks us to forgo the emphasis on the Chicano movement as index and look to other experiences that support an aesthetic invested in politics and shaped by the international sensibilities of artists who trained in the United States while also studying Mexican art. These sensibilities and experiences are directly portrayed, for instance, in Ulloa's work, such as *Painters on Strike* (1948), *Racism/Incident at Little Rock* (1957), *Braceros* (1960), and *Going Home* (1964); however, some works make indirect references to Mexican American struggle, culture, and history. That is, the international influences on de Larios's ceramic sculptures, the surrealist figurative compositions of Chavez, and the domestic interiors of Carrillo should not be dismissed as "vaguely Chicano." With a new index, we may place their work squarely within Chicana/o art.

CHAPTER 7. CONCLUSION

1 Ybarra-Frausto, "Rasquachismo," 156.

2 For a cogent discussion of art historical methods derived from Western thought and the normative emphasis on binary thinking, see Jones, *Seeing Differently*.

3 Palumbo-Liu, "Introduction: Unhabituated Habituses," 4.

4 Garcia, *Margaret Garcia*, interview by Davalos, 56.

5 Vásquez, *Triangulations*.

6 Graciela Iturbide does not discretely label her photographs. Several works have the same title.

7 I witnessed the same exuberance at another event on March 7, 2008. The Getty Center featured a panel consisting of scholars Charlene Villaseñor Black, Stanley Brandes, and John Pohl, and the artist Christina Fernandez, in the Museum Lecture Hall. The

panel was sparsely attended by forty to fifty people, many of whom did not remain for the late afternoon tour of the exhibition led by Fernandez. The artist's tour, on the other hand, was packed, and the crowd giddy with excitement as I describe above.

8   With this notion, I would count the first Chicana/o Day at the Museum as the events in 1963, when the exhibition of *Master Works of Mexican Art* forced LACMA to extend the show for an additional two months and to offer longer daily hours.

9   Hernández and Rodriguez y Gibson, introduction to *The Un/Making of Latina/o Citizenship*, 3–4.

10  Noriega, "Orphans of Modernism," 20.

11  For an example of the illogical critique of identity politics and the argument that ethnic minorities enjoy their victim status, see Brown, *State of Injury*, 73–74. Brown cannot account for the decades of Chicana feminist scholarship and creative writing that theorizes loss differently. Eliza Rodriguez y Gibson, for example, in *Stunned into Being*, offers a theory for the poetics of loss that comprehends agency, power, complexity, and resistance that is beyond immobility and mimicry of the hegemonic order. This position drives most Chicana feminist scholarship.

12  Noriega, introduction to Noriega, Romo, and Tompkins Rivas, *L.A. Xicano*, xi.

13  Quotations are from the didactic label accompanying the installation.

14  On a larger scale, the two exhibitions function as errata to the omission of Chicana/o art in the PST shows *Proof: The Rise of Printmaking in Southern California*; *Collaboration Labs: Southern California Artists and the Artist Space Movement*; and *Doin' It in Public: Feminism and Art at the Woman's Building*. These three PST shows included little or no mention of Chicana/o artists, even though these artists had made important contributions to printmaking through Self Help Graphics & Art and in Richard Duardo's print studios, had fostered alternative artist spaces, and had produced feminist art and collaborated with the Woman's Building. The exhibition I document here, *Las Venas de la Mujer*, was the only substantial Chicana/o presence in *Doin' It in Public*. I acknowledge Armando Durón for carefully documenting each PST exhibition that could have recognized Chicano and Chicana artists but did not.

15  Ortega, "Photographic Representation of Racialized Bodies."

16  Alcoff, *Visible Identities*, 38, 44.

17  Mills, *The Racial Contract*.

18  One would need to travel to the National Hispanic Cultural Center of Albuquerque, New Mexico, to see three or more concurrent exhibitions of Chicana/o art.

19  "Pacific Standard Time: LA/LA," Getty Foundation, www.getty.edu.

20  Romo, "Re-Searching for an American Art."

Acuña, Rodolfo F. *A Community under Siege: A Chronicle of Chicanos East of the Los Angeles River, 1945–1975*. Monograph 11. Los Angeles: Chicano Studies Research Center Publications, 1984.

Alarcón, Norma. "Chicana Feminism: In the Tracks of 'the' Native Woman." In *Living Chicana Theory*, edited by Carla Trujillo, 371–82. Berkeley: Third Woman Press, 1998.

———. "Making *Familia* from Scratch: Split Subjectivities in the Work of Helena María Viramontes and Cherríe Moraga." In *Chicana Creativity and Criticism: Charting New Frontiers in American Literature*, edited by María Hererra-Sobek and Helena María Viramontes, 220–32. Albuquerque: University of New Mexico Press, 1996.

———. "The Theoretical Subject(s) of *This Bridge Called My Back* and Anglo-American Feminism." In *Making Face, Making Soul: Haciendo Caras*, edited by Gloria Anzaldúa, 365–69. San Francisco: Aunt Lute, 1990.

Alcoff, Linda Martín. *Visible Identities: Race, Gender, and the Self*. New York: Oxford University Press, 2006.

Aldana, Erin. Review of *L.A. Xicano* and *Asco: Elite of the Obscure, A Retrospective, 1972–1987*. CAA Reviews, College Art Association, February 8, 2013. doi: 10.3202/caa.reviews.2013.17.

Alejandre, Abel Mora. *Resurrected Histories: Voices from the Chicano Arts Collectives of Highland Park*. DVD. Avenue 50 Studio, 2012.

Anzaldúa, Gloria. *Borderlands/La Frontera: The New Mestiza*. San Francisco: Aunt Lute, 1987.

———. "Chicana Artists: Exploring *Nepantla, en Lugar de la Frontera*." In *The Latino Studies Reader: Culture, Economy, and Society*, edited by Antonia Darder and Rodolfo D. Torres, 163–69. Malden, MA: Blackwell, 1998.

———. *Interviews/Entrevistas*. Edited by AnaLouise Keating. New York: Routledge, 2000.

Aranda, José F., Jr. *When We Arrive: A New Literary History of Mexican America*. Tucson: University of Arizona Press, 2003.

Arreola, Linda. "Vaguely Chicana." *Chicana/Latina Studies: Journal of MALCS* 8, nos. 1–2 (2008): 6–7.

Avila, Eric R. "The Folklore of the Freeway: Space, Culture, and Identity in Postwar Los Angeles." *Aztlán: Journal of Chicano Studies* 23, no. 1 (1998): 15–31.

———. *Popular Culture in the Age of White Flight: Fear and Fantasy in Suburban Los Angeles.* Berkeley: University of California Press, 2006.

Baca, Judith. *Judy Baca.* Interview by Karen Mary Davalos, January 29, March 16 and 26, May 10, June 3, September 29, October 13, 20, and 27, and November 3, 2010. CSRC Oral Histories Series 14. Los Angeles: UCLA Chicano Studies Research Center Press, 2014.

Baekeland, Frederick. "Psychological Aspects of Art Collecting." In *Interpreting Objects and Collections*, edited by Susan M. Pearce, 205–19. New York: Routledge, 1994.

Baram, Uzi, and Yorke Rowan. "Archaeology after Nationalism: Globalization and the Consumption of the Past." In *Marketing Heritage: Archaeology and the Consumption of the Past*, edited by Yorke Rowan and Uzi Baram, 3–23. Walnut Creek, CA: Altamira, 2004.

Barrows, H. D. "Antonio F. Coronel." *Annual Publication of the Historical Society of Southern California and Pioneer Register, Los Angeles* 5, no. 1 (1900): 78–82. doi: 10.2307/41169640.

Baudrillard, Jean. *Simulacra and Simulation.* Ann Arbor: University of Michigan Press, 1994.

Beardsley, John, and Jane Livingston, eds. *Hispanic Art in the United States: Thirty Contemporary Painters and Sculptors.* Houston: Museum of Fine Arts; New York: Abbeville, 1987. Exhibition catalog, with an essay by Octavio Paz.

———. "Preface and Acknowledgments." In *Hispanic Art in the United States: Thirty Contemporary Painters and Sculptors.* Houston: Museum of Fine Arts; New York: Abbeville, 1987. Exhibition catalog.

Belk, Russell W. *Collecting in a Consumer Society.* New York: Routledge, 1995.

———. "The Double Nature of Collecting: Materialism and Anti-Materialism." *Etnofoor* 11, no. 1 (1998): 7–20.

Benjamin, Walter. "The Work of Art in the Age of Mechanical Reproduction." In *Illuminations: Essays and Reflections.* Edited by Hannah Arendt. Translated by Harry Zohn, 217–51. New York: Schocken, 1968.

Berger, John. *Ways of Seeing.* New York: Viking, 1972.

Berger, Martin A. *Sight Unseen: Whiteness and American Visual Culture.* Berkeley: University of California Press, 2005.

Berkeley, George. *Journals of Travel in Italy*, vol. 7 of *The Works of George Berkeley, Bishop of Cloyne.* 9 vols. Edited by A. A. Luce and T. E. Jessop. London: Nelson, 1948–1957.

Black, Jeremy. *The British Abroad: The Grand Tour in the Eighteenth Century.* Stroud, UK: Sutton, 1992.

———. *Italy and the Grand Tour.* New Haven: Yale University Press, 2003.

Blaine, John, and Decia Baker. "Finding Community through the Arts: Spotlight on Cultural Pluralism in Los Angeles." *Arts in Society* 10, no. 1 (1973): 125–38.

Bojórquez, Charles "Chaz." *The Art and Life of Chaz Bojórquez.* Edited by Marco Klefisch and Alberto Scabbia. Bologna: Grafiche Damiani, 2009.

————. *Charles "Chaz" Bojórquez*. Interview by Karen Mary Davalos, September 25, 27, and 28, and October 2, 2007. CSRC Oral Histories Series 5. Los Angeles: UCLA Chicano Studies Research Center Press, 2013.

Botello, David. *David Botello*. Interview by Karen Mary Davalos, September 23 and 30, October 1 and 15, 2007, and May 21, 2009. CSRC Oral Histories Series 7. Los Angeles: UCLA Chicano Studies Research Center Press, 2013.

Bowron, Edgar Peters, and Peter Björn Kerber. "British Patrons and the Grand Tour." In *Pompeo Batoni: Prince of Painters in Eighteenth-Century Rome*, 37–87. New Haven: Yale University Press, 2007.

Brady, Mary Pat. *Extinct Lands, Temporal Geographies: Chicana Literature and the Urgency of Space*. Durham: Duke University Press, 2002.

Brown, Wendy. *State of Injury: Power and Freedom in Late Modernity*. Princeton: Princeton University Press, 1995.

Buckley, Annie. "Asco Elite of the Obscure." *Art in America*, January 10, 2012. www.artinamericamagazine.com.

Bürger, Peter. *Theory of the Avant Garde*. Minneapolis: University of Minnesota Press, 1984.

Buzard, James. *The Beaten Track: European Tourism, Literature, and the Ways to Culture, 1800–1918*. Oxford: Clarendon, 1993.

Calaresu, Melissa. Review of *Italy and the Grand Tour*, by Jeremy Black. *European History Quarterly* 35, no. 1 (2005): 179–81.

"Califas: Chicano Art and Culture in California." Transcripts Book 4. Archival documents of the Califas Conference held at Mary Porter Sesnon Gallery, University of California, Santa Cruz, 1982. Transcripts and video recordings housed at Stanford University Libraries.

Camacho, Alicia Schmidt. "Hailing the Twelve Million: U.S. Immigration Enforcement and the Imaginary of Lawful Violence." *Social Text* 28, no. 4 (2010): 1–24.

Camille, Michael, and Adrian Rifkin, eds. *Other Objects of Desire: Collectors and Collecting Queerly*. Oxford: Blackwell, 2001.

Carrasco, Barbara. *Barbara Carrasco*. Interview by Karen Mary Davalos, August 30, September 11 and 21, and October 10, 2007. CSRC Oral Histories Series 3. Los Angeles: UCLA Chicano Studies Research Center Press, 2013.

Castellanos, Leonard. "Chicano Centros, Murals, and Art." *Art in Society* 12, no. 1 (Spring–Summer 1975): 38–43.

————. *Leonard Castellanos*. Interview by Karen Mary Davalos, October 15, 2011. CSRC Oral Histories Series 15. Los Angeles: UCLA Chicano Studies Research Center Press, 2014.

————. Oral history interview by Allen Bassing, December 26, 1972. Smithsonian Archives of American Art, Washington, DC. www.aaa.si.edu/collections/interviews.

Chabram-Dernersesian, Angie. "Introduction to Part One." In *The Chicana/o Cultural Studies Reader*, edited by Angie Chabram-Dernersesian, 3–25. New York: Routledge, 2006.

Chaney, Edward. *The Evolution of the Grand Tour: Anglo-Italian Cultural Relations since the Renaissance*. London: Frank Cass, 2000.

Chávez, Ernesto. *"¡Mi Raza Primero!" (My People First!): Nationalism, Identity, and Insurgency in the Chicano Movement in Los Angeles, 1966–1978*. Berkeley: University of California Press, 2002.

Chavoya, C. Ondine. "Orphans of Modernism: Chicano Art, Public Representation, and Spatial Practice in Southern California." PhD diss., University of Rochester, 2002.

Chavoya, C. Ondine, and Rita Gonzalez. "Asco and the Politics of Revulsion." In *Asco: Elite of the Obscure, A Retrospective, 1972–1987*, edited by C. Ondine Chavoya and Rita Gonzalez, 37–106. Ostfildern, Germany: Hatje Cantz Verlag, 2011. Exhibition catalog.

———. "Documents." In *Asco: Elite of the Obscure, A Retrospective, 1972–1987*, edited by C. Ondine Chavoya and Rita Gonzalez, 384–91. Ostfildern, Germany: Hatje Cantz Verlag, 2011. Exhibition catalog.

———. "Elite of the Obscure: An Introduction." In *Asco: Elite of the Obscure, A Retrospective, 1972–1987*, edited by C. Ondine Chavoya and Rita Gonzalez, 18–27. Ostfildern, Germany: Hatje Cantz Verlag, 2011. Exhibition catalog.

Cheng, Scarlet. "Asco." *Art Ltd.*, November–December 2011. www.artltdmag.com.

*Chicanismo en el Arte*. Los Angeles: Los Angeles County Museum of Art, 1975. Exhibition catalog.

Cockcroft, Eva Sperling. "From Barrio to Mainstream: The Panorama of Latino Art." In *Handbook of Hispanic Cultures in the United States: Literature and Art*, edited by Francisco Lomelí, 192–217. Houston: Arte Público; Madrid: Instituto de Cooperación Iberoamericana, 1993.

Cockcroft, Eva Sperling, and Holly Barnet-Sánchez, eds. *Signs from the Heart: California Chicano Murals*. Venice, CA: SPARC; Albuquerque: University of New Mexico Press, 1993.

Cockcroft, Eva Sperling, John Pitman Weber, and James D. Cockcroft. *Toward a People's Art: The Contemporary Mural Movement*. New York: Dutton, 1977.

Codell, Julie F. "Indian Crafts and Imperial Policy: Hybridity, Purification, and Imperial Subjectivities." In *Material Cultures, 1740–1920: The Meanings and Pleasures of Collecting*, edited by John Potvin and Alla Myzelev, 149–70. Burlington: Ashgate, 2009.

Coffey, Mary K. "Banking on Folk Art: Banamex-Citigroup and Transnational Cultural Citizenship." *Bulletin of Latin American Research* 29, no. 3 (2010): 296–312.

*Community Arts Los Angeles*. Los Angeles: Community Arts Alliance, 1973.

Cooks, Bridget R. *Exhibiting Blackness: African Americans and the American Art Museum*. Amherst: University of Massachusetts Press, 2011.

Coomaraswamy, Ananda. *Christian and Oriental Philosophy of Art*. New York: Dover, 1956. First published as *Why Exhibit Works of Art?* London: Luzac, 1943.

Corrin, Lisa G. "*Mining the Museum*: Artists Look at Museums, Museums Look at Themselves." In *Mining the Museum: An Installation by Fred Wilson*, edited by Lisa G. Corrin, 1–22. Baltimore: The Contemporary; New York: New Press, 1994. Exhibition catalog.

Cortez, Constance. "The New Aztlan: Nepantla (and Other Sites of Transmogrification)." In *The Road to Aztlan: Art from a Mythic Homeland*, edited by Virginia M. Fields and Victor Zamudio-Taylor, 358–73. Los Angeles: Los Angeles County Museum of Art, 2001. Exhibition catalog.

Davalos, Karen Mary. "'All Roads Lead to East L.A.': Goez Art Studios and Gallery." In *L.A. Xicano*, edited by Chon A. Noriega, Terezita Romo, and Pilar Tompkins Rivas, 29–39. Los Angeles: UCLA Chicano Studies Research Center Press, 2011. Exhibition catalog.

———. "The Art of Place: The Work of Diane Gamboa." In *Performing the US Latina and Latino Borderlands*, edited by Arturo J. Aldama, Chela Sandoval, and Peter J. García, 73–93. Bloomington: Indiana University Press, 2012.

———. "Centro de Arte Público/Public Art Center." *Aztlán: A Journal of Chicano Studies* 36, no. 2 (2011): 171–78.

———. *Exhibiting Mestizaje: Mexican (American) Museums in the Diaspora*. Albuquerque: University of New Mexico Press, 2001.

———. "The Mexican Museum of San Francisco: Creating New Contexts for Chicano and Mexican Art." In *The Mexican Museum of San Francisco Papers, 1971–2006*, 1–69. Chicano Archives, vol. 3. Los Angeles: UCLA Chicano Studies Research Center Press, 2010.

———. "A Poetics of Love and Rescue in the Collection of Chicana/o Art." *Latino Studies* 5, no. 1 (2007): 76–103.

———. "The Visual Art of Linda Vallejo: Indigenous Spirituality, Indigenist Sensibility, and Emplacement." *Chicana/Latina Studies: The Journal of MALCS* 15, no. 1 (2015): 24–54.

———. *Yolanda M. López*. A Ver: Revisioning Art History, vol. 2. Los Angeles: UCLA Chicano Studies Research Center Press, 2007.

Davalos, Karen Mary, and Colin Gunckel. "The Early Years, 1970–1985: An Interview with Michael Amescua, Mari Cárdenas Yáñez, Yreina Cervántez, Leo Limón, Peter Tovar, and Linda Vallejo." In *Self Help Graphics & Art: Art in the Heart of East Los Angeles*, edited by Colin Gunckel, 2nd ed., 49–88. Chicano Archives, vol. 1. Los Angeles: UCLA Chicano Studies Research Center Press, 2014.

Dávila, Arlene. *Barrio Dreams: Puerto Ricans, Latinos, and the Neoliberal City*. Berkeley: University of California Press, 2004.

———. *Culture Works: Space, Value, and Mobility across the Neoliberal Americas*. New York: New York University Press, 2012.

———. *Latinos, Inc.: The Marketing and Making of a People*. Berkeley: University of California Press, 2001.

———. *Latino Spin: Public Image and the Whitewashing of Race*. New York: New York University Press, 2008.

Davis, Carlyle Channing, and William A. Alderson. *The True Story of "Ramona": Its Facts and Fictions, Inspiration and Purpose*. New York: Dodge, 1914. www.library.arizona.edu.

de la Loza, Ernesto. Interview by Karen Mary Davalos, Los Angeles, July 13, 2012.

de la Loza, Sandra. Interview by Karen Mary Davalos, Boyle Heights, CA, December 2, 2011.

———. "La Raza Cósmica: An Investigation into the Space of Chicana/o Muralism." In *L.A. Xicano*, edited by Chon A. Noriega, Terezita Romo, and Pilar Tompkins Rivas, 53–61. Los Angeles: UCLA Chicano Studies Research Center Press, 2011. Exhibition catalog.

———. "Mural Remix: An Artist's Intervention into the Discourse of Chicano Muralism." Paper presented at College Art Association annual conference, Los Angeles, February 25, 2012.

Delgado, Roberto. *Roberto "Tito" Delgado*. Interview by Karen Mary Davalos, November 5, 7, 9, and 16, 2007. CSRC Oral Histories Series 8. Los Angeles: UCLA Chicano Studies Research Center Press, 2013.

del Olmo, Frank. "Murals Changing Face of East LA." *Los Angeles Times*, December 3, 1973, B1.

Diaz, David R. "Barrio Logic and the Consolidation of Chicanas/os in the City: 1945–1975." In *Barrio Urbanism: Chicanos, Planning, and American Cities*, 49–62. New York: Routledge, 2005.

———. Interview by Karen Mary Davalos, Los Angeles, June 26, 2011.

———. "Open Space and Recreation." In *Barrio Urbanism: Chicanos, Planning, and American Cities*, 126–39. New York: Routledge, 2005.

Diaz, Ella Maria. "Flying under the Radar with the Royal Chicano Air Force: The Ongoing Politics of Space and Ethnic Identity." PhD diss., College of William and Mary, 2010.

———. "The Necessary Theater of the Royal Chicano Air Force." *Aztlán: A Journal of Chicano Studies* 38, no. 2 (2013): 41–70.

Driskell, David C. *The Other Side of Color: African American Art in the Collection of Camille O. and William H. Cosby Jr.* San Francisco: Pomegranate, 2001.

Duardo, Richard. *Richard Duardo*. Interview by Karen Mary Davalos, November 5, 8, and 12, 2007. CSRC Oral Histories Series 9. Los Angeles: UCLA Chicano Studies Research Center Press, 2013.

Duggan, Lisa. *The Twilight of Equality? Neoliberalism, Cultural Politics, and the Attack on Democracy*. Boston: Beacon, 2003.

Durón, Armando. *Other Footprints to Aztlan: Works from the Collection of Mary and Armando Durón*. Venice, CA: Social and Public Art Resource Center, 2001.

Duvernoy, Sophie. "Asco at LACMA: Glitter, Face Paint, Velvet and Chiffon in the Name of Politics." *Public Spectacle* (*LA Weekly* blog), September 8, 2011. www.laweekly.com.

Elsner, John, and Roger Cardinal, eds. *The Cultures of Collecting*. London: Reaktion, 1994.

Eng, David L. "The Civil and the Human." *American Quarterly* 64, no. 2 (2012): 205–12.

Estrada, William David. *The Los Angeles Plaza: Sacred and Contested Space*. Austin: University of Texas Press, 2008.

———. *Los Angeles's Olvera Street*. Charleston: Arcadia, 2006.

Fabian, Ann. "The Curious Cabinet of Dr. Morton." In *Acts of Possession: Collecting in America*, edited by Leah Dilworth, 112–37. New Brunswick: Rutgers University Press, 2003.

Fabian, Johannes. "Presence and Representation: The Other and Anthropological Writing." *Critical Inquiry* 16, no. 4 (1990): 753–72.

Fe, Sonya. "Mechicano Art Center: Discovering the Center" and "Mechicano Art Center: Creating Awareness." Videotaped interview. *Departures*, KCET website, n.d. www.kcet.org.

Feifer, Maxine. *Tourism in History*. New York: Stein and Day, 1985.

Fernandez-Sacco, Ellen. "Check Your Baggage: Resisting Whiteness in Art History." *Art Journal* 60, no. 4 (2001): 58–61.

Fields, Virginia M. Interview by Karen Mary Davalos, Los Angeles, January 23, 2002.

Fields, Virginia M., and Victor Zamudio-Taylor. "Aztlan: Destination and Point of Departure." In *The Road to Aztlan: Art from a Mythic Homeland*, edited by Virginia M. Fields and Victor Zamudio-Taylor, 38–77. Los Angeles: Los Angeles County Museum of Art, 2001. Exhibition catalog.

———, eds. *The Road to Aztlan: Art from a Mythic Homeland*. Los Angeles: Los Angeles County Museum of Art, 2001. Exhibition catalog.

Foley, Douglas E., Clarice Mota, Donald E. Post, and Ignacio Lozano. *From Peones to Politi-cos: Ethnic Relations in a South Texas Town, 1900 to 1977*. CMAS Monograph 3. Austin: Center for Mexican American Studies, University of Texas, 1977.

Foster, Hal, Rosalind Krauss, Yve-Alain Bois, Benjamin H. D. Buchloh, and David Joselit. *Art since 1900: Modernism, Antimodernism, Postmodernism*. London: Thames and Hudson, 2011.

Fox, Howard N. "Theater of the Inauthentic." In *Phantom Sightings: Art after the Chicano Movement*, edited by Rita Gonzalez, Howard N. Fox, and Chon A. Noriega, 74–98. Berkeley: University of California Press; Los Angeles: Los Angeles County Museum of Art, 2008. Exhibition catalog.

Franco, Victor. Oral history interview by Barry Schwartz, July 1972. Smithsonian Archives of American Art, Washington, DC. www.aaa.si.edu/collections/interviews.

Fusco, Coco. "The Other History of Intercultural Performance." In *English Is Broken Here: Notes on Cultural Fusion in the Americas*, 37–64. New York: New Press, 1995.

Gamboa, Fernando, ed. *Master Works of Mexican Art from Pre-Columbian Times to the Present*. Los Angeles: Los Angeles County Museum of Art, 1963. Exhibition catalog.

Gamboa, Harry, Jr. "Gronk and Herrón: Muralists." *Neworld* 2, no. 3 (1975).

———. Oral history interview by Jeffrey Rangel, April 1–16, 1999. Smithsonian Archives of American Art, Washington, DC, www.aaa.si.edu/collections/interviews.

Garcia, Margaret. *Margaret Garcia*. Interview by Karen Mary Davalos, August 27 and September 10, 12, 19, and 24, 2008. CSRC Oral Histories Series 11. Los Angeles: UCLA Chicano Studies Research Center Press, 2013.

Garvey, Ellen Gruber. "Dreaming in Commerce: Advertising Trade Card Scrapbooks." In *Acts of Possession: Collecting in America*, edited by Leah Dilworth, 66–87. New Brunswick: Rutgers University Press, 2003.

Goldman, Shifra M. *Contemporary Mexican Painting in a Time of Change*. Albuquerque: University of New Mexico Press, 1995.

———. *Dimensions of the Americas: Art and Social Change in Latin America and the United States*. Chicago: University of Chicago Press, 1994.

———. "How, Why, Where, and When It All Happened: Chicano Murals of California." In *Signs from the Heart: California Chicano Murals*, edited by Eva Sperling Cockcroft and Holly Barnet-Sánchez, 23–53. Venice, CA: SPARC; Albuquerque: University of New Mexico Press, 1993.

———. "A Public Voice: Fifteen Years of Chicano Posters." *Art Journal* 44, no. 1 (1984): 50–57.

———. "Response: Another Opinion on the State of Chicano Art." In *Dimensions of the Americas: Art and Social Change in Latin America and the United States*, 383–93. Chicago: University of Chicago Press, 1994. Originally published in *Metamórfosis: Northwest Chicano Magazine of Literature Art and Culture* 3, no. 2 (1980)/4, no. 1 (1981): 2–7.

Goldman, Shifra M., and Tomás Ybarra-Frausto, eds. *Arte Chicano: A Comprehensive Annotated Bibliography of Chicano Art, 1965–1981*. Berkeley: Chicano Studies Library Publications Unit, University of California, 1985.

———. "The Political and Social Contexts of Chicano Art." In *Chicano Art: Resistance and Affirmation, 1965–1985*, edited by Richard Griswold del Castillo, Teresa McKenna, and

Yvonne Yarbro-Bejarano, 83–95. Los Angeles: Wight Art Gallery, University of California, 1991.

Gonzales-Day, Ken. *Lynching in the West, 1850–1935*. Durham: Duke University Press, 2006.

González, Jennifer A. *Subject to Display: Reframing Race in Contemporary Installation Art*. Cambridge: MIT Press, 2008.

Gonzalez, José Luis. Interview by Lourdes Karina Olivares, Los Angeles, May 19, 2004. Available from the author.

Gonzalez, Juan. *Johnny Gonzalez, with Irma Núñez*. Interview by Karen Mary Davalos, October 28, November 4, 11, and 18, and December 17 and 20, 2007. CSRC Oral Histories Series 7. Los Angeles: UCLA Chicano Studies Research Center Press, 2013.

Gonzalez, Rita. "Frida, Homeboys, and the Butch Gardens School of Fine Art." In *Asco: Elite of the Obscure, A Retrospective, 1972–1987*, edited by C. Ondine Chavoya and Rita Gonzalez, 318–25. Ostfildern, Germany: Hatje Cantz Verlag, 2011. Exhibition catalog.

———. "Phantom Sites: The Official, the Unofficial, and the Orificial." In *Phantom Sightings: Art after the Chicano Movement*, edited by Rita Gonzalez, Howard N. Fox, and Chon A. Noriega, 46–73. Berkeley: University of California Press; Los Angeles: Los Angeles County Museum of Art, 2008. Exhibition catalog.

———. *An Undocumented History: A Survey of Index Citations for Latino and Latina Artists*. CSRC Research Report 2. Los Angeles: UCLA Chicano Studies Research Center Press, 2003.

Gonzalez, Rita, Howard N. Fox, and Chon A. Noriega. Introduction to *Phantom Sightings: Art after the Chicano Movement*, edited by Rita Gonzalez, Howard N. Fox, and Chon A. Noriega, 13–14. Berkeley: University of California Press; Los Angeles: Los Angeles County Museum of Art, 2008. Exhibition catalog.

———, eds. *Phantom Sightings: Art after the Chicano Movement*. Berkeley: University of California Press; Los Angeles: Los Angeles County Museum of Art, 2008. Exhibition catalog.

Gonzalez, Rosalie. Interview by Karen Mary Davalos, Montebello, CA, June 25, 2011.

Gonzalez, Yolanda. Interview by Karen Mary Davalos, Alhambra, CA, July 12, 2013.

Govan, Michael. "Los Angeles County Museum of Art." In *Asco: Elite of the Obscure, A Retrospective, 1972–1987*, edited by C. Ondine Chavoya and Rita Gonzalez, 16. Ostfildern, Germany: Hatje Cantz Verlag, 2011. Exhibition catalog.

Grimm, Tracy. *Identifying and Preserving the History of the Latino Visual Arts: Survey of Archival Initiatives and Recommendations*. CSRC Research Report 6. Los Angeles: UCLA Chicano Studies Research Center Press, 2005.

Griswold del Castillo, Richard, Teresa McKenna, and Yvonne Yarbro-Bejarano, eds. *Chicano Art: Resistance and Affirmation, 1965–1985*. Los Angeles: Wight Art Gallery, University of California, 1991. Exhibition catalog.

Gudiol, José. *Goya*. Translated by Kenneth Lyons. Barcelona: Ediciones Polígrafa, 2008.

Guerrero, Tony, Jr. "Chicano Art Center Showcases Minorities, Gives Opportunity." *Campus News* (East Los Angeles College), October 17, 1973, 4.

Gunckel, Colin. "It Is the Artist's Function to Act Like a Camera for Society." Presentation at "L.A. Xicano: A Symposium on Art and Place over Time," Fowler Museum, University of California, Los Angeles, November 6, 2011. YouTube.

————. "'I Was Participating and Documenting': Chicano Art through the Photography of Oscar Castillo." In *The Oscar Castillo Papers and Photograph Collection*, edited by Colin Gunckel, 1–17. Chicano Archives, vol. 5. Los Angeles: UCLA Chicano Studies Research Center Press, 2011.

————. "'We Were Drawing and Drawn into Each Other': Asco's Collaboration through *Regeneración*." In *Asco: Elite of the Obscure, A Retrospective, 1972–1987*, edited by C. Ondine Chavoya and Rita Gonzalez, 151–78. Ostfildern, Germany: Hatje Cantz Verlag, 2011. Exhibition catalog.

Gutierrez-O'Neill, Ava. "Oportunidad para el artista ofrece una galería de E. L.A." *La Opinión* (Los Angeles), July 25, 1971.

Guzmán, Kristen. "Self Help Graphics & Art: Art in the Heart of East Los Angeles." In *Self Help Graphics & Art: Art in the Heart of East Los Angeles*, edited by Colin Gunckel, 2nd ed., 1–30. Chicano Archives, vol. 1. Los Angeles: UCLA Chicano Studies Research Center Press, 2014.

Haecki, John. "Goez Art Studios and Gallery KOs Doubters." *Montebello News–East Los Angeles Gazette–Pico Rivera News*, August 25, 1979, 9A.

Hames-García, Michael. *Identity Complex: Making the Case for Multiplicity*. Minneapolis: University of Minnesota Press, 2011.

Harris, Enriqueta. *Goya*. London: Phaidon, 1994.

Harvey, David. *The Condition of Postmodernity: An Inquiry into the Origins of Cultural Change*. Malden, MA: Blackwell, 1990.

Hayes, Jeffreen M. "On the Cusp: Young Collectors." *International Review of African American Art* 22, no. 2 (2008): 25–29.

Hernández, Ellie D., and Eliza Rodriguez y Gibson. Introduction to *The Un/Making of Latina/o Citizenship: Culture, Politics, and Aesthetics*. New York: Palgrave Macmillan, 2014.

Hernández, Judithe. Interview by Karen Mary Davalos, Santa Monica, CA, July 24, 2014.

Hollinshead, Keith. "Tourism and Third Space Populations: The Restless Motion of Diaspora Peoples." In *Tourism, Diasporas and Space*, edited by Tim Coles and Dallen J. Timothy, 33–49. New York: Routledge, 2004.

hooks, bell. "Homeplace: A Site of Resistance." In *Yearning: Race, Gender, and Cultural Politics*, 41–53. Boston: South End, 1990.

Huacuja, Judith. "Borderlands Critical Subjectivity in Recent Chicana Art." In *Gender on the Borderlands: The Frontiers Reader*, edited by Antonia Castañeda with Susan H. Armitage, Patricia Hart, and Karen Weathermon, 104–21. Lincoln: University of Nebraska Press, 2002.

Ianco-Starrels, Josine. "Art News: 'Video Anthology' Opens Today." *Los Angeles Times*, June 8, 1975, T75.

Ibarra, María de la Luz. "Frontline Activists: Mexicana Care Workers, Subjectivity, and the Defense of the Elderly." *Medical Anthropology Quarterly* 27, no. 3 (2013): 434–52.

"Images of Aztlan at Méchicano." *Chismearte* 1, no. 1 (1976): 2–4.

Jackson, Carlos Francisco. *Chicana and Chicano Art: ProtestArte*. Tucson: University of Arizona Press, 2009.

James, David E. "No Movies." In *Asco: Elite of the Obscure, A Retrospective, 1972–1987*, edited by C. Ondine Chavoya and Rita Gonzalez, 179–206. Ostfildern, Germany: Hatje Cantz Verlag, 2011. Exhibition catalog.

Jansen-Verbeke, Myriam, and Els Lievois. "Analyzing Heritage Resources for Urban Tourism in European Cities." In *Contemporary Issues in Tourism Development*, edited by Douglas G. Pearce and Richard W. Butler, 81–107. New York: Routledge, 1999.

Johnson, Ken. "They're Chicanos and Artists. But Is Their Art Chicano? Review of Phantom Sightings." *New York Times*, April 9, 2010.

Johnson, Reed. "Carlos Almaraz's Time Is Coming, Nearly 30 Years after Death." *Los Angeles Times*, March 8, 2014.

Jones, Amelia. *Seeing Differently: A History and Theory of Identification and the Visual Arts.* New York: Routledge, 2012.

———. "'Traitor Prophets': Asco's Art as a Politics of the In-Between." In *Asco: Elite of the Obscure, A Retrospective, 1972–1987*, edited by C. Ondine Chavoya and Rita Gonzalez, 107–41. Ostfildern, Germany: Hatje Cantz Verlag, 2011. Exhibition catalog.

Kastner, Carolyn. "Collecting Mr. Ayer's Narrative." In *Acts of Possession: Collecting in America*, edited by Leah Dilworth, 138–62. New Brunswick: Rutgers University Press, 2003.

Katzew, Ilona. "'Only If It Bothers You': Ruminations on the Display of Latin American Art." *Unframed: The LACMA Blog*, June 17, 2013. https://unframed.lacma.org.

Keating, AnaLouise. "Introduction: Reading Gloria Anzaldúa, Reading Ourselves . . . Complex Intimacies, Intricate Connections." In *The Gloria Anzaldúa Reader*, edited by AnaLouise Keating, 1–16. Durham: Duke University Press, 2009.

"Keeping It Real: An Open Roundtable Discussion." Tropico de Nopal Gallery Art-Space, August 30, 2008. Hosted by Christina Fernandez, Reyes Rodriguez, and Arturo Ernesto Romo-Santillano. Audio file available on *The Sickly Season* website, www.sicklyseason.com.

Keller, Gary, Mary Erickson, Kaytie Johnson, and Joaquín Alvarado, eds. *Contemporary Chicana and Chicano Art*. Tempe, AZ: Bilingual Press/Editorial Bilingüe, 2002.

Kennicott, Philip. "Art Review: 'Our America' at the Smithsonian." *Washington Post*, October 25, 2013. http://wapo.st.

Kilday, Gregg. "Chicano Review Opens: Crash Course for Anglos." *Los Angeles Times*, September 2, 1971, I17.

Knight, Christopher. "Art Review: 'Asco: Elite of the Obscure, 1972–1987' at LACMA." *Culture Monster (Los Angeles Times* blog), September 9, 2011. www.latimesblogs.latimes.com.

Kun, Josh. "This Is Chicano Art? The New Chicano Movement." *Los Angeles Times Magazine*, January 9, 2005.

Kwon, Miwon. *One Place after Another: Site-Specific Art and Locational Identity*. Cambridge: MIT Press, 2002.

Latorre, Guisela. *Walls of Empowerment: Chicana/o Indigenist Murals of California*. Austin: University of Texas Press, 2008.

"Lectures Slated." *Herald-American* (Los Angeles), October 17, 1963. Clippings folder. "Masterworks of Mexican Art," Research Library, Los Angeles County Museum of Art.

Lerner, Jesse. "Asco's Super-8 Cinema and the Specter of Muralism." In *Asco: Elite of the Obscure, A Retrospective, 1972–1987*, edited by C. Ondine Chavoya and Rita Gonzalez, 237–55. Ostfildern, Germany: Hatje Cantz Verlag, 2011. Exhibition catalog.

Lewallen, Constance M., and Karen Moss. *State of Mind: New California Art circa 1970*. With additional essays by Julia Bryan-Wilson and Anne Rorimer. Berkeley: University of California, Berkeley Art Museum, Pacific Film Archive, and Orange County Museum of Art; Berkeley: University of California Press, 2011. Exhibition catalog.

Limón, Leo. *Leo Limón*. Interview by Karen Mary Davalos, October 2, 4, and 18, 2007. CSRC Oral Histories Series 6. Los Angeles: UCLA Chicano Studies Research Center Press, 2013.

Lippard, Lucy R. *Mixed Blessings: New Art in a Multicultural America*. New York: New Press, 1990.

Lipsitz, George. "Not Just Another Social Movement: Poster Art and the *Movimiento Chicano*." In *Just Another Poster? Chicano Graphic Arts in California*, edited by Chon A. Noriega, 71–89. Santa Barbara: University Art Museum, University of California, 2001. Exhibition catalog.

———. *Time Passages: Collective Memory and American Popular Culture*. Minneapolis: University of Minnesota Press, 1990.

Londoño, Johana. "An Aesthetic Belonging: The Latinization of Space, Urban Design and the Limits of Representation." PhD diss., New York University, 2011.

Loper, Mary Lou. "Giving Her All for Mechicano Center." *Los Angeles Times*, July 12, 1973, E6.

López, Tiffany Ana. "'Stunned into Being': The Practice of Critical Witnessing in Lorna Dee Cervantes's *Drive*." In *Stunned into Being: Essays on the Poetry of Lorna Dee Cervantes*, edited by Eliza Rodriguez y Gibson, 177–95. San Antonio: Wings Press, 2012.

Lorde, Audre. "The Master's Tools Will Never Dismantle the Master's House." In *Sister Outsider: Essays and Speeches*. Berkeley: Crossing Press, 1984.

Los Angeles Chamber of Commerce. *Antonio F. Coronel Collection: Exhibition Room, Third Floor, Chamber of Commerce Building*. Los Angeles: Baumgardt, 1906.

Luján, Gilbert Sánchez. Oral history interview by Jeffrey Rangel, November 7–17, 1997. Smithsonian Archives of American Art, Washington, DC. www.aaa.si.edu/collections/interviews.

Lummis, Charles Fletcher. "Relics of Old Mexico." *Land of Sunshine: A Southern California Magazine* 14 (1901): 111–18.

Macleod, Dianne Sachko. *Enchanted Lives, Enchanted Objects: American Women Collectors and the Making of Culture, 1800–1940*. Berkeley: University of California Press, 2008.

Mahood, Ruth I. "The Coronel Collection." *Los Angeles County Museum Quarterly* 14, no. 4 (1958): 4–7.

———, ed. *The 20 Dioramas of California History in the California Hall of the Los Angeles County Museum of History and Science*. History Division Bulletin, no. 2. Los Angeles: Los Angeles County Museum of History and Science, 1965.

Marin, Cheech. Interview by Karen Mary Davalos, Malibu, CA, June 24, 2011.

———. Remarks on panel discussion of *Artifex* exhibition with Susana Smith Bautista, Einar and Jamex de la Torre, Shizu Saldamando, John Valadez, and Harry Gamboa Jr., at Koplin Del Rio Gallery, Culver City, CA, May 29, 2013. Audio recording posted on *Off-Ramp* (KPCC Los Angeles blog), June 4, 2013. www.scpr.org.

"Masterworks of Mexican Art." *Los Angeles Times*, October 16, 1963, 1.

Mathes, Valeria Sherer, and Phil Bringandi. "Charles C. Painter, Helen Hunt Jackson, and the Mission Indians of Southern California." *Journal of San Diego History* 55, no. 3 (2009): 89–118.

McCaughan, Edward J. *Art and Social Movements: Cultural Politics in Mexico and Aztlán.* Durham: Duke University Press, 2012.

McWhorter, Ladelle. *Racism and Sexual Oppression in Anglo-America: A Genealogy.* Bloomington: Indiana University Press, 2009.

"Mechicano Art Center Works on Display at Junior Art Center." *Eastside Journal/Belvedere Citizen*, May 31, 1973.

Mendoza, Ruben R. "Deciphering the Decoy: Phantom Transformations and the Decolonial Imaginary of Chicana/o Art." Review of *Phantom Sightings: Art after the Chicano Movement.* LatinArt.com, [2008]. www.latinart.com.

Mercer, Kobena. "Black Art and the Burden of Representation." In *Welcome to the Jungle: New Positions in Black Cultural Studies*, 233–58. New York: Routledge, 1994.

Mesa-Bains, Amalia. "Art of the Other Mexico: Sources and Meanings." In *Art of the Other Mexico: Sources and Meanings*, edited by René H. Arceo-Frutos, Juana Guzman, and Amalia Mesa-Bains, 14–73. Chicago: Mexican Fine Arts Center Museum, 1993. Exhibition catalog.

———, ed. *Ceremony of Spirit: Nature and Memory in Contemporary Latino Art.* San Francisco: Mexican Museum, 1993. Exhibition catalog.

———. "El Mundo Feminino: Chicana Artists of the Movement: A Commentary on Development and Production." In *Chicano Art: Resistance and Affirmation, 1965–1985*, edited by Richard Griswold del Castillo, Teresa McKenna, and Yvonne Yarbro-Bejarano, 131–40. Los Angeles: Wight Art Gallery, University of California, 1991. Exhibition catalog.

Mills, Charles W. *The Racial Contract.* Ithaca: Cornell University Press, 1997.

Miranda, Anita. Interview by Karen Mary Davalos, Pico Rivera, CA, May 13, 2004.

Miranda, Caroline A. "How Chicano Is It?" *ARTnews*, September 1, 2010. www.artnews.com.

Mondloch, Kate. "The *Difference* Problem: Art History and the Critical Legacy of 1980s Theoretical Feminism." *Art Journal* 71, no. 2 (2012): 18–31.

Monteverde, Mildred. "Contemporary Chicano Art." *Aztlán: Chicano Journal of the Social Sciences and the Arts* 2, no. 2 (1971): 51–61.

Montoya, Malaquias, and Lezlie Salkowitz-Montoya. "A Critical Perspective on the State of Chicano Art." *Metamórfosis* 3, no. 1 (1980): 3–7.

Moraga, Cherríe. *The Last Generation: Prose and Poetry.* Boston: South End, 1993.

———. *Loving in the War Years: Lo que nunca pasó por sus labios.* Boston: South End, 1983.

Moraga, Cherríe, and Gloria Anzaldúa, eds. *This Bridge Called My Back: Writings by Radical Women of Color.* New York: Kitchen Table/Women of Color Press, 1983.

Moravec, Michelle. "Historicizing the Chicana." *Politics of Women's Culture* website. Accessed February 2013; essay no longer available.

———. "Judithe Hernandez's Altar." *Politics of Women's Culture* website. Accessed February 2013; essay no longer available.

———. "The Past Put into Chicanismo Perspective." *Politics of Women's Culture* website. Accessed February 2013; essay no longer available.

Muchnic, Suzanne. "Emerson Woelffer, 88; Abstract Artist, Teacher." *Los Angeles Times*, February 5, 2003, B12.

Muensterberger, Werner. *Collecting: An Unruly Passion: Psychological Perspectives*. Princeton: Princeton University Press, 1994.

Muñoz, José Esteban. *Disidentifications: Queers of Color and the Performance of Politics*. Minneapolis: University of Minnesota Press, 1999.

Muñoz, Ricardo, and Maria Teresa "Terry" Muñoz. Interview by Karen Mary Davalos, South Pasadena, CA, June 13, 2011.

*The National Cyclopaedia of American Biography*. S.v. "de Smith, Mariana Coronel (Williamson)," 566. New York: James T. White, 1904.

Newmark, Maurice H., and Marco R. Newmark, eds. *Sixty Years in Southern California, 1853–1913, Containing the Reminiscences of Harris Newmark*. New York: Knickerbocker, 1916.

Noriega, Chon A. "The City of Dreams . . . and Shoes." *Tate Etc.* (blog), no. 23 (September 1, 2011). www.tate.org.uk.

———. "Collectors Who Happen to Be . . ." In *East of the River: Chicano Art Collectors Anonymous: From the Collections of Martha Abeytia Canales and Charles Canales . . . [et al.]*, edited by Chon A. Noriega, 8–16. Santa Monica, CA: Santa Monica Museum of Art, 2000. Exhibition catalog.

———. "Conceptual Graffiti and the Public Art Museum: *Spray Paint LACMA*." In *Asco: Elite of the Obscure, A Retrospective*, edited by C. Ondine Chavoya and Rita Gonzalez, 256–61. Ostfildern, Germany: Hatje Cantz Verlag, 2011. Exhibition catalog.

———. *The Ethnic Eye: Latino Media Arts*. Minneapolis: University of Minnesota Press, 1996.

———. Introduction to *L.A. Xicano*, edited by Chon A. Noriega, Terezita Romo, and Pilar Tompkins Rivas, xi–xii. Los Angeles: UCLA Chicano Studies Research Center Press, 2011. Exhibition catalog.

———. "Many Wests." In *From the West: Chicano Narrative Photography*, 9–16. San Francisco: Mexican Museum, 1995. Exhibition catalog.

———. "The Orphans of Modernism." In *Phantom Sightings: Art after the Chicano Movement*, edited by Rita Gonzalez, Howard N. Fox, and Chon A. Noriega, 16–45. Berkeley: University of California Press; Los Angeles: Los Angeles County Museum of Art, 2008. Exhibition catalog.

Noriega, Chon A., and Pilar Tompkins Rivas. "Chicano Art in the City of Dreams: A History in Nine Movements." In *L.A. Xicano*, edited by Chon A. Noriega, Terezita Romo, and Pilar Tompkins Rivas, 71–102. Los Angeles: UCLA Chicano Studies Research Center Press, 2011. Exhibition catalog.

Ortega, Mariana. "Photographic Representation of Racialized Bodies: Afro-Mexicans, the Visible, and the Invisible." *Critical Philosophy of Race* 1, no. 2 (2013): 163–89.

Padilla, Debra. Interview by Karen Mary Davalos, Venice, CA, March 25, 2004.

Pagel, David. "Monique Prieto." *BOMB* 72 (Summer 2000): 75–82. http://bombsite.com.

Palumbo-Liu, David. "Introduction: Unhabituated Habituses." In *Streams of Cultural Capital: Transnational Cultural Studies*, edited by David Palumbo-Liu and Hans Ulrich Gumbrecht, 1–21. Stanford: Stanford University Press, 1997.

Panicacci, Lorraine. "The History of Goez." *Eastside Journal/Belvedere Citizen* (East Los Angeles), January 1, 1976.

Pearce, Susan M., ed. *Interpreting Objects and Collections*. New York: Routledge, 1994.

———. *Museums, Objects and Collections: A Cultural Study*. Washington, DC: Smithsonian Institution Press, 1992.

———. *On Collecting: An Investigation into Collecting in the European Tradition*. New York: Routledge, 1995.

Pearce, Susan, and Alexandra Bounia, eds. *The Collector's Voice: Critical Readings in the Practice of Collecting*. Vol. 1, *Ancient Voices*. Burlington: Ashgate, 2000.

———. Introduction to *The Collector's Voice: Critical Readings in the Practice of Collecting*, vol. 1, *Ancient Voices*, edited by Susan Pearce and Alexandra Bounia, xiii–xx. Burlington: Ashgate, 2000.

Peña, Elaine. *Performing Piety: Making Space Sacred with the Virgin of Guadalupe*. Berkeley: University of California Press, 2011.

Pérez, Emma. *The Decolonial Imaginary: Writing Chicanas into History*. Bloomington: Indiana University Press, 1999.

Pérez, Laura E. *Chicana Art: The Politics of Spiritual and Aesthetic Altarities*. Durham: Duke University Press, 2007.

———. "The Poetry of Embodiment: Series and Variation in Linda Arreola's Vaguely Chicana." In *Vaguely Chicana: Linda Arreola*, edited by Marialice Jacob, 3–4. Los Angeles: Tropico de Nopal Gallery Art-Space, 2008. Exhibition catalog.

Pérez-Torres, Rafael. *Mestizaje: Critical Uses of Race in Chicano Culture*. Minneapolis: University of Minnesota Press, 2006.

Pineda-Madrid, Nancy. "Notes toward a ChicanaFeminist Epistemology (and Why It Is Important for Latina Feminist Theologies)." In *A Reader in Latina Feminist Theology: Religion and Justice*, edited by María Pilar Aquino, Daisy L. Machado, and Jeanette Rodríguez, 241–66. Austin: University of Texas Press, 2002.

Pollock, Griselda, and Joyce Zemans, eds. *Museums after Modernism: Strategies of Engagement*. Malden, MA: Blackwell, 2007.

Pomian, Krzysztof. *Collectors and Curiosities: Paris and Venice, 1500–1800*. Translated by Elizabeth Wiles-Portier. Cambridge, UK: Polity, 1990.

Powell, Richard J. "The Deep." Paper presented at the symposium "Performing Race in African American Visual Culture," University of Maryland, College Park, September 15–16, 2010.

Prado Saldivar, Reina Alejandra. "On Both Sides of the Los Angeles River: Mechicano Art Center." In *L.A. Xicano*, edited by Chon A. Noriega, Terezita Romo, and Pilar Tompkins Rivas, 41–51. Los Angeles: UCLA Chicano Studies Research Center Press, 2011. Exhibition catalog.

Quirarte, Jacinto. *Mexican American Artists*. Austin: University of Texas Press, 1973.

Ramírez, Catherine S. "Afrofuturism/Chicanafuturism: Fictive Kin." *Aztlán: A Journal of Chicano Studies* 33, no. 1 (2008): 185–94.

————. "Deus ex Machina: Tradition, Technology, and the Chicanafuturist Art of Marion C. Martinez." *Aztlán: A Journal of Chicano Studies* 29, no. 2 (2004): 55–92.

Ramírez, Mari Carmen. "Beyond 'the Fantastic': Framing Identity in U.S. Exhibitions of Latin American Art." *Art Journal* 51, no. 4 (1992): 60–68.

Richter, Linda K. "The Politics of Heritage Tourism Development: Emerging Issues for the New Millennium." In *Contemporary Issues in Tourism Development*, edited by Douglas G. Pearce and Richard W. Butler, 107–26. New York: Routledge, 1999.

Rodríguez, Jeanette. *Our Lady of Guadalupe: Faith and Empowerment among Mexican-American Women*. Austin: University of Texas Press, 1994.

Rodríguez, Richard T. *Next of Kin: The Family in Chicano/a Cultural Politics*. Durham: Duke University Press, 2009.

Rodriguez y Gibson, Eliza, ed. *Stunned into Being: Essays on the Poetry of Lorna Dee Cervantes*. San Antonio: Wings Press, 2012.

Román-Odio, Clara. *Sacred Iconographies in Chicana Cultural Production*. New York: Palgrave Macmillan, 2013.

Romo, Terezita. "Conceptually Divine: Patssi Valdez's Virgen de Guadalupe Walking the Mural." In *Asco: Elite of the Obscure, A Retrospective, 1972–1987*, edited by C. Ondine Chavoya and Rita Gonzalez, 270–75. Ostfildern, Germany: Hatje Cantz Verlag, 2011. Exhibition catalog.

————. "Curating without a Rear View Mirror: The Mexican-American Generation." Paper presented at College Art Association annual conference, Los Angeles, February 25, 2012.

————. *Malaquias Montoya*. A Ver: Revisioning Art History, vol. 6. Los Angeles: UCLA Chicano Studies Research Center Press, 2011.

————. "Mexican Heritage, American Art: Six Angeleno Artists." In *L.A. Xicano*, edited by Chon A. Noriega, Terezita Romo, and Pilar Tompkins Rivas, 3–27. Los Angeles: UCLA Chicano Studies Research Center Press, 2011. Exhibition catalog.

————. "Points of Convergence: The Iconography of the Chicano Poster." In *Just Another Poster? Chicano Graphic Arts in California*, edited by Chon A. Noriega, 91–115. Santa Barbara: University Art Museum, University of California, 2001. Exhibition catalog.

————. "Re-Searching for an American Art." Paper presented at the conference "Latino Art Now!," Washington, DC, November 7–9, 2013.

Rony, Fatimah Tobing. *The Third Eye: Race, Cinema, and Ethnographic Spectacle*. Durham: Duke University Press, 1996.

Saavedra, Denise Lugo. "Arte de 'East Los' y el movimiento muralista público de los setenta." In *Los Chicanos: Origen, presencia, destino*, 121–26. Colima, Mexico: Universidad de Colima, 1990.

Sacco, Ellen. "Racial Theory, Museum Practice: The Colored World of Charles Willson Peale." *Museum Anthropology* 20, no. 2 (1996): 25–32.

Saldívar, José David. *Trans-Americanity: Subaltern Modernities, Global Coloniality, and the Cultures of Greater Mexico*. Durham: Duke University Press, 2012.

Sanchez, John. Interview by Karen Mary Davalos, Walnut, CA, July 7, 2011.

Sanchez-Brown, Olivia. Interview by Karen Mary Davalos, Los Angeles, CA, July 7, 2011.

Sandoval, Chela. *Methodology of the Oppressed*. Minneapolis: University of Minnesota Press, 2000.

Santillano, Dianna Marisol. "Asco." In *Phantom Sightings: Art after the Chicano Movement*, edited by Rita Gonzalez, Howard N. Fox, and Chon A. Noriega, 115–19. Berkeley: University of California Press; Los Angeles: Los Angeles County Museum of Art, 2008. Exhibition catalog.

Schiller, Nina Glick. "Editor's Foreword: The Dialectics of Race and Culture." In "(Multi) Culturalisms and the Baggage of 'Race,'" special issue, *Identities: Global Studies in Culture and Power* 1, no. 4 (1995): iii–iv.

Schmal, John P. "The Four Latino Mayors of Los Angeles." HispanicVista.com, May 23, 2005. www.hispanicvista.com.

Schor, Naomi. "Collecting Paris." In *The Cultures of Collecting*, edited by John Elsner and Roger Cardinal, 252–74. Cambridge: Harvard University Press, 1994.

Schumach, Murray. "Mexican Art Seen by Many on Coast." *New York Times*, October 25, 1963.

Selz, Peter. *Art of Engagement: Visual Politics in California and Beyond*. Berkeley: University of California Press, 2006.

Shaked, Nizan. "Event Review: Phantom Sightings: Art after the Chicano Movement." *American Quarterly* 60, no. 4 (2008): 1057–72.

Simpson, Eve. "Chicano Street Murals." *Journal of Popular Culture* 8, no. 3 (1980): 642–52.

Simpson, Mary Caroline. "Modern Art Collecting and Married Women in 1950s Chicago— Shopping, Sublimation, and the Pursuit of Possessive Individualism: Mary Lasker Block and Muriel Kallis Steinberg Newman." *Women's Studies* 39, no. 6 (2010): 585–621.

Singh, Nikhil Pal. "Liberalism." In *Keywords for American Cultural Studies*, edited by Bruce Burgett and Glenn Hendler, 139–44. New York: New York University Press, 2007.

Smith, Valene L. Introduction to *Hosts and Guests: The Anthropology of Tourism*, edited by Valene L. Smith, 1–17. Philadelphia: University of Pennsylvania Press, 1989.

Sorell, Victor. "Barrio Murals in Chicago: Painting the Hispanic-American Experience on 'Our Community' Walls." *Revista Chicano-Riqueña* 4, no. 4 (1976): 51–72.

Sotomayor, Frank. "*Chicanarte* Exposition Opening in Barnsdall." *Los Angeles Times*, September 14, 1975, S24.

Stewart, Susan. *On Longing: Narratives of the Miniature, the Gigantic, the Souvenir, the Collection*. Baltimore: Johns Hopkins University Press, 1984.

"Supplement to Los Four." *Los Angeles County Museum of Art Members' Calendar* 12, no. 2 (1974): n.p.

"Symposium on the Politics of the Arts: Minorities and the Arts." *Arts in Society* 10, no. 3 (1973): 66–73. Transcript of a panel discussion with Donald Bushnell, Leonard Castellanos, James Wood, Decia Baker, and Lawrence Perea.

Tejada, Roberto. "Los Angeles Snapshots." In *Now Dig This! Art and Black Los Angeles, 1960–1980*, edited by Kellie Jones, 69–84. New York: Prestel, 2011. Exhibition catalog.

Torres, Luis R. "A Profile of an Hispano Artist: Charlie 'Clavos' Felix." *La Luz* 4, nos. 6–7 (1975): 3–4.

Torres-Saillant, Silvio. "Introduction: Inscribing Latinos in the National Discourse." In *Recovering the U.S. Hispanic Literary Heritage*, vol. 4, edited by José F. Aranda Jr. and Silvio Torres-Saillant, 1–10. Houston: Arte Público, 2002.

Urry, John. *Consuming Places*. New York: Routledge, 1995.

Valadez, John. *John Valadez*. Interview by Karen Mary Davalos, November 19 and 21 and December 3, 7, and 12, 2007. CSRC Oral Histories Series 10. Los Angeles: UCLA Chicano Studies Research Center Press, 2013.

Vallejo, Linda. *Linda Vallejo*. Interview by Karen Mary Davalos, August 20 and 25, 2007. CSRC Oral Histories Series 2. Los Angeles: UCLA Chicano Studies Research Center Press, 2013.

Vargas, George. *Contemporary Chican@ Art: Color and Culture for a New America*. Austin: University of Texas Press, 2010.

———. "Contemporary Latino Art in Michigan, the Midwest, and the Southwest." PhD diss., University of Michigan, 1988.

Vásquez, David J. *Triangulations: Narrative Strategies for Navigating Latino Identity*. Minneapolis: University of Minnesota Press, 2011.

Venant, Elizabeth. "Hispanic Art Sparks Ethnic Pride." *Los Angeles Times*, March 15, 1989, Calendar (part 6), 1.

———. "On-the-Wall Latino Art at LACMA." *Los Angeles Times*, February 4, 1989, V1.

Venegas, Sybil. "The Artists and Their Work—The Role of the Chicana Artist." *Chismearte* 1, no. 4 (1977): 3, 5.

———. "Conditions for Producing Chicana Art." *Chismearte* 1, no. 4 (1977): 2, 4.

———. *Image and Identity: Recent Chicana Art from "La Reina del Pueblo de Los Angeles de la Porciúncula,"* Art of Greater Los Angeles in the 1990s, vol. 2, no. 1. Los Angeles: Laband Art Gallery, Loyola Marymount University, 1990. Exhibition catalog.

———. "Mi Corazon/My Sacrifice, Mi Sacrificio/My Heart: Art and Faith in East L.A." *ChicanoArt.org*, n.d. www.chicanoart.org.

———. "Walking the Road: The Art and Artistry of Linda Vallejo." In *Fierce Beauty: Linda Vallejo, A Forty-Year Retrospective*, curated by Betty Ann Brown, 101–3. Los Angeles: Plaza de la Raza and Cultural Center for the Arts and Education, 2010. Exhibition catalog.

Verstraete, Ginette. *Tracking Europe: Mobility, Diaspora, and the Politics of Location*. Durham: Duke University Press, 2010.

Wald, Priscilla. "American Studies and the Politics of Life." *American Quarterly* 64, no. 2 (2012): 185–204.

Wilson, William. "30 Works from the Grass Roots." *Los Angeles Times*, June 4, 1973, I2.

———. "Chicano Exhibition 'Cheerfully Angry.'" *Los Angeles Times*, February 22, 1971, I10.

———. "A Distressing Overlap in 'Mechicano.'" *Los Angeles Times*, September 24, 1973, C9.

———. "Gallery Shows Chicano Art." *Los Angeles Times*, December 5, 1971, SE2.

———. "'Los Four' a Statement of Chicano Spirit." *Los Angeles Times*, March 10, 1974, O64.

———. "The Troubled Gift of Carlos Almaraz: Art." *Los Angeles Times*, June 27, 1992, F1.

Wolf, Bryan Jay. *Vermeer and the Invention of Seeing*. Chicago: University of Chicago Press, 2001.

Woolsey, Ronald C. "Antonio Coronel and Southern California's Romantic Lore, Ramona." In *Migrants West: Toward the Southern California Frontier*, 138–59. Sebastopol, CA: Grizzly Bear, 1996.

Yarbro-Bejarano, Yvonne. "The Female Subject in Chicano Theatre: Sexuality, 'Race' and Class." *Theatre Journal* 38, no. 4 (1986): 389–407.

Ybarra-Frausto, Tomás. "The Chicano Movement/The Movement of Chicano Art." In *Exhibiting Cultures: The Poetics and Politics of Museum Display*, edited by Ivan Karp and Steven D. Lavine, 128–50. Washington, DC: Smithsonian Institution Press, 1991.

———. "Post-Movimiento: The Contemporary (Re)Generation of Chicana(o) Art." In *A Companion to Latina/o Studies*, edited by Juan Flores and Renato Rosaldo, 289–96. Malden, MA: Blackwell, 2007.

———. "Rasquachismo: A Chicano Sensibility." In *Chicano Art: Resistance and Affirmation, 1965–1985*, edited by Richard Griswold del Castillo, Teresa McKenna, and Yvonne Yarbro-Bejarano, 155–62. Los Angeles: Wight Art Gallery, University of California, 1991. Exhibition catalog.

Yzaguirre, Raúl, and Mari Carmen Aponte. *Willful Neglect: The Smithsonian Institution and U.S. Latinos*. Report of the Smithsonian Institution Task Force on Latino Issues. Washington, DC: Smithsonian Institution, 1994.

Zabala, Ro. "*Chicanarte*: A Cultural Statement." In *Chicanarte: An Exhibition Organized by the Comité Chicanarte with Cooperation of the Los Angeles Municipal Art Gallery, Barnsdall Park, September 14–October 12, 1975*, iii. Los Angeles: Comité Chicanarte, 1976. Exhibition catalog.

Zamudio-Taylor, Victor. "Inventing Tradition, Negotiating Modernism: Chicano/a Art and the Pre-Columbian Past." In *The Road to Aztlan: Art from a Mythic Homeland*, edited by Virginia M. Fields and Victor Zamudio-Taylor, 342–57. Los Angeles: Los Angeles County Museum of Art, 2001. Exhibition catalog.

# INDEX

abstract art, 47, 64, 208, 244n53
accountability, politics of visibility and, 14, 60, 67, 96
*Action Portraits* (S. de la Loza), 6–12, 208, 214, 237nn22–27, 238n28
aesthetic/aesthetics: aestheticization of social space, 81–82, 86; assimilationist, 110; avant-garde, 30–31, 33, 60, 70, 76–77, 100, 198, 199, 201, 209; barrio/urban, 64, 73, 78, 84, 100; borderlands, 58, 61, 66, 190; challenging aesthetic exclusion, 26–38; Chicana/o, 38, 39, 40–42, 58, 60, 68, 73, 75–76, 82, 100, 101, 190, 195, 200–201, 212; diverse/hybrid, 31, 60, 92, 101, 110–11, 117–18, 150, 189–90, 206, 209, 212, 226, 231; dominant, 52, 73, 102; Eastern/ Asian, 102, 103, 116, 118, 119–25, 141, 142, 145, 147, 227; global/universal, 24, 42, 120–21, 125, 209, 228, 231; graffiti, 66, 121–22; indigenous, 100, 110, 112, 128–29; Latin American, 159; Latino, 95; Mexican, 40–42, 46, 64, 72, 78, 100; minimalist, 41, 53, 64, 100, 206, 208; mural, 7, 9, 10, 20, 108, 208; political, 203, 208, 226, 266n77; postidentity/postethnic, 2, 3, 49, 51, 65, 241n19; postmodern, 41, 42, 45, 149, 209; of poverty, 171, 196; queer, 101, 173, 176, 198, 208, 263n27; rasquache, 54, 213, 262n18; regional, 101, 155, 179, 206, 207; spatial and aesthetic positions, 86–92; subaltern, 25, 188, 202, 228; travel as source of aesthetic inspiration, 101, 106–12, 118, 119–25, 145–50; vernacular, 69, 72, 78, 82, 100, 111, 121; Western/European, 17, 25, 64, 100, 105, 108, 110,

127, 139, 148, 149, 150, 227 (*see also* European influence/inspiration); women-centered, 31–38, 171
aesthetic autonomy, 121, 146
aesthetic politics, 23
African American art/artists, 89, 235nn2–3, 240n13, 264n38
Aguilar, Laura, 35, 38
Alarcón, Margaret "Quica," 173, 259n51
Alarcón, Norma, 244n71
Alcaraz, Lalo, 47
Alcoff, Linda Martín, 227–28, 238n29, 246n14, 267n16
Aldama House/Corazon Productions, 69, 70, 224, 247n21
Alejandre, Abel Mora, 222–24, 226, 246n20
allegory, 41, 87, 128, 142, 205; European, 135–39
Almaraz, Carlos, 5, 64, 70, 104, 190, 224, 239n1, 240n9, 257n27, 263n32, 265n66; exhibitions of, 185, 193, 194, 206, 207, 208–9; works discussed, 64, 65–66, 207, 245n6. *See also* Los Four
*Almost* (Arreola), 53–54
altars/*altares*, 31–32, 60, 209
Amerasia Bookstore, 89
American Council for the Arts in Education, 88
American Dream, 131, 132
American triumphalism, 66
Amescua, Michael, 141, 170, 253n33
*Angelenos/Chicano Painters of L.A.: Selections from the Cheech Marin Collection, Los*, 260n7
anti-immigrant legislation/groups, 47, 180
Antonio F. Coronel Collection, 151–58, 255n1

Chisme Arte, 224

*Chismearte* (literary magazine), 71, 247n27

*Cholas, White Fence, East L.A.* (Iturbide), 217, 218, 219

*Cholos, Harpys, East L.A.* (Iturbide), 217–18

Chouinard Art Institute, 63, 118

*Cielos, Los* (Vallejo), 115, 116

Círculo de Bellas Artes, 103

Cisneros, Sandra, 173

Citywide Mural Program, 69

civil rights movements, 65, 69, 79, 118, 246n17

coalition-building strategies and spaces, 88–92

Coalition for Humane Immigrant Rights of Los Angeles (CHIRLA), 171

Coatlicue, 48

Cockcroft, Eva Sperling, 239n1, 246n19, 254n59

codetermination, 101, 111, 252n16

Coffey, Mary K., 162, 178, 258n39, 259n59, 260n65

COLA (City of Los Angeles) Individual Artist Fellowship, 142

collections, private, 5, 230; as corrective to record, 17, 152; early Californian, 151–58; family/community and, 165–70, 171, 175–76; with feminist content, 167–68, 169, 173, 176; as noncommercial venture, 163–64; represented in exhibitions, 230; as scholarly resource, x, xi, 175; with spiritual content, 167–69

collections, public, 151–58, 160, 179, 261n12. *See also specific institutions*

collectors, private, 42, 151–80, 227, 257n24; as advocates, 160, 164, 174–75, 176; backgrounds of, 152–53, 169, 170–72; collecting as act of critical witness, 158–59, 161, 164, 166–69, 172, 173, 176–80, 222; community formation and, 159, 161, 165–70; as curators, 42, 166–67, 175–76; as custodians of art/culture, 151, 152, 153, 155–59, 161, 175, 177, 230; groups of, 17, 163–64; motivation for, 151, 152–53, 154, 159–60, 161, 162, 166, 167–70, 171, 173–74, 175, 257n34, 258n35–36; public museums and, 151–52, 160, 175, 177; as social agents, 161–62, 165–66

*Colonial Failure Kit* (Gamboa), 208

coloniality of art historical method, 22, 188

*Colossus* (attributed to Goya), 115, 253n43

commercial/noncommercial art, 189; alternative modes of exchange and agency, 92–96; arts organizations and, 67, 68, 69, 74, 77–80, 92–96, 245n8; commercial galleries, 93, 245n8; fiscal instability and, 95; heritage tourism and, 80–86; vs. political art, 67

Community Arts Alliance, 88–92

"Community Arts and Community Survival" (symposium), 88

community arts movement, 88–92

community-based arts, 75–78; bench art competition, 81–82; heritage tourism and, 65, 68, 80–86, 109–10, 250n79; neighborhood arts festivals, 82

community-based arts organizations, 6, 24–25, 65, 67, 68–80, 93, 96, 185, 224–25; alternative modes of exchange and agency, 92–96; collaborations and cultural authority, 221–32; public museums and, 224–26; women's involvement in, 71, 247n24. *See also* Goez Art Studios and Gallery; Los Angeles Community Arts Alliance; Mechicano Art Center

Compton Junior College, 266n70

conceptualism, 100

Concilio de Arte Popular, 70

"Conditions for Producing Chicana Art" (Venegas), 71

consumerism/consumer analysis, 131, 132, 159, 257n27. *See also* collectors, private

contributory model, xii

Coomaraswamy, Ananda, 92, 251n94

coparticipatory research, x–xii, 159, 162–65

Corazon Productions, 224

Cordova, Cary, 235n5

Cordova, Ruben C., 235n5

Coronel, Antonio F., 151–58, 180, 255n6, 256n17

Coronel, Mariana Williamson, 151–58, 180, 256n19–20

Corrin, Lisa G., 23, 240n11

Cortez, Constance, 189–90, 191, 235n5, 242n41, 250n88, 255n67, 262n24, 263n25, 263n27

Courbet, Gustave, 100

Covarrubias, Teresa, 198

Coyolxauhqui, 48–49

critical consciousness, 68, 69, 78, 132, 133, 146, 153, 185–86, 199, 249n56

critical education, 65, 68, 75–78, 89, 92; heritage tourism as, 84–86

critical witness, acting as, 158–59, 161, 164, 166–69, 172, 173, 176–80, 222

Cruz, Manuel, 64

CSRC Oral Histories Series, ix, 233n2, 246n20. *See also* UCLA Chicano Studies Research Center

Cuauhtemoc, 110

cubism, 142

*Cucaracha, La* (Alcaraz), 47

cultural authority, 221–32; closing gap between cultural resource and, 221

cultural politics, 4, 38, 67, 104, 127, 188, 199, 204, 235n4

cultural tourism, 80, 249n68, 250n79

KAREN MARY DAVALOS is Professor of Chicano and Latino Studies at the University of Minnesota. She is an independent curator and an author of three books about Chicana/o art. Her research explores questions of space, subjectivity, agency, power, and spirituality and religion. She pursues feminist editorial methods, the archive, and the infrastructure of US Latino Art.

CPSIA information can be obtained
at www.ICGtesting.com
Printed in the USA
BVHW021329270121
598897BV00020B/188